D0339347

DISCOVERING THE WORLD OF THE BIBLE

DISCOVERING THE WORLD OF THE BIBLE

THIRD EDITION
REVISED & UPDATED

LaMar C. Berrett
D. Kelly Ogden

GRANDIN BOOK COMPANY PROVO, UTAH

Copyright © 1996 LaMar C. Berrett & D. Kelly Ogden

All Rights Reserved

ISBN 0-910523-52-5

Grandin Book Company
116 West Center St., Provo, UT 84601

PREFACE

The most popular book on earth is the Holy Bible, and often its many readers wish to walk the paths of the prophets, see where the miracles were performed, and witness the scenes and culture of the lands which gave birth to three of the world's great religions: Judaism, Christianity, and Islam. This book is an invitation to help you discover the world of the Bible. It is intended particularly for the tourist but is also useful for the student and the armchair reader.

The most popular biblical countries visited in this period of time are Israel, Egypt, and Jordan, and to include all three countries in one book is convenient for the traveler. Information on virtually all the identifiable biblical sites, along with the significant pertinent scriptural references, will be especially helpful to the student of the Scriptures. Important nonbiblical sites are also included.

These features, along with the easy-to-read maps and line diagrams and photographs, will make this book a valuable companion for the traveler or student intent on discovering the world of the Bible.

Dr. LaMar C. Berrett
Dr. D. Kelly Ogden
1996

HOW TO USE THIS BOOK

Throughout this book, the usual American units of measurement are used, including inches, feet, yards, and miles, accompanied occasionally by the corresponding metric figures. Temperatures are expressed in Fahrenheit degrees.

Both historical and modern sites important to every visitor are discussed in this volume. All cities are listed in a logical sequence of travel to avoid backtracking. Sites within cities are also listed in the same manner, so that the traveler will see the most in the time available.

City names in the text employ three type faces: (1) biblical names appear first, in bold capitals; (2) modern names are in bold upper- and lowercase letters; (3) variants, translations, and other explanatory matter are in italics. Hence for a city whose biblical name is *Beeroth*, translated as "wells," and whose modern name is *Bira*, with a variant name *el-Bireh*, the head appears this way:

BEEROTH *("wells"),* **Bira,** *el-Bireh*

Cities and sites of scriptural significance are followed by the pertinent scriptural references.

Points of interest within a city or things to see at a site – such as statues, paintings, or archaeological artifacts – are in smaller bold capitals in the text. The numbers of sites in the text correspond to the numbers of the same sites on the maps.

Throughout this book, square dots and boxes identify sites or references having to do with the King James Bible: square dot leaders introduce Bible references; square dots mark biblical sites on maps (except for capital cities, which are identified by stars); and square boxes enclose the number of biblical points of interest on maps and diagrams where numbered keys are used. All others use circles, including round dot leaders introducing references from other scripture such as *The Book of Mormon, Doctrine and Covenants, The Pearl of Great Price,* from the Apocrypha, the Qur'an, and such sources as Josephus and other ancient documents. Occasionally, for purposes of comparison, we have included a scripture reference elsewhere than in its appropriate section, preceded by *cf.* ("compare").

Scripture references are arranged chronologically in their respective sections.

For greater ease in reading and in quickly extracting data from the text, we have shown even small numbers in figures rather than words where such a practice seems helpful for the reader.

Since most languages of the Near East employ different characters, names have to be transliterated into English. Consequently, spellings frequently vary. Although they have been kept consistent enough in this volume to avoid confusion, different spellings occasionally have been allowed to remain, orienting the traveler to the same kind of variation he will encounter on road maps, street signs, and elsewhere. *Qiryat,* for example, could just as well be spelled *Kiryat;* the common Hebrew word *beit* ("house of"), which often begins place names, may also be spelled *bet* or *beth.*

An index of place names gives the reader immediate access to references concerning any important site.

ABBREVIATIONS

Old Testament

Gen.	Genesis	2Chron.	2 Chronicles	Dan.	Daniel
Exod.	Exodus	Ezra	Ezra	Hos.	Hosea
Lev.	Leviticus	Neh.	Nehemiah	Joel	Joel
Num.	Numbers	Esther	Esther	Amos	Amos
Deut.	Deuteronomy	Job	Job	Obad.	Obadiah
Josh.	Joshua	Ps.	Psalms	Jon.	Jonah
Judg.	Judges	Prov.	Proverbs	Mic.	Micah
Ruth	Ruth	Eccles.	Ecclesiastes	Nah.	Nahum
1Sam.	1 Samuel	Song of Sol.	Song of Solomon	Hab.	Habakkuk
2Sam.	2 Samuel	Isa.	Isaiah	Zeph.	Zephaniah
1Kings	1 Kings	Jer.	Jeremiah	Hag.	Haggai
2Kings	2 Kings	Lam.	Lamentations	Zech.	Zechariah
1Chron.	1 Chronicles	Ezek.	Ezekiel	Mal.	Malachi

New Testament

Matt.	Matthew	Eph.	Ephesians	Heb.	Hebrews
Mark	Mark	Phil.	Philippians	James	James
Luke	Luke	Col.	Colossians	1Pet.	1 Peter
John	John	1Thess.	1 Thessalonians	2Pet.	2 Peter
Acts	Acts	2Thess.	2 Thessalonians	1John	1 John
Rom.	Romans	1Tim.	1 Timothy	2John	2 John
1Cor.	1 Corinthians	2Tim.	2 Timothy	3John	3 John
2Cor.	2 Corinthians	Titus	Titus	Jude	Jude
Gal.	Galatians	Philem.	Philemon	Rev.	Revelation

Apocrypha

Esd.	1 Esdras	Bar.	Baruch
Esd.	2 Esdras	Song of the Three Children	The Song of the Three Holy Children
Tob.	Tobit	Sus.	Susanna
Jud.	Judith	Bel and Dragon	Bel and the Dragon
Rest of Esther	The Rest of Esther	Pr. of Man.	Prayer of Manasses
Wisd. of Sol.	The Wisdom of Solomon	1 Macc.	1 Maccabees
Ecclus.	Ecclesiasticus	2 Macc.	2 Maccabees

Book of Mormon

1 Ne.	1 Nephi	Mos.	Mosiah	3 Ne.	3 Nephi
2 Ne.	2 Nephi	Al.	Alma	Morm.	Mormon
Om.	Omni	Hel.	Helaman	Eth.	Ether

Other Scripture

D&C	Doctrine and Covenants
JST	Joseph Smith Translation
Abr.	Abraham (in the Pearl of Great Price)
JS-M	Joseph Smith-Matthew
JS-H	Joseph Smith-History

Miscellaneous

ca.	about, approximately
cf.	compare
b.	born
d.	died
esp.	especially

Israel

"And the Lord said to Abram...Lift up now thine eyes, and look from the place where thou art northward, and southward, and eastward, and westward: For all the land which thou seest, to thee will I give it, and to thy seed for ever" (Gen. 13:14-15).

This 4,000-year-old promise forms the basis and the essence of a spirit of return that has been an essential part of the Jewish spirit. Though dispersed throughout the earth, the Jews have never forgotten that the prophets of old foresaw not only a "dispersion" but also a "gathering." To Jews all over the world, the creation of a modern state for them is the answer to daily prayers for the past twenty centuries.

HISTORY

The modern state of Israel was brought into existence on May 15, 1948, with Dr. Chaim Weizmann as its first president and David Ben-Gurion as prime minister. Jerusalem was the capital. The new nation was born after about 2,000 years of foreign rule. It was bounded on the north by Lebanon, on the east by Syria and Jordan, and on the southwest by Egypt. During the six-day war of June 1967, Israel enlarged her land area from 8,000 to 26,000 square miles.

HISTORY OF THE HOLY LAND IN BRIEF

Pre-biblical Period (4000-2000 B.C.)

The oldest known communities on the earth were in the Holy Land.

Biblical Period (Beginning with Abraham, 2000 B.C.)

In approximately 2000-1900 B.C., Abraham arrived in Canaan from Ur of Chaldea. When he arrived, the land was controlled by Amorites and Canaanites (local powers). Prior to Joshua's entry into the land, the Hyksos, Egyptians, and local dynastic leaders held control at various times. At the end of the thirteenth century, Joshua victoriously led the Israelites into the Promised Land.

Ca. 1630. Jacob went to Egypt to be with Joseph

Ca. 1250. Joshua entered the Promised Land.

Ca. 1200. The Philistines from Crete invaded Canaan. They occupied much of the land by 1050 B.C.

1025. Saul was crowned the first king of Israel.

1004-965. David reigned as king of Israel.

965-922. Solomon reigned.

Ca. 920. Israel was divided into Israel and Judah.

721. The Assyrians captured Samaria and took Israel into captivity. Israel became lost to history.

Aqsa Mosque, Old Jerusalem

Babylonian Period (605-562 B.C.)

586. Nebuchadnezzar destroyed Jerusalem and took the tribe of Judah into captivity in Babylon.

Persian Period (549-332 B.C.)

539. Cyrus, who conquered Babylon, allowed the Jews to return to Jerusalem

Greek Period (332-167 B.C.)

334. Alexander the Great conquered the Holy Land, and after his death it was controlled by the Ptolemies of Egypt.

197. The country passed into the hands of the Seleucid Empire when Antiochus III defeated the Egyptians at Caesarea Philippi (Paneas).

175. The Seleucid Antiochus IV (Antiochus Epiphanes) became king. He abolished the worship of Jehovah. He desecrated the Temple by offering swine on the Temple altar and installing a statue of the Olympian Zeus.

Hasmonean Period (167 B.C.-63 B.C.)

Under the leadership of Mattathias, his sons, and other Jews, there was a Jewish revolt against the Seleucids. The Jews had nearly 100 years of independence.

Division of the Promised Land among the Tribes of Ancient Israel

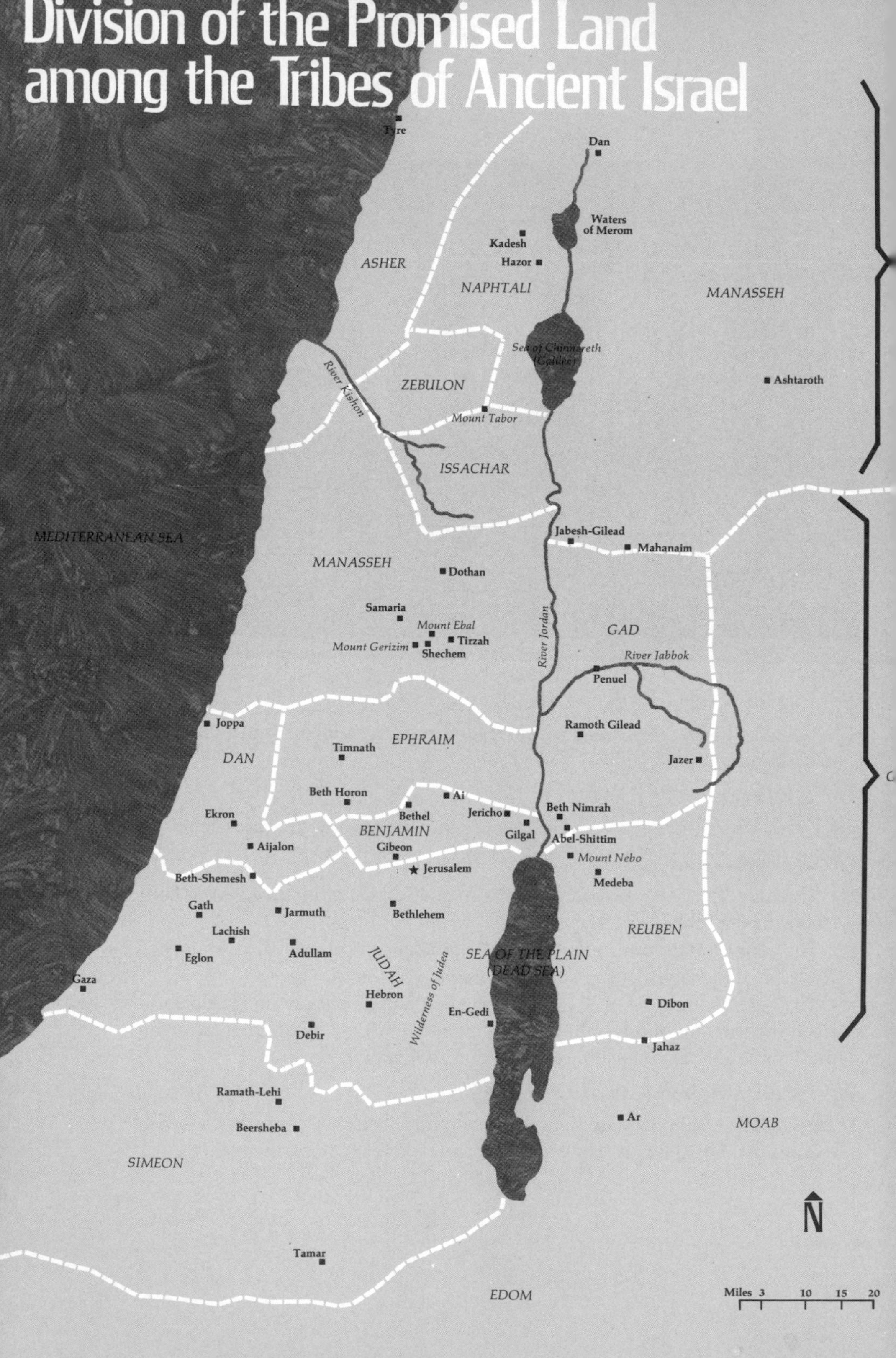

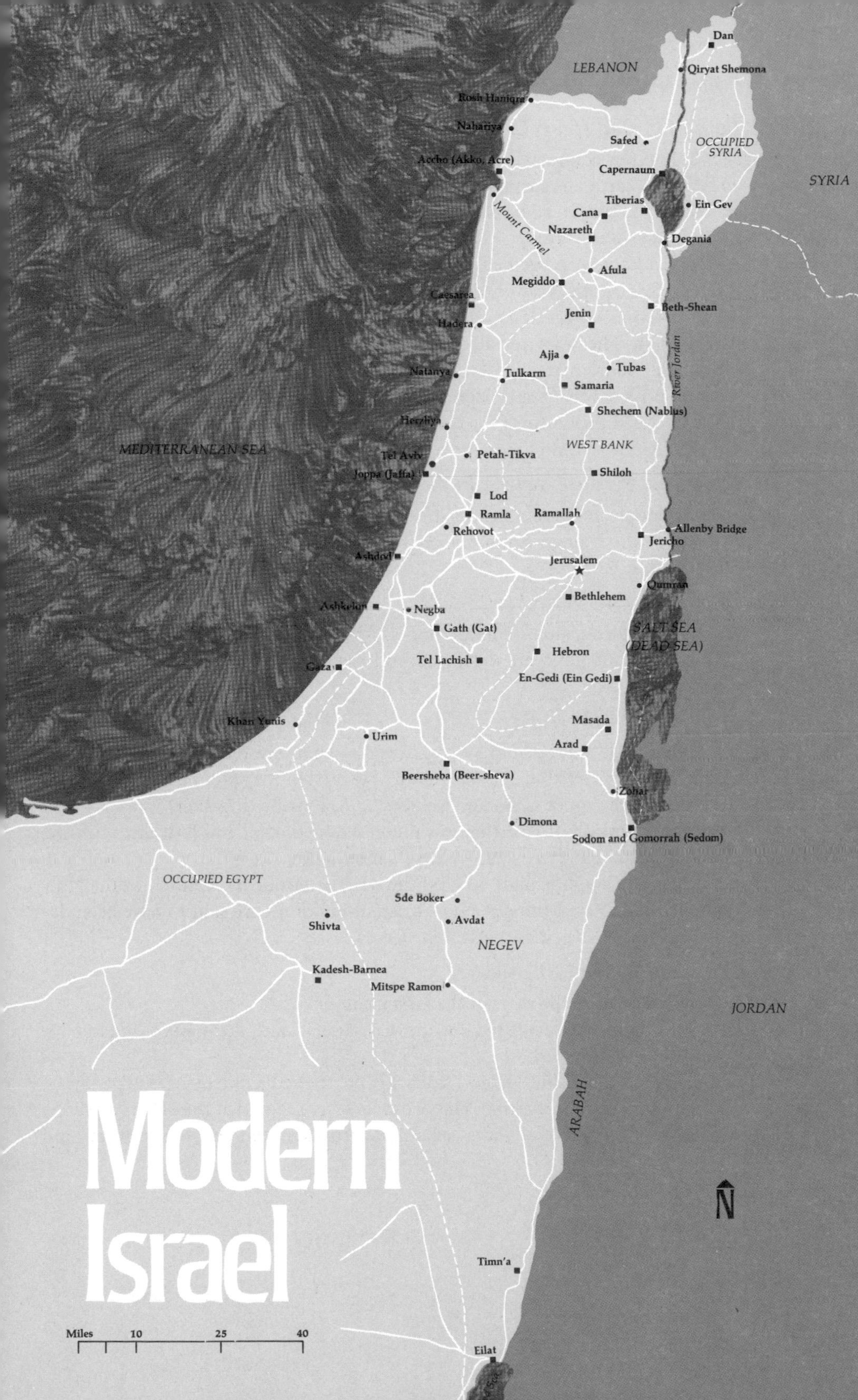

Modern Israel
Dan
LEBANON
Qiryat Shemona
Rosh Haniqra
Nahariya
Safed
OCCUPIED SYRIA
Accho (Akko, Acre)
Capernaum
SYRIA
Tiberias
Ein Gev
Cana
Mount Carmel
Nazareth
Degania
Afula
Megiddo
Caesarea
Beth-Shean
Jenin
Hadera
Ajja
River Jordan
Tubas
Natanya
Tulkarm
Samaria
Shechem (Nablus)
Herzliya
WEST BANK
MEDITERRANEAN SEA
Tel Aviv
Petah-Tikva
Joppa (Jaffa)
Shiloh
Lod
Ramla
Ramallah
Rehovot
Allenby Bridge
Jericho
Ashdod
Jerusalem
Qumran
Bethlehem
Ashkelon
Negba
SALT SEA (DEAD SEA)
Gath (Gat)
Hebron
Tel Lachish
Gaza
En-Gedi (Ein Gedi)
Khan Yunis
Masada
Urim
Arad
Beersheba (Beer-sheva)
Zohar
Dimona
Sodom and Gomorrah (Sedom)
OCCUPIED EGYPT
Sde Boker
Shivta
Avdat
NEGEV
Kadesh-Barnea
Mitspe Ramon
JORDAN
ARABAH
N
Timn'a
Miles 10 25 40
Eilat
Red Sea

Roman Period (63 B.C.-A.D. 330)

63 B.C. Pompey conquered Judea for Rome.

40 B.C. The Parthians surprised the Romans and took the land.

39 B.C. Herod the Great expelled the Parthians. Herod then reigned until 4 B.C.

4-1 B.C. Jesus was born.

A.D. 28-34. Jesus was crucified.

A.D. 66. This was the year of the first Jewish revolt under the Zealots.

A.D. 70. Jerusalem was destroyed by Titus, son of Vespasian.

A.D. 132-135. The Jews revolted a second time, under the leadership of Bar Kokhba. Hadrian rebuilt Jerusalem as a Roman city, and under penalty of death, no Jew was to approach the city. Hadrian called it *Aelia Capitolina.* He also changed the name of the country from *Judea* to *Syria Palestina* – "Syria of the Philistines" – and hence the name, *Palestine* (Isa. 14:29, 31).[1]

Byzantine Period (eastern Roman) (330-634)

Constantinople, or Byzantium, as it was called, was made the capital of the eastern half of the Roman Empire. Christianity spread rapidly after Constantine's conversion.

Second Persian Period (607-629)

May 20, 614. Jerusalem was taken, and 33,877 people were slain by the Persians. Christian churches were destroyed and the work of 300 years' construction obliterated.

Arab Period (634-1099)

570. Muhammad was born in Mecca. At age 43 he received a series of revelations, which later became the *Qur'an (Koran).* He died in 632, after he had established the world religion of Islam and welded the Arab tribes together.

636. By this time all of Palestine was under Arab control, and Jerusalem became Islam's third sacred city, next to Mecca and Medina.

1009. Fatimid Caliph Hakim ordered the destruction of the Church of the Holy Sepulcher. In Asia Minor 30,000 Christian buildings are said to have been destroyed. These atrocities sparked the Crusades.

Crusader Period (1099-1263)

1098-99. These were the years of the First Crusade.

1099. Jerusalem was captured by the Crusaders, and the Latin Kingdom of Jerusalem was formed.

1187. Saladin, a Muslim prince from Egypt, gained control of Egypt, Syria, Mesopotamia, and Palestine. The Crusaders were routed at the Horns of Hittin in Galilee. The Christians later controlled Jerusalem for a short time in 1229 and

1241. Mongol tribes from central Asia also took Jerusalem, with a terrible slaughter, early in the thirteenth century.

Mameluke Period (1263-1516)

1263. The Mameluke Sultan Baybars of Egypt captured the remaining Crusader strongholds. The Mamelukes held the coastal cities intermittently for the next 250 years.

1400. Another Mongol invasion took place under Tamerlane.

Turkish Period (1517-1917)

1517. The Turkish Ottoman Empire conquered Palestine and held it for 400 years.

1799. Napoleon made an unsuccessful attempt to add Palestine to his French empire. He captured Joppa but failed at Acre.

1917. Jerusalem was taken by the Allies in World War I under General Allenby.

Modern Period (1917-)

1878. Petah Tikvah was the first pioneering village.

1911. Degania, the first kibbutz, was founded.

1917. This was the year of the Balfour Declaration and liberation from Turkey by Great Britain.

1921. Nahalal, the first moshav, was founded.

1922. The British Mandate over Palestine was confirmed by the League of Nations.

1947. The United Nations adopted a Partition Plan, and Palestine was to be partitioned between Israel and Jordan by the United Nations.

May 15, 1948. The State of Israel was established, the British withdrew, and the Jewish-Arab war began.

July 18, 1948. This marked the end of the war officially. Palestine was partitioned between Israel and Jordan by the United Nations.

Feb. 16, 1949. Dr. Chaim Weizmann was elected president. David Ben-Gurion was the prime minister. (He was the prime minister again in 1955.)

1956. When Egypt nationalized the Suez Canal on July 26, 1956, Israel attacked and occupied nearly all of the Sinai Peninsula. Peace terms were made, and Israel withdrew to her 1949 armistice lines.

June 1963. Prime Minister David Ben-Gurion resigned and Levi Eshkol took his place. Eshkol died in 1969, and Ben-Gurion in 1973.

May 23, 1967. President Gamal Abdel Nasser of Egypt closed the Gulf of Aqaba to Israeli shipping, and a war began on June 5 between Israel and Egypt. Six days later, under the leadership of the defense minister, Moshe Dayan, it concluded with Israel occupying the entire Sinai Peninsula to the Suez Canal, the Golan Heights east of the Sea of Galilee, the west bank of the Jordan River, and all of Jerusalem. The Jews had access to the Western Wall (Wailing Wall) for the first time since 1948.

March 1969. Golda Meir was installed as Israel's fourth premier, or prime minister.
1973. Yom Kippur War: Egypt and Syria launched coordinated surprise attack on Israel.
1974. Yitzhak Rabin became prime minister.
1977. Likud political party came to power with Menahem Begin, ending 30 years of Labor party dominance. Egyptian President Anwar Sadat visited Jerusalem.
1978. Camp David Accords were signed, with potential basis for settlement of the Arab-Israel conflict.
1979. A peace treaty was signed between Israel and Egypt.
1982. Israeli withdrawal from the Sinai Peninsula was completed. Israel's "Operation Peace for Galilee" with massive military thrust into Lebanon.
1983. Yitzhak Shamir became prime minister.
1984. A National Unity Government was instituted (Labor + Likud); Shimon Peres became prime minister (then Shamir again in '86).
1987. Brigham Young University's Jerusalem Center for Near Eastern Studies was completed on Mt. Scopus, Jerusalem. Outbreak of Palestinian Uprising (*Intifada*).
1989. Soviet Jews immigrated en mass to Israel.
1991. The Persian Gulf War involved Israel.
1992. Yitzhak Rabin again became prime minister.
1994. Agreement was reached between Israel and the Palestine Liberation Organization (P.L.O.). Yasser Arafat arrived in Jericho to start the process leading to a Palestinian state.
1995. November 4. Assassination of Prime Minister Yitzhak Rabin.
1995. The peace process continued through on-going negotiations with Egypt, Jordan, Syria, and others.

LAND AREA

Israel's area is 10,840 square miles (27,817 sq. km.), which is about one-eighth the size of the State of Utah in the USA. About 15 Israels could fit inside the State of California. The country is 290 miles long (450 km.) and about 85 miles (135 km.) at its widest point.

POPULATION

Since the beginning of the State of Israel the flow of immigration has been enormous. Jews have come from all over the world to what they consider to be their homeland. In 1948 there were 710,000 Jews in Israel, and 20 years later the population had reached a total of nearly 3,000,000, about 2,500,000 of whom were

Jews, 325,000 were Muslims, 75,000 were Christian, and about 36,000 were Druzes and others. In June 1967 another million people became a part of Israel because of the "expansion" during the war, and by 1970 the population of Israel exceeded 4,000,000. Of the million that were added after the war, 960,000 were Muslims, 40,000 were Christians, and 5,000 were Druzes. In 1995 the population reached a total of 5,500,000. Eighty-one percent of the populace is Jewish, with 19%, mostly Arab, non-Jewish. Recent estimates show world Jewish population at about 13 million. Some 32% now lives in Israel (49% in North and South America, and 18% in Europe, including the former Soviet Union).

Between 1989 and 1993, over 550,000 immigrants were welcomed to Israel.

ISRAEL TODAY

Modern Israel has large airports, an airline, a merchant fleet, an efficient military organization, and rapidly expanding industry. She exports goods to many nations. Imports totalled $29 billion in 1992, with exports at $20 billion, leaving a deficit of $9 billion. Inflation, which reached 445% in 1984 was reduced to only 11% in 1993. Tourism is an essential part of her economy. Two million tourists visit Israel each year. The average length of stay of a tourist in Israel is one of the highest in the world. Secular and religious history is of prime interest to many tourists. The country's past is revealed, in part, at 3,500 registered archaeological sites.

Even though Israel has had four major wars with her Arab neighbors (1948, 1956, 1967, and 1973) and has poured hundreds of millions of dollars into defense, she has also spent many millions on farming, education, and industry. The result has been a fulfilling of prophecy that the desert would blossom like a rose.

In Israel there are two seasons: winter, with its cold, rainy season, and summer, with its hot, dry season. The first rains start about October and the latter rains usually end in April. Galilee has an average of 60 to 70 rainy days a year, and the Negev has between 10 and 20.

Spring comes to Israel in March, and the whole country is softly green and carpeted in wild flowers. The stony Judean hills are brilliant with red anemones, yellow daisies, mauve cyclamen, tiny cream-colored lupines, and almond blossoms, making the hills rich in color – all prepared for the spring festivals: Jewish Passover and Christian Easter.

The national language is Hebrew, but Israel's second language is English, which most youth can speak. A few Hebrew words from the tourist are warmly appreciated; the Israelis are accustomed to the tourists' mistakes.

Israeli currency is based on the new shekel, divided into 100 *agorot* (singular *agora*).

Useful Everyday Expressions

hello – *shalom*
goodbye – *shalom*
thank you very much – *to-dah rah-bah*
please – *be-va-ka-sha*
yes – *ken*
no – *lo*
good morning – *bo-ker tov*
good evening – *erev tov*
bad – *rah*
good – *tov*
hotel – *ma-lon*
room – *khe-der*
water – *my-im*
toilet – *bait key-say*
how much is it? – *ka-mah zeh oh-leh*
doctor – *row-feh*
café – *café*
waiter – *mel-tsar*
menu – *taf-reet*
ice cream – *glee-dah*

Jerusalem and the Dome of the Rock, from the Mount of Olives

patience – *sav-la-noot*
good night – *lila tov*
excuse me – *slee-kha*
where is – *ay-fo*
money – *ke-sef*
bus – *auto-boos*
taxi – *taxi*
to the right – *yah-meenah*
to the left – *smo-lah*
milk – *kha-lav*
mountain – *har*
Sunday – *yom ree-shon*
Monday – *yom shay-nee*
Tuesday – *yom shlee-shee*
Wednesday – *yom reh-vee-ee*
Thursday – *yom kha-mee shee*
Friday – *yom shee-shee*
Saturday – *shabbat (as in "hot")*

Map Reading in Israel

The following words often recur in the place names of Israel:

beit, beth, bet – house of, place of
be'er – well, cistern
ein – spring of
emek – valley
eretz – land of
gan – garden
gesher – bridge
migdal – tower
rehov – street
sha'ar – gate
ya'ar – forest
derech – road
kvish – highway
givat – hill of
har – mountain
kerem – vineyard
kfar – village
kiriat – suburb of
ma'ayan – spring
meshek – farm
ramat – height of
sdeh – field of
tel, tell – hill, mound
sderot – boulevard

CITIES AND SITES

JERUSALEM

Jerusalem has also been known by the following terms: *Salem; Jebus; City of Peace; Urusalimu; Sion of God; Zion; City of David; the Holy City; and al-Quds.*

At the time of Abraham it was called *Salem*, and before David's conquest it was an Amorite city called *Jebus.*

The first mention of Jerusalem in the scriptures is in Gen. 14:18: "And Melchizedek King of Salem brought forth bread and wine: and he was the priest of the most high God."

Although its name means "peace," there have probably been more wars fought at its gates than at any other city in the world. It is located "in the tops of the mountains" (Judean range), about 2,500 feet above sea level, about 40 miles east of the Mediterranean and 20 miles west of the Dead Sea. The natural water supply is rather poor, and conduits have brought water into the city from earliest times.

About 996 B.C. David took the city and made it his capital, and Solomon made it a beautiful city (965-922 B.C.), built a Temple and palaces, strengthened the walls, and brought treasures into the city.

After the division of Israel, Jerusalem had both good and bad kings, and during the reign of Rehoboam (921 B.C.) it was raided and the treasures of the Temple removed by Shishak of Egypt. It was strengthened by Uzziah, Jotham, and Hezekiah, but it was soon (701 B.C.) besieged by the Assyrians under Sennacherib and the people of Jerusalem were compelled to pay heavy tribute (2 Kings 18:3-16; 20:12-19; 19:35). The *Taylor Prism,* located now in the British Museum, tells of the tributes being given to Sennacherib of Assyria – especially by Hezekiah. In 609 B.C. Pharaoh Necho captured Jerusalem for Egypt.[2]

The Babylonians, under Nebuchadnezzar, captured Jerusalem in 605, and again in 598 B.C., and destroyed it in 586 B.C. After 70 years of captivity, some of the Jews returned to Jerusalem in 538 B.C. and restored the walls and Temple.

The *Babylonian Chronicle,* an archaeological find in Mesopotamia and a source independent from the Bible, tells about Nebuchadnezzar's capture of Jerusalem. The accounts in the Babylonian Chronicle and the Bible compare in detail (2 Kings 24:10-18; 2 Chron. 36). The Chronicle is now in the British Museum.

The *Jehoiakin Tablets* throw light on the treatment of Judah's king, Jehoiakin, while he was in captivity in Babylon. The tablets were found in Babylon.

The *Cyrus Cylinder* tells about Cyrus, the great Persian who restored the Jews to their homeland (538 B.C.), and of his life in Babylon. Isaiah felt Cyrus was anointed of the Lord (Isa. 45:1); Cyrus felt his god, Marduk, called him to be the ruler. Cyrus, said Isaiah, was elected by Jehovah (Isa. 44:28; 45:1-4). Concerning the liberation of the Jews, Cyrus said on his cylinder: "I gathered together all their inhabitants and restored to them their dwellings." Isaiah and Micah prophesied of the restoration by Cyrus (Isa. 44:24-28; 45:12-13; Mic. 5). The prophecies were fulfilled in the time of Zerubbabel (Ezra 1:1-11).

In 332 B.C. the Greeks, under Alexander the Great, captured Jerusalem. In 320 B.C. Ptolemy Soter captured it. In 302 B.C. it was annexed to Egypt. In 170 B.C. its walls were razed by Antiochus Epiphanes. Later the Maccabees fought the Greeks, and from 167 to 63 B.C. the Jews enjoyed independence under the Hasmonean kings. But finally the Romans came in 63 B.C. and besieged the city. In 37 B.C. Herod (half Idumaean) was appointed king of the Jews. He married a Jewess, among others. He was a great builder. He rebuilt Jerusalem with a palatial Temple area more magnificent than Solomon's. He also built a palace and the city walls, including the Western Wall (Wailing Wall). Herod died in 4 B.C., and thus the city Herod built was the city that Jesus knew.

After the Jews unsuccessfully revolted in A.D. 66, the Romans under Titus destroyed the city in A.D. 70. This fulfilled Jesus' prophecy (Luke 19:41-44; 21:20-24) and was another part of the Jewish dispersion. Bar Kokhba's Jewish revolt (A.D. 132-135) returned Jerusalem to the Jews for 3 short years. The city was rebuilt and named *Aelia Capitolina* by Hadrian in 138. Roman temples were built on sacred sites, and Jews were forbidden to enter the city on penalty of death. Constantine converted Jerusalem into a Christian city. It was conquered by the Persians in 614 and by the Arab Muslims (Saracens) in 637, and remained under the latter's rule for almost 500 years. It fell into the hands of the Turks in 1076, suffered in the wars of the Christian Crusades that began in 1099, and finally, by 1517, it came under the control of the Turks and continued so for the next 400 years until it was taken by General Allenby of the British Army in 1917. It remained in the hands of the Arab Palestinians under the British Mandate until 1948, when it became the capital of the new State of Israel.

When the Jews captured Old Jerusalem in 1967, Moshe Dayan said on June 7, 1967, "We have returned to our holy places, never to part from them again." Jerusalem was united again, and the 70,000 Arabs from East Jerusalem were free to come and go as they desired. For the first time in 19 centuries the Old City was again under Jewish rule.

The City has been besieged many times and its walls built and rebuilt. It has been totally destroyed at least 5 times. The present city walls were built in 1542 during the Turkish reign of Sultan Suleiman, called "the Magnificent." In the walls there are 8 gates and 34 towers. The walls are 2½ miles in length and average 40 feet in height.

The Old City of Jerusalem is divided into four quarters: Muslims in the northeast; Christians in the northwest; Armenians (who are also Christians) in the southwest; and Jews in the southeast.

Rubble has filled the streets so that one now walks several feet *above* where Jesus walked in some places.

Jerusalem is the most sacred city in the world, and the most important one in biblical history. Its role in history is out of proportion to its size and economic importance. It is sacred to Christian, Muslim, and Jew, and is the most oriental of Israel's cities. On the streets you can see the black-bearded Hasidim (the Orthodox element in broad fur hats and black gowns), darker-skinned peoples from Morocco and Yemen, copper-faced Indians in saris, and hawk-nosed men from Iraq and Persia. It is truly a melting pot of over half a million people.

Yemin Moshe, the first modern Jewish suburb of Old Jerusalem, was founded outside the city walls in 1860. Sir Moses Montefiore led this movement. By 1995 the population of Jerusalem had reached 565,000. Jews comprise approximately 404,000, with Muslims at nearly 146,000, and Christians around 15,000.

- *Abraham paid tithes to Melchizedek here (Gen. 14:17-24).*
- *Joshua killed Jerusalem's king, who conspired against him (Josh. 10:1-27).*
- *The tribe of Judah conquered it (Judg. 1:1-8; 19:10, 11; 1 Chron. 11:4).*
- *The city was captured, strengthened, and beautified by David (2 Sam. 5:6-16; 1 Chron. 11:4-7).*
- *The ark was brought here and the city made the capital by David (2 Sam. 6:1-2; 1 Chron. 13-16; Ps. 24).*
- *David planned the Temple (2 Sam. 7; 1 Chron. 17:22-27).*
- *The city was preserved from pestilence (2 Sam. 24).*
- *It was the scene of Solomon's building enterprises (1 Kings 6-9).*
- *It was sacked by Shishak and others (1 Kings 14:25-28; 2 Kings 14:13-14).*
- *It was strengthened by Uzziah (2 Chron. 26:9-15).*
- *It was saved from Assyria (2 Kings 18:13-20; Isa. 36-39; Ps. 46, 48).*
- *Jerusalem suffered from many wars (2 Kings 25; 2 Chron. 12, 25, 36; Jer. 39, 52).*
- *Jeremiah was a prophet in Jerusalem when Zedekiah was king of Judah (2 Kings 24:17, 18; 2 Chron. 36:15-16).*
- *King Zedekiah's sons were slain by the king of Babylon (2 Kings 25:7).*
- *Jerusalem was captured by Nebuchadnezzar in 605 B.C. and many of its inhabitants were taken to Babylon (2 Kings 24-25; 2 Chron. 36:15-21; Jer. 39:9-14).*
- *The word of the Lord is to come from Jerusalem (Isa. 2:3).*
- *Jerusalem was lamented by the exiles (Lam. 1-2; Ps. 130, 137).*
- *The return to Jerusalem was foretold (Isa. 35; 40; 43:1-21; 52).*
- *The walls of the city were rebuilt by Nehemiah (Neh. 2:4-20; 6:15-26; Pss. 126, 147).*

- *Jesus was here as a babe (Luke 2:22), at twelve years of age (Luke 2:41-52), and at the triumphal entry (Matt. 21:1-11).*
- *Jesus wept over it and foretold its doom (Matt. 23:37-24:51; Mark 13).*
- *Jesus was tried and crucified here (Matt. 27; Mark 15; Luke 23; John 19).*
- *The Holy Spirit descended here on the day of Pentecost (Acts 2).*
- *Abraham paid tithes to Melchizedek here (Al. 13:14-19).*
- *Melchizedek gave the priesthood to Abraham. Melchizedek was translated (D&C 84:14; JST Gen. 14:32-34), and the priesthood was named after him (D&C 107:1-7; JS-H 1:72).*
- *Lehi and Jeremiah were contemporary prophets in Jerusalem when Zedekiah was king of Judah (1 Ne. 1:4; 5:13; cf. 2 Kings 24:17-18; 2 Chron. 36:15-16).*
- *Lehi received a vision of the Twelve Apostles, the destruction of Jerusalem, and the captivity in Babylon (1 Ne. 1:8-18).*
- *Lehi prophesied concerning the coming of a Messiah and the redemption of the world (1 Ne. 1:19).*
- *The Jews sought Lehi's life (1 Ne. 1:20).*
- *Lehi departed into the wilderness from Jerusalem (1 Ne. 2:4; D&C 17:1).*
- *Jerusalem was the home of Laban (1 Ne. 3:4).*
- *The record of the Jews (plates of brass) was taken from Laban after Nephi cut off Laban's head (1 Ne. 3-4; D&C 17:1).*
- *Zoram, a servant of Laban, joined Lehi (1 Ne. 4:35).*
- *Ishmael lived in the land of Jerusalem and had daughters and sons that married into the family of Lehi (1 Ne. 7:1-6, 19, 22; 16:7, 27).*
- *Lehi traveled in the wilderness near the Red Sea (1 Ne. 2:5).*
- *Mulek, infant son of Zedekiah, king of Judah, was preserved when the rest of his brothers were slain by the king of Babylon (Hel. 8:21).*
- *About 11 years after Lehi left Jerusalem, the Lord led another colony from that city to America; among them was Mulek (Mos. 25:2; Hel. 6:10; 8:21). The land northward in America was named after Mulek at one time (Hel. 6:10).*
- *Jerusalem was captured by Nebuchadnezzar in 605 B.C. and many of its inhabitants were taken to Babylon (1 Ne. 1:13; 10:3; 2 Ne. 25:10; Om. 1:15).*

POINTS OF INTEREST

Within the Walls of Old Jerusalem[3]

1. **TEMPLE MOUNT/MOUNT MORIAH** (Haram esh-Sharif). This is an area enclosed by walls measuring 913 by 1,515 by 1,586 by 1,050 feet on the sides and covering over 35 acres. Near the center of the area is the Dome of the Rock. This area

was known early as the Hill of Zion, the dwelling place of God, and the position for the Temple on Mount Moriah was indicated by God.

Solomon's Temple was built here (ca. 950 B.C.). David collected the materials, but his son built the Temple. The plan followed that of the tabernacle, and the ark of the covenant was placed in the Temple. It was lavishly built and later burned to the ground by Nebuchadnezzar in 586 B.C. The Jews were taken captive to Babylon and the ark was lost.

After the return of the Jews from captivity, they rebuilt the Temple in 515 B.C. It is called the Second Temple, or the Temple of Zerubbabel. In comparison to Solomon's Temple, the second Temple was modest. In 168 B.C. Antiochus the Great desecrated the Temple by stripping it of its sacred items and offering swine upon the altar. It was left desolate. Judas Maccabaeus cleansed it and restored it to use in 165 B.C.

Construction was begun on the Temple of Herod about 20 B.C., to try to win for Herod popularity with the Jews and certainly an eternal name for himself. He built up the walled area to 600 feet square, and the work was proceeding all during the Savior's life. It was not completely finished until A.D. 64, six years before its final destruction.

After the destruction of Herod's Temple, the Romans built a temple to Jupiter on the site. Early Christians felt Mount Moriah had been cursed by God, and left it desolate, but when the Muslims captured Jerusalem in 639, the Mount became a sacred Muslim shrine. A mosque was built here first about 690, and when the Crusaders captured Jerusalem in 1099 they converted the mosque into a church. A century later, when the Crusaders were defeated by the Arabs, the Dome of the Rock again became a place sacred to the Muslims. The cross was replaced by the crescent, and although the mosque has undergone many changes it has been a Muslim shrine ever since.

(For detailed treatment of the on-going debate regarding the precise position of the ancient Temples on the Temple Mount, along with photos, maps, and diagrams, see *Biblical Archaeology Review* Mar/Apr 1983, 40-59; Nov/Dec 1989, 23-53; Mar/Apr 1992, 24-45, 64-65.)

- *It was here, according to tradition, that Abraham took his son, Isaac, to offer him as a sacrifice (Gen. 22:1-2).*
- *The threshing floor of Araunah the Jebusite was purchased by David to build an altar (2 Sam. 24:18-25).*
- *The exact position on Mount Moriah was indicated by God (2 Sam. 24:18-25; 1 Chron. 21:15, 18, 28; 22:1; 2 Chron. 3:1).*
- *David collected materials and his son Solomon built a Temple (1 Chron. 22:14-15; 28:11-20).*
- *The Temple of Solomon included the threshing floor site (2 Chron. 3:1).*

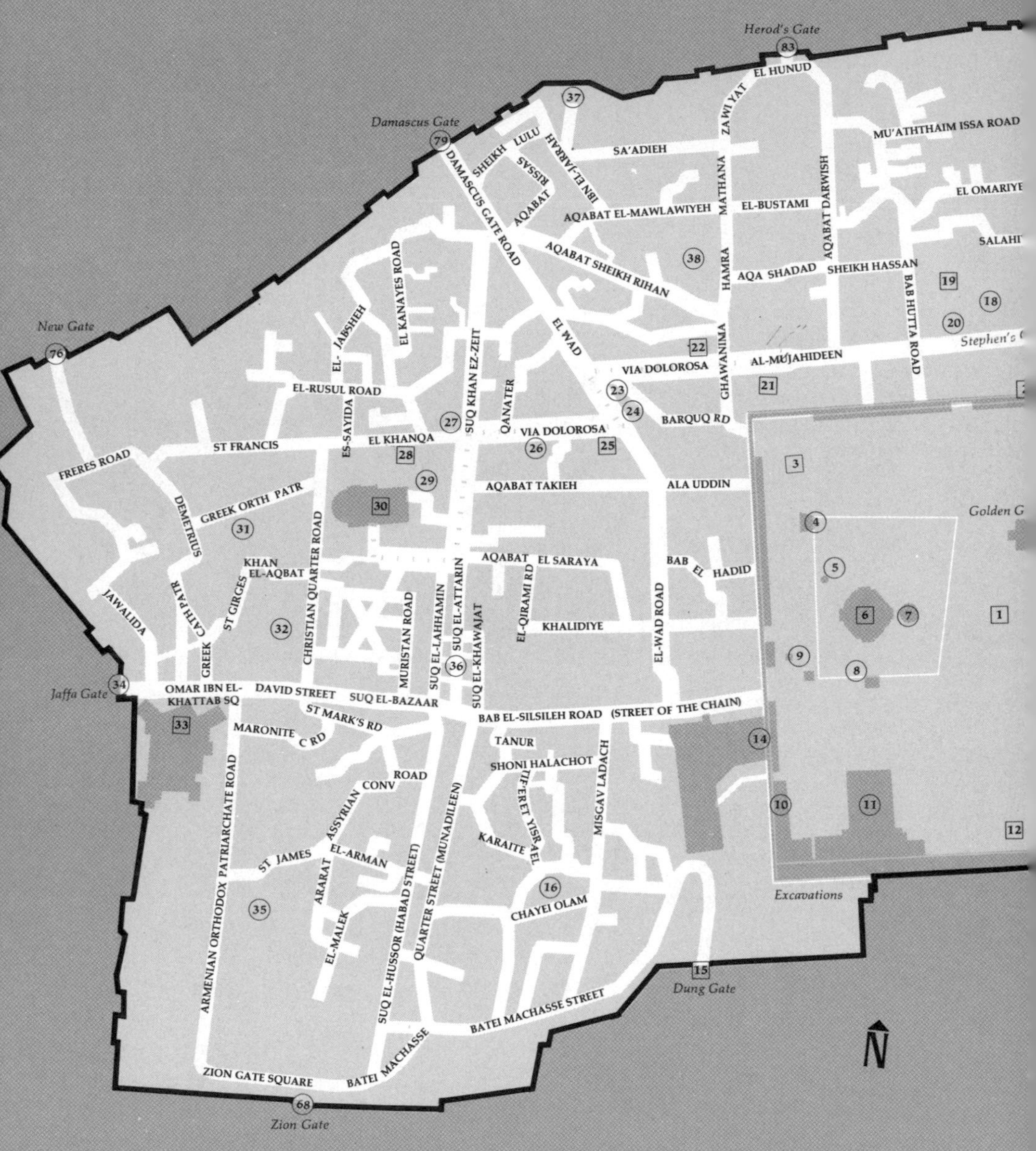

Jerusalem
Old City

Miles ¼ ½

1 Temple Square on Mount Moriah
2 Gate of the Tribes
3 Threshing floor
4 Arcades
5 Dome of Ascension
6 Dome of the Rock
7 Dome of the Chain
8 Summer Pulpit
9 Sabil Quait Bey
10 Islamic Museum
11 Aqsa Mosque
12 Solomon's Stables
13 Golden Gate
14 Western Wall
15 Dung Gate
16 Jewish Quarter
17 Saint Stephen's Gate
18 Church of Saint Anne
19 Pool of Bethesda
20 Saint Anne Seminary
21 Pilate's Judgment Hall
22 Where Jesus received the cross
23 Where Jesus fell for the first time
24 Where Jesus met his mother
25 Where Simon was compelled to bear the cross
26 Where Saint Veronica wiped Jesus' face
27 Where Jesus fell the second time
28 Where Jesus consoled the women of Jerusalem
29 Where Jesus fell the third time.
30 Church of the Holy Sepulcher
31 Christian Quarter
32 Pool of Hezekiah
33 Citadel, David's Tower, and Herod's Palace
34 Jaffa Gate
35 Armenian Quarter
36 Bazaars
37 Spafford Children's Center
38 Muslim Quarter

- *The Temple of Solomon was burned by Nebuchadnezzar in 586 B.C. (2 Kings 25:8-9).*
- *When the Jews returned from captivity, they built the Second Temple. It was called the Temple of Zerubbabel (Ezra 3:8-13; 4:23-24; 5:15; 6:15-18; Haggai).*
- *Herod started to build a Temple for the Jews about 20 B.C. It was completed in A.D. 64 (John 2:20).*
- *Gabriel announced to Zacharias that Elisabeth would bear a son (Luke 1:5-25). That son was later known as John the Baptist.*
- *Jesus was named (Luke 2:21-39).*
- *Jesus visited the Temple at age 12 (Luke 2:41-50).*
- *Jesus carried out the first cleansing of the Temple (John 2:12-25).*
- *Jesus healed the blind and the lame and taught the multitudes (John 8:20; Mark 12; Luke 19:47; John 8).*
- *Here it was that Jesus said, "He that is without sin among you, let him first cast a stone at her" (John 8:7).*
- *Jesus watched the widow cast in her mites (Mark 12:41-44).*
- *The second cleansing of the Temple was done by Jesus (Matt. 21:12-16; Mark 11:15-18; Luke 19:45-48).*
- *Jesus taught the chief priests and elders concerning authority, the parable of the two sons, the parable of the wicked husbandman, the marriage of the king's son, rendering unto Caesar, the resurrection, marriage, the great commandment, and eight woes to the scribes and Pharisees (Matt. 21:23-23:29).*
- *Jesus foretold the destruction of the Temple (Matt. 24; Mark 13; Luke 21:5-38).*
- *The veil of the Temple was rent in twain from top to bottom when Jesus died (Matt. 27:51; Mark 15:38; Luke 23:45).*
- *Judas cast down pieces of silver (betrayal money) in the Temple (Matt. 27:5).*
- *Peter healed the cripple at the Temple and taught in the Temple (Acts 3).*
- *Paul was seized in the Temple and was eventually imprisoned in Rome (Acts 21:11-15).*
- *The Temple is to be rebuilt (Zech. 8:7-9; Ezek. 40-48).*
- *Water is to come out from under the Temple (Ezek. 47:1-2).*
- *The Lord will "suddenly come to his temple" (Mal. 3:1).*

- *The Doctrine and Covenants refers to Abraham's obedience in taking his son, Isaac, to offer him as a sacrifice (D&C 132:36, 50).*
- *Jesus became a "son of the law" and taught the "doctors" in the Temple (JST Luke 2:41-50). Jesus' first recorded words indicated that he must be about his Father's business.*
- *Jesus foretold the destruction of the Temple (D&C 45:18-20).*
- *The Temple is to be rebuilt (D&C 124).*
- *The Lord will "suddenly come to his temple" (3 Ne. 24:1; D&C 36:8; 133:2).*

2. **GATE OF THE TRIBES** (Sheep Gate, Jericho Gate). North of the Golden Gate is the Gate of the Tribes, which leads out of the Temple site to the Lion's Gate.

- *A gate near the Lion's Gate on the east side of the city was rebuilt by Nehemiah (Neh. 3:1, 32; 12:39).*

3. **THRESHING FLOOR.** Northwest of the Dome of the Rock, near the Mameluke Arch, is a threshing floor that is believed by some to have been owned by Araunah the Jebusite and purchased by David to build the altar.

- *David bought the threshing floor from the Jebusite (2 Sam. 24:18-25; 1 Chron. 21:18-22:1; 2 Chron. 3:1).*

4. **ARCADES.** Eight stairways lead to the raised platform of the Dome of the Rock, and at the head of the stairs are beautiful arcades. According to tradition, the souls of men will be weighed at the final judgment by scales that hang from the arcades.

5. **DOME OF ASCENSION.** Northwest of the Dome of the Rock is a dome representing Muhammad's ascent into heaven. It dates back to 1200 and seems to be a

Dome of the Rock, Old Jerusalem

copy of the Byzantine dome on the Mount of Olives which, according to tradition, marks the site of Jesus' ascension.

6. **DOME OF THE ROCK**. This is a golden-domed octagonal-shaped mosque or shrine, built between A.D. 687 and 691 and decorated with brilliant blue, green, yellow, and white Persian tiles. The octagon is 180 feet in diameter, and each side measures 63 feet. The dome rises 105 feet from the ground, has a diameter of 78 feet, and is designed after the fourth-century shrine on the Mount of Olives which marks the site of the ascension of Jesus. It is covered with aluminum bronze alloy (anodised aluminum) and a small percentage of actual gold. The inside of the dome is decorated with stained glass windows and stones of marble. The columns within were taken from different Byzantine churches; hence their differences. Some still have Christian crosses on them. The Dome of the Rock is located on Mount Moriah, the site of Solomon's, Zerubbabel's, and Herod's Temples (2 Chron. 3:1).

Many mistakenly refer to the Dome of the Rock as the Mosque of Omar. The truth is that Omar did not build the Dome. Another caliph, Abd-al-Malik, built it. However, the "true" Mosque of Omar is located in front of the Church of the Holy Sepulcher. When the Caliph Omar accepted the surrender of Jerusalem from the Christians in A.D. 638, the Patriarch of Jerusalem, Sophronius, showed Omar around the Church of the Holy Sepulcher. It was the hour of prayer, and the Patriarch suggested that Omar pray within the sacred walls. The great caliph refused, saying: "If I prayed inside the church, thou wouldst have lost it; the believers would have taken it from thee, saying, 'Omar prayed here.'" He stepped outside to make his prayer, and the true Mosque of Omar was built there. It stands to this day across the narrow street from the Church of the Holy Sepulcher. Omar did, however, build a wooden mosque on the Temple Mount right after he captured Jerusalem. During the past 13 centuries the Dome of the Rock has been repaired many times, but it remains essentially the same as it was in 691. The Crusaders used the Dome of the Rock as a Christian church in 1099.

The Dome of the Rock is built over an immense rough-hewn rock about 40 by 52 feet, rising 7 feet above the ground level. The rock is the summit of Mount Moriah. According to Jewish legend, the rock marks the center of the earth, and it was marked as such on maps. It formed the base of the Jewish altar of burnt offering. There is a hole in the rock through which blood would drain into a cave under the rock, called the "well of souls" because the souls of the dead supposedly meet there every week.

The Muslims hold this site as one of three most holy places – next to Mecca and Medina in importance. The Muslims believe that Muhammad went to heaven from this point on his winged steed, al- Buraq (lightning). When he ascended, the rock began to rise with him, but an angel appeared and held the rock down. The fingerprints of the angel can be seen on the side of the rock. Footprints of Muhammad are also pointed out on the rock. A tall cupboard southeast of the rock is said to contain a few hairs from Muhammad's beard. The Muslims also believe Adam and Eve offered up sacrifices here and that Abraham took his son Ishmael (not Isaac) to offer him as a sacrifice on Mount Moriah. (Muslims keep Friday as their sabbath. They refrain from pork, alcohol, gambling, and making paintings or sculptures of human beings. They practice polygamy – up to four wives if they are rich. They pray five times a day and are monotheistic.)

Many believe the Dome of the Rock marks the site of Solomon's Temple, but others believe it was located straight in from the Golden Gate, and that just inside of the northwest arcades, a small cupola covers bedrock where perhaps the Holy of Holies was located. (See source references from *Biblical Archaeology Review*, listed under #1, Temple Mount/Mount Moriah).

- *Abraham prepared to sacrifice his son Isaac (Gen. 22:1-22).*
- *David bought the threshing floor of Araunah (2 Sam. 24:18-25; 1 Chron. 21).*
- *The submissiveness of Abraham's son when told he was to be sacrificed is poignantly told in the Qur'an (xxxvii:99-111).*

7. **DOME OF THE CHAIN**. On the east side of the Dome of the Rock is a small eighth-century treasury that resembles the Dome of the Rock. Arabs have stored their silver in the dome of this small structure over the years. Crusaders used it as a church and named it after Saint James. Most of the 17 columns may be seen at once when viewed from any angle. It received its name from an iron chain suspended from its cupola.

8. **SUMMER PULPIT**. This structure was built by Burhan ed Din in 1456.

9. **SABIL QUAIT BEY**. This is a beautifully decorated Mameluke fountain provided by Sultan Quait Bey in 1487.

10. **ISLAMIC MUSEUM**. In the southwest corner of the mount is a museum with Byzantine and Islamic antiquities.

11. **AL-AQSA MOSQUE**. In the southern part of the mount, over the area where Solomon built his palace, is the al-Aqsa (or Aksa) Mosque. It is considered by many to have been built in honor of Saint Mary by Justinian in 536. The first mosque was built between 709 and 715 by Caliph Walid, son of Abd-al-Malik, who built the Dome of the Rock. It was built on the foundation of a Byzantine church and still follows the general lines of a basilica. It has been rebuilt many times and can presently hold 5,000 worshipers. In 1099 the Knights Templars used the mosque as their headquarters. In 1187 Saladin captured it for the Muslims.

The al-Aqsa Mosque is used for group prayers, and the Dome of the Rock is used for individual worship. Just left of the door as you enter is the place where the Jordanian king Abdullah was murdered by the Mufti's men in 1951. Abdullah's grandson, Al-Hussein ibn Talal, was with him. One of the bullets glanced off a medal of Al-Hussein, the future ruler of Jordan. In 1969, an Australian set fire to the mosque, which caused a major furor among the Arabs.

Al-Aqsa, mentioned in the Qur'an in a vision of the ascension of Muhammad, means the "distant place" or the "farthest point," with reference to its being removed from Mecca. This mosque is one of Islam's holiest shrines after Mecca and Medina.

The *EL KAS FOUNTAIN,* in front of the mosque, is used by Muslims for ritual washing. Jews and Latter-day Saints also perform ritual cleansings preparatory to worshipping in holy places.

12. **"SOLOMON'S STABLES"**. These are located under the southeast corner of the Temple esplanade. When Herod the Great rebuilt the Temple area in Jerusalem, he made it more expansive by building up the southern end with a series of arches. A huge platform was built, resting on 88 pillars. Holes in the pillars indicate that horses may have been kept here during Herod's or the Crusaders' time. Having been constructed by Herod just before the time of Jesus, these so-called "Solomon's Stables" have nothing to do with Solomon, who reigned a thousand years earlier.

Though some are now suggesting the southwest corner as the "pinnacle of the temple," yet the southeast corner may still be the more likely candidate. It is the most precipitous man-made height ever achieved in the history of the Holy Land (over 300 feet above the floor of the Kidron).

Note the **"SEAM"** about 100 feet (32 meters) north of the corner. An obvious difference in cut of stone is visible; to the north, stones were left rough on the exterior and to the south, they are very smooth. North of the seam is pre-Herodian work, but the extension south is definitely Herod's addition to the platform of the Temple Mount. (The stone work above is later, from Suleiman's restoration of the walls, so it shows no seam.)

- *This corner of the Temple Mount is also known as the "pinnacle of the temple," where Satan tempted Jesus (Matt. 4:5; Luke 4:9).*

13. **GOLDEN GATE** (Eastern Gate, Gate of Mercy). This seventh-century Byzantine structure is located in the eastern wall of the Temple complex. Legend has it that this will be the spot where the trumpet will sound and the dead will be raised. In the hope of postponing the day of judgment and the end of the world, therefore, the Turkish governor of Jerusalem blocked up the gate in 1530.

It is the only gate that leads directly into the Temple area, and according to Jewish tradition, the Messiah will enter through this gate when he comes to Jerusalem. On the east side of the gate is a Muslim cemetery.

- *The gate is said to be built on the place where Jesus made his triumphal entry into Jerusalem (Matt. 21:8-11; Mark 11:8-11; Luke 19:35-38).*

- *This was the traditional route Jesus took to Gethsemane (Matt. 26:30, 36; Mark 14:26; Luke 22:39).*
- *Many Christians believe that at Jesus' second coming the gate will be opened (unblocked) and he will enter the city (Ezek. 44:1-3).*

14. **WESTERN WALL** (Wailing Wall, Kotel Ha Ma'aravi). The Western Wall is a portion of the wall Herod built around the west side of his Temple area and is the holiest shrine of the Jewish world. This part of the wall is 60 yards in length and 60 feet high. Many stones of the wall measure 30 feet by 3 feet by 5 feet. The wall is located by the western entrance to the Temple area.

The wall received its name "Wailing" for at least two traditional reasons: (1) Early in the morning and late at night the wall is covered with drops of dew which legend says are tears that the wall sheds while weeping with Israel in her exile. Legend also has it that in the dead of night a white dove representing the presence of God appears and coos sadly with the mourners. Actually, a family of white doves lives in the holes of the wall. (2) The second reason is that the Jews come here to bewail the loss of their Temple. Today the tears shed are tears of joy, for Israel has returned from exile and is once more able to pray at the wall. Before the six-day war of 1967, Jews were not able to visit the wall.

Jews may be seen praying at the wall at nearly any time; but Friday evening, the beginning of the Jewish Sabbath *(Shabbat)*, is the time when crowds of Orthodox Jews gather to this sacred site and hold regular Shabbat services. Here one sees bits of paper (containing prayers) placed in the cracks of the walls. Torah scrolls, contained in arks, are brought out, and prayer shawls, phylacteries, and prayer books are available. At the north end of the wall is a large synagogue, used in the event of rain or an exceptionally hot day. Hassidim pray, "shokel," and sing at the wall, while small groups dance and sing. Orthodox Jews rock back and forth and put their whole bodies into their prayers, to help maintain concentration and avoid distractions.

Before the six-day war, the wall was hemmed in by houses or buildings and only a few could participate at it. Bulldozers cleared the buildings away after the six-day war and now there is a large plaza that will accommodate thousands of worshippers. To avoid distraction while worshipping, men and women are separated (as Latter-day Saints also do in their Temples). Not only is this a place of holy worship, but here also young recruits to the Israeli army take the oath.

Visitors at the wall have to be careful to observe Jewish customs: heads covered, no picture taking or having pens or pencils in view on the Shabbat and so forth.

To the right of the Western Wall, on the southeast corner of the Temple complex, the Department of Antiquities conducted archaeological digging after 1968 under the direction of Professor Benjamin Mazar of the Hebrew University. The

excavators have found items and buildings dating back to Herod's time and most intervening periods to modern times.

To the left of the Western Wall is **WILSON'S ARCH**, and under the arch the Jews gather to say prayers. It is a section of a bridge, erected on arches, which connected the Temple site with the upper city in the Second Temple period, or the beginning of the Christian period. It is named after a British officer who first explored the site in the 1860s. Excavations within the area show that the stones of Herod go down about 60 feet, or 15 layers below the present ground level to the original soil.

To the right (south) of the Western Wall is **ROBINSON'S ARCH**. The spring of the arch projects from the wall. It was also a royal bridge used to get to the Temple site from the Tyropeon Valley. It is named after Edward Robinson, an American scholar. North of Robinson's Arch huge ashlars (cut building stones) are visible, lying right where they landed when knocked off the Herodian wall at its destruction in A.D. 70, landing on the Roman road – at the level where Jesus walked. Notice the difference in stonework at the top and bottom, the much more impressive lower courses being Herodian and the upper courses being the work of Suleiman the Magnificent in the 16th century A.D.

By 1982 workers had cleared a tunnel the full length of the Western Wall to the site of the ancient Antonia Fortress. At 485 meters, the Western Wall is the longest wall of the four sides of the Temple Mount. There were at least 7 courses of Herodian stone above the level of today's Western Wall, and 19 below today's ground level to bedrock. The beautiful ashlar blocks of stone, which give strength and stability to the wall, were quarried from the area of the present Russian Compound. One of these giant stones measures over 36 x 9 feet! Columns in secondary use are visible sticking out of the inferior upper levels of the present wall. The southwest corner is where the stone of trumpeting, now seen in the Israel Museum, was found lying in the rubble when excavated – lying directly below where it was apparently knocked off by Roman soldiers. (See *Biblical Archaeology Review* Nov/Dec 1986, 20-38, 40-52.)

Herodian stairs (the **GRAND STAIRCASE**) used by pilgrims on their way to the Second Temple (Herod's) have in recent decades been unearthed by archaeologists. They lead up to the two **HULDA GATES** cut into the southern wall of Herod's Temple Mount in the first century B.C. The elaborate stairway in front of the Double Gate was originally 210 feet wide. There are 30 steps, alternating steps and landings – conducive to a slow, reverent ascent or descent. On these steps Jesus may have taught. During his scathing denunciation of hypocrites, he may have gestured toward the east where whited sepulchers gleamed in the mid-day sun. (See Luke 11:47-51 and Matt. 23:27-31.)

Entrance to the Temple area may be made on the right side of the Western Wall through **MOORS GATE**. It is also called the Gate of the Maghrebians, as Muslims from North Africa (Maghreb) once lived near the gate.

15. **DUNG GATE** *(Bab el Maghariba ["gate of the Moors"])*. South of the Wailing Wall is the Dung Gate, so named because past citizens of Jerusalem have taken their garbage and refuse out of the city at this point.

- *Nehemiah mentioned the gate (Neh. 2:13; 3:13-14; 12:31).*

16. **JEWISH QUARTER**. Immediately west of the Wailing Wall and Dung Gate is the old Jewish Quarter, the center of Jewish life in the Holy City for 800 years, until 1948. The **SYNAGOGUE OF RAMBAN**, built on ancient ruins in A.D. 1267, is the most ancient synagogue in the old city. The **JOHANAN BEN ZAKKAI SYNAGOGUE** still stands, but other synagogues have been destroyed. The giant newly-constructed Yeshiva called "Porat Yosef" gets its name from Joseph's patriarchal blessing (Gen. 49:22) – "Joseph is a fruitful bough."

HERODIAN QUARTER. Excavations by archaeologists under the direction of Prof. Nahman Avigad between 1969 and 1983 revealed remains of a wealthy and religious residential quarter, dating from the Herodian period (37 B.C. to A.D. 70). Spacious mansions belonging to Jerusalem's nobility feature beautiful frescoes and mosaic floors, bathrooms and ritual baths (*mikvehs*), stone furniture and vessels, and luxurious ornamental decor. Romans destroyed these villas in A.D. 70. Another structure the Romans destroyed is the "**BURNT HOUSE**," which features an audio-visual presentation of the tragic effects of the war. **THE CARDO** (Gr. "heart") is the colonnaded main street of late Roman, Byzantine, and Crusader Jerusalem. Displayed along the partly restored Cardo is a mosaic recreation of the Jerusalem portion of the Medeba Map. A column is visible in the mosaic Map at today's Damascus Gate. In Arabic it is still called *Bab el Amud*, "gate of the column." The Jerusalem Municipality spent over $20,000 to set up a hologram display of the column with Hadrian's statue on top. It may be seen under the Damascus Gate.

Also in the Jewish Quarter is a **MODEL OF FIRST TEMPLE-PERIOD JERUSALEM** at the Ben Zvi Institute, which features an audio-visual presentation.

Excavations of Old Testament Jerusalem may be studied at the "**BROAD WALL**," which is located a few steps away from the Ben Zvi Institute. The Broad Wall (see Nehemiah 3:8 and 12:38) extended the limits of the City of David to include the Mishneh Quarter, a newer residential district of ancient Jerusalem. (The word "college" in KJV 2 Kings 22:14 and "the second" in Zephaniah 1:10 are both *Mishneh* in Hebrew, apparently designating the second and wealthier housing district of the ancient city.) The exposed section of the Broad Wall is 200 feet long and 22 feet (!) wide, and was part of the fortifications of Hezekiah in preparation for an Assyrian attack in the year 701 B.C. Houses were destroyed to allow for the building of the Broad Wall (as Isaiah reported - see Isa. 22:9-10; *Biblical Archaeology Review* May/Jun 1992, 22-40).

17. **SAINT STEPHEN'S GATE** *(Lion's Gate, Bab Sitti Miriam ["Saint Mary's Gate"])*. This gate is on the east side of the city. It was built with reliefs of lions on the gate's facade because of a dream of Sultan Suleiman. Through this gate the Israel army penetrated into the Old City on June 6, 1967. South of the entrance about one-half block is the **GATE OF THE TRIBES**, which opens into the Temple area. Note the window above the gate. Most ancient gates had an immediate right-angle turn (as Damascus and Zion Gates). While an attacking army was slowed down at the gate, boiling oil could be poured out on them – not an uncommon defensive ploy in antiquity.

The tradition that Stephen was stoned to death outside this gate must be incorrect because the wall was extended northward and the gate built in it by Herod Agrippa, after the time of Stephen.

- *Some believe that this is near the place where Stephen was martyred, while Saul of Tarsus looked on (Acts 7:54-60).*
- *Jesus spoke often of gates (Matt. 7:13-14).*
- *Similar references to gates occur in the Doctrine and Covenants (D&C 22:2, 4; 43:7; 132:22-25).*

18. **CHURCH OF SAINT ANNE**. This church is one of the finest examples of Crusader construction in the Holy Land. It was built in 1100 on the site of a fifth-century Byzantine church, which had in turn been built over a cave believed to be the home of Joachim and Anne, parents of the Virgin Mary – hence the site of the "immaculate conception" (the doctrine that the Virgin Mary was kept free from original sin from the moment of her conception in Saint Anne's womb). At the right center of the church are steps leading down into the **GROTTO OF THE VIRGIN'S BIRTH**. At the end of the twelfth century the church was turned into a school of Islamic studies by Saladin. The "White Fathers," a Greek Orthodox missionary order, took possession of the site in 1878. Groups should sing inside; the church has marvelous acoustics.

A **BIBLICAL MUSEUM** is located near Saint Anne's Church. It was built by the White Fathers and houses artifacts found in the area.

19. **POOL OF BETHESDA** ("house of mercy," *Beth-Zatha*). An ancient double pool, identified as the Pool of Bethesda, has been excavated near Saint Anne's Church by the White Fathers. Only a part of the double pool has been excavated, which shows that the pool was built about 60 feet below the present ground level. The twin pools had five porticoes or porches surrounding them: four around the

sides and one dividing them, and according to Eusebius, they were used to wash sheep before sacrificing them in the Temple. Certain medicinal or curative properties were ascribed to the pool. A superstitious tradition had an angel coming down and "troubling" the waters – probably the result of a siphon-karst spring flowing into the pool, causing bubbling at the surface. At this pool, Jesus met an invalid man, lame or paralyzed for thirty-eight years. On the Sabbath day, he raised him up, completely healed. (See John 5:1-16). A very large fifth-century Church of the Paralytic was built over the pool, but it was destroyed by the Persians in 614. The Crusaders built a chapel over the Byzantine ruins, and the apse and entrance are still visible above the remains of the excavated pool. Schick, Vincent, and Van der Vliet helped excavate the area.

- *Jesus healed a lame man at the troubled waters of the pool of Bethesda (John 5:1-16).*

20. The **SAINT ANNE SEMINARY** is located just west of the Church of Saint Anne.

VIA DOLOROSA

The **VIA DOLOROSA** ("way of sorrow," Way of the Cross) is the traditional pathway Jesus took from Pilate's judgment hall to Calvary. Millions of pilgrims have walked this path. Each Friday at 3:00 P.M. a ceremony led by Franciscan priests is conducted along the Via Dolorosa, beginning at station number 1, and prayers are made at each of 14 **STATIONS OF THE CROSS** as originally pointed out by the Crusaders. Nine stations are based on the gospel accounts and five are based on tradition. Originally the Catholics had 36 stations. The Protestants have 7. Every Catholic who "makes" the Way of the Cross, either in Jerusalem or in his chapel at home, may receive indulgences for his efforts.

The 14 Catholic stations are as follows:

21. (1) **PILATE'S JUDGMENT HALL** (the Praetorium), where Jesus was condemned to death (Matt. 27:2-31). This is traditionally the site of Herod's great fortress, the Antonia, named after Mark Antony. Within the fortress Jesus was condemned, mocked, crowned, and given the cross to bear. The first station is now a Muslim boys' school, El Omariye, and the school stands on the ruins of the Antonia. The original staircase, known as the *Scala Santa* (the holy steps), where Pilate washed his hands, was transferred by Constantine's mother, Saint Helena, to Rome, where it is located in a church near San Giovanni in Laterano.

22. (2) **WHERE JESUS RECEIVED THE CROSS**, at the foot of the Antonia. Located opposite the Praetorium is the Franciscan Bible School, with its **CHURCH OF THE FLAGELLATION** (Matt. 27:28-32). It stands on the traditional site where Jesus was scourged and a crown of thorns was placed on his head

(John 19:1-2). A crown of thorns hangs over the sanctuary, and in the chapel an altar dedicated to Saint Paul commemorates his imprisonment in the Antonia (Acts 21-23).

The "**ECCE HOMO" ARCH**, over the Via Dolorosa, was built by Hadrian in the second century. The Latin phrase *ecce homo* means "behold the man," Pontius Pilate's declaration when he pointed to Jesus (John 19:5). Archaeological investigation has shown that the arch is a portion of a triple gateway leading to the Roman city of Aelia Capitolina. The **NOTRE DAME DE SION CONVENT DE L'ECCE HOMO** (Church of the Sisters of Zion) is located by the Gate (arch) of Ecce Homo, and a former tradition says it was built over the top of the "pavement" of Pilate's courtyard, where Jesus was condemned to death.

For many years pilgrims and tourists visited the Sisters of Zion Convent and the pavement (Gr. *lithostrotos*) below it, believing that to be the place where Jesus might have stood before Pilate. That has now been proved incorrect. The striated (grooved) Roman pavement, with its etchings of Roman games, etc., on the lowest level of the Convent was laid by Hadrian above the vault of the Struthion Pool or cistern. The pavement served as a plaza and marketplace for Aelia Capitolina, the city Hadrian built over the ruins of Jerusalem destroyed by Titus in A. D. 70.

The **ECCE HOMO BASILICA**, west of the striated flagstone, is called such because the northern section of Hadrian's triple triumphal gateway into Aelia Capitolina has been incorporated into the basilica, where it frames the main altar.

Just west of the Sisters of Zion Convent is a **GREEK ORTHODOX MONASTERY.**

23. (3) **WHERE JESUS FELL FOR THE FIRST TIME.** Here the polish Roman Catholic Biblical-Archaeological Museum and store now stand, on the corner as you turn left along El-Wad Street. From here the visitor walks about 75 feet to station number 4.

24. (4) **WHERE JESUS MET HIS MOTHER.** This is marked by an Armenian Catholic church, "Our Lady of the Spasm." The church is thought to stand on the site of the Byzantine church of Saint Sophia. In the crypt a sixth-century mosaic shows the outline of a pair of sandals that is said to be on the spot where Mary stood. About 75 feet from this point the visitor turns right. On the left-hand corner, station number 5 is located.

25. (5) **WHERE SIMON THE CYRENIAN WAS COMPELLED TO BEAR THE CROSS OF JESUS.** A small chapel, a nineteenth-century Franciscan oratory, is located here, and a stone in the wall of the chapel shows a light depression where, according to tradition, Jesus in his weariness rested his hand (Matt. 27:32; Mark 15:21; Luke 23:26). This station is located on the Via Dolorosa street. It is about 240 feet to station number 6.

26. (6) **WHERE SAINT VERONICA WIPED JESUS' FACE.** This is the house of the traditional Saint Veronica, who, after wiping the sweat and blood from Christ's forehead, is supposed to have found the imprint of Christ's facial features on the cloth. According to tradition, this was the woman who was cured by touching the hem of Jesus' garment. The site is served by the Little Sisters, a congregation of Greek Orthodox Catholics. Station number 7 is approximately 250 yards from station number 6.

27. (7) **WHERE JESUS FELL THE SECOND TIME** (up the large steps through the vaulted alley). This is located on the main market street (Suq Khan Ez-Zeit) opposite the junction with the Via Dolorosa. Two Franciscan chapels are attached to the station. One of the chapels has a red column of stone from Aelia Capitolina. This is the location of the Gate of Judgment, through which Jesus was led outside the city walls. Here a copy of the death sentence was fastened to one of the columns of the portico. From here the visitor enters El-Khanqa Street to station number 8.

28. (8) **WHERE JESUS CONSOLED THE WOMEN OF JERUSALEM.** "Weep not for me, but weep for yourselves," Jesus said (Luke 23:27-32). The site is marked by the large Greek Orthodox Monastery of Saint Charalambos, about on hundred yards up El-Khanqa Street.

29. (9) **WHERE JESUS FELL FOR THE THIRD TIME.** A Coptic monastery with a shaft of column built into the door marks the site. This site is located up an alley leading west from Suq Khan Ez-Zeit. A huge underground cistern lies within the convent. A circular cupola on a nearby terrace is the roof of Saint Helena's Chapel within the Church of the Holy Sepulcher. The Coptic Abyssinian monks and their ancient Ethiopian dialect are of interest.

Via Dolorosa

30. (10-14) **CHURCH OF THE HOLY SEPULCHER.** Stations 10-14 are all inside the Church of the Holy Sepulcher. As you enter, bear to the right and go up the steps for stations 10-13. For details of stations 10-14, see the subsection "Church of the Holy Sepulcher," below.

(10) **WHERE JESUS WAS STRIPPED OF HIS GARMENTS** and received gall to drink (Matt. 27:34; Mark 15:23-24; Luke 23:34; John 19:23). This site is located behind the Roman Catholic altar.

(11) **WHERE JESUS WAS NAILED TO THE CROSS** (Golgotha) (Matt. 27:35; Mark 15:25; Luke 23:33; John 19:18).4 The rock of Calvary, Catholic version, may be seen under a glass in the Greek Orthodox chapel, which is built right by the Catholic chapel.

(12) **WHERE JESUS WAS CRUCIFIED AND DIED ON THE CROSS** (Golgotha) (Matt. 27:50; Mark 15:25, 37; Luke 23:46; John 19:30). This location may be seen in the Greek Orthodox chapel under the altar, and a star marks the exact site. A split rock at the station was caused, according to tradition, by the earthquake when Jesus was crucified.

(13) **WHERE JESUS WAS TAKEN DOWN FROM THE CROSS** and given over to Mary. The exact site, according to Catholic tradition, is under the Roman Catholic altar.

(14) **WHERE JESUS WAS LAID IN THE CHAMBER OF THE SEPULCHER** (tomb) and from there **RESURRECTED** (Matt. 27:57-61; 28:1-10; Mark 15:42-16:8; Luke 23:50-24:8; John 19:38-20:31).[5]

CHURCH OF THE HOLY SEPULCHER

The **CHURCH OF THE HOLY SEPULCHER** (*Golgotha*, Catholic version) is the most sacred site on earth for a majority of Christians. The church is built over the traditional hill of Calvary and the tomb of Joseph of Arimathea (Catholic version). Several churches have been built on this site since Hadrian built a temple to Jupiter and Venus in A.D. 135. This he did hoping to wean the Christians from their veneration of sacred places. This temple remained until Constantine built a church in 335, which was destroyed in 614 by the Persians. Other churches were built on the site in the seventh and eleventh centuries and finally in the twelfth. The Crusaders' church of the twelfth century is still the basic outline of the present building.

Saladin defeated the Crusaders in 1187, and he allowed the Christians to use the shrine only if the key to the building remained in Muslim hands. It has been in the hands of the Arab Nuseibeh family since 1330. Various renovations and additions have been made over the years. In 1927 an earthquake left the building in a weak condition, and between 1936 and 1944 the British shored up the facade with ugly iron girders and tied up the interior with wood supports.

Since 1958 a "total restoration" has been in progress; but since the 6 communities cannot agree on "rights" and "renovations," the building is in a poor state of repair. Since reconstruction implies possession, it is difficult to get agreement on repair procedures. To have unity among those interested seems to be wishful thinking. The communities are classified as 3 "major" and 3 "minor" when it pertains to rights. Those who have major rights are the Roman, Greek Orthodox, and Armenian Orthodox Catholics. Those who have minor rights are Syrian (Jacobite), Coptic, and Abyssinian Catholics.

As you enter the building, the steps on the right lead to Latin and Greek chapels representing the tenth, eleventh, twelfth, and thirteenth stations of the Way of the Cross. They are built on the top of "Calvary," where tradition says Adam's skull was buried (*Golgotha*, "place of a skull") (Matt. 27:33; John 19:17).[6]

The Latin Franciscan chapel on the right has stations 10, where Jesus was stripped of his garments, and 11, where Jesus was nailed to the cross. The Greek altar in the left chapel represents station 12, where Jesus died on the cross. Between the columns which support the altar, a silver disc, with an opening in the center, covers the **SPOT WHERE THE CROSS OF JESUS STOOD**. It is possible to touch the rock of Golgotha through the hole in the center of the silver disc.

Station 13, which represents **JESUS' BODY BEING TAKEN FROM THE CROSS**, is marked by a wooden bust of the virgin Mary in a glass case. It is decorated with jewels and gold. Black discs on both sides of the altar mark the places where the **THIEVES' CROSSES STOOD**. On the right of the altar is shown the split in the rocks that were rent at the time of the crucifixion. It can also be seen in the **CHAPEL OF ADAM**, below which is housed an altar dedicated to Melchizedek. Legend has it that Adam was buried here, and that on the day of the Crucifixion the blood of the Redeemer fell upon that "first guilty head." This has given rise to the custom, mainly of the Greek Orthodox church, to represent, at the foot of the crucifix, a skull and crossbones.

As the visitor leaves this chapel, to the left is the Greek sacristy, with many relics. The superior will allow people to visit the Greek treasury, which is kept in a room above "Calvary." The relics include "two big pieces of the **TRUE CROSS**, jewelled mitres, vestments, and "the sword of Peter the Great of Russia."

Close to the entrance of the building is the **STONE OF UNCTION**, or "Stone of the Anointing," marking the spot where tradition indicates Jesus' body was prepared for burial.

The Holy Sepulcher, where Jesus was laid, is the fourteenth station of the Way of the Cross. This tomb, with a Muscovite cupola, is entered through a small Chapel of the Angel, which has a fragment of the **STONE UPON WHICH AN-**

GELS SAT after they had rolled it back from the entrance (Mark 16:6). The Holy Sepulcher has a marble slab raised above the floor, marking the **PLACE WHERE JESUS WAS BURIED**. According to tradition, the original stone slab is beneath the one that is displayed. Behind the edicule is a small Coptic chapel, where the rock of the Holy Sepulcher can be seen and touched. Behind the Holy Sepulcher is the chapel of the Syrian Jacobites in a dark chamber. A narrow opening leads to rock-hewn empty burial niches. This is a part of the traditional **TOMB OF JOSEPH OF ARIMATHEA**.

In the Greek cathedral, a large stone **CHALICE** on the Crusader floor is supposed to mark the **CENTER OF THE EARTH**. A flight of steps leads down to the **CHAPEL OF SAINT HELENA**, then on down to the Latin **CHAPEL OF THE FINDING OF THE CROSS**, where, according to tradition, the crosses of Jesus and the thieves were found by Saint Helena in 327 at the bottom of an unused cistern cut into Calvary. On the north side of the church is the **CHAPEL OF THE APPARITION**, commemorating Jesus' appearance to the Virgin. It contains a reddish **COLUMN OF THE FLAGELLATION**. Sword and spurs of the first Crusader king Godfrey of Bouillon are on display in the sacristy east of the chapel.

On the Church of the Holy Sepulcher as the burial place of Jesus, consult *Biblical Archaeology Review* May/Jun 1986, 26-45.

OTHER SITES IN OLD JERUSALEM

31. **CHRISTIAN QUARTER**. Surrounding the Church of the Holy Sepulcher, in the northwest section of the Old City of Jerusalem, is the Christian Quarter. The Lutheran **CHURCH OF THE REDEEMER** was built in 1898 over the gateway and cloister of the Crusader Church of Saint Mary Latina. A magnificent view of the city may be had from the spire of the church. South of the Holy Sepulcher Church is an area known as *Muristan*, which means "hospice" in Arabic. Here thousands of pilgrims stayed during Crusader times. The **CHURCH OF SAINT JOHN THE BAPTIST** was built in the eleventh century. Excavations on the site have disclosed a reliquary which contains a fragment of the "true cross."

The **GREEK PATRIARCHATE** is a large building embracing Crusader churches. The visitor can walk along the roof of the Patriarchate to the cupola of the Holy Sepulcher Church, where, in Saint Thecla's chapel, there is a stone coffin which tradition says belonged to Mariamne, Herod's murdered wife. A nearby small ladder gives access to the galleries over the rotunda, where the edicule over the Holy Sepulcher can be seen.

The **MOSQUE OF OMAR** is south of the entrance to the Church of the Holy Sepulcher. The minaret dates back to 1465 and commemorates Omar's prayer that he gave outside the entrance of the Church of the Holy Sepulcher. The **MOSQUE**

OF KHANQA is north of the Church of the Holy Sepulcher. Many schools, monasteries, churches, and souvenir shops are located within the Christian Quarter.

32. **POOL OF HEZEKIAH.** Southwest of the Church of the Holy Sepulcher, in the Muristan quarter of the Old City, is the large, dry Pool of Hezekiah, or Bath of the Patriarchs. It can be seen by going through one of the shops on the west side of Christian Street, or on the north side of David Street.

33. **CITADEL, DAVID'S TOWER,** and **HEROD'S PALACE.** The **CITADEL** was built by Herod. It stands alongside Jaffa Gate and was the only part of the walls of Jerusalem to remain standing after Titus and the Roman army destroyed the city in A.D. 70. It has always been an important point for the various battles of Jerusalem and was a scene of fierce fighting during the Israeli-Arab conflict of 1948. The present citadel stands on Crusader foundations, but most of the citadel was built by Suleiman the Magnificent in 1540. Only part of the moat that surrounded the citadel is visible today.

The **TOWER OF DAVID** is the name given to the tower on the right of the Citadel's entrance. On the same site that General Allenby proclaimed the start of British rule in Palestine in 1917 is the entrance to the new, state-of-the-art **MUSEUM OF THE HISTORY OF JERUSALEM,** established 1988. This Citadel or Tower of David Museum offers four different tours: Exhibit Tour, Excavation Tour, Panorama Tour, or Brief Tour, ranging from many hours and several different visits to just an introductory film, view of the city, and a look at excavations. Exhibit rooms show the history of Jerusalem during the Canaanite period, the First and Second Temple periods, Roman, Byzantine, Early Muslim, Crusader, Mamluke, Ottoman, and British Mandate periods. Jerusalem's illustrious history is taught by means of holograms, maps, models, dioramas, reliefs, videos, and animated films. Portable tape-recorded guides are available. From April to October a **SOUND AND LIGHT SHOW** lasting approx. 45 minutes is presented beginning at 8:30, 9:30, and 10:30 p.m., depending on the language. Warm clothing is recommended.

HEROD'S PALACE was located south of the citadel where the police barracks now stand.

- *Wise men from the east came to Jerusalem and asked Herod (the Great), "Where is he that is born King of the Jews?" (Matt. 2:1-2).*
- *Pilate sent Jesus to Herod (Antipas) to be accused (Luke 23:7-12).*

34. **JAFFA GATE** *(Bab el Khalil* ["gate of the friend"]). The road from Jerusalem to Jaffa on the Mediterranean Sea starts here. It is also the road to Hebron; and as it makes its way through Jerusalem it is the main thoroughfare. It was the first street built outside the old city walls (1870). The gate is located by the Citadel of

David. General Allenby entered this gate in 1917 in his march through Palestine after defeating the Turks. After the six-day war in 1967 the Jaffa Gate was restored by funds collected from South African Jewry. An Arab inscription over the entrance reads "There is no God but Allah and Abraham is his friend."

When George A. Smith, Lorenzo Snow, Albert Carrington, Eliza R. Snow and their party came to Palestine in 1873, their "travel agency" furnished the horses, tents, beds, food, etc., for their thirty days' trip. When they arrived at Jerusalem on Feb. 25, their tents were pitched "near" and "in front of" the Jaffa Gate. On Sunday, March 2, after dedicating the land while on the Mt. of Olives, they held a "sacramental" meeting in one of their tents that was 16 feet in diameter. In the meeting, George A. Smith, Feramorz Little, and Paul Schettler, who had been re-baptized in the Jordan River at Bethabara, were re-confirmed members of the Church. (*Correspondence of Palestine Tourists,* Salt Lake City, 1875).

When David O. McKay arrived in Jerusalem on Oct. 31, 1921, he stayed in the Allenby Hotel "just outside the walls near the Jaffa Gate" (*Cherished Experiences from the Writings of David O. McKay,* p. 116).

35. **ARMENIAN QUARTER**. The **SAINT JAMES CATHEDRAL**, in the south-western part of the Old City, is the most famous site in the Armenian Quarter. It is named after James the apostle, who, according to tradition, was flung from the pinnacle of the Temple into the Kidron Valley and then stoned and buried. His bones were transferred to the church, and tradition says they are under the main altar.

The **ARMENIAN MUSEUM** has displays of the Patriarchate's priceless treasures.

The traditional site of the **HOUSE OF ANNAS**, the ex-high priest and father-in-law of the high priest Caiaphas in Jesus' day, is located in the southern portion of the Armenian Quarter. By the northeastern corner of the chapel is an olive tree to which, according to tradition, Jesus was tied while waiting to see Annas.

- *Jesus was compelled to appear before the high priest Caiaphas (John 18:13-14).*
- *Peter and John were brought before the council composed of Annas, Caiaphas, and other high priests (Acts 4:5-19).*

36. **BAZAARS**. Many small, narrow streets have their bazaars. For one you will always remember, turn down Suq el-Lahhamin (Butcher Street); it is to the east of the Holy Sepulcher, at the junction with Dabbage Road. Don't be alarmed at the begging of little children. The cry for "baksheesh" is a respectable pastime in the Muslim world. They help Allah by making it possible for Muslims to give alms. Don't be taken in by "official guides" along the way – who want "baksheesh" also.

The Arabs call a market a "souk" (*suq*). The three covered "souks" at the end of Bab el-Khan Zeit date from Crusader times.

37. **SPAFFORD CHILDREN'S CENTER.** Just inside the walls of the Old City, on a hill that originally extended north to include the hill designated by the Protestants as Golgotha, is a building used for decades as a center to train young mothers in child care.

The Center operated under the direction of two granddaughters of Horatio Gates Spafford. He brought his family from Illinois, USA, in 1881 after tragedy took the lives of four daughters at sea and a son died. They came to find peace and give themselves to God in the Holy Land.

When World War II was waging, Horatio's daughter, Bertha Spafford Vester, and her husband, with other members of the American colony, offered their services to both British and Turkish forces by operating a hospital and dishing out food rations. Bertha spent her long life in the charitable hospital service. She saw three wars in Jerusalem.

In 1971 the hospital became a center of education and child care.

38. **MUSLIM QUARTER.** In the northeast section of Old Jerusalem is the Muslim Quarter.

Immediately East of the Old City

39. **MOUNT SCOPUS** ("to look over," *Har Hatsofim* = "the Mount of Watchmen"). The north end of the Mount of Olives range is called Mount Scopus. (*Skopeo* is Greek and means "to watch.") It has played a decisive role in the many battles that have been fought for the Holy City since time immemorial. Babylonian armies between 605-586 B.C. camped and watched the city they were besieging. Roman legions of Titus camped here in A.D. 70, the Crusaders in 1099, the British in 1917, and the Arabs in 1948 and 1967.

40. **BRITISH WAR CEMETERY.** This is the final resting place of soldiers who fell in the area during the battles of World War I. A Jewish section is on the northwest.

41. **HADASSAH HOSPITAL.** Near the cemetery are the buildings of the Hadassah University Hospital. Between 1948 and 1967 it was moved to a new location near Ein Karem, and finally re-established after 1967 on its original site on Mount Scopus. It was built in 1939 and was used as a medical school.

42. **HEBREW UNIVERSITY ON MOUNT SCOPUS.** The cornerstone of the Hebrew University was laid on Mount Scopus in 1918, and the university opened in 1925 with Lord Balfour present. The complex received a "demilitarized" status in 1948, and for 19 years it was controlled by the Jews. When access to Mount Scopus was so difficult, the Jews built a campus at Givat Ram in western Jerusalem. In 1968 foundation stones were again laid for a new university city on Mount Scopus, and it has since become the main campus of the two.

43. **TRUMAN RESEARCH CENTER.** Named after Harry S. Truman, president of the United States, this edifice was built as a study center for international scholars, scientists, and philosophers engaged in research to advance peace and prosperity among all nations. It houses a 350-seat auditorium, 2 seminar rooms, and a large library, including the complete library of philosopher Martin Buber.

44. **AMPHITHEATER.** North of the Truman Research Center is an amphitheater overlooking the Judean wilderness. It has a beautiful setting and good acoustics. It is used for lectures, concerts, recitals, and other such events.

45. **AUGUSTA VICTORIA HOSPITAL.** In 1910 a German hospice and sanatorium was opened and named after Kaiser Wilhelm's wife. (The hospice was erected for German Protestant pilgrims and the Church of the Dormition, Dormition Abbey, on Mount Zion was erected for German Catholic pilgrims). It is built between Mount Scopus and the Mount of Olives. Its high, square tower is a landmark, but removed from its natural setting on the Rhine. It served as a government house for the British from 1920 to 1927, when it was badly damaged in an earthquake. Here in 1921, British Colonial Secretary, Winston Churchill, met with Abdullah, King Hussein's grandfather, and created the Arab State of Transjordan. Now the hospital is operated by the Lutheran World Federation.

THE JERUSALEM CENTER FOR NEAR EASTERN STUDIES

After more than a decade of study abroad programs in the Holy Land, Brigham Young University began a search for property to build their own study center in Jerusalem. Following several years of searching and negotiations with the Jerusalem Municipality, the District Lands Administration, and ministries of the Israeli Government, a site on Mount Scopus was selected, financial and political arrangements made, and construction begun. Ground-breaking for the multi-million-dollar Center took place in August of 1984 and earth-moving and construction commenced shortly thereafter.

Opposition was voiced by some orthodox and nationalist Jewish individuals and groups who supposed the "Mormons" were building a "missionary center" to bring their young people to Israel and train them to go out and convert Jews. Various arguments were raised by certain Jewish activists to stop construction of the Center. Objections were met by the University and the Church making commitments to not use this Center or its study programs and tours to proselyte.

Students moved into the facility in March of 1987, and it was dedicated in May, 1989. The 125,000-square-foot, eight-story structure is built on 6 acres of land terraced down the slope of Mount Scopus, with an extraordinary panoramic view out over the Holy City and the Temple Mount/Haram esh-Sharif. The

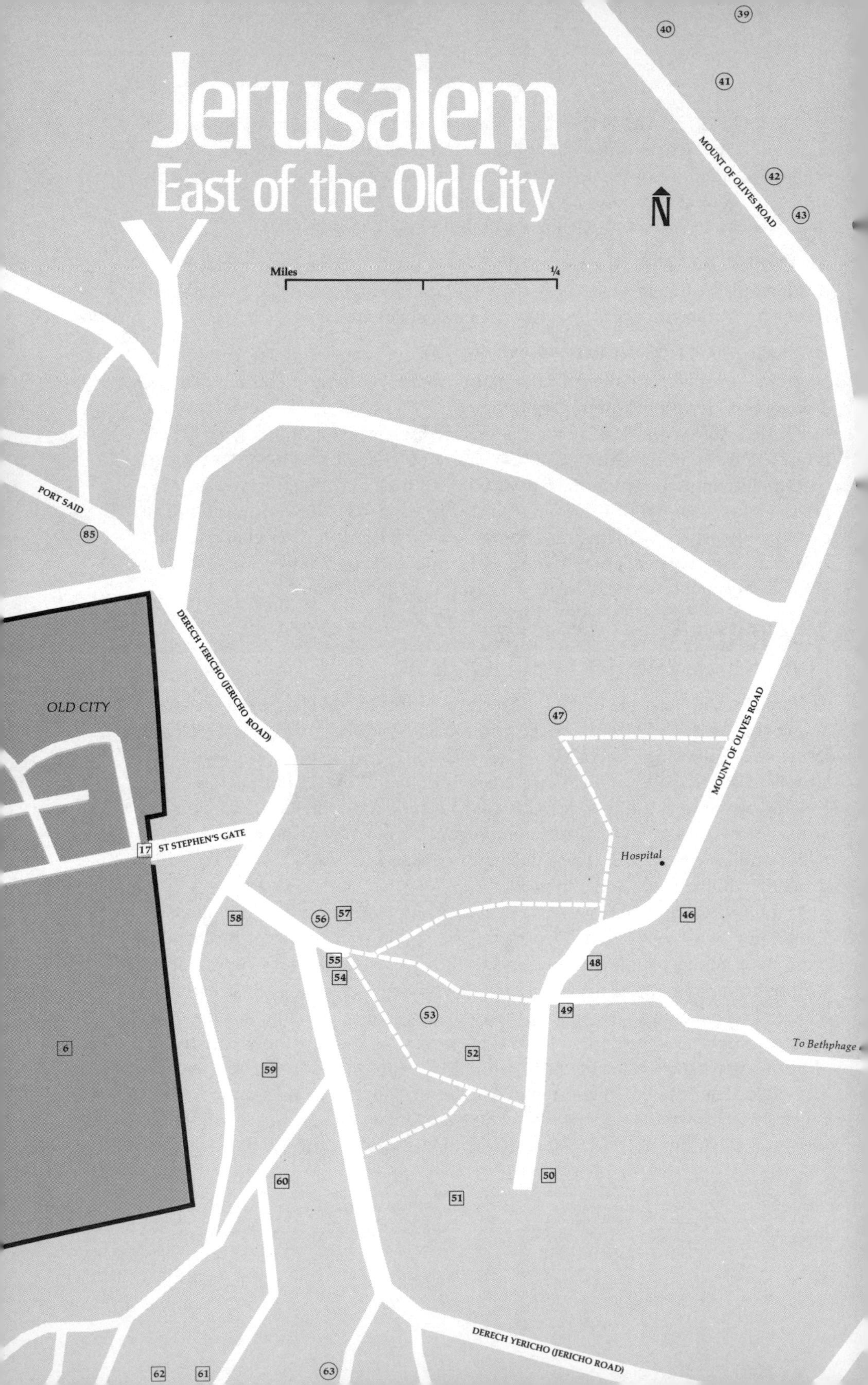
Jerusalem
East of the Old City
N
Miles
¼
MOUNT OF OLIVES ROAD
39
40
41
42
43
PORT SAID
85
DERECH YERICHO (JERICHO ROAD)
OLD CITY
47
MOUNT OF OLIVES ROAD
Hospital
17
ST STEPHEN'S GATE
58
56
57
46
55
54
48
49
53
To Bethphage
6
59
52
60
50
51
DERECH YERICHO (JERICHO ROAD)
62
61
63

39. Mount Scopus
40. British War Cemetery
41. Former Hadassah Hospital
42. Hebrew University on Mount Scopus
43. Truman Research Center
44. Amphitheater
45. Augusta Victoria Hospital
46. Mount of Olives
47. Hill where angels addressed the disciples after Ascension
48. Hill where Jesus ascended into heaven
49. Church of the Pater Noster
50. Mount of Offense
51. Jewish cemetery
52. Dominus Flevit
53. Russian Othodox Church of Mary Magdalene
54. Basilica of the Agony
55. Gethsemane
56. Tomb of the Virgin Mary
57. Grotto of Gethsemane
58. Church of Saint Stephen
59. Kidron Valley
60. Absalom's Pillar, Tomb of Jehoshaphat,
    Grotto of Saint James, and Tomb of Zechariah
61. Gihon Spring
62. Hill Ophel and the City of David
63. Royal Tomb of Shebna
64. Mount of Offense and Mount of Evil Counsel
65. Pool of Siloam and Hezekiah's Tunnel
66. Hinnom Valley
67. Potter's Field
    (For sites 64–67, see map on page 58.)

Center includes dormitory rooms for 200 L.D.S. students, faculty, and staff, classrooms, kitchen and cafeteria, gymnasium, computer room, offices, parking garage, two auditoriums, seminar/video rooms, domed theater, library, and learning resource center. The upper auditorium features a remarkable, custom-made organ. Exquisitely landscaped biblical gardens surround the facility. The Center is occupied year-round by students, young and old, who come to study the Scriptures on site, plus learn more about the history, geography, archaeology, languages, culture, politics, and current events of the peoples who have lived and now live in this land. The Center hosts thousands of touring visitors each month.

MOUNT OF OLIVES

46. **MOUNT OF OLIVES** (Olivet).[7] The Mount of Olives, holy to three great faiths, is separated from Old Jerusalem by the Kidron Valley. It has four eminences extending from north to south:

47. (1) The **NORTHERNMOST** (south of Mt. Scopus) is supposed to be the hill where the two **ANGELS ADDRESSED THE DISCIPLES** after the Ascension and said, "Ye men of Galilee, why stand ye gazing up into heaven?" (Acts 1:11). *Viri*

Mount of Olives, with the Church of All Nations and Garden of Gethsemane in the foreground

Galilaei is the name given to a wooded compound on the hill which belongs to the Greeks. A modern chapel and a Byzantine chapel mark the site.

48. (2) The **SECOND EMINENCE** is supposed to be the hill where **JESUS ASCENDED INTO HEAVEN** (Luke 24:50-53; Acts 1:9-12). (Acts 1:12 is at variance with Luke 24:50. Luke indicates Bethany is the site.) The **CHURCH OF THE ASCENSION** was built on this site before A.D. 387, and in 1187 the church was converted into a mosque. Only one small domed building remains of the original. Within this small octagonal building are, according to tradition, the **FOOTPRINTS LEFT BY JESUS** just before he ascended into heaven. This is a Christian shrine under Muslim control. The Muslims revere Jesus as a prophet and believe in the doctrine of the Ascension. Jesus, they believe, will raise Muhammad on resurrection day. A panoramic view of the area can be seen from the roof. The Church of the Ascension seems to have been the main inspiration for the architecture of the Dome of the Rock Mosque.

On October 24, 1841, Elder Orson Hyde dedicated the Holy Land on the central western slope of the Mount of Olives, which is directly east from and slightly higher than the Temple Mount. One hundred thirty-eight years later, on October 24, 1979, President Spencer W. Kimball and 2,000 other Church officials and members gathered at the same location to dedicate the **ORSON HYDE MEMORIAL GARDEN**, a 5½-acre park developed with a $1. million gift from the Orson Hyde Foundation. The Garden is one of the largest and most prestigious parts of the Jerusalem National Park, a green-belt of small parks and landscaped gardens around the Old City. It features a 150-seat stone amphitheater near the top of the Garden, and on the north side of the amphitheater a bronze plaque was placed with excerpts of Elder Hyde's prayer in English and Hebrew. Olive trees and other indigenous vegetation are growing throughout the park and a stone path winds back and forth in a gradual descent to the lower slope of the Mount of Olives and the Garden of Gethsemane.

In his dedicatory prayer of the Memorial Garden in 1979, Pres. Kimball noted that "the city of Jerusalem has flourished and we know that in thine own due time other things will also be prospered and bring peace and joy to this land. We pray for Abraham's children, both those of blood and those by their faithfulness through adoption. . . . Help us to embrace strangers with love and draw them to us and to thee. Help us to realize in our lives the special responsibility of a chosen people, quick to do thy will. . . . Protect this garden from the ravages of war and storm and depredation of every kind. Let it be a haven, where all may meditate on the glory thou hast shed upon Jerusalem in ages past and the greater glory yet to be."

In 1872, President Brigham Young sent his counselor, George A. Smith, to dedicate the land of Palestine for the return of the Jews. Pres. Smith took with him two apostles, Lorenzo Snow and Albert Carrington, and also Eliza R. Snow, Feramorz Little, Thomas W. Jennings, Paul A. Schettler, and Clara S. Little.

On Sunday, March 2, 1873, they ascended the Mt. of Olives and visited the Church of the Ascension while a tent was being erected for a sacred and solemn occasion. Most of the group assembled in the tent in the robes of the priesthood, and Albert Carrington, Lorenzo Snow, and George A. Smith each dedicated the land of Palestine for the return of the Jews. The tent was arranged with a table, seats and carpet, and was located about 100 feet northeast of the Church of the Ascension (a mosque today). Of the location of the tent, Pres. Smith said, "We concluded it to be as likely a spot of the Ascension as the one which the Mohamedans had selected; we had no doubt but the mountain was correct" (Private Journal of George A. Smith).

The **RUSSIAN COMPOUND** was built in the late nineteenth century. At the southeast corner of the church is a **STONE** where, according to tradition, the **VIRGIN MARY STOOD** at the time of the Ascension, which, according to the Russians, took place where the tower is. The **TOWER OF ASCENSION** has 6 stories and 214 steps, and is the most noticeable landmark on the Mount of Olives.

On March 4, 1902, Pres. Francis M. Lyman visited the Russian Compound and ascended the Bell Tower of Ascension with its large and beautifully decorated bells. From the tower he saw a quiet spot for a dedicatory prayer, located fifty yards east from the base of the tower in a little grove of young cypress trees. In that quiet spot, he placed his rug, knelt down with Brothers Herman and Sylvester by his side, and dedicated the land of Palestine for the return of the Jews. Pres. Lyman's prayer by the Bell Tower of Ascension was one of at least twelve dedicatory prayers that concerned Palestine and the return of the Jews. These dedicatory prayers were offered by apostles and one "pastor" [mission president], between the years 1841 and 1933. Eight of the prayers were offered on the Mt. of Olives, one in the Casa Nova hospice in Old Jerusalem, a block from the New Gate, two on Mt. Carmel at Kaiser's Watch, and what appears to be the last one, in the mission home in Haifa.

East of the main church is another **CHURCH WITH A MOSAIC** over a hollow, where, according to a document on the wall, the **HEAD OF JOHN THE BAPTIST WAS DISCOVERED** at the time of Constantine.

49. (3) On the **THIRD EMINENCE** the **CHURCH OF THE PATER NOSTER** ("our father") stands on the traditional spot where Jesus instructed his disciples on the Lord's Prayer (Matt. 6:9-15; Luke 11:1-4). (Since the instructions on the Lord's Prayer were given as a part of the Sermon on the Mount, this site is questionable.) The original church was built by Saint Helena in 333 and later destroyed by the Persians. Tiles along the walls of the cloister are inscribed with the Lord's Prayer in more than 60 languages.

The **CARMELITE CONVENT** and **BASILICA OF THE SACRED HEART** are on a hill adjoining the Church of the Pater Noster.

The **TOMB OF THE PROPHETS HAGGAI, MALACHI, AND ZECHARIAH** is located southwest of the Church of the Pater Noster. It contains 36 burial niches.

50. (4) The **SOUTHEAST EMINENCE** is called by some the **MOUNT OF OFFENSE OR MOUNT OF SCANDAL** because it is supposed to be the "Mount of Corruption" on which Solomon erected the high places for the worship of strange gods (1 Kings 11:7). Some believe Solomon erected the high places on the mount south of the Jericho Road.

- *David fled over the Mount of Olives from Absalom (2 Sam. 15:30; 16:14).*
- *Jesus taught concerning the destruction of Jerusalem, his second coming, and the end of the world (Matt. 24-25; Mark 13).*
- *Jesus taught the parable of the ten virgins and the talents, and about the last judgment: "Inasmuch as ye have done it unto one of the least of these my brethren..." (Matt. 25).*
- *The Mount of Olives was the scene of Christ's triumphal entry (Luke 19:29-44).*
- *The fig tree was cursed (Matt. 21:17-22; Mark 11:12-14, 20-26).*
- *Here Jesus wept over Jerusalem (Matt. 27:37-39; Luke 19:37-44).*
- *This was the place of the ascension of Jesus and the appearance of the angels to the apostles (Matt. 28:16-20; Luke 24:50-53; Acts 1:4-12).*
- *At the Lord's coming the Mount of Olives will split in two (Zech. 14:4). Into the valley made by the split the Jews will flee and meet the Lord and his saints (Mal 3:2; Zech. 14:3-9).*
- *The "touching-down scene" is mentioned in the New Testament (1 Thess. 4:16-18; Rev. 19:7).*

- *Jesus taught concerning the destruction of Jerusalem, his second coming, and the end of the world (1 Ne. 1:18-19: 3:17; 7:13; 10:3-4; 2 Ne. 25:14-19; Hel. 8:20-21; JS-M 1:1-55; D&C 33:17; 65:3; 88:92).*
- *The Doctrine and Covenants speaks of the last judgment (D&C 45:57).*
- *Jesus will return, the mount will "cleave in twain," and the Jews will recognize Jesus as their Messiah (D&C 45:48-53; 133:1-42, esp. 20; 5:20; 34:7; 45:16; 78:21; 109:75).*
- *Destruction will be caused by the brightness of Jesus' coming (D&C 5:19; 29:11-12; 34:7; 45:16, 44, 56; 65:5).*
- *Jesus is to be in red apparel at his coming (D&C 133:48; cf. Isa. 63:1-6).*
- *The "touching-down scene" is referred to in the Doctrine and Covenants (D&C 88:96; 29:9-11).*

51. **JEWISH CEMETERY**. On the Mount of Olives is the largest and oldest Jewish cemetery in the world. It dates to biblical times. Today there are over 70,000 graves here. Many a Jew has made a pilgrimage to Jerusalem in order to live, die, and then be buried in this cemetery. Jews were anguished over the building of a large hotel in the middle of the cemetery. They were shocked when the Jordanians used tombstones to pave pathways to army latrines. The Jews believe that the resurrection will take place here.

- *The final judgment and resurrection are expected to take place here (Ezek. 37:1-14).*
- *The Lord will stand upon the Mount of Olives (Zech. 14:4).*

OTHER CHURCHES ON THE MOUNT OF OLIVES:

52. **DOMINUS FLEVIT** ("the Lord wept"). This Franciscan church is the only church in the area with contemporary church lines. It is located down the path on which Jesus came to Jerusalem and honors the spot where, according to tradition, Jesus wept over Jerusalem (Matt. 23:37-39; Luke 19:37-44).

53. The **RUSSIAN ORTHODOX CHURCH OF MARY MAGDALENE** is marked by 7 striking onion-shaped spires in Slavic style. It was built in 1888 by the Czar of Russia, Alexander III, and is maintained by the White Russian nuns. It is located next to the **RUSSIAN ARCHAEOLOGICAL MUSEUM.**

54. The **BASILICA OF THE AGONY** (**CHURCH OF ALL NATIONS**) adjoins the Garden of Gethsemane. This Roman Catholic basilica is a Byzantine-style chapel, built in 1924 on the site of a Crusader church. It houses the **ROCK OF AGONY**, where Jesus is supposed to have prayed. Sixteen nations contributed to the construction of the basilica, including the United States, whose seal is located on the southwest area of the ceiling. The facade pictures Jesus weeping over the fate of the Holy City.

Standing in front of the church by the noisy road, note the following: Franciscans, a Catholic order (distinguished by brown robes with rope belt and sandals) own the property, and the Franciscan cross stands at the pinnacle of the church. On each side of the cross is a deer. The motif comes from Psalm 42:2 – "As the hart [deer] panteth after the water brooks, so panteth my soul after Thee, O God." In front of the mosaic facade are four statues of the Gospel writers. On the doorway/entry of the church, note the stylized metal olive trees. Before entering the church it is helpful to realize that the basilica is intentionally dark, portraying nighttime on a cool spring evening as when Jesus knelt here; stars are visible in the ceiling. The rock outcropping at the east end is one of the traditional places of Jesus' prayer and Atonement.

Kidron Valley Area

55. **GETHSEMANE** ("wine and oil press"). The traditional Garden of Gethsemane is maintained by the Franciscans and contains eight ancient olive trees, the oldest in the country, which botanists claim may be over 2,000 years old. Josephus tells us Titus cut down all the trees in the environs of Jerusalem in A.D. 70. Whether these are trees which somehow escaped destruction or whether they grew later from the roots of previous trees is difficult to say. The Church of All Nations, discussed above (site 54), stands here.

- *Gethsemane was a garden across the Kidron from Jerusalem (John 18:1).*
- *It lay across the Kidron from the Golden Gate (Luke 22:39).*
- *Here Jesus took upon himself the sins of all mankind (Matt. 26:36-56; Mark 14:32-49; Luke 22:39-53).*
- *This was the place of Jesus' betrayal and arrest (Matt. 26:47-56; John 18:1-13).*

• *Here Jesus took upon himself the sins of all mankind (D&C 19:15-19; 3 Ne. 11:11).*
• *Jesus shed his blood for a purpose (D&C 20:40, 79; 27:2; 45:4-5; 76:69).*

56. The **TOMB OF THE VIRGIN MARY** (Church of the Assumption of Mary) is a deep underground chamber that supposedly houses the tombs of Mary and Joseph. Forty-seven steps lead down into the darkened tomb. Some believe this is the place of Mary's ascension ("assumption") into heaven. This doctrine was defined as a Catholic article of faith on November 1, 1950. The Greek Orthodox church has possession of the shrine, which has suffered from floods several times since 1948. The church dates back to the Crusader period, but was built on a sanctuary site dating from the fifth century. Mary's tomb is located in the bottom to the right, and halfway up the staircase are two chapels: the one on the left contains the tomb of Joachim and Anne, Mary's parents; the one on the right is built over the tomb of Joseph, Mary's spouse. Beneath the church is a large cistern supported by 146 columns.

57. **GROTTO OF GETHSEMANE** (Cavern of Agony). A few steps east of the Church of the Assumption of Mary is a grotto maintained in its primitive form. Tradition has it that Jesus and his disciples prayed here, and that this is where Jesus took upon himself the sins of all mankind (see scriptural references of #55, Gethsemane; see also *Biblical Archaeology Review* Jul/Aug 1995, 26-35). The grotto has belonged to the Franciscans since 1392. Franciscans, a Catholic order, are distinguished by brown robes with rope belts and sandals.

- *Traditionally this is where Jesus prayed in the Garden of Gethsemane (Luke 22:41).*

58. **CHURCH OF SAINT STEPHEN**. The modern Greek Orthodox Church of Saint Stephen is located northwest of the Garden of Gethsemane. This is a traditional site where Stephen was stoned to death (Acts 8:58-59). Directly across the

road to the north is an abstract iron memorial to Jewish paratroopers who fell here in June of 1967. One wing is up, symbolizing victory, the other wing is broken and hanging down, signifying lives sacrificed.

59. **KIDRON VALLEY** (Valley of Jehoshaphat). This is a wadi nearly 3 miles long lying between Jerusalem and the Mount of Olives. It is usually dry unless fed by rainfall. Opposite the Temple area, the brook Kidron is 300 feet below the Temple platform. Further south, it runs between the villages of Silwan on the east and Ophel on the west.

From Israelite times, the valley has been a favorite burial site. Some call it the *Valley of Kings* because they believe David, Solomon, and other kings of Israel were buried here. Joel mentioned that judgments will take place in the Valley of Jehoshaphat (Joel 3:2, 12), and Muslims have a similar belief. Muhammad will sit on a pillow by the Dome of the Rock. A wire will be stretched from there to the Mount of Olives, where Jesus will be. All mankind will walk across the wire. The righteous will reach the other end safely, while the wicked drop off into the Valley of Jehoshaphat and perish.[8]

60. **ABSALOM'S PILLAR, TOMB OF JEHOSHAPHAT, GROTTO OF SAINT JAMES, TOMB OF ZECHARIAH.** In the Kidron Valley, opposite the southern portion of the Temple area, are four stone tombs. The first is a prominent stone pillar known as **ABSALOM'S PILLAR** (see 2 Sam. 18:18), or Absalom's Tomb; but his body is probably not buried here because it is generally accepted that the stone structure was built during the period of the Second Temple (700 years after Absalom's death). To the left rear of Absalom's Tomb is the **TOMB OF JEHOSHAPHAT.** A beautiful frieze of acanthus leaves is carved over the entrance.

The **GROTTO OF SAINT JAMES** is a tomb hewn out of rock, to the right of the pillar of Absalom. According to tradition, the apostle James hid here at the time of Jesus' arrest. Jewish tradition, along with a Hebrew inscription found above and between the central pillars of the tomb, indicate that this is the **TOMB OF THE PRIESTLY HOUSE OF HEZIR** (Neh. 10:20). Uzziah (Azariah) allegedly spent time here when he had leprosy (2 Kings 15:5).

To the right of Saint James Grotto is the first-century **TOMB OF THE ANCIENT PROPHET ZECHARIAH.** It has a top built like a pyramid, with three pillars carved on the side of the rock. The whole monument was carved out of the living stone of the mountainside. Some believe this is the tomb of Zacharias, the father of John the Baptist, however. It is likely the tomb of some wealthy, aristocratic Jerusalem family in the 1st century B.C.

It was customary for the Jews to whitewash their tombs each year, and it has been suggested that Jesus was referring to these very tombs in the Valley of the

Kidron when he accused the hypocritical Pharisees of being like whited sepulchers – beautiful on the outside but inside full of dead men's bones (Matt. 23:27).

- *Burying Israelites in the Kidron Valley was a custom (2 Kings 23:6; 2 Chron. 34:4).*
- *David fled over the Kidron from Absalom (2 Sam. 15:13-23).*
- *Josiah cast out the idols (2 Kings 23:4-14).*
- *Perhaps this was the scene of Ezekiel's vision of the dry bones (Ezek. 37:1-14).*
- *It is closely associated with the great day of judgment (Joel 3:2, 12).*
- *Jesus crossed the Kidron to Gethsemane (John 18:1).*
- *Many saints were resurrected and appeared in the Holy City (Matt. 27:52-53).*
- *Perhaps Jesus referred to the tombs in the Kidron valley when he likened the Pharisees to whited sepulchers (Matt. 23:27).*

61. **GIHON SPRING** ("gushing spring," Fountain of the Virgin). This spring is located in the Kidron Valley on the west side of the road in the Arab village of Silwan. It was one of Jerusalem's earliest sources of water, and it supplies the water for Hezekiah's Tunnel and the Pool of Siloam. It is called the Fountain of the Virgin because legend tells of Mary washing Jesus' clothes with water from this spring.

WARREN'S SHAFT. A water system was in place from the Jebusite (pre-Israelite) period, consisting of a diagonal, stepped tunnel one hundred twenty-eight feet long from inside the city to outside the city, underground, where vessels could be lowered down a vertical shaft some forty feet deep, which was connected to a horizontal feeder tunnel sixty-six feet long with water channelled from the city spring (later called Gihon). This water system continued in use for more than a thousand years, through Old and New Testament periods. Significant diversions and additions to this original system were made in the days of Solomon and Hezekiah.

The word "gutter" in King James Version 2 Sam. 5:8, *tsinnor* in Hebrew, in other translations is rendered "water channel" or "water shaft." According to this signification, David's general was able to "get up" into the Jebusite city through their water system, through the same tunnel and up the same shaft that were discovered by Charles Warren in 1867 and cleared out by Yigal Shiloh in 1980. See reports in *Biblical Archaeology Review* Jul/Aug 1981, 24-39; Jul/Aug 1994, 34-35.

- *It was at the Gihon spring that Solomon received his coronation (1 Kings 1:33, 38, 45).*
- *This was the spring that supplied water for Hezekiah's Tunnel (2 Chron. 32:30).*

62. **HILL OPHEL** and **THE CITY OF DAVID**. The southern ridge of Mount Moriah extends from Mount Moriah to the Pool of Siloam. The City of David was located on this small ridge, and excavations have shown walls from Jebusite to Hellenistic-Roman periods. It is estimated that the City of David had a popula-

tion of 2-3,000 people; in Solomon's day the city expanded to 4-5,000. Hezekiah's city, in the late 8th century B.C., expanded to include (besides the City of David and the Temple Mount) part of the western hill (today's Mt. Zion).

The city swelled with Israelites from the Northern Kingdom after the Assyrian conquest in 721 B. C. Many ceramic fertility figurines have been found not far from the Temple, suggesting the apostate nature of the Judahite religion, and signalling why prophets spoke out vehemently against idolatry and other perversions of true religion.

Built into the side of the hill of the City of David is **THE HOUSE OF AHIEL**, which dates from the late 7th century B.C., the time of Lehi. Lehi's family apparently lived outside of Jerusalem proper – they went down to their home to bring silver, gold, and other precious things to try to "buy" the Brass Plates and then came back up into the city. Somewhere on this very hill, however, **LABAN** must have lived.

The value of finding houses like Ahiel's, which were destroyed in the Babylonian siege of the city, is underscored by the fact that as late as 1962 the most widely used textbook on Biblical archaeology lamented the fact that "from Jerusalem no archaeological evidence of the Babylonian destruction has been recovered." (G. E. Wright, *Biblical Archeology*, p. 182.) The excavations of Dame Kathleen Kenyon and of Prof. Yigal Shiloh make such a statement no longer true. Now there is a great quantity of physical evidence of the fulfillment of Lehi's and Jeremiah's prophecies concerning the destruction of Jerusalem!

Excavations in the City of David attest to the destructive burning in the 587-586 B. C. siege of Jerusalem; the war atmosphere is evidenced by many arrowheads, a burnt room, and **CLAY BULLAE** (letter seals or stamps) baked hard by a great conflagration which swept over the whole city. The bullae were found in what has come to be known as "the bullae house," which the excavator Yigal Shiloh speculated may have been an official administrative archive. Inscribed on the bullae were fifty-one different names of scribes, court officials, and ministers, a high percentage of them with the theophoric suffix *-yahu* (Jehovah). Most of the names are known from the Bible and other inscriptions. One such name is Gemariah son of Shaphan, likely the same as mentioned in Jeremiah 36, a sort of secretary of state in the court of Jehoiakim, king of Judah from 609-598 BC. Another seal mentions the scribe and friend of the Prophet Jeremiah, Berechiah son of Neriah. Berechiah is the long form of Baruch. This same Baruch ben Neriah is he who served as scribe for Jeremiah and recorded his teachings, including predictions of the downfall of Judah and Jerusalem (see Jer. 36:10-25). (For additional information on the City of David, see *Biblical Archaeology Review* Mar/Apr 1988, 17-27.)

In the Kidron Valley, south of the ancient city, are the green trees of the ancient **KING'S GARDEN.**

- *David took "the stronghold of Zion: the same is the city of David." It became the capital of the Israelite kingdom and David's empire (2 Sam. 5:4-9).*

63. **ROYAL TOMB OF SHEBNA.** In the Arab village of Silwan (the ancient Siloam), on the eastern side of the Kidron Valley, is a rock-cut chamber tomb believed to have been built by Sheban-yahu, the royal steward of Hezekiah, king of Judah, who was rebuked by Isaiah for having built such an elaborate tomb in his lifetime. This tomb was discovered by a French archaeologist, Charles Clermont-Ganneau, in 1870. The text above the door, dating from the eighth century B.C., was deciphered in 1953 by Professor N. Avigad, an Israeli scholar. It is the first known text of a Hebrew sepulchral inscription from the preexilic period. (See *Biblical Archaeology Review* May/Jun 1994, 38-51.)

- *Isaiah rebuked Shebna for building his elaborate tomb (Isa. 22:15-19).*

64. **MOUNT OF OFFENSE** and **MOUNT OF EVIL COUNSEL.** East of the Pool of Siloam is the Arab village of Silwan. Behind the village rises the traditional Mount of Offense, or Mount of Scandal – so called because Solomon erected on this mount altars to the pagan gods of his foreign wives. This hill east of the City of David was used anciently as the necropolis, or burial place, of the city. There are hundreds of rock-cut tombs, most from the Israelite period, 9th-7th centuries B.C.

The Mount of Evil Counsel is south of the ancient city of David. A legend indicates that the high priest Caiaphas had a house there and conspired against Jesus. The Jewish village of Abu Tor and United Nations buildings are located on the mount.

- *Solomon erected altars to pagan gods on the Mount of Offense (1 Kings 11:7-8; 2 Kings 23:13).*
- *Tradition says that Judas hanged himself on the Mount of Evil Counsel (Matt. 27:5; Acts 1:18).*

65. **POOL OF SILOAM** ("sending forth") and **HEZEKIAH'S TUNNEL.** Siloam's Pool is located on the south end of the City of David, near the point where the Valley of Hinnom and the Tyropoeon Valley (Cheesemaker's Valley) run into the Kidron Valley. It was originally constructed by King Hezekiah as a reservoir at the southern end of the water tunnel. In the fifth century a church was built over the pool, but it was destroyed by the Persians in 614 and never rebuilt. A small modern mosque marks the site.

In the time of David, Jerusalem's main supply of water was the Gihon Spring, just outside the wall in the Kidron Valley. Lying just below the wall of the City of David, it was thus exposed to an attacking enemy. In 701 B.C. Sennacherib, king of

Assyria, invaded Judah and was soon to besiege Jerusalem (2 Kings 18:17-21). However, Isaiah prophesied that the king of Assyria would not come against the city nor shoot an arrow against it (2 Kings 19:32-33). The *Sennacherib Prism*, found at Nineveh, tells of Sennacherib's invasion into Judah and his failure to capture Jerusalem.

In order to protect the water supply from the invading Assyrians, Hezekiah had a 1,777-foot conduit (1,090 feet in a direct line) cut through the solid rock to carry the waters of Gihon Spring to the Pool of Siloam. The Gihon Spring was then covered over from the outside. It was probably completed just before Sennacherib besieged Jerusalem, but after Sargon had captured Samaria in 721 BC.

Workmen began on each end and accomplished a remarkable engineering feat to meet in the middle. The tunnel averages 6 feet high. In 1880 a boy discovered the Siloam Inscription 5 feet from the floor and 19 feet from the Siloam end of the tunnel. The inscription, which is the longest Biblical Hebrew inscription ever found in the Holy Land, told of "the meeting of workmen." The original stone is located in the Archaeological Museum at Istanbul. The inscription reads: "The completing of the piercing through. While the stone cutters were swinging their axes, each toward his fellow, and while there were yet three cubits to be pierced through, there was heard the voice of a man . . . then ran the waters from the spring to the pool for twelve hundred cubits, and a hundred cubits was the height of the rock above the head of the stone cutters."

The Sennacherib Prism said that "considerable preparations" had been made by the Jews to "strengthen Jerusalem."

Estimated time for the two teams to dig the tunnel, working 24 hours around the clock, would have been 7-8 months. It takes 30-40 minutes to walk through the tunnel, and water in some places – especially at the southern end – comes up to the waist of a 6-foot tall person. There's approx. 150 feet of limestone overhead. A flashlight is necessary since it is totally dark in the tunnel. It is possible for the adventurous explorer to look up Warren's Shaft: after walking 65 feet inside the tunnel, you will come to a sharp left turn; immediately in front of you is a stone ledge, which if you climb over, you can take a few steps and look up the Shaft.

About half-way, approximately 20 minutes into the tunnel, there is an S-shaped bend. At the end of that bend the ceiling rises about two feet, and chisel marks may be seen coming from both directions. This is where the two teams of workers met each other as they worked from both ends of the tunnel toward the center.

At the exit of the tunnel people often wonder, "why is the ceiling of the tunnel so much higher on the south end than on the north? What happened?" Answer: The southern team started too high, the water wouldn't flow; they had to carve their section even lower, which left a higher ceiling.

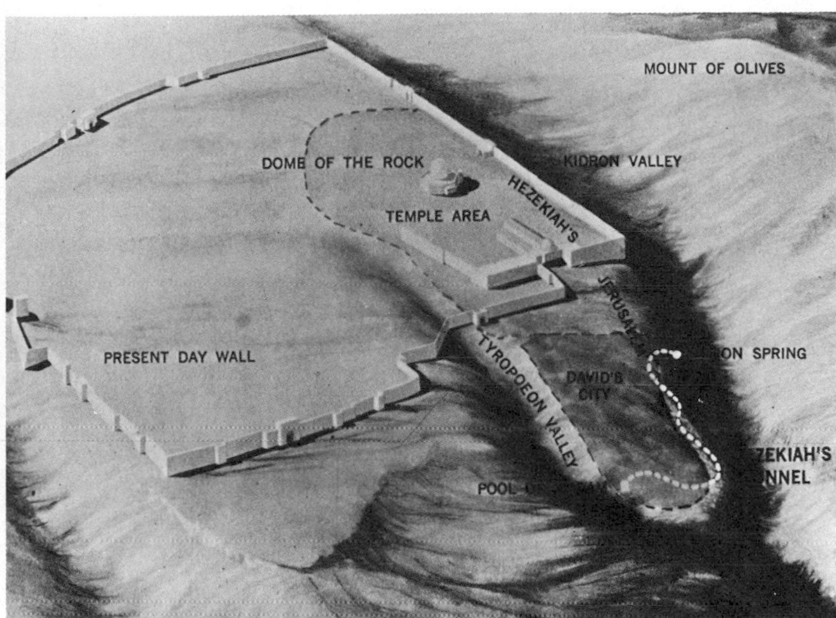

Map of Hezekiah's Tunnel, Jerusalem

(For details about the construction of Hezekiah's Tunnel, see *Biblical Archaeology Review* Jul/Aug 1994, 20-33, 64).

- *Ophel is the hill where Jotham repaired the city wall (2 Chron. 27:3).*
- *Manasseh enclosed the hill in a high wall (2 Chron. 33:14).*
- *It is believed to be the same as the "pool of Siloah by the king's garden" (Neh. 3:15) and the "waters of Shiloah that go softly" (Isa. 8:6).*
- *Hezekiah's Tunnel is mentioned in the Old Testament (2 Kings 20:20; 2 Chron. 32:2-4, 30; Isa. 36-37; 22:11).*
- *Isaiah prophesied that the king of Assyria would not come against Jerusalem (2 Kings 19:32-33).*
- *The angel of God smote the Assyrian army (2 Kings 19:35).*
- *A tower fell at Siloam, killing 18 people (Luke 13:4).*
- *Jesus healed a blind man, who washed in this pool (John 9:7-11).*

66. **HINNOM VALLEY** (Valley of Slaughter, *Gehenna, Wadi er-Rababi*). The Hinnom Valley runs from west of the Old City, around Mount Zion, and eastward to join the Kidron Valley. It formed part of the boundary between the tribes of Judah and Benjamin. Here perpetual fires are said to have been kept burning to consume the rubbish of the city. It was a place of defilement, and the New Testament likens it to eternal punishment. A small bridge with an ornate drinking

fountain erected by Suleiman the Magnificent (1520-66) traverses the Valley of Hinnom west of Mount Zion.

- *This was the boundary between Judah and Benjamin (Josh. 15:8; 18:16).*
- *It was the scene of Molech worship and pollution by Josiah (2 Kings 23:10; 2 Chron. 28:3; 33:6; Jer. 7:29-34).*
- *Here kings Ahaz and Manasseh are said to have offered their sons to the god Molech (2 Chron 28:3; 33:6; 2 Kings 23:10; Jer. 32:35).*
- *Gehenna was referred to as a type of "hell," a lake of fire, outer darkness, and so forth (Matt. 5:22, 29-30; 10:28; 18:9; 23:15, 33; Mark 9:43, 45, 47; Luke 12:5; James 3:6).*

67. **POTTER'S FIELD** (*Aceldama* ["the field of blood"]). On the southern side of the Valley of Hinnom, where it meets the Kidron Valley at the foot of the hill Ophel, is the Potter's Field, called *Aceldama* ("the field of blood"). This is possibly the field of which Zechariah prophesied. It may have been purchased by the high priests with the 30 pieces of silver Judas threw down in the Temple after he realized the enormity of his crime of betraying Jesus. The field was to be a place in which to bury strangers. The Greek Orthodox Convent of Saint Onuphrius marks the site, which has many rock-hewn tombs full of the skulls and bones of pilgrims who had been buried here. Tombs are shown where, according to tradition, the apostles hid during Jesus' trial.

The high hill south of the Old City of Jerusalem, behind Potter's Field, is sometimes called the **MOUNT OF EVIL COUNSEL**. The United Nations headquarters are housed here in the government buildings of the British Mandate.

For further archaeological analysis of this site, see *Biblical Archaeology Review* Nov/Dec 1994, 22-46, 76.

- *Zechariah prophesied of this field (Zech. 11:12-13).*
- *It was purchased by the high priests with Judas's 30 pieces of silver (Matt. 27:3-10; Acts 1:18-19).*

Immediately South, West, and North of the Old City

68. **ZION GATE** (*Bab en Nabi Daoud* ["gate of David the prophet"]). This is a city gate at the southwest end of the Old City. Mount Zion and "David's Tomb" are located outside the gate.

South of Zion Gate is a partially finished **ARMENIAN CHURCH** built over ancient ruins believed by the Armenians to be the ruins of the **HOUSE OF CAIAPHAS**. Southwest of Zion Gate, and near the southwest corner of the Old City walls, is an Armenian cemetery. In this cemetery is buried an **ARMENIAN MORMON**, Garabed Kamajian (1914-1981), who was baptized a member of the Church of Jesus Christ of Latter-day Saints at age eight in Aintab, Turkey. He moved to Jerusalem in the 1930s, and died in May, 1981. His white marble tomb, with a black stone slab in the center, is located about 40 feet east of the west wall of the cemetery and about 80 feet south of the north wall of the cemetery, which is just outside of the southwest corner of the walls around the Old City. Brother Kamajian is the only known baptized Latter-day Saint to be buried within the walls of Jerusalem that once enclosed Mt. Zion.

69. **MOUNT ZION**. Zion was the name of the citadel of the Jebusite city of Jerusalem, captured by David. Today, mistaken tradition dating from at least the Roman period says this was on the southwest hill of the city. Zion was also a title applied to the Temple area. The present traditional site of Mount Zion is on a hill close to the southwest corner of the old walled city. In A.D. 340 a large basilica, called *Hagia Zion*, was built on the mount. The basilica was destroyed by the Persians in 614. This area was once within the city wall, and is sacred to some Jews because they believe David is buried here. On the slope of Mount Zion is a Protestant cemetery in which Sir Flinders Petrie, the noted archaeologist, is buried.

The **BASILICA OF THE DORMITION** is the most imposing building on the mount and is served by the Benedictine Fathers. This marks the spot (one of three traditional locations) where Mary, the mother of Jesus, died, or "fell into eternal sleep." Some Roman Catholics believe that it was from this spot that Mary was taken into heaven, body and spirit (the *Assumption*). In the crypt is a stone effigy of Saint Mary asleep on her deathbed. *Dormition Sanctae Mariae* is Latin for "the sleep of Saint Mary." In the chapel are beautiful mosaic pieces of art. The circular mosaic floor has symbols of the Trinity and representations of the apostles and the signs of the zodiac. One mosaic above an altar shows Mary as if she were the head of the Twelve Apostles.

North of the Dormition Church is a small Armenian chapel called the **HOUSE OF CAIAPHAS** because it marks the traditional archaeological site of Caiaphas's house.

The **AMERICAN INSTITUTE OF HOLY LAND STUDIES** is located on the southern slope of Mount Zion.

- *"Out of Zion shall go forth the law" (Isa. 2:3).*
- *Mount Zion was spoken of as Temple Hill (Isa. 8:18; Jer. 31:6; Mic. 4:7).*
- *Zion was the name of the whole city (Ps. 102:21; Mic. 3:10-12).*
- *Here Jesus was taken before Annas and Caiaphas (Matt. 26:3-5, 57-75; John 18:12-24).*
- *Here Peter denied knowing Jesus at the palace of Caiaphas (Matt. 26:59-75; Luke 22:54-62).*

70. **UPPER ROOM OF THE LAST SUPPER** (*Coenaculum*, Cenacle). The upper story of David's building is the Hall of the Last Supper, or Coenaculum (Latin for

Jerusalem
South, West, and North of the Old City
Miles
¼
SHEIKH JARRAH
NAHLAT SHIMON
AMERICAN COLONY
WADI EL JOZ
BEIT ISRAEL
MORASHA
OLD CITY
MISHKENOT SHA'ANANIM
SHAMA
VALLEY OF HINNOM
DERECH SHECHEM (NABLUS ROAD)
SHMUEL HANAVI
BEIT YISRAEL
G'MUL
REEM
ST GEORGE
YMCA
MANDELBAUM
PIKUD HAMERKAZ
SALAH ED DIN (SALADIN) STREET
AZ-ZAHRA
NUR-ED-DIN
KHALID IBN-AL-WALID
HAROUN AL-RASHID
SULTAN SULEIMAN
P.O.
Herod's Gate
Arab Bus Station
Damascus Gate
Stephen's Gate
Golden Gate
New Gate
Jaffa Gate
Dung Gate
Zion Gate
EIN YA'AKOV
MEA SHEARIM
AVRAHAM MISLONIM
SALANT
DEVORA HANEVIA
ADMON
SHIFTEI YISRAEL
HAHOMA HASHELISHIT
IDO HANAVI
HANEVIIM
HAVATZELET
MONBAZ
HELENA HAMALKA
GRUZENBERG
NATAN HANAVI
HA'AYIN HET
ELISHA
CHESHIN
HATIVAT HATZANHANIM (PARATROOPERS)
YAFO (JAFFA)
YOHNAN MIGUSH HALAV
KORESH
SHLOMZION HAMALKA
YEDIDYA
SHIMON BEN SHETTAH
BEN SIRA
YANAI
SHLOMO HAMELECH
MAMILLA
AGRON
HAEMEK
DAVID HAMELECH
ELIYAHU SHAMA
JULIANUS
WALLENBERG
ZAMENHOF
ELIOT
HESS
EMILE BOTTA
ABRAHAM LINCOLN
WASHINGTON
KEREN HAYESOD
MAPU
HATAHANA
HAMIGDAL
YEMIN MOSHE
MISHKENOT SHA'ANANIM
HATIVAT YERUSHALAYIM
HAR ZION
DERECH HEVRON
DERECH YERICHO
To Mount
91
90
87
86
88
85
89
84
80
82
83
81
17
79
78
13
77
76
34
15
62
68
65
75
69
71
72
73
70
74
66
67

68. Zion Gate
69. Mount Zion
70. Upper Room of the Last Supper
71. Tomb of David
72. Chamber of Martyrs and Yeshiva of the Diaspora
73. Palace of Caiaphas and Saint Peter's in Gallicantu
74. Yemin Moshe
75. Herod's Family Tomb
76. New Gate
77. Notre Dame de France Monastery
78. Armenian Mosaic
79. Damascus Gate
80. Garden Tomb
81. Solomon's Temple Stone Quarries
82. Jeremiah's Grotto
83. Herod's Gate
84. Calvary (Golgotha)
85. Rockefeller Museum
86. Albright Institute of Archaeological Research
87. Tomb of the Kings
88. Mandelbaum Gate
89. Mea Shearim
90. Bukharian Quarter
91. Tomb of Simon the Just

"dining hall"), according to Christian tradition. It is a medieval Franciscan building dating back to 1335. The roof of the building offers a commanding view of the Old City. According to recent archaeological investigations, this long-standing traditional site could very well be the site of the "Church of the Apostles," and earlier – the Upper Room of the Last Supper. (See *Biblical Archaeology Review* May/Jun 1990, 16-35, 60).

- *This was the traditional site of the "last supper" (Matt. 26:17-30; Mark 14:12-25; Luke 22:7-30; John 13:1-30).*
- *According to tradition, the apostles met here after the Ascension (Acts 1:13-14).*
- *The upper room is believed by some to have been the place where 120 disciples were gathered when the Holy Spirit came upon them on the day of Pentecost (Acts 2:1-42; cf. D&C 109:36).*

71. **TOMB OF DAVID.** The tomb or cenotaph of David, held sacred by Muslims and Christians and Jews, is made of stone and has silver crowns of the Torah on top of it. This site has been marked since about A.D. 1173, and is located on the

first floor of the same building complex that houses the traditional upper room of the Last Supper.

This is one of the most sacred of all sites to the Jews, second only to the Western Wall. A devout Jew will light a candle for you and say a few prayers if you desire. According to 1 Kings 2:10, it appears David was buried in the City of David, south of the Temple area.

72. **CHAMBER OF MARTYRS** (*Martef Hashoa*, Cellar of the Holocaust), **YESHIVA OF THE DIASPORA**. In the basement of a building by the tomb of David is a memorial to the 6,000,000 Jews slain by the Nazis during World War II.

On the floor above the Chamber of Martyrs is an English-speaking yeshiva where the visitor can see the traditional method of studying the Torah and Talmud.

73. **PALACE OF CAIAPHAS. SAINT PETER'S IN GALLICANTU** (Latin for "cock-crow"). Southwest of the Dung Gate, on the eastern slope of Mount Zion, is a traditional site of the palace of Caiaphas, the high priest at the time of Jesus' arrest and crucifixion. Jesus came here from Gethsemane. A French Catholic Order, the Assumptionist Fathers, built a church on the site in 1931. The site also has remains of a Byzantine monastery and a grotto where, according to tradition, Peter wept. The **STEPS** of the ancient street are shown, the **CELL DUNGEON** of Caiaphas where Jesus stayed, the **COURTYARD**, and the **SERVANTS' QUARTERS**. A complete set of Jewish weights and measures was discovered in excavations, possibly indicating judicial purposes. Also, a large lintel inscription was found apparently featuring the Hebrew word "corban" (offering), suggesting the residents served in priestly functions. In Jesus' day the site was within the walls of Jerusalem.

In 1990 archaeologists discovered a burial cave in the Peace Forest in south Jerusalem which contained several ossuaries (burial boxes). One of the ossuaries has two inscriptions bearing the name *Caiaphas;* it is generally agreed that this refers to the same high priest involved in securing the death penalty for Jesus. (See *Biblical Archaeology Review*, Sep/Oct 1992, 29-44, 76.)

- *This was the scene of Jesus' first trial (Matt. 26:57-63; Mark 14:53-65; Luke 22:54, 63-71; John 18:12-14, 19-24).*
- *Here Peter denied knowing the Lord three times (Matt. 26:69-75; Mark 14:66-72; Luke 22:54-62; John 18:15-18, 25-27).*
- *The prison could have been the place where the apostles were imprisoned (Acts 4:3; 5:17-23).*

74. **YEMIN MOSHE**. This is the first quarter to be built outside the walls of the Old City. It is now a quaint artists' quarter, across the valley from Mount Zion. At the entrance is the windmill constructed by Moses Montefiore in the nineteenth

century, to provide the Jewish inhabitants with work. It is now a museum, housing the benefactor's original carriage. The long, one-story house, built in 1860, was the first dwelling constructed outside the walls of the Old City. It was financed by Judah Touro of New Orleans, and was one of the first efforts of American Jewry in Israel. The name comes from Isaiah 63:12 "[He] led them by the *right hand of Moses* [Heb. "yemin Moshe"] with his glorious arm."

75. **HEROD'S FAMILY TOMB** (*Just off David Hamelekh Street*). This family tomb, just east of the King David Hotel, was uncovered in 1892. It is believed that members of Herod's family were buried here, including Mariamne, whom he murdered. The mausoleum is built out of huge stone blocks in the form of a cross. Note the rolling stone used to block the door – one of the best preserved in Israel. The beautiful stone sarcophagi found in the tomb are now at the Greek Patriarchate in the Old City. Herod is supposed to have been buried at the Herodion (Josephus, *Wars of the Jews*, I:23:8–9; *Antiquities of the Jews*, XVII:8:3–4).

76. The **NEW GATE**, opposite the Monastery of Notre Dame de France, was opened in 1889 in the time of the Turks by Sultan Abdul-Hamid and was thus known as the *Gate of the Sultan*. It was closed during the Jordanian occupation, 1948-67. About two blocks east of the New Gate, on Casa Nova Road, is the Casa Nova Hospice, where Francis M. Lyman dedicated Palestine for the return of the Jews, on March 2, 1902.

77. **NOTRE DAME DE FRANCE MONASTERY.** Opposite the New Gate is this monastery, founded in 1887 and managed by the Assumptionist Fathers. The Notre Dame is a Christian hospice for pilgrims and is one of the largest buildings in Jerusalem.

78. **ARMENIAN MOSAIC.** On Prophets Street, just outside the Damascus Gate, is the oldest monument to an "unknown soldier" ever found. A beautiful mosaic with representations of birds, plants, and flowers was part of a fifth-century chapel above the tombs of Armenian soldiers who died in A.D. 451 while fighting the Persians.

79. **DAMASCUS GATE** (Shechem Gate, *Bab el Nasr* ["gate of victory"], Bab el Amud ["gate of the column"]). The Damascus Gate is located on the northwest side of Old Jerusalem, where the highway starts toward Damascus, capital of Syria. The Jews call it the *Shechem* or *Nablus* Gate because the highway goes there also. This is the most picturesque and busiest of the gates and is the main entrance to the city. It has always been considered the proper entry for crowned heads. It was built by Suleiman the Magnificent in 1537. Beneath the gate are remains of the ancient second-century wall and gate, recently discovered through

Damascus Gate, Jerusalem

excavations. It is now possible to enter the left side of the triple-arched triumphal gate which dates to the time of Hadrian. On its lintel was inscribed the name of the city, "Aelia Capitolina." This is the level of the street where Jesus walked as he went in and out of the city a century before. The sixth-century Medeba Map of Jerusalem has a large column standing just inside the gate, with a statue of Hadrian on top of it. This detail is preserved in the Arabic name for the gate. (See *Biblical Archaeology Review* May/Jun 1988, 48-56.)

80. **GARDEN TOMB** (A traditional Protestant Version). Immediately west of Golgotha and a short block north of the Damascus Gate on the Nablus road is the rock-cut Jewish tomb called the *Garden Tomb*, discovered by General Gordon of Khartoum fame. It has been occupied formerly by a church. Jewish tombs were often composed of two chambers: the first served as a vestibule, and in it the relatives congregated to mourn for the dead; in the second, on a shelf cut into the rock, the corpse was laid. The entrance to the monument was closed by a round

massive slab, like a millstone, which rolled in a groove. In the Garden is one of the biggest water cisterns ever found which dates from ancient times. A wine press has also been found. The cistern and wine press suggest the ancient use of this property as a garden. The Garden Tomb is now owned and kept beautiful by the Garden Tomb Association of London. A traditional site of Calvary/Golgotha adjoins the Garden to the east.

In this garden the Jerusalem Branch of the Church was organized in Sept. 1972 by Pres. Harold B. Lee, with David B. Galbraith as the first president of the branch. Of his visit to the Garden Tomb, President Lee said, "something seemed to impress us as we stood there that this was the holiest place of all, and we fancied we could have witnessed the dramatic scene that took place there" (*The Ensign*, April 1972, p.6).

- *Jesus was buried in a garden (Matt. 27:57-66; Mark 15:42-47; Luke 23:50-56; John 19:41-42).*
- *Jesus' tomb was guarded (Matt. 27:62-66).*
- *"Who shall roll us away the stone...?" (Mark 16:3-4).*
- *Mary Magdalene saw the resurrected Christ in the garden (Mark 16:9; John 20:11-18).*
- *Peter and John raced to the garden (Luke 24:12; John 20:1-4).*
- *Jesus was resurrected (Matt. 28:1-15; Mark 16:1-11; Luke 24:1-12; John 20:1-18).*
- *Nephi prophesied Jesus' entombment (2 Ne. 25:13).*
- *Jesus was resurrected (2 Ne. 25:13; Eth. 12:7; D&C 20:23).*

81. **SOLOMON'S QUARRIES** or Cave of Zedekiah. Just east of the Damascus Gate is a seven-foot fissure in the natural rock on which the city wall is built. It is covered by a small iron gate. This fissure leads to an extensive underground cavern – the famous quarries from which Solomon and later kings cut stone for their building projects. The huge cavern goes 214 yards into the heart of the mountain, below the buildings of the Old City. It branches off in several directions.

Members of the Masonic Movement regard the first 3,600 overseers, who put the people to work on the stones for Solomon's Temple, as the first Freemasons. Many blocks of the virgin stone have been shipped around the world for use as foundation stones in Masonic lodges.

- *Stone was used for the Temple of Solomon (1 Kings 5:15; 6:7).*
- *Solomon's Temple was described (2 Chron. 3).*
- *This was the possible hiding place of Zedekiah (according to legend) during the Babylonian siege under Nebuchadnezzar in 587 B.C. (2 Kings 25:1-5).*

82. **JEREMIAH'S GROTTO** (*Hazor Hamatara* ["court of the prison"]). This cavern, once a part of "Solomon's Quarries", is located behind the Arab bus station across from Solomon's Quarries, at the end of a small lane.

- *According to tradition, Jeremiah wrote his Lamentations here (Jer. 38:6-13).*

83. **HEROD'S GATE** (Gate of Flowers). This gate on the northeast side of the Old City, is located across from the Arab post office, and is one of 8 gates in the Old City wall. It is believed that its name was given by medieval pilgrims who believed that the house of Herod Antipas, where Jesus was sent by Pilate, was nearby.

84. **CALVARY** (*Golgotha* ["skull"] in Protestant version, Gordon's Calvary). This is a knoll north of the Old City and over the top of Jeremiah's Grotto. It is presently used as a Muslim cemetery. Its entrance is from Salah ed Din Street, at a point one-half block northwest of the post office. The entrance is marked with a crescent, indicating a Muslim cemetery, across the street from the Metropole Hotel. The knoll is also called *Gordon's Calvary*, after the English General Gordon, the hero of Khartoum.

- *Jesus was crucified (Matt. 27:32-56; Mark 15:21-41; Luke 23:26-46; John 19:16-37).*
- *Jesus was crucified (1 Ne. 11:33; 3 Ne. 27:14; Eth. 4:1; D&C 20:23; 35:2; 45:52; 46:13; 76:41).*
- *The prophecies of his crucifixion were fulfilled (1 Ne. 19:10-13; Mos. 15:7; 2 Ne. 6:9; 10:3, 25; 25:13; Moses 5:9, 7:55).*

85. **ROCKEFELLER MUSEUM** (Palestine Archaeological Museum). This excellent museum, built with a $2,000,000 fund from John D. Rockefeller in 1927, stands just north of the city wall near Herod's Gate. It contains one of the most extensive archaeological collections in this part of the world. Pottery, tools, and household effects are arranged by periods of time. This museum has been a workshop to piece together the many manuscript fragments of the Dead Sea Scrolls. Note the following items of interest: a display of **LAMPS** used in different periods of time; a limestone **CANAANITE ALTAR** for burnt offerings, dating back to 1000 B.C. and found at Megiddo, used for incense of sin offering as described in Leviticus 4:7, 18-20, and 1 Kings 1:50 and 2:28 (note the horns on the corners); a **COPPER SWORD** from Megiddo, dating back as far as 3000 B.C.; **CANAANITE IDOLS** of the Patriarchal period (Gen. 35:4; Josh. 24:23); reliefs from Sennacherib's palace at Nineveh (700 B.C.).

A fine library deals with the history, geography, and archaeology of the Holy Land.

86. **ALBRIGHT INSTITUTE OF ARCHAEOLOGICAL RESEARCH**. This is a branch of the American Schools of Oriental Research, a professional organization instituted to promote archaeological and related research in the world of the Bible. The school has branches in Baghdad, Amman, and on Cyprus as well as Jerusalem. The Institute sponsors work on the Dead Sea Scrolls, and a great deal

of archaeological research and excavation. The school is located on Salah ed Din (Saladin) Street northwest of the National Palace Hotel.

87. **TOMB OF THE KINGS.** Near the top of Saladin Street one may see a hollowed-out courtyard with small cave openings and 25 stone steps leading to a cistern that was used for ritual ablutions or preparation for burial. Inside one of the tombs, four carved sarcophagi were found. The family of Queen Helena of Mesopotamia, who was converted to Judaism around A.D. 50, was buried here. The tomb is misnamed. It is one of the most interesting burial tombs in the Holy Land. Here the visitor can see one of the best-preserved examples of a rolling stone closing the entrance to a tomb. The sarcophagi from the tomb are located in the Louvre. A canal system brings water to the cisterns.

- *The tomb of Joseph of Arimathea, where Jesus was buried, had a rolling stone (Matt. 27:60, 66; 28:2; Mark 15:46; 16:3-4; Luke 24:2, 12; John 20:1).*
- *To enter, one had to "stoop down" (John 20:5, 11).*

88. **MANDELBAUM GATE** (Command Square). This was a gate that existed be tween Jordan and Israel during the period 1948-67. It was removed after the six-day war in 1967. It was named after Dr. S. Mandelbaum, whose house was bisected by the armistice line.

89. **MEA SHEARIM** Around 1877 this area was built as the Orthodox Jews' religious quarter. Here they live as they did in the ghettos of Europe, with crowded but clean living quarters, schools, and synagogues. The name was taken from the account concerning Isaac in the Book of Genesis (Gen. 26:12), where the patriarch was promised blessings an *hundredfold* (Heb. *mea shearim*).

Mea Shearim Street starts from Prophets Street and is one of the main streets in the area. It is the center of the religious Hassidic sect. Long beards, black robes, beaver fur hats (shetrained), broad-brimmed hats, side curls (peot), and high black socks are worn here. The women wear bandannas over their shaved heads. These religious Jews oppose the blasphemous modern life of Israel. Some of them recognize no state of Israel before the coming of the Messiah. They clash with police in demonstrations protesting burial laws, the driving of cars on Saturday (the Jewish Sabbath), and the use of swimming pools by men and women simultaneously. Signs in the area request women to dress modestly. The streets close on Friday evening and Saturday.

90. **BUKHARIAN QUARTER.** Jews from Bukhara (Central Asia, former Soviet republics) came to Jerusalem as early as 1862 and by 1895 had established their own quarters. The main Bukharian synagogue is called *Baba Tama.* The services in the synagogue are very oriental in flavor. The Bukharian Quarter lies northwest of Mea Shearim.

91. **TOMB OF SIMON THE JUST.** Northeast of the Sheikh Jarrah Mosque is a tomb that belonged to the high priest Simon (335-270 B.C.), one of the last members of the "Great Synod," which gathered the writings of the Hebrew Bible (Old Testament).

WEST JERUSALEM

In 1841 the Anglican Church, supported by the king of Prussia, founded a bishopric in Jerusalem. After 1860 new settlements arose outside of the old walls. The first important buildings outside the Old City were the Russian buildings. In 1881 a small colony of Americans was founded by a Mr. Spafford and his wife, based upon the original communistic teaching of the Bible. In 1868 an attempt to found an ideal Christian community in Palestine was made by Germans from Wurtemberg, who revived the name of *Templer* and who had several flourishing colonies in Palestine in 1939.

Jaffa Road is the new city's main street, and where it crosses King George Street (king at the time of the Balfour Declaration) and Ben Yehuda Street (Father of Modern Hebrew) is the center of the city. Jaffa Road and Ben Yehuda Street offer the best in shopping – souvenirs, antiques, and so forth. The Mea Shearim market and the markets in Old Jerusalem are also good for shopping. In West Jerusalem there is little "bargaining," but in East Jerusalem the oriental culture expects you to haggle over the price.

NEAR THE CENTER OF THE NEW CITY

92. **HALL OF HEROISM.** Just off Shiftei Yisrael Street, behind the Russian Compound Cathedral, is a small museum dedicated to the men involved in the underground resistance during the British Mandate. The museum is housed in a former British prison.

93. **RUSSIAN COMPOUND.** Located on Jaffa Road, the Russian Compound was once one of the world's largest hotels, accommodating between 1000-2000 Russian pilgrims at one time. During the 1920s the Russians were the most numerous pilgrims to Israel. The green-domed cathedral stands on the highest ground of the compound, where the Assyrians camped when they besieged Jerusalem about 700 B.C. The Romans were also here in A.D. 70. The buildings of the compound are now used by the Israeli government. By the cathedral is a pillar that is thought to have been quarried for Herod's Temple.

94. **MAHANE YEHUDA.** This is a colorful open-air market that is especially lively on Fridays and before holidays. It is located west of the War of Independence Memorial, on the south side of Jaffa Street.

95. **HECHAL SHLOMO** ("Palace, or Temple, of Solomon"). This is the seat of Israel's chief rabbinate, the supreme religious center. It stands opposite Independence Park on King George Street. It has a synagogue with beautiful stained glass windows, a library, and the Abraham Wax Collection of Jewish religions and folk art. It has an excellent series of dioramas portraying certain biblical events.

Adjacent to Hechal Shlomo is **THE JERUSALEM GREAT SYNAGOGUE**, built and dedicated in 1982-83. Total cost of the project was $14 million, with funding largely provided by Sir Isaac Wolfson of London. Entrance to the Synagogue is via a large forecourt paved with Jerusalem stone. Inside the visitor may see the largest and most modern synagogue in Israel, with luxury fixtures and seating for nearly 1,000 men and 650 women. The diamond-shaped synagogue hall has no pillars to obstruct the view of worshippers. There is a raised platform in front of the ark, which can be used as a foundation for wedding canopies. A large stained-glass window features prominent Jewish artistic motifs. Also included in the Great Synagogue are a banquet hall, preparatory chambers for bride and groom, reception areas and kitchens.

96. **INDEPENDENCE PARK AND MAMILLA POOL**. This is one of the largest of Jerusalem's parks and is located on Agron Street and Mamilla Road, near the city center. A large reservoir, called Mamilla Pool, is believed to be a part of an ancient water system connected to Hezekiah's Pool in the Old City.

97. **YMCA BUILDING**. Built on King David Road in 1928 by James Jarvie of New Jersey, this building affords one of the best panoramic views of the city. The sixth-century Medeba Map of Jerusalem is reproduced in the vestibule.

98. **PRESIDENT'S RESIDENCE** (*Beit Hanassi*). In May 1972 the president of Israel moved into this new residence just southwest of the Academy of Sciences, on Hakeshet Street.

99. **JASON'S TOMB** (Alfasi Cave). On Alfasi road southwest of Hechal Shlomo, in a section of the city called Rehavia, is a second-century BC tomb with a pyramidal roof. Burial niches, etchings of a menorah, representations of a naval battle, and the name of Jason carved in the stone are of interest. Perhaps the tomb belonged to Jason, father of Antipater, a commissioner of Judas Maccabaeus in 161 BC.

POINTS OF INTEREST IN OUTLYING MODERN JERUSALEM

100. **MONASTERY OF THE CROSS**. Built originally by Georgian Monks in the eleventh century at Abu Tor, this monastery, according to legend, stands on the spot where once stood the tree from which the cross of Jesus was made. The

Knesset, Jerusalem

Greek Orthodox church maintains it now. It is called the **CHURCH OF EVIL COUNSEL**. It contains interesting catacombs, crypts, frescoes, and mosaics.

101. **KNESSET** (Parliament Building). This is a multi-million-dollar structure of peach-colored stone on Jerusalem's "acropolis." It has a 24-foot-high Chagall mosaic in the reception hall, a synagogue, separate kitchens for milk and meat meals, and exhibition rooms. The grill-work entrance way is the work of Israeli sculptor Polombo, who also designed the doors at Yad Vashem.

A large 16-foot-high bronze **MENORAH**, executed by sculptor B. Elkan and donated by Great Britain, stands in front of the building. Twenty-nine panels on the menorah depict highlights in Jewish history.

Israel is a republic with a president, who is elected for 5 years by a majority of the members of the Knesset (Parliament). The first president of Israel was Dr. Chaim Weizmann. The president is not head of the executive as in the United States; his powers resemble those of the British constitutional monarch.

The Knesset is a single house with 120 members. The members are elected by simple ballot, with proportional representation. Each party puts up a list of candidates, who then receive the number of seats proportional to the percentage they win of the total national vote. Over the decades the *Mapai* (Labor Party) has been the largest single party. The first prime minister was David Ben-Gurion who was given this office in 1948. He resigned in 1964 as the leader of this group, and Levi

Eshkol succeeded him until 1967. Golda Meir took Eshkol's place. She was followed by Yitzhak Rabin, Menachem Begin, Yitzhak Shamir, Shimon Peres, and Yitzhak Rabin.

102. The **NATIONAL MUSEUM** is a very large and beautiful museum that houses Israel's treasures. It opened in 1965 and contains the following four components:

(1)The **BEZALEL MUSEUM OF ART AND FOLKLORE** displays such items as Hanukkah lamps, Torah scrolls, stylized menorahs, reconstructed synagogues, costumes, jewelry from different Jewish communities, and paintings by Chagall, Van Gogh, Renoir, Monet, Dali, Rembrandt, Picasso, and prominent Israeli artists.

(2)The **BRONFMAN ARCHAEOLOGICAL AND ANTIQUITIES MUSEUM** houses exhibits dating from the stone age to the Ottoman period. Of particular interest are the following: recent discoveries from the biblical city of Dan; statues, figurines, and other cultic objects from the worship of idol gods and goddesses; sacrificial altars from Arad and Hazor; horned altars from Megiddo; ivory plaques from Samaria; important, recent finds from the City of David (including silver amulets with the name "Jehovah," and clay seal impressions with the names of biblical personalities); inscribed potsherds from Lachish; a copy of wall reliefs from Sennacherib's royal palace at Nineveh that tell of the Assyrians' siege of Lachish in Southwest Judah; objects from caves identified with the Bar Kokhba revolt; and portions of writings found on the walls of the Jerusalem Cave.

(3)The **BILLY ROSE ART GARDEN** is laid out in semicircular rock terraces and contains sculpture by Rodin, Daumier, Epstein, Lipschitz, and others. The garden was laid out by a Japanese landscape artist, Isamu Naguchi.

(4)The **SHRINE OF THE BOOK** is an onion-top-shaped building contoured to resemble the jar covers in which the Dead Sea Scrolls were discovered. It has 275,000 glazed bricks on the roof. It houses the Dead Sea Scrolls, scrolls found at Masada, and the Bar Kokhba letters.

Like a huge jar lid, the architectural design of the Shrine of the Book is unique. The concern of the scrolls – and indeed the Qumran community to which they belonged – with the struggle of light against darkness, good against evil, knowledge against ignorance, finds architectural expression through the play of contrasts between the white dome and the nonfunctional rectilinear black wall. The black wall calls to mind by its color or shape the heavy burden which lay on the people of Israel for more than 2,000 years.

Bronze gates open on a cavelike manuscript corridor leading to the **SANCTUARY**, which has a double parabolic dome, ribbed as by the hand of some giant potter. It swings upward from its 80-foot diameter to a 6-foot opening. A facsim-

New Jerusalem
N
Miles
1/4
1/2
1
To Nablus
To Tel Aviv
Mandelbaum Gate
OLD CITY
Israel-Jordan Boundary before 1967
SHMUEL HANAVI
HARAV BAR IIAN
YEHEZKEL
YIRMIY
MALCHEI YISRAEL
MEA SHEARIM
SHIFTEI YISRAEL
HANEVI'IM
SAREI YISRAEL
SDEROT WEIZMANN
YAFO (JAFFA)
AGRIPPAS
SHLOMZION HAMALKA
YAFO
BEN YEHUDA
HILLEL
BEZALEL
SDEROT BEN ZVI
SDEROT HERZL
RUPPIN
KAPIAN
AGRON
DAVID HAMELECH
KEREN HAYESOD
RAMBAN
METU
DELLA
DERECH AZA
HARAV HERZOG
DERECH BEIT LEHEM
DERECH HEVRON (HEBRON ROAD)
EIN GEDI
KORE H
LEIB YAFE
HAZIKARON
EIN KAREM
HANTKE
TEHON
DERECH MANAHAT
HARAV UZIEL
DERECH GOLOMB
SZOLD
92
93
94
95
96
97
98
99
100
101
102
103
104
105
106
107
108
109
110
112
113
114

92. Hall of Heroism
93. Russian Compound
94. Mahane Yehuda
95. Hechal Shlomo
96. Independence Park and Mamilla pool
97. YMCA building
98. President's residence
99. Jason's Cave
100. Monastery of the Cave
101. Knesset
102. National Museum
103. Kiriya
104. Hebrew University
105. Mount Herzl
106. Yad Vashem Memorial
107. Ein Karem
108. Hadassah Hospital
109. Kennedy Memorial
110. Model of Ancient Jerusalem
111. Ramat Rachel
112. Biblical Zoo (former site)
113. Sanhedrin Tombs
114. Ammunition Hill

ile of the scroll of Isaiah, 24 feet long, girdles a jar-shaped fountain, and below the Isaiah scroll are simulated caves with scrolls and other objects. The building is buried like the Dead Sea Scrolls and is one of the very few public buildings in the world planned to be essentially subterranean.

SMALLER MUSEUMS. In addition to the museums already noted, there are smaller museums worth visiting: The **AGRICULTURAL MUSEUM**, at the Ministry of Agriculture on Helena Hamalka Street; the **NATURAL HISTORY MUSEUM**, on Mohiliver Street; the **MUSICAL INSTRUMENTS MUSEUM**, in the Rubin Academy of Music, on Smolenskin Street; the **TAXATION MUSEUM**; the **MUSEUM OF ISLAMIC ART**, attached to the Meyer Center, near the president's residence and the Hechal Shlomo.

The main purpose of the **BIBLE LANDS MUSEUM**, located a short distance northwest of the Shrine of the Book, is to promote deeper understanding of the Bible. On permanent exhibit in the museum are thousands of artifacts presented in chronological order illustrating the material culture of Egypt, Assyria, Babylon,

Bronze menorah, Jerusalem

Persia, Greece, Rome, Byzantium, and other ancient cultures which provide a foundation for the Biblical world and Judeo-Christian civilization. The Museum is the life-work of Dr. Elie Borowski, who collected the artifacts.

103. The **KIRIYA** (**Kiryat Ben-Gurion**). Northwest of the Knesset are several large buildings that house some of the more than twenty government ministries: the Prime Minister's Office, Ministries of the Interior, Finance, State Archives, and others.

104. **HEBREW UNIVERSITY** (**Givat Ram**). This modern university was dedicated in 1954. The campus is built around the National Library, the largest in the Near East with over 2,000,000 volumes. This is one of two campuses of the Hebrew University; the other and larger one is located on Mount Scopus.

105. **MOUNT HERZL**. This is the burial site of jurist, dramatist, and journalist, Dr. Theodore Benjamin Herzl, who forecast the state of Israel 50 years before its birth and is known as the father of modern Zionism and the state of Israel. His black granite tomb stands on the summit of Mount Herzl, surrounded by gardens. Herzl's remains were interred here in 1949, 45 years after his death in Vienna. In the Herzl cemetery are buried Vladimir Jabotinsky, revisionist philosopher, and also Levi Eshkol, an early prime minister of Israel. The **HERZL MUSEUM** is located near the main entrance. On the northern slope of Mount Herzl is the **MILITARY CEMETERY**, where war casualties of 1948 are buried.

106. **YAD VASHEM MEMORIAL** ("Hill of Remembrance"). Built in 1957 on the top of Mount Memorial is this beautiful memorial dedicated to the 6,000,000 Jews killed in Nazi Germany, at Bergen-Belsen, Auschwitz, Dachau, and other places. The archives in the memorial house contain the documentary evidence of the slaughter. From here the evidence was produced against Adolf Eichmann in 1961. The memorial stands a thousand yards west of Mount Herzl, and an eternal flame is housed in the **OHEL VIZKOR** ("tent, or hall, of remembrance") (Isa. 56:5), built of large unhewn boulders. Its mosaic floor is inscribed with the names of the 21 largest concentration and death camps. The 70-foot **PILLAR OF HEROISM** was erected in honor of the resistance fighters.

The **AVENUE OF THE RIGHTEOUS** leads to the memorial. The trees that line this avenue were all planted by and in honor of non-Jews who had risked their lives to help Jews escape from the Nazis.

The new **CHILDREN'S MEMORIAL** features the unique use of subdued light, mirrors, and a continuous recording of names in various languages – all honoring, in an emotionally provocative way, the one and a half million children slaughtered by the Nazis.

107. **EIN KAREM** ("spring of the vineyard"). On the terraced slopes of western Jerusalem is a quaint village noted traditionally as the **BIRTHPLACE OF JOHN THE BAPTIST** (for an alternative site, see Yuttah, south of Hebron). There are a number of educational institutions in the village, as well as homes of many artists.

On the north side of the village is the Franciscan **CHURCH OF SAINT JOHN**, built over the traditional site of John the Baptist's birthplace. A small stairway left of the nave of the church leads into the grotto, where a hollow niche is pointed out as John's birthplace. A church was built on the site as early as the fifth century A.D. Behind the church is a seventeenth-century monastery.

The **SPRING OF THE VINEYARD** (*Ein Karem*) **MOSQUE** is south of the Church of Saint John and the main road through the village. The mosque is built over a rock, from which the spring emerges. The spring was called *Mary's Fountain* in Crusader times because it was associated with the visit of the Virgin Mary to Elisabeth (Luke 1:26-40).

Southwest of the Spring of the Vineyard Mosque is the Franciscan **CHURCH OF THE VISITATION**. It may be reached by ascending the broad stone stairway outside the entrance gate of the Russian compound. The mosaic facade of the church portrays Mary's journey from Nazareth. The church was built in 1955 above the grotto that marks the traditional site of the visitation of the angel Gabriel to Elisabeth (Luke 1:26-40). In the lower church a cavity hollowed out of a large stone marks the traditional place of concealment where John the Baptist was hidden from Herod's soldiers.

According to one tradition, when Herod issued his edict to slay children under two years of age John was taken into the mountains, where he was raised on locusts and wild honey. When Zacharias refused to disclose the hiding palace of his son, John, he was slain by Herod's order. The tradition identifies John's father as the Zacharias who was killed "between the temple and the altar" (Matt. 23:31-35).

- *Gabriel visited Zacharias in the Temple (Luke 1:5-23).*
- *Gabriel visited Mary; then Mary came to the hill country of Judea to be with Elisabeth (Luke 1:26-40).*
- *Mary and Elisabeth spoke by the Holy Ghost (Luke 1:41-55).*
- *John was named, and Zacharias regained his speech (Luke 1:57-79).*
- *John baptized Jesus in the Jordan (Matt. 3:1-17; Mark 1:4-11).*
- *John was one of the greatest of prophets (Matt. 11:7-11).*
- *John was filled with the Holy Ghost from his mother's womb (D&C 84:27).*
- *John was baptized while a child and ordained by an angel of God at eight days of age (D&C 84:28).*
- *It was prophesied that John the Baptist would baptize Jesus (1 Ne. 10:7-10).*
- *John baptized Jesus in the Jordan (D&C 93:15-18).*
- *John restored the Aaronic Priesthood (D&C 13).*

108. **HADASSAH HOSPITAL.** On the extreme west side of the city of Jerusalem is the largest medical center in the Near East – a $30,000,000, 11-floor complex – opened in 1961. It has over 1,000 beds, medical, dental, and pharmacy schools, and laboratories. *Hadassah*, the Women's Zionist Organization of America, organized in 1912, sponsored this hospital. In the hospital's synagogue are Marc Chagall's world-famous monumental stained glass windows, depicting in abstract the Twelve Tribes of Israel.

109. **KENNEDY MEMORIAL** and **PEACE FOREST**. On Mount Orah, near the village of Aminadav, is a 60-foot-high poured-concrete memorial, opened in May 1966 and shaped like the lower half of a tree trunk, symbolizing the president whose life was cut short in his prime. It has an eternal fire burning and is encircled by 50 columns, each bearing the emblem of a state of the Union, plus the District of Columbia. The John F. Kennedy Peace Forest is planted to the southwest of the monument.

110. **MODEL OF ANCIENT JERUSALEM.** This model city of Herodian-period Jerusalem (A.D. 66) near the Holyland Hotel, took 7 years to build. The scale is 1 to 50 (¼ inch equals 1 foot), and it occupies a quarter of an acre. The owner of the hotel had it built as a memorial to his son, who was killed in one of Israel's wars. Professor Michael Avi-Yonah of the Hebrew University made the plans. Original materials of marble, limestone, wood, iron, and copper have been used in the

Shechem (Nablus)
Shiloh (Shilon)
JORDA
Phasaelis
River Jordan
Ai
Ramallah
Caliph Hisham's Palace
Refugee Camp
Synagogue
Old Jericho
Elisha's Fountain
Allenby Bridge
Mount of Temptation
New Jericho
Herod's Winter Palace
Musa al-Alami
Wadi Kelt
Gilgal
Refugee Camp
Brook Cherith
Adummim
Bethabara
Bethphage
Jerusalem
Bethany
Nabi Musa
N
Qumran
Bethlehem
Ein Fashkha
Israel
East of the
Mount of Olives
SALT SEA (DEAD SEA)
Miles
5
10

model's construction. It is updated whenever archaeological evidence warrants changes.

For a detailed tour of the Model City, see **GUIDE TO THE MODEL CITY AND TO NEW TESTAMENT JERUSALEM** in the Appendix.

111. **RAMAT RACHEL.** South of the Old City and west of the Government House area is the Kibbutz Ramat Rachel (hill of Rachel). It is the only kibbutz within the confines of Jerusalem. It is the city's southern bastion. Archaeologists have uncovered levels of occupation, dating from the seventh century B.C. to the seventh century A.D. The Romans had a bath house and palace here, and the Byzantines built a church and monastery here in the fifth century A.D. Brigham Young University's Study Abroad programs were centered here in the Kibbutz's guesthouse for nine years.

112. **BIBLICAL ZOO.** The Biblical Zoo contains birds and animals described in the Bible. It is one of the most unusual animal collections in the world. Nearly all of the 100 different animals and 30 birds mentioned in the Bible are housed here. Relevant biblical quotations and paraphrases are displayed with each animal: "Can the leopard change his spots?" (Jeremiah 13:23). The Zoo was founded in 1939.

Note: The site of the Biblical Zoo has recently been changed to southwest Jerusalem.

113. **SANHEDRIN TOMBS** (Tombs of the Judges). Near the end of Samuel Street, on the northern edge of Jerusalem, is a series of tombs in a public garden, called by the Christians the *Tombs of the Judges.* The judges of Israel's supreme court during the first and second century may have been buried in the Sanhedrin Tombs. There are over 21 tombs in the area, dating back to the first century of the Christian era. The richest and most monumental tomb is **NUMBER 14**, a 3-level catacomb carved out of rock. The entrance is decorated with relief carvings of pomegranates and acanthus leaves. There are 80 burial places in the tomb, and because of the large size it is believed by some to have been the burial place of the Sanhedrin. Others believe it was a very large family tomb.

- *Jesus was arraigned before the Sanhedrin (John 11:47).*

114. **AMMUNITION HILL.** This hill was the main Jordanian outpost in the 1967 six-day war. It was in this area that the Maccabees made their way to deliver Jerusalem from the hands of the Greeks in 165 B.C. The Roman legions also had their main camp here when they battled Jerusalem in A.D. 70.

EAST OF THE MOUNT OF OLIVES

BETHPHAGE ("*place of young figs*"), Keft et-Tur

On the eastern slopes of the Mount of Olives, between the summit and Bethany, is Bethphage, the traditional starting point of the Palm Sunday procession. Rabbinic literature cites Bethphage as the eastern limits of the city of Jerusalem. Jesus' first coming, at his Triumphal Entry, was from the east, as his Second Coming will be. A Franciscan convent chapel houses the very stone (traditionally) upon which Jesus mounted the donkey for his triumphal entry into Jerusalem. The paintings on the stone date back to the Crusader period and were restored by C. Vagarini in 1950. Tombs with rolling stones, cisterns, presses, and pottery found in the area indicate that this slope had a sizable population.

- *From here Jesus sent two disciples to bring a colt for him to ride in his triumphal entry into Jerusalem (Palm Sunday) (Matt. 21:1-11; Mark 11:1-11; Luke 19:29-40; Zech. 9:9).*

BETHANY ("*house of dates*"), *Azereyeh, el-Azariye*

Bethany is 1.7 miles from Jerusalem, on the eastern slope of the Mount of Olives and on the road to Jericho. The town's Arabic name today, *el-Azariye*, preserves the name of its famous former citizen, Lazarus. The **CHURCH OF SAINT LAZARUS**, run by the Franciscans, was built near the tomb of Saint Lazarus in 1953. The church has beautiful mosaics depicting the events that took place here. Next to the Church of Saint Lazarus is a sixteenth-century **MOSQUE**, standing by Lazarus' tomb. West of the mosque is a **GREEK ORTHODOX CHURCH** and the remains of the traditional house of Mary and Martha, these remains dating from the Crusader period. All these holy structures honor Lazarus and his sisters, Mary and Martha.

- *This was the home of Mary, Martha, and Lazarus (John 11:1).*
- *Jesus often stayed here (especially during the Passion Week). This was his home in Judea (Matt. 21:17; Mark 11:11).*
- *Jesus taught Martha the better way (Luke 10:38-42).*
- *Jesus raised Lazarus from the dead (John 11:1-44).*
- *In the house of Simon the leper, Mary anointed Jesus for burial (Matt. 26:1-13; Mark 14:3-9; Luke 7:36-50; John 12:1-8).*
- *Jesus ascended into heaven from here (Luke 24:50-51).*

ADUMMIM ("*red places*"), *Maale Adummim, the Good Samaritan Inn, Khan Hathrour, Tal at ed-Damm* ("*the ascent of blood*")

About 12 miles east of Jerusalem, between Jerusalem and Jericho, is the traditional site of the Samaritan's Inn mentioned in Jesus' story of the Good Samaritan. A Turkish police station was built here in 1903 and was destroyed in 1917. On a hill north of the highway are the remains of a Crusader castle, built by the Templars. Between the castle and Jerusalem is a new Israeli city built up in the Judean Desert, also called Maale Adummim. The Hebrew name *Maale Adummim*, meaning "ascent of blood," has reference to the fact that desert marauders and robbers were often at work along the highway between Jerusalem and Jericho, as also attested in Jesus' parable of the Good Samaritan.

- *This was a boundary of the tribe of Judah, between Jericho and Jerusalem (Josh. 15:7; 18:17).*
- *Tradition places the Good Samaritan inn here (Luke 10:34-35).*

WADI KELT or QELT, *Qilt*

About 2 miles east of Maale Adummim the road forks, and the road to the left follows the old Roman road through Wadi Kelt, a beautiful gorge in the desert, where stands the **GREEK MONASTERY OF SAINT GEORGE**. St. George's Monastery is the traditional place of Elijah's being fed by the ravens. Edward Robinson, and others, have equated Cherith with Kelt (1 Kgs. 17:1-7). Alongside Wadi Kelt is an ancient aqueduct which is still used.

At the mouth of the wadi are ruins of the New Testament Jericho. Here Herod had his winter palace.

- *A tradition also places the Good Samaritan inn here (Luke 10:34-35).*

NABI MUSA, *Nebi Moussa*

About 18 miles east of Jerusalem a road leads to the south where Arab tradition says Moses was buried. A mosque marks the site.

- *Deuteronomy indicates Moses died in Moab and was buried there (Deut. 34:5-6).*
- *Some believe Moses was translated (Alma 45:18-19; cf. Deut. 34:5-6; Matt. 17:3).*

Refugee Camps

South and north of Jericho were the largest refugee camps built in Jordan at the time of the 1948 war. Thousands of Palestinian refugees lived here for nearly 20 years. In the six-day war of 1967, most of the refugees fled to Amman, Jordan, across the Jordan River from Jericho. A few refugees still live in the camps at Jericho.

NEW TESTAMENT JERICHO AND HEROD'S WINTER PALACE

A luxurious palace was built by Herod the Great near the mouth of Wadi Kelt. Ruins may still be seen. Mark Antony made a present of the New Testament Jericho to Cleopatra, who leased it to Herod the Great; the latter died here in 4 B.C. Nearby are the remains of a Herodian fortress. This area was the New Testament Jericho.

- *Zacchaeus was converted here (Luke 19:1-27).*
- *Great multitudes followed Jesus in Jericho (Matt. 20:29).*
- *Jesus cured Bartimaeus and his companion (Matt. 20:29-34; Mark 10:46-52; Luke 18:35-43).*

JERICHO ("*fragrant*"), *Tell es-Sultan*, "*City of Palm Trees*"

Five miles west of the Jordan River, 6 miles north of the Dead Sea, and 850 feet below sea level is the **NEW, TWENTIETH-CENTURY CITY OF JERICHO**. It is the lowest city on the globe. It is 17 miles northeast of Jerusalem.

OLD JERICHO is a mound 1,200 feet long and 50 feet high, supporting 4 smaller mounds. It is located in the northwest part of modern Jericho. The ten-acre mound was excavated by British archaeologist, Dame Kathleen Kenyon, and a stone tower was found that is claimed to be 8,000 years old – the "oldest building on the earth". It is 35 feet in diameter. (See further in *Biblical Archaeology Review* Mar/Apr 1990, 44-58.)

NEW TESTAMENT JERICHO was situated at the mouth of Wadi Kelt, where Herod had his winter palace. (See above.)

- *Jericho was called "the City of Palm Trees" (Deut. 34:3; 2 Chron. 28:15).*
- *Israel was numbered here (Num. 26:3, 63).*
- *It was a walled city ruled by a king (Josh. 2:2-3).*
- *Joshua's spies went to Jericho (Josh. 2:1-15).*
- *The walls fell. It was captured and cursed by Joshua (Josh. 6:13-17, 26).*
- *Achan sinned by keeping some of the spoils of the city (Josh. 7).*
- *Its overthrow led other kings to try to make peace (Josh. 10:1-30).*
- *It belonged to Benjamin and Manasseh (Josh. 16:1-7; 18:11-12).*
- *It was rebuilt by Hiel the Bethelite (1 Kings 16:34), in spite of Joshua's curse (Josh. 6:26).*
- *Elijah and Elisha and "the sons of the prophets" were at Jericho (2 Kings 2:4-18).*
- *Here David's messengers suffered indignities (2 Sam. 10:1-5; 1 Chron. 19:1-5).*
- *Elisha healed its waters (2 Kings 2:19-22).*
- *Zedekiah was captured near here (2 Kings 25:5-7; Jer. 39:5-7; 52:8-11).*
- *Israel returned captives and spoils of Judah by way of Jericho (2 Chron. 28:1-15).*

MOUNT OF TEMPTATION, *Quarantana*

Just west of the ancient tel of Jericho is the traditional Mount of Temptation, where immediately after his baptism Jesus went to be with God. He fasted 40 days and was tempted by the devil. The **GREEK MONASTERY OF THE FORTY DAYS** is on the Mount. The top of the mount offers an excellent panorama of the Jordan Valley.

- *Jesus fasted and was tempted by Satan (Matt. 4:1-11; Mark 1:12-13; Luke 4:1-13).*

ELISHA'S FOUNTAIN, *Spring of the Sultan*

Elisha's Fountain is located across the street from the Old Jericho mound. Here, according to tradition, Elisha found polluted waters and threw salts in them to make them pure. The Arabs have a legend that barren women will become fruitful if they drink of the spring.

- *Elisha healed its waters (2 Kings 2:19-22).*

ANCIENT SYNAGOGUE

Three-quarters of a mile northeast of Elisha's Fountain, a row of cypress trees leads to a house built over the floor of a synagogue that is 1,500 years old.

Caliph Hisham's Palace

This is about a mile northeast of Old Jericho. It was a winter resort for the Umayyad caliphs, whose capital was Damascus in Syria. Well preserved, it dates back to A.D. 724. A beautiful mosaic bath is worth seeing.

PHASAELIS, *El Fasayil*

Twelve miles directly north of New Jericho are the remains of a town built by Herod and named after his brother Phasael.

ALLENBY BRIDGE

Five and one-half miles east of Jericho is the Allenby Bridge. It was near here that the children of Israel crossed the Jordan River and entered the Promised Land. The river stopped its flow and twelve stones were taken from the river bed. The blockage of the Jordan that allowed the Israelites to cross near today's Allenby Bridge occurred 16 miles upstream at a place called Adam (Josh. 3:16). Note the coincidental rendering of the name in English: A-*dam*! It is still called by the same name today, Adam Bridge. In 1927 tremors caused the collapse of high clay riverbanks *at the same place*, and the river stopped flowing for over 21 hours (see further in *Encyclopedia Judaica, Geography*, p. 86).

- *The children of Israel crossed the Jordan River near here (Josh. 3:14-4:13, 20-24; Ps. 114:3).*

ACHOR ("trouble"), el-Buquei'ah

- *In this valley near Jericho Achan and his family were stoned and buried and his property destroyed (Josh. 7:24, 26).*
- *It was within the borders of Judah (Josh. 15:7).*
- *The valley of Achor will be a place of pasture (Isa. 65:10).*
- *It will be a door of hope (Hos. 2:15).*

GILGAL ("*circle*"), *Riba, Khirbet el-Mefjer*

One of the traditional locations of Gilgal is 3 miles southeast of Jericho. (Another site called Gilgal is about 19 miles north of Jerusalem.)

- *Here Joshua set up twelve stones taken from the Jordan (Josh. 4:1-3, 20-24).*
- *This was the Israelites' first camp after they crossed the Jordan, and here they were circumcised (Josh. 4:19-24; 5:2-10; 9:6; 10:7, 15; 14:6; 15:7; Deut. 11:30).*
- *This is where the Israelites ate the Passover, manna ceased, and messengers of God came to Joshua (Josh. 5:10-15).*
- *Israel camped here while besieging Jericho (Josh. 6).*
- *Here the Gibeonites tricked Joshua (Josh. 9, 10).*
- *Here Saul was crowned and rejected as a king (1 Sam. 11:14-15; 15).*
- *Here Saul was denounced (1 Sam. 13:8-15).*
- *Samuel preached here (1 Sam. 12).*
- *Here was a place of sacrifices (1 Sam. 10:8; 13:8-10; 15:21).*
- *Agag was slain here (1 Sam. 15).*
- *People welcomed David as he returned from exile beyond the Jordan (2 Sam. 19:15).*
- *Elisha and Elijah seem to have lived here (2 Kings 2:1).*
- *Elisha purified the pottage (2 Kings 4:38-41).*
- *Gilgal was referred to by prophets as a place of idolatry (Hos. 4:15; Mic. 6:56).*

RIVER JORDAN

The Jordan River is 125 miles long between the Sea of Galilee and the Dead Sea; yet the distance it covers is only 65 miles in a straight line. This is due to its meandering course as it lazily flows down the Jordan (Rift) Valley. Its average width is 100 feet. It is the only river in the world that flows for most of its course below sea level. The name Jordan (Yarden) comes from the Hebrew verb "yarad," which means to descend. Of the three rivers holy to mankind, the Ganges, the Nile, and the Jordan, the last is the smallest and least impressive. Though the other two possess mighty currents and are broad and long, they remain most important locally, their spell limited mainly to those who live along their banks. But the Jordan, hardly a river at all, modest in every measure, is yearned for by many to whom it has ceased to be – and indeed never was – a living reality. Instead it exists for them as a symbol and a dream.

According to John 1:28 and 1 Nephi 10:9, John was baptizing at a place along the river called **BETHABARA**. Hebrew *Beth* means "house of" or "place of" and the verb *la'avor* means to cross; therefore, the toponym means place of crossing, or fording place across the river. It is likely the same natural fording place today called Allenby Bridge, or King Hussein Bridge.

When President Brigham Young sent his counselor, George A. Smith, and others to Palestine in 1873 to dedicate the land for the return of the Jews, they visited Bethabara, where Jesus was baptized, and Pres. Smith, along with Feramorz Little and Paul A. Schettler, were re-baptized here (*Correspondence of Palestine Tourists*, 1875).

In 1893, while he was president of the Turkish Mission, Don C. Musser visited Bethabara, and later wrote about his visit here:

"A half hour's ride from where we took our Dead Sea bath, brings us to the banks of the Jordan at the reputed place of Joshua's crossing with the children [of Israel, and Jesus' baptism].

"Here is a bathing place resorted to by thousands of the Greek Church. I saw a party of over a thousand Greeks here one day last spring and a very interesting sight it was to see them all, old and young, male and female, without any regard for propriety, plunge nude and heedless into a promiscuous bath.

River Jordan, near where Jesus was baptized

"Some of these pilgrims were old and feeble, and had saved a life-time for money to bring them these thousands of miles to bathe in this stream, alike sacred to the Christian, Jew and cast out Ishmaelite" (*Millennial Star,* vol. 56, Jan. 8, 1894, p. 28).

- *Lot chose the plains of the Jordan (Gen. 13:10-11).*
- *Israel miraculously crossed it and gathered twelve stones from the river bottom (Josh. 3:13-17; 4:1-9, 20-24; Ps. 114:3).*
- *Elijah divided its waters (2 Kings 2:6-8).*
- *Elisha divided its waters (2 Kings 2:14).*
- *Naaman was cured of leprosy by washing in it (2 Kings 5:10-14).*
- *Elisha made an axe head float (2 Kings 6:1-7).*
- *John baptized many here (Matt. 3:6).*
- *Jesus was baptized here (Matt. 3; Mark 1:4-11).*
- *Jesus won his first disciples here (John 1:25-51).*
- *Jesus was baptized in the Jordan (1 Ne. 10:7-10; 2 Ne. 31:4-13; D&C 93:15-18).*

SALT SEA, Dead Sea, *Sea of the Plain*

The Dead Sea is 47 by 10 miles in length and width. It is nearly 1300 feet deep and lies 1300 feet below sea level. Annual average rainfall at the Dead Sea is less than 2 inches and it usually has high temperatures. The highest ever recorded was 124 degrees F. (The lowest and driest point in North America, California's Death Valley, is also a rift valley, and is one of the hottest places on earth - a temperature of 135° F. was recorded there in 1913, the highest shade temperature ever recorded anywhere). The Dead Sea region is one of the driest climates in the world. The low altitude makes it richer in oxygen than any other place on earth (10% more than at sea level). High atmospheric pressure, the highest in the world, reduces the sun's ultra violet rays and greatly lessens danger of sunburn on the more than 300 cloudless days of the year. The Dead Sea has the highest salinity and density of any body of water in the world - over 30%, which is eight times more than ocean water (the Great Salt Lake was once about 27%); with so much solid matter, water of the Dead Sea is proportionately heavier than the human body – that's why people float on the sea.

Six million tons of water has evaporated off the Dead Sea *daily* (which is one reason for the thick haze usually hanging over the lake). That's how much water once entered the lake daily, and since it had no outlet and maintained a fairly constant level, it lost that great quantity by evaporation. Freshwater is what evaporates, leaving the heavy mineral residue. Oceans maintain a constant salinity of about 3.5 per cent. The Mediterranean at 3.9% and the Red Sea at 4% are both saltier than ocean waters. This, again, is because of rapid rate of evaporation. The Mediterranean loses 100,000 tons of water *per second!*

The Dead Sea has been receding tremendously the past two decades because Israelis are drawing off the freshwater. Israel's National Water Carrier and Jordan's East Ghor Canal have caused a 75% reduction in flow into the salt lake. Since the 1960s it is ten meters lower! Photos of several decades ago show a water connection between northern and southern bays – which no longer exists (it's dry from Israel to Jordan, across the Lisan Peninsula, opposite Masada). Closing off the shallow pools at the south end, and controlling flow of freshwater into them, increases the rate of evaporation and concentration of salts produced. The Dead Sea is an enormous natural mineral reservoir. Chemicals extracted include potash, salts, bromine, gypsum, calcium chloride, and magnesium. On the northern shore are remains of the buildings of the phosphate works that were used prior to 1948 but were destroyed in the war. Israel has built a large, modern plant at Sodom, on the southern end of the lake, that processes the various minerals.

- *In the Valley of Salt David smote 18,000 men of Edom (1 Chron. 18:12).*
- *Here Amaziah destroyed 10,000 Edomites (2 Kings 14:7; 2 Chron. 25:11).*
- *It is called by various names (Gen. 14:3; Num. 34:3, 12; Josh. 15:2, 5; 18:19; Deut. 3:17; Josh. 3:16).*

Qumran

The Dead Sea Scrolls, considered the greatest archaeological find of the twentieth century, made Qumran famous. Many of the scrolls are now housed in the Shrine of the Book, at Jerusalem. Qumran, a National Parks Authority site, lies 13 miles north of Ein Gedi, 2 miles north of Ein Fashkha, and 10 miles south of Jericho. At the time of Jesus an ascetic group of Essenes, an off-shoot from mainstream Judaism, lived here. Qumran is the Greco-Roman name of the former biblical City of Salt (or "Salt Lake City"). Excavations began at Qumran in 1951. Ruins are of the community center, not living quarters; people may have lived in tents roundabout. Aqueducts brought water from the wadi for mikvaot (ritual baths or immersion pools, what Christians would call "baptismal fonts"). Communal dining is evidenced by the great quantity of pots, dishes, and bowls found neatly stacked in the room called "store of pottery." The cemetery to the east contained at least 1,100 graves, 15 of women. It may have been a regional cemetery.

The scrolls the Essenes hid in the caves and the habits of the community have caused some to question the "uniqueness" of Jesus, speculating that Jesus probably and John the Baptist almost assuredly were Essenes. Most Christians do not share this view, however.

Muhammad adh-Dhib, a 15-year-old Bedouin, discovered cave number 1 in February or March of 1947. Archbishop Metropolitan Samuel of the Syrian Orthodox Church in Jerusalem purchased four of the scrolls from the Bethlehem antique dealer Kando, and Dr. Eleazar L. Sukenik purchased three. Sukenik purchased the scrolls on November 29, 1947, the very day the United Nations voted

caves near Qumran

for the re-creation of the Jewish state after nearly 2,000 years of nonexistence.

Over 850 scrolls have been discovered in and around Qumran (also 14 at Masada). Forty percent of the scrolls are biblical.

The seven main scrolls from cave number 1 were as follows: *Isaiah, Commentary on Habakkuk, Manual of Discipline, Genesis Apocryphon, War of the Sons of Light with the Sons of Darkness, Thanksgiving Psalms,* and an *Isaiah Fragment.* They date between 250 B.C. and A.D. 70. Cave 4 was discovered in Sept. of 1952. An estimated 15-40,000 fragments from hundreds of documents were found 4 inches thick on the floor of the cave. Work on them continues at Jerusalem's Rockefeller Museum and elsewhere. In the eastern part of the ruins, a major crack is visible right down the stairs leading into a large water cistern. It is the result of a severe earthquake that rocked the country in the spring of 31 B.C., killing 30,000 in Judea alone.

POINTS OF INTEREST CONCERNING THE SCROLLS

(1) The **GENESIS APOCRYPHON** is another book about Abraham, and the original manuscript may have been written by Abraham. (Compare Gen. 12:10-13 with Abr. 2:22-25.)

(2) **ISAIAH** seems to have been the most read and revered by the Essenes. It reads essentially the same as in the King James Version of the Old Testament; yet this scroll is 1,000 years older than any known Hebrew texts.[9]

(3) **THE WAR OF THE SONS OF LIGHT WITH THE SONS OF DARKNESS** discusses military tactics and mentions such things as an "improvised banner" and a "consultation with the prophet."

(4) The **BEATEN COPPER SCROLL** tells of buried treasures – $200,000,000 worth, according to some estimates. It is now housed in the Amman Archaeological Museum in Jordan.

(5) The **TEMPLE SCROLL** gives a detailed description of the temple, a command to build it, and instructions as to how. It differs from hitherto known ancient sources that were concerned with the first, second, and Herodian Temples (1 Kings 5-9; 2 Chron. 2-7; Ezek. 40-47). Another major portion of the Temple Scroll is devoted to statutes, laws, and duties of the king, and description of various holy days and festivals, the Essene calendar, and laws of purity. Much of the scroll has God speaking in first person. Passages from the Torah are quoted extensively. The Temple Scroll was discovered later than other scrolls, only in 1955, in Cave 11. It is the longest of all, over 8 meters. Among another 16 scrolls found in the same Cave 11 were the Leviticus Scroll, the Targum of Job, Psalms, and Melchizedek.

(6) The **APOCRYPHAL WRITINGS** bear testimony of the coming of Messiah and tell of Adam's baptism.[10]

PARALLELS

The religious structure of the Qumran community has many parallels in the Church and Gospel as organized and taught by Jesus and understood by many Christian churches today:

(1) **ORGANIZATION**: priesthood, three priests, twelve men as a council, overseers, bishops, teachers, and elders.

(2) **ORDINANCES**: baptism by immersion, baptism of the spirit, sacrament, Temple covenants, and being just and true.

(3) **DOCTRINES**: love of God, a God with bodily parts, a Messiah, a premortal existence inferred, earth life as a probationary period, new revelation, a new covenant, community of goods, sabbath observance, the last days, judgment, resurrection, and others.

(4) **LOVE OF THE SCRIPTURES**: the hiding of records, flight into the desert, peculiar literature, reading and writing of scriptures, metal used to write on, anticipation of the Temple, a divine plan, the elect of God, typical New Testament expressions, denunciation of the Jews in Jerusalem, observance of the law of Moses, secrets, revelation, inspired leadership, the literary period of New Testament times, and others.

Although there are a number of fascinating parallels, it should be kept in mind that there are also many striking differences. From the point of view of mainstream Judaism and mainstream "Mormonism," this group of Qumran Covenanters carried on various apostate practices. For example, Jesus and His Apostles never preached separation, isolation, or withdrawal from society; they encouraged the Saints to live within the community and set a living example for others.

Ein Fashkha, *En Eglaim*

Ein Fashkha is a freshwater spring a little south of Qumran. The Israelis flock to these springs to bathe off the salt after a swim or float in the nearby Dead Sea. It has been a favorite bathing site since the six-day war. Showers and dressing facilities are available to the bather.

NORTH FROM JERUSALEM TO NABLUS (SHECHEM)

BAHURIM ("*low grounds*"), **Ras et-Tmim**

This is 1 mile from Old Jerusalem and near the ancient road from Jerusalem to Jericho, northeast of the Mount of Olives.

- *It was located in Benjamin (2 Sam. 19:16).*
- *Shimei lived here (2 Sam. 16:5; 1 Kings 2:8).*
- *It was the home town of Azmaveth (2 Sam. 23:31).*
- *Jonathan and Ahimaaz hid in the well here (2 Sam. 17:18).*
- *Phaltiel, son of Laish, was ordered to relinquish Michal (2 Sam. 3:14-16).*

NOB ("*height*"), **Ras Umm et-Tala**

Two miles northeast of Jerusalem, near Anathoth, is the ancient site of Nob.

- *Here David received Goliath's sword from the priest Ahimelech (1 Sam. 21:1, 8-9).*
- *David fled here from Saul (1 Sam. 21:1, 10).*
- *Saul took vengeance on its inhabitants and slew the priests (1 Sam. 22:6-23).*
- *The house of Judah is to return to Nob (2 Ne. 20:32).*

ANATHOTH ("*answers,*" *name related to the Canaanite goddess Anath*), **Anata**, *Ras el-Kharrubeh*

This is a Levitical city in Benjamin, 3 miles northeast of Jerusalem.

- *It was the birthplace of Jeremiah (Jer. 29:27).*
- *It is mentioned many times in the Old Testament (Josh. 21:17-18; 1 Kings 2:26; 1 Chron. 6:60; Ezra 2:23; Neh. 7:27; 11:31-32; Isa. 10:30; Jer. 1:1; 11:21, 23; 29:27; 32:7-9).*

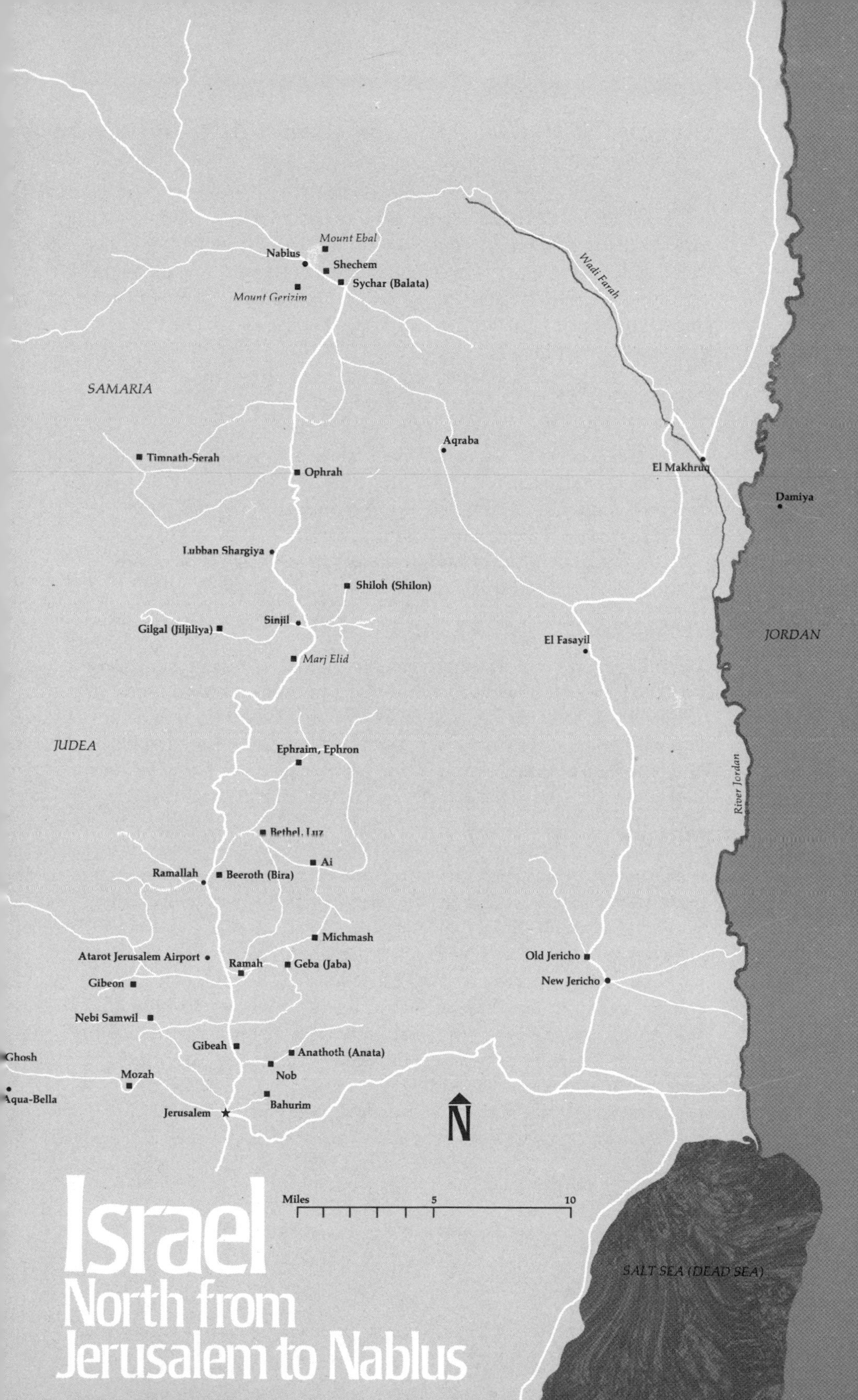

Israel
North from Jerusalem to Nablus

GIBEAH ("*hill Gabaah*"), **Shuafat**, *Gibeath, Tell el-Ful* (literally, "*hill of beans*")

Located 2 miles north of Jerusalem, Gibeah is on the east of the high road to Shechem. This is the place where David played music to soothe Saul's agitated feelings, where Saul tried to put a javelin through David, and even through his own son, Jonathan. Four fortresses have been built here, one on another. It was the capital of Saul, the first king of Israel. On the ruins of Saul's fortress, King Hussein of Jordan started to build a palace, but his construction was interrupted by the six-day war in 1967.

- *Gibeah belonged to Benjamin (Josh. 18:28; 1 Sam. 13:2).*
- *It was the scene of the destruction of most of the tribe of Benjamin (Judg. 20:12-48).*
- *It was Saul's home town and his home after he was elected king (1 Sam. 10:26; 11:14; 13:16; 15:34; Isa. 10:29).*
- *Here Saul summoned the people to war (1 Sam. 11:1-13; 13; 14).*
- *It was the place of Saul's court (1 Sam. 14:2-3).*
- *The bodies of seven sons of Saul were hung up in Gibeah (2 Sam. 21:6).*
- *It is referred to as "Gibeah of Saul" (2 Ne. 20:29.)*

Nebi Samwil ("*prophet Samuel*")

Four miles directly northwest of Jerusalem, in the territory of Benjamin, is the ancient site now called Nebi Samwil. It was a prominent religious center, particularly in the time of Samuel the prophet. Some believe Samuel is buried here, though the Bible clearly indicates that he died and was buried in his hometown Ramah (1 Sam. 25:1; 28:3). From the highway going north out of Jerusalem a high minaret may be seen in the distance to the west. This marks the site.

GIBEON ("*hill*"), *el-Jib*

Approximately 5 miles directly northwest of Jerusalem is Gibeon. Here an attempt was made to settle a quarrel between the armies of Ishbosheth, under Abner, and of David, under Joab, by having 12 men from each side fight. The plan failed because the 24 men killed each other at the pool.

Gibeon has a spectacular **WATER SYSTEM**. Cut entirely from solid rock, it includes a pool 82 feet deep, 37 feet in diameter, and equipped with a circular stairway of 79 steps. Beyond the pool a tunnel, again carved from solid rock a distance of 167 feet, leads to a spring outside the ancient city. The unusual contest of arms probably took place beside this great pool.

When 5 kings of the Amorites fought against Gibeon, Joshua came to the rescue. Hailstones from heaven destroyed more of the enemy than the Israelites did.

The sun and moon stood still so the Israelites could win the battle. The kings were slain by Joshua.

Gibeon was the only city that made peace with the Israelites in their conquest of Canaan, and its inhabitants were made servants to Israel (Josh. 11:19).

Unlike most archaeological sites, excavators were able to identify Gibeon because of written evidence: 27 jar handles were found with the name "Gib'on" inscribed on them. Also of interest are 11 wine cellars, the total storage capacity of which amounted to about 25,000 gallons.

- *David defeated the Philistines here (1 Chron. 14:16; 2 Sam. 5:25).*
- *Gibeon was allotted to Benjamin and the Levites (Josh. 18:21, 25).*
- *Hailstones came, the sun and moon stood still for Joshua, and five kings were killed by Joshua (Josh. 10:1-27).*
- *At the pool of Gibeon 24 men killed each other when Abner defeated Joab (2 Sam. 2:12-28).*
- *Saul slew Gibeonites (2 Sam. 21:1-9).*
- *When David brought the ark of God back to Jerusalem, it seems that the tabernacle of the congregation was at Gibeon (2 Chron. 1:3-6).*
- *This was the place of Solomon's sacrifice and famous prayer and dream (1 Kings 3:4-15; 9:2; 2 Chron. 1:2-17).*
- *Here captives from Mizpah were freed (Jer. 41:11-18).*

RAMAH ("*height*", "*loftiness*")

Five miles north of Jerusalem, between Gibeah and Geba, is Ramah.

This is a high place in the hill country of Benjamin. It can hardly be dissociated from the name of Mizpah nearby. Its chief distinction is its connection with Samuel.

- *The palm tree of Deborah was near here, between Ramah and Bethel (Judg. 4:5).*
- *It was the birthplace of Samuel (1 Sam. 1:18-20; 2:11).*
- *The house of Elkanah and Hannah, Samuel's parents, was here (1 Sam. 1:19; 2:11).*
- *Samuel lived here and judged Israel (1 Sam. 8:4; 15:34; 16:13).*
- *Samuel anointed Saul the first king of Israel here (1 Sam. 10:1).*
- *David fled from Saul and came here to seek safety with Samuel (1 Sam. 19:18).*
- *Samuel died and was buried here (1 Sam. 25:1; 28:3).*
- *Ramah was built up by Baasha, king of Israel, in a war against Judah (1 Kings 15:17; 2 Chron. 16:1).*
- *Building material was taken by Asa to build Geba and Mizpah (2 Chron. 16:6).*
- *The people of Ramah returned after captivity and settled here (Ezra 2:1, 26; Neh. 7:6, 30; 11:1-4; 32-33).*
- *There was lamentation in Ramah, Rachel weeping for her children (Jer. 31:1; cf. Matt. 2:18).*

- *Jeremiah was released from chains here (Jer. 40:1-4).*

GEBA ("*hill*"), Jaba

Geba lies 6 miles north of Jerusalem, on the border of Benjamin's inheritance (Josh. 18:23-24).

- *It was a city of the Levites (Josh. 21:1, 17; 1 Chron. 6:60).*
- *Jonathan fought the Philistines here (1 Sam. 14:1-23).*
- *It was reoccupied by Judah after the 70-year exile in Babylon (Ezra 2:26; Neh. 11:1-4, 31-33).*

MICHMASH, Mukhmas

This site is 7 miles north of Jerusalem, on the northeast of Ramah.

- *The contests between the courageous Jonathan and the Philistines took place here (1 Sam. 13-14; Isa. 10:28).*
- *It was resettled by the Jews as they returned from their captivity in Babylon (Ezra 2:1, 27; Neh. 7:6, 31).*

Atarot Jerusalem Airport

Five miles north of Jerusalem is the Atarot Jerusalem Airport (Kalandia).

MIZPAH ("*watch tower*"), Mizpeh, *Tell en-Nasbeh*

- *It was in the territory of Benjamin (Josh. 18:21, 26).*
- *Israel conferred here about the outrage of the Levite concubine (Judg. 20:1-3).*
- *Samuel rededicated the people and attacked the Philistines (1 Sam. 7:3-14).*
- *Saul was proclaimed the first king of Israel (1 Sam. 10:17-25).*
- *Mizpah was fortified by King Asa (1 Kings 15:22; 2 Chron. 16:6).*
- *Here Gedaliah reigned over the remnant left by Nebuchadnezzar (2 Kings 25:22-26; Jer. 40:5-16).*

Ramallah ("*the high place of God*"), *Ram-Allah*

Eight miles north of Jerusalem and 2,930 feet above sea level is the city of Ramallah. It is true to its name because it overlooks the entire area. The majority of the city is Christian Arab.

BEEROTH ("*wells*"), Bira, *al-Bireh*

Beeroth is 8 miles north of Jerusalem, by the town of Ramallah. This was the first stopping place for caravans going from Jerusalem to Galilee.

- *This is thought to be the place where Mary and Joseph first missed Jesus when he was still in the Temple at age twelve (Luke 2:41-45).*

BETHEL (*"house of God"*), **LUZ, Beitin**

Bethel is 11 miles north of Jerusalem and 2 miles (3 kilometers) east of the main road between Ramallah and Nablus. It was first called *Luz.* The name Luz is Aramaic for "almond." Tradition has the name *Bethel* refer to the stone set up by Jacob and anointed as a symbol of God's presence. After the division of the kingdom, Bethel became the Northern Kingdom's religious center. In 721 B.C. the Assyrians captured it, along with Samaria. Bethel was fortified during the Maccabean period, but was taken by Vespasian as the Romans approached Jerusalem. Very little remains of the ancient city today. The Arab village of Beitin is built up on the historical Bethel. At Burj Beitin are the ruins of a 6th century A.D. church. According to tradition, the stone that Jacob set up as a pillar is the same stone that is now under the seat of the coronation chair in Westminster Abbey, in London.

- *Bethel was known as Luz (Gen. 28:19) and as Beth-aven (Hos. 4:15).*
- *It was the place of Abraham's second altar of worship in Canaan (Gen. 12:7-8).*
- *Here Abraham and Lot separated (Gen. 13).*
- *Here Jacob had his dream of the ladder. He used the stone for a pillow and then set it up as a pillar and altar (Gen. 28:10-22).*
- *Jacob lived here (Gen. 35:1-15).*
- *Jacob revisited Bethel, and Deborah, Rebekah's nurse, died here (Gen. 35:1-8).*
- *Israel conquered Bethel, a royal city of the Canaanites (Judg. 1:22-26).*
- *Samuel judged here (1 Sam. 7:16).*
- *Jeroboam set up a golden calf as a shrine (1 Kings 12:25-33).*
- *Jeroboam was warned by a prophet (1 Kings 13).*
- *Because Amos foretold the death of the king and the captivity of Israel, he was forbidden by Jeroboam from prophesying in Bethel (Amos 7:10-17).*
- *Here was one of the "schools of the prophets," as they are often called (2 Kings 2:2-3).*
- *Elisha cursed the youth, and bears tore them, according to the "bear story" (2 Kings 2:23-24).*
- *King Josiah overthrew idol worship (2 Kings 23).*
- *Bethel was the frequent subject of prophecy (Jer. 4:3-13; Amos 3:14; 4:4; 5:5; 7:10, 13).*
- *Here Abraham built his second altar in Canaan (Abr. 2:20).*

AI (*"the ruined mound"*)

Two to three miles southeast of Bethel is the traditional site of Ai. Excavations by Mme Marquet-Krause showed that a palace, a sanctuary, and fortifications existed here and some ruins date back to the third millennium B.C. Ai means "ruin"; the place is elsewhere called Hai, the initial letter representing the Hebrew definite article "the" – thus "the ruin." The hill between Bethel and Ai is as sacred as Mt. Sinai, the Sacred Grove, the Kirtland Temple, and other such places.

- *Ai was connected with Abraham's journeys (Gen. 12:8; 13:3).*
- *It was the first city captured by the Israelites in Canaan (Josh. 7; 8; 9:3).*
- *It was mentioned in the time of Ezra (Ezra 2:28).*
- *Its captivity was prophesied (Jer. 49:3).*
- *Perhaps this is the Aiath of Isaiah's description (Isa. 10:28) and the Aija mentioned in Nehemiah's account (Neh. 11:31.)*
- *The Book of Abraham gives another account of Abraham erecting an altar and worshipping God at Hai, the same as biblical Ai (Abr. 2:20).*

EPHRAIM ("*doubly fruitful*"), OPHRAH, EPHRON, Taiyibe

Twelve miles north of Jerusalem and a few miles from Bethel is the traditional site of Ephraim.

- *It was a town in Benjamin (Josh. 18:21, 23).*
- *An angel met Gideon here (Judg. 6:11).*
- *This was the scene of the activities of Gideon and Abimelech (Judg. 6:11; 9:5-7).*
- *It was the house and burying place of Gideon (Judg. 8:27-32).*
- *Here Abimelech slew 69 of his brethren (Judg. 9:1-5).*
- *Gideon built an altar here (Judg. 6:24).*
- *It was near Absalom's sheep farm (2 Sam. 13:23).*
- *Abijah took Ephraim from Jeroboam (2 Chron. 13:19).*
- *Here Jesus retired after raising Lazarus from the dead (John 11:54).*

Sinjil

The site of the ancient Crusader town of Saint Giles is located on the road that goes west to Gilgal.

GILGAL ("*circle*," "*wheel*"), Jiljiliya

Approximately 19 miles north of Jerusalem and 3 miles west of the highway is another ancient site called Gilgal. (Another site is 3 miles southeast of Jericho. See above.)

SHILOH, Shilon, *Seilun* ("*peaceful*," "*place of rest*"), *Turmus-Aya*

Shiloh's location, about 20 miles north of Jerusalem, has always been known because of Judges 21:19, possibly the most detailed geographical verse in the Bible – describing where Shiloh is. Shiloh was the first capital of Israel for 300 years before the conquest of Jerusalem. It was destroyed by the Philistines about 1050 B.C. A lintel with "horned altars" in bas-relief was found here. There are also remains of an ancient synagogue or mosque that are over a thousand years old. Full-scale excavations were carried out between 1981-1984. (See *Biblical Archaeology Review* Jan/Feb 1986, 22-41.) The **VALLEY OF THE DANCERS** is somewhere near Shiloh.

- *Here the tribes of Israel assembled after the conquest and received their allotment of territory (Josh. 18-22).*
- *Shiloh was the home of the ark and tabernacle at the time of the judges (Josh. 18:1; Judg. 18:31).*
- *Here the Benjaminites captured maidens for wives (Judg. 21:16-25).*
- *Here Eli judged and Hannah prayed for a son (1 Sam. 1:1-10).*
- *This was the scene of the wickedness of Eli's sons (1 Sam. 2:12-36).*
- *Samuel grew up here in the service of the Lord under the high priest Eli (1 Sam. 3).*
- *Here Eli died (1 Sam. 4).*
- *Here Samuel judged Israel (1 Sam. 7:16-17).*
- *Ahijah prophesied against Jeroboam (1 Kings 14:1-20).*
- *The Assyrian king restored Jeremiah to liberty (Jer. 40:1-6).*
- *Shiloh was used as an illustration and warning (Ps. 78:59-61; Jer. 7:12, 14; 26:6).*

Lubban Sharqiya

In the beautiful valley of Lebona (meaning "frankincense") is Lubban Sharqiya, and less than a mile north of the city was the boundary line between Samaria on the north and Judea on the south in the days of the Savior. The line was also located 1½ miles north of Shiloh. As the traveler nears the valley of Lebona from the south, he can see two **WATCHTOWERS** built on the right side of the road to guard against intruders.

- *Watchtowers were built in biblical times (Isa. 5:2; Matt. 21:33).*
- *The parable of the wicked husbandmen mentions watchtowers (Matt. 21:33-44).*
- *A parable in the Doctrine and Covenants also mentions such a tower (D&C 101:43-62.)*

TIMNATH-SERAH

Timnath-Serah is where Joshua was buried (Josh. 19:50; 24:30). The exact location in the tribe of Ephraim is unknown.

SYCHAR, Balata, *Balatah*, Askar, Jacob's Well

Jacob's Well is located at the fork of the road at Balata near Shechem, on the ground designated as "Jacob's parcel of ground," or the land that Jacob gave Joseph. Jews, Samaritans, Muslims, and Christians associate this well with Jacob. The well is 7½ feet in diameter, lined with rough masonry, and over 100 feet deep to the water. The Greek Orthodox church owns the well and has partially built a chapel over it.

Some believe that Sychar was at Shechem. Others believe that Askar, about 1 mile north of Jacob's Well, was the ancient site of Sychar. Two hundred yards northwest of Jacob's well is **JOSEPH'S TOMB**, similar to Rachel's tomb. Here is the traditional spot where Joseph's bones were buried after being carried from Egypt. Joseph was born in Paddan-Aram, in Mesopotamia, and he died in Egypt. Altogether he spent 93 years in Egypt. As far as we know, his sons Ephraim and Manasseh were born, lived their lives, died, and were buried in Egypt. Joseph had visions of Moses and Joseph Smith Sr. and Jr. (see 2 Ne. 3), and the Book of Joseph was among the papyri in the possession of Joseph Smith. D&C 27 notes that Joseph will be among those that will be on the earth at the Second Coming. Joseph is one of the greatest prophets who ever lived: "he truly prophesied concerning all his seed. And the prophecies which he wrote, there are not many greater" (2 Ne. 4:2).

- *Detailed location of Jacob's property in Shechem is given (Gen. 33:18-20).*
- *This was the land that Jacob gave Joseph (Gen. 48:22).*
- *Here Joseph's bones were buried (Josh. 24:32).*
- *Jesus talked to the Samaritan woman here (John 4:3-26).*

SHECHEM ("*shoulder*"), *Sechem*, Nablus (*from Greek Neapolis meaning "New City"*), *Tell Balatah*

Shechem, the first capital of the Northern Kingdom under Jeroboam, lies in a valley between Mount Gerizim and Mount Ebal, in the eastern part of the present city of Nablus. The ancient tel is located just northwest of the traditional burial site of Joseph. Genesis 33:18 says Jacob pitched his tent "before the city" – *before* in Hebrew means "in front of" or "to the east." Jacob's Well and Joseph's Tomb are indeed east of the city, in the parcel of ground Jacob had purchased from the local inhabitants. With no natural fortification, the Canaanite city had to have strong walls; to this day sections of the massive, "cyclopean" wall are still standing, and it is possible to walk through the ancient city gate to the middle of the tel. The large *matzeva* or pillar standing in the forecourt of the Middle Bronze Age temple may be the very stone referred to in the covenant ceremony of Joshua and the Israelites upon their incursion into the land (see Josh. 24:24-27). It is interesting to note that the temple had been in use for some four centuries, but was abandoned at the end of the 13th century B. C. We have evidence of a drastic disruption of local worship practices at the time that the Bible indicates the Israelites penetrated to this site. Joshua 24 records that Israelites covenanted to keep the commandments, and they did – two generations remained faithful (see Judg. 2:7,10). Shechem is mentioned 48 times in the Bible.

Nablus is an Arab Palestinian city and noted for its soap and pastry making. Nablus is presently the home of several hundred Samaritans, who live on the southwest side of the city. Here in the **SAMARITAN SYNAGOGUE** is the *Samaritan Pentateuch*, reputed by the Samaritans to be the oldest copy of the writings of Moses (they claim over 3,000 years old) and written on parchment. Modern scholars date the document to A.D. 1100-1200, however. The Samaritans, remnants of the Ten Tribes, are those who stayed in Samaria when the Ten Tribes were carried north by the Assyrians (2 Kings 17:6, 23). They intermarried with non-Israelites (2 Kings 17:24) and were thus shunned by the Jews of Jesus' day. They claim, however, that their blood is pure to Aaron, and they marry within their own group. There are over 600 Samaritans – some in Nablus and some at Holon, near Tel Aviv – belonging to 7 major families.

Many Samaritans are very poor and live in houses near their synagogue. They wear white robes, they do not shave or cut their hair, and their hats are covered with red cloth. The Samaritan temple on Mount Gerizim was destroyed by John Hyrcanus in 126 B.C., but the Samaritans still celebrate the Passover feast every year on Mount Gerizim on the evening before the full moon of Nisan (April).

The creed of the Samaritans includes the following:

(1) God is one, incorporeal.
(2) Moses is the only prophet and the intercessor for man in the final judgment.
(3) The law of Moses is the only divine revelation.
(4) Mount Gerizim is the chosen place of God, the only center of worship, the "navel of the earth," and "the place where Adam offered sacrifices."
(5) On Judgment Day the righteous will be resurrected in paradise and the wicked will roast in eternal fire.
(6) Six thousand years after creation a Restorer will arise to ameliorate their fortunes. He will live 110 years.

- *This was the first place Abraham dwelt and built an altar in Canaan (Gen. 12:1-7).*
- *Jacob bought land and lived here after meeting Esau (Gen. 33:16-20).*
- *Jacob's daughter was defiled (Gen. 34).*
- *Jacob hid strange gods here (Gen. 35:1-4).*
- *Joseph came here to seek his brethren, who were feeding their flocks. On this journey he was sold to the Ishmaelite traders (Gen. 37:13-14).*
- *Near here Joseph's bones were buried in land purchased after he was carried from Egypt (Gen. 50:25; 33:18-19; Josh. 24:32).*
- *Blessings and cursings of Israel were pronounced here, and covenants were made (Deut. 11:26-30; 27; 28; Josh. 8:30-35).*
- *This was the scene of Joshua's final address and Israel's dedication to God: "We will serve the Lord" (Josh. 24:1-25, esp. 15).*
- *The pillar was a sacred stone erected by Joshua (Josh. 24:26.)*
- *Abimelech, son of Gideon, set himself up as head over all Israel at Shechem. He slew 69 of his brothers and reigned 3½ years (Judg. 9).*

a Samaritan and the Pentateuch, Nablus

- *The sacred oak of the pillar was here, beside which Abimelech was crowned (Judg. 9:6).*
- *Rehoboam was rejected, and the kingdom was divided (1 Kings 12:1-24).*
- *Jeroboam was elected and fortified it as his capital (1 Kings 12:25-33; 13-14).*
- *It was a city of refuge (Num. 35:11-32; Deut. 19:1-13; Josh. 20).*
- *The king of Assyria brought people from Babylon and placed them in cities of Samaria (2 Kings 17:24).*
- *The Samaritans hindered the building of the walls of Jerusalem (Neh. 2:19-20; 4:1-9; 6:1-14).*
- *This was the first place Abraham offered sacrifices in Canaan (Abr. 2:18-19).*

MOUNT GERIZIM ("*waste places*"), *Jebel et Tor* (*Mount of Blessing*)

On the south of Nablus is Mount Gerizim, 2,848 feet above sea level and held sacred by the Samaritans. The Samaritans claim they have the **ALTARS BUILT BY ADAM AND NOAH** on the top of the mount. They claim that it was on this mountain that Abraham prepared to offer up his own son Isaac as a sacrifice.

At the beginning of the fourth century B.C. a Samaritan temple was built. It was destroyed by Hyrcanus in 126 B.C. In the walls of the Justinian Castle, built on the top in A.D. 583, are **TWELVE STONES** that the Samaritans say came from the bottom of the Jordan River as the Israelites crossed. The Samaritans spend a week of celebrating on the mount during the Passover. Sheep are slaughtered and roasted for the occasion.

- *This was known as the "Mount of Blessing" (Deut. 11:29-30; Josh. 8:33).*
- *Jotham spoke his parable to Shechem from Mount Gerizim (Judg. 9:7).*
- *At the Well of Jacob the Samaritan woman spoke about worshipping "in this mountain" (John 4:20).*

MOUNT EBAL ("*bare*"), *Jebel Eslamiyeh* (*Mount of Cursing*)

On the north of Nablus, directly across from Mount Gerizim, is Mount Ebal, 3,077 feet above sea level. Both Gerizim and Ebal mountains are important because it was here that Israel renewed her covenants with God. Joshua stationed half of the tribes on Ebal and half on Gerizim and the ark with the priests and Levites in the center. From Gerizim they shouted out the blessings of God that they would receive if they were faithful, and from Ebal they proclaimed the curses that would overtake them if they were disobedient to God.

- *This was the "Mount of Cursing" (Deut. 11:29-30; 27:11-26: Joshua 8:30-34).*
- *Joshua built an altar and erected a monument bearing the law of Moses (Josh. 8:30).*

NORTH FROM NABLUS (SHECHEM) TO THE SEA OF GALILEE

TIRZAH ("*delight*"), **Tell el Farah**

Four or five miles north of Shechem is the site of Tirzah. Its king was slain by Joshua. Tirzah at one time superseded Shechem as the capital of the northern kingdom of Israel.

- *Its king was slain by Joshua (Josh. 12:1, 24).*
- *It was a capital of the Northern Kingdom under Jeroboam (1 Kings 14:17).*
- *Here Menahem matured his rebellion against Shallum (2 Kings 15:14).*

SAMARIA ("*watch*"), *Sebaste, Sebastia,* **Sabastiya**

Forty-two miles north of Jerusalem, 9 miles north of Nablus, and on a hill 300 feet high are the extensive ruins of the ancient capital city of Samaria. Omri, the sixth king of Israel, secured the site from one Shemer (Heb. *Shomeron*) and founded Samaria as Israel's capital city, and it was to the kings of Samaria that the northern tribes of Israel turned for leadership. The whole country took its name from the city, and the immediate area was occupied by the tribes of Ephraim and Manasseh.

Omri lived here 6 years, and when he died his son Ahab reigned in his place. Here Ahab built his ivory palace, which Amos spoke of and denounced. Samaria

Israel

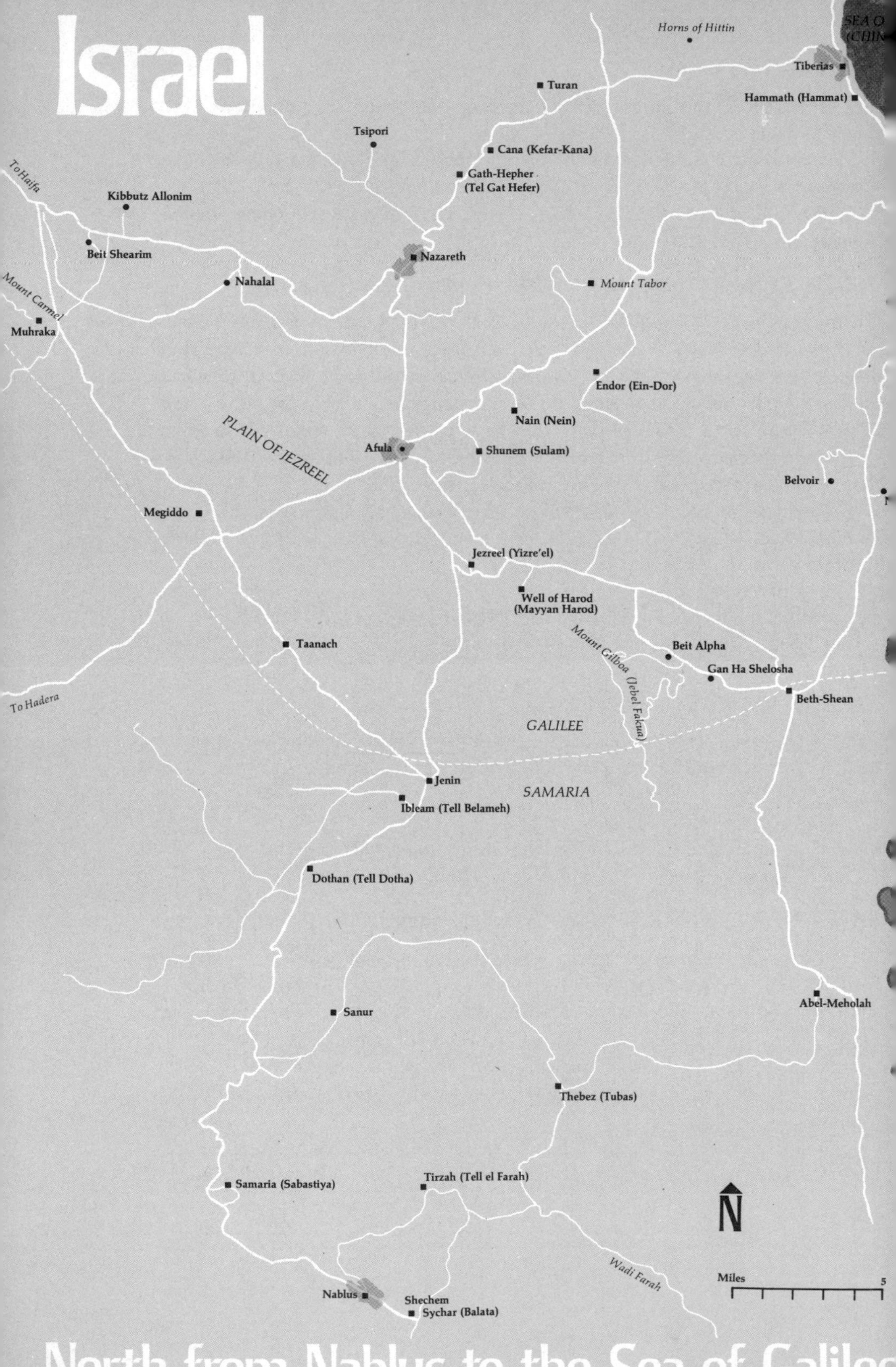

North from Nablus to the Sea of Galilee

saw the wickedness of Jezebel, who induced Ahab to build a temple to Baal right in the capital city.

In addition to Omri and Ahab, Samaria was also the summer palace and burial place of 4 other kings of Israel: Jehu, Jehoahaz, Joash, and Jehoash. The prophets of Israel denounced the city for its transgressions and prophesied its doom.

Samaria was besieged by Shalmaneser V in the seventh year of Hosea and taken by Sargon in 722-721 B.C. Its inhabitants, along with others of the Ten Tribes, were carried captive "over the river" and became lost to history. Some Israelites remained in the area, however, and intermarried with those who were brought from Babylon, Cuthah, Ava, Hamath, and other places to take the place of the lost Israelites. Descendants from these mixed marriages were called Samaritans.

The *Black Obelisk of Shalmaneser III*, found in Nimrod and dated 859-824 B.C., contains the only known portrait of an Israelite king – Jehu. This Victory Monument shows Jehu, son of Omri, giving tribute to Shalmaneser III and tells about his capture.

The *Royal Annals*, found at Nineveh, are a part of several Mesopotamian documents that tell of Sargon's capture of Samaria in 721 B.C. Sargon told of taking 27,290 Israelites prisoner at Samaria (Annals 10-18).

In 331 B.C. Alexander the Great besieged Samaria, and it was later destroyed by John Hyrcanus in 120 B.C. It was rebuilt by Pompey and built again by Gabinius.

Herod the Great carried out very important building works here (35 B.C.), large portions of which remain. He built a promenade that covered the top of the hill, with huge columns in three rows. Some of the 600 columns once adorning the entry to the Herodian city are still visible. He is responsible for changing the name to *Sebaste* in honor of Caesar Augustus. Here he had his son and wife, Mariamne, killed.

Excavations at Samaria under the direction of J. W. Crowfoot resulted in the discovery of hundreds of finely carved ivory fragments from an ivory building identified as Ahab's palace, which Amos denounced. The fragments included inlays of glass paste in ivory, representing floral motifs, and figured scenes that were apparently made by Phoenician artisans. They were probably a part of the furniture decorations in the royal palace. The ivory fragments are owned by the University Museum of Philadelphia, the Rockefeller Museum in Jerusalem, and the Palestine Exploration Fund of London. Harvard University began excavations at Samaria in 1908, financed by Jacob Schiff, a Jewish millionaire; and beginning in 1931 a joint expedition began excavating again. Ruins that have been uncovered include the **PALACE OF OMRI AND AHAB**, the **TEMPLE OF AUGUSTUS**, the

ROMAN FORUM, the **BASILICA**, the **HIPPODROME**, the **THEATER**, the **STREET OF COLUMNS**, the **GATEWAY**, the **WALLS**, and the **CHURCH OF SAINT JOHN THE BAPTIST**, which dates from the Crusader period. Ostraca, ivories, and other remains and ruins make this one of the most important archaeological sites in Israel.

It is a National Parks Authority site.

SABASTIYA is the village on the east side of the hill at Samaria. Its name is a corruption of the Greek *Sebaste* (which is the Greek name of Augustus). Local tradition holds that the prophets Elisha and Obadiah are buried at Samaria in a subterranean cave in the courtyard of a mosque. The minaret is built inside a Crusader cathedral, dating back to 1160. Some Christians believe that this is where John the Baptist was imprisoned and that his head is buried here. A church is named in his honor, the "Church of the Invention of the Head of St. John the Baptist," what we might call the "Shrine of the Head." A dungeon is pointed out as *the* dungeon in which John suffered imprisonment. (Machaerus in Jordan is a more likely site for this event.)

- *Samaria was the capital, residence, and burial place of the kings of Israel, the Northern Kingdom (1 Kings 16:23-24, 28; 22:37; 2 Kings 6:24-30).*
- *Under the influence of Jezebel, Ahab made it a center of Baal worship (1 Kings 16:29-33).*
- *Amos denounced Ahab's house of ivory (Amos 6:1, 4; 1 Kings 22:39).*
- *Jezebel killed many prophets here (1 Kings 18:2, 4).*
- *Benhadad, king of Syria, twice besieged it and was unsuccessful (1 Kings 20; 2 Kings 6).*
- *Elijah destroyed the messengers of King Ahaziah and prophesied his death (2 Kings 1).*
- *Naaman, the Syrian leper, went to Samaria to be healed by Elisha (2 Kings 5).*
- *Elisha smote Benhadad's army with blindness and led some of them into Samaria (2 Kings 6, 7).*
- *Jehu killed Ahab's seventy sons and destroyed the idolatry (2 Kings 10).*
- *Samaria was captured and finally overthrown by Sargon (Shalmaneser's successor) and the Assyrians in 721 B.C. (2 Kings 17; 18:9-12).*
- *Many prophecies concerned its sin and doom (Isa. 8:4; 9:8-24; 10:9; 28; 36:19; Jer. 23:13; Ezek. 23:1-4; Hos. 7; 13:16; Amos 3:12; Mic. 1:6).*
- *As some have thought, this is where John's head was brought at the request of Salome (Matt. 14:1-12; Mark 6:17-29).*
- *Here Philip preached (Acts 8:5-25).*

- *Samaria's capture by Assyria was prophesied (2 Ne. 18:4).*
- *There were other prophecies of its doom (2 Ne. 19:9-11; 20:9-11).*

THEBEZ, Tubas

In a fruitful valley 10 miles northeast of Nablus is Tubas, the site of the ancient city of Thebez.

- *In the reduction of this fortified city Abimelech met his death (Judg. 9:54; 2 Sam. 11:21).*

ABEL-MEHOLAH ("*meadow of the dance*") (*location uncertain, possibly Tell el-Maqlub or Tell Abu Sifri*)

This is a city in Issachar, at the north of the Jordan Valley and 10 miles south of Beth-Shean. It is the birthplace of Elisha, a leading prophet of Israel after the death of Elijah. His prophetic career lasted more than 50 years during the reigns of Jehoram, Jehu, Jehoahaz, and Joash.

- *This was the limit of Gideon's pursuit of the Midianites (Judg. 7:22).*
- *It was the birthplace of Elisha (1 Kings 19:16; 4:12).*
- *Elisha was the prophet who healed Naaman (2 Kings 5; Luke 4:27).*
- *The people forsook the Lord and served Baal and Ashtoreth (1 Sam. 31:10; 1 Kings 11:5).*

DOTHAN ("*double feast*"), Tel Dothan

Dothan is about 14 miles north of Sabastiya (Samaria). It is a strategic military point at the entrance of a pass leading to the Dothan Valley and then the Jezreel Valley (Plains of Esdraelon). At the end of the Dothan Valley is a "knocked out" Jordanian tank – a grim reminder of the six-day war. The city site, the tel of Dothan, is visible to the east of the highway upon entering the valley from the south.

- *Joseph's brothers tended their flocks here and Joseph was sold to Ishmaelites to be carried to Egypt (Gen. 37:13-28).*
- *Joseph's coat of many colors was rent by his brothers (Gen. 37:31-32).*
- *It was the home of Elisha (2 Kings 6:13).*
- *Here the Syrian army surrounded Elisha and his servant (2 Kings 6:13-23).*
- *Alma referred to the rending of Joseph's coat (Al. 46:23-24).*

IBLEAM ("*place of victory*"), *Bileam*, Tell Belameh

This town was about 1 mile southwest of Jenin.

- *It was given to Manasseh (Josh. 17:11).*
- *Here the Canaanites successfully resisted the people of Manasseh (Josh. 17:12; Judg. 1:27).*
- *As a Levitical city it was called Bileam (1 Chron. 6:70).*
- *Near here Jehu killed King Ahaziah (2 Kings 9:27).*
- *Zechariah, king of Israel, was killed here by Shallum (2 Kings 15:10).*

EN-GANNIM, Jenin (*"fount of gardens"*)

This is a typical oriental town, in a fertile region on the southern edge of the plain of Jezreel and 13 miles north of Dothan. It lies about a mile south of the Galilee-Samaria boundary line. On its western outskirts is a hill, which has a tower and a sacred tree. It is known as Khirbet Belame.

- *It is mentioned in Joshua 15:34; 19:21; 21:29.*
- *According to tradition, it was here that Jesus healed ten lepers (Luke 17:11-19).*

GALILEE (*"the circle," home of Jesus*)

Galilee was the northern region of the Holy Land in the days of Jesus. The south boundary was the Carmel mountain range to the west and a line from Jenin to Beth-Shean on the east. To the northeast and northwest it was bounded by Syria and Phoenicia. The area was about 60 miles long and 30 miles wide.

When the Israelites conquered this region it was allotted to the tribes of Asher, Naphtali, Zebulon, and a part of Issachar. It was later conquered by the Assyrians, still later by Babylonians, Persians, and Greeks, then by the Romans. Under Rome, Herod the Great was ruler in 47 B.C. and was succeeded by his son Antipas as Tetrarch in 4 B.C. In the third century A.D., Galilee became the center of Rabbinic life. Remains of Jewish synagogues of this era are to be seen among the ruins of Galilean cities.

Galilee is important because Jesus spent most of his life here. Eleven of his disciples were Galileans, as also had been the prophets Jonah, Elisha, and possibly Hosea. A population of two or three million people may have lived in 204 towns of Galilee in Jesus' day. They were Aramaean, Phoenician, Greek, and Jewish.

A vast blanket of green covers Galilee through most of the year. One Galilee lover said, "In March, Galilee is so green it hurts your eyes." Here you can witness sleepy villages that characterize biblical days. Wells, jugs, shepherds, donkeys, and robes take us back 2,000 years to Jesus' day. The Israelis had to fight malaria to settle the area, but it is now a beautiful paradise for the Israeli and Palestinian farmers.

- *There are many Old Testament references to this area (Josh. 20:7; Judg. 4:6-10; 1 Kings 9:11; 2 Kings 15:29, etc.).*
- *Jesus went into Galilee (Matt. 4:12-25).*
- *Jesus made his first preaching tour of Galilee; a leper was healed (Matt. 4:23-25; 8:2-4; Mark 1:35-45; Luke 4:42-44; 5:12-16).*
- *He made a second tour of Galilee (Luke 8:1-3; Matt. 11:2-30; Luke 7:18-35). He raised the widow's son at Nain from the dead (Luke 7:11-17).*
- *He made a third tour of Galilee; the Twelve were sent forth (Matt. 9:35-11:1; Mark 6:6-13; Luke 9:1-6).*
- *Jesus foretold his death (Matt. 17:22-23).*

- *Jesus took his final departure from here (Matt. 19:1; Mark 10:1; Luke 9:51).*
- *He appeared here after his resurrection (Matt. 28:16-20; Mark 16:15-18).*

TAANACH ("*battlement*"), *Ta'annek*

This is a modern village located on the eastern half of the base of the Tell Ta'annek and 5 miles southeast of Megiddo. The tel was first excavated in 1899 and was one of the first sites of excavation in Palestine. The largest Akkadian tablet group ever found in the Holy Land was discovered here. A water system and one of the best preserved ancient buildings are at the site. A complete figurine mold, dating as far back as the eighth to eleventh century B.C. was also found.

- *This was a Canaanite town undefeated by Joshua (Judg. 1:27; Josh. 12:21).*
- *It was a famous battleground where Sisera gathered his forces to battle against Barak and Deborah (Judg 5:19).*
- *There are other biblical references to the place (Josh. 17:11; 1 Chron. 7:29; Josh. 21:25; 1 Kings 4:12).*

PLAIN OF JEZREEL ("*God sows*"), *Valley of Armageddon, Plain of Esdraelon, the Emek, Merj Ibn Amir*

This is the largest and most fertile valley in Israel and cuts in two the central ridge of mountains of Galilee in the north and Samaria in the south. It is a historic battleground, lying between Nazareth, Mount Carmel, Mount Gilboa, and Mount Moreh – a triangle about 15 by 15 by 20 miles. This was a malarial swampland until, in the early 1920s, the Jewish National Fund launched its biggest land reclamation project (not unlike malarial swampland along the Mississippi River in the 1830s that the Latter-day Saints cleared and where they created a city and gave it a Hebrew name: *Nauvoo* = "Beautiful"). Israel's oldest and best-known settlements are here. One of the most famous is the large moshav, Nahalal, where many families farm on "spokelike" farms that fan out from the settlement's center.

The Jezreel Valley is the classic warpath and battlefield of empires. Egyptians, Hittites, Israelites, Philistines, Assyrians, Syrians, Babylonians, Persians, Greeks, Romans, Crusaders, Turks, and the British under Allenby (1918) have marched and fought on these plains. The apostle John saw the gathering in the valley of Armageddon, in connection with the last great battle.

- *It was named the Valley of Jezreel (Josh. 17:16).*
- *It was located in the area allotted to the tribes of Manasseh and Issachar (Gen. 49:14-15).*
- *It was the scene of Deborah and Barak's strategy against Sisera (Judg. 4-5).*
- *It was the place of Gideon's victory (Judg. 7).*
- *Here Elijah ran before the chariot of Ahab (1 Kings 18:46).*
- *King Josiah was mortally wounded in battle (2 Chron. 35:20-24).*

- *King Saul and his son Jonathan died at Mount Gilboa near here in a clash with the Philistines (1 Sam. 31; 2 Sam. 1; 21:12-14).*
- *It will be involved in the last great battle of Armageddon (Zech. 12:10-11; Rev. 16:13-16).*
- *Great blessings are to come upon Israel at this very place – probably in the Millennium (Hos. 2:21-23).*

MEGIDDO, *Tell el-Mutesellim ("hill of the governor")*

This was a royal city of the Canaanites, 22 miles north of Shechem on the southwest edge of the plains of Jezreel, the most famous battlefield in the world. Thutmose III battled with Megiddo in 1468 B.C.; the walls of his temple at Thebes tell of his war plans. His famous comment was, "Taking Megiddo is like taking a thousand cities." The mound, which was extensively excavated between 1925 and 1939 by the Oriental Institute of the University of Chicago, covers 13 acres and reveals 20 cities – each built on the ruins of the preceding one – dating from earliest times to 400 B.C. Its **WATER SYSTEM** dates back 2,800 years. A shaft 120 feet deep connects with a spring outside the city walls by a **TUNNEL** 215 feet long, which protected the city's water supply. Sunken **GRAIN SILOS** from the time of Jeroboam II protected the grain. Exquisite **IVORIES**, a fragment of an **EGYPTIAN STELA** bearing the name *Shishak*, an elaborate **CITY GATE**, and the **SEAL OF SHEVA** are among the important discoveries at Megiddo. The Hebrew Seal of Sheva has the following words inscribed on it: *Eved Yravam*, which means "servant of Jeroboam." Although this seal is in a museum in Istanbul, most of the finds at Megiddo have been placed in the Rockefeller Museum and the Israel Museum in Jerusalem. A limestone **ALTAR WITH HORNS** like those used by the children of Israel is very interesting to Old Testament students (1 Kings 1:50). It is in the Rockefeller Museum in Jerusalem. (See *Biblical Archaeology Review* Jan/Feb 1994, 26-49.)

It is hard to overemphasize the strategic importance of Megiddo's position at the intersection of ancient international highways. It is the single most important site on the Via Maris, the "Way of the Sea." Megiddo and its surrounding valley is one of the most celebrated battlefields in the history of the world. Among those who have passed through and fought here are: Egyptians Amenhotep, Thutmose, Seti, Ramses, Shishak, Necho; Assyrians Tiglath-pileser, Shalmaneser, Sargon, Sennacherib; Babylonian Nebuchadnezzar; Greeks Alexander, Seleucids, Ptolemies, Cleopatras; Romans Pompey, Mark Antony, Vespasian, Titus; modern day Napoleon, and British General Allenby. Because of all the above, Megiddo has given its name to the last great battle: *Armageddon*, which derives from two Hebrew words, *Har Megiddo,* meaning the hill or mound of Megiddo.

Right: Canaanite altar with horns, found at Megiddo

Below: Megiddo, with a large Canaanite altar in the center

This tel's excavation was in part a model for James Michener's Tel Makor in *The Source* (along with Hazor in Galilee). Megiddo is a National Parks Authority site.

- *Joshua killed the king and took the city (Josh. 12:7, 21).*
- *The city was possessed by Manasseh (Josh. 17:11; 1 Chron. 7:29).*
- *Sisera and his armies were defeated "by the waters of Megiddo" (Judg. 5:19-20).*
- *Solomon fortified the city and it served as one of his defense posts (1 Kings 9:15). Some believe stables capable of taking care of 450 horses and 150 chariots have been excavated; others identify the structures as store houses. Archaeologists have recently dated them to the time of King Ahab. Solomon may have erected something similar on this spot a century earlier.*
- *Ahaziah, king of Israel, was slain here by Jehu (2 Kings 9:27).*
- *Josiah was killed in a battle with Pharaoh Necho and the Egyptian army at Megiddo in 609 B.C. (2 Chron. 35:20-24; 2 Kings 23:29-30).*
- *The last great battle of this world's history will involve Armageddon – in Hebrew Har Mageddon, "Mount of Megiddo" (Rev. 16:13-16; Ezek. 38-39; Zech. 14:2-3).*

MOUNT CARMEL (*Heb. Kerem El = "vineyard of God"*), Mukhraka (*Arabic: "sacrifice"*), *Jebel Mar Elyas*

This is a mountain range 13 miles long projecting into the Mediterranean Sea at Haifa. Its highest point is 1,810 feet above sea level. Mount Carmel has had no political or military history. In the Old Testament Carmel was a symbol or a sanctuary. It is green the year round and has been venerated since antiquity. It is covered with lush, verdant forests and other thick vegetation, and has thousands of caves (see Isa. 5:2; Jer. 46:18; 50:19; and Amos 1:2; 9:3). It was a sanctuary for the worship of Baal. The **CARMELITE MONASTERY OF SAINT ELIJAH** stands at Mukhraka on the eastern end of the mount. A grotto is located here, where tradition indicates Elijah dwelt. Other buildings include a monument to French soldiers; a building to care for pilgrims; a lighthouse; a chapel at "the place of burning," where, tradition says, Elijah challenged the priests and prophets of Baal; and another where they are said to have been killed. A large statue of Elijah killing the priests and prophets of Baal is located near the chapel.

Mount Carmel is a National Parks Authority site.

- *An ancient altar to Jehovah stood here (1 Kings 18:30).*
- *Elijah's contest with the prophets of Baal was here (1 Kings 18:19-40).*
- *The 3½-year drought was ended by Elijah's prayer (1 Kings 18:41-45).*
- *It was visited by Elisha (2 Kings 2:25).*
- *From earliest times it was the site of altars, shrines, and caves where hermits found solitude (Amos 9:3).*

- *It was used as a symbol of beauty, fruitfulness, majesty, and prosperity (Isa. 35:2; Jer. 46:18; 50:19; 2 Chron. 26:10; Song of Sol. 7:5).*
- *"As the dews of Carmel, so shall the knowledge of God descend upon [the Saints]" (D&C 128:19). Note that Mt. Carmel averages 250 dew-nights a year!*

Kibbutz Allonim

Three miles northeast of Beit Shearim is a beautiful farm where a hard-working group of Jews have built a kibbutz with hothouses for roses, sorting, and packing sheds for fruit, and a "merry-go-round" that is used for milking sheep.

Beit Shearim (*"house of gates"*)

About 12 miles east of Haifa are the Beit Shearim burial caves, which are reminiscent of the Sanhedrin Tombs in Jerusalem. In the second century A.D. Beit Shearim was the home of Israel's Supreme Court, the Sanhedrin, as well as the headquarters of the famous Rabbi Yehuda Hanassi, compiler of the Mishna. He was buried here. Many famous rabbis and sages lived in Beth Shearim, and it became a central burial place of Jews of Palestine and the Diaspora.

SARCOPHAGI carved with rams' horns, eagles, human faces, gates, a star of David, ships, shells, lions' heads, and a menorah are an unparalleled phenomenon in Jewish sepulchers. There were originally 200 sarcophagi here, but grave robbers looted them hundreds of years ago. On a tomb there is a **COMBINATION SAILING SHIP AND STAR OF DAVID** dating from the second or third century A.D.[11]

The city of Beit Shearim was destroyed about A.D. 350, but artifacts remain. Israeli archaeologist B. Mazar started to dig here in 1936. Near the remains of an ancient synagogue – once the largest and most important in the region – is an interesting fourth-century **OIL PRESS**. A small **MUSEUM** is located here, and above the catacombs on the hillside the **STATUE OF ALEXANDER ZEID** stands near **SHEIKH AVREKH**, a tomb holy to the Muslims.

Beit Shearim is a National Parks Authority site.

Nahalal

Eight miles west of Nazareth is Nahalal, the first moshav in the land of Israel, founded in 1920 and built in the form of a wheel with farms like spokes going out from the center. The houses are grouped around the center and the public buildings are in the center. Moshe Dayan, hero of the Six-day War of 1967, grew up here and is buried here.

A moshav is an agricultural settlement where every settler lives separately with his family and tills a plot of land leased to him by the Jewish National Fund at a nominal rent. Each farmer works his farm with the help of his family and he is supposed to have only that amount of land that his family can manage.

Purchases and sales are made on a cooperative basis. The moshav is the most common type of rural settlement in Israel.

- *The name Nahalal comes from a biblical town of Zebulun, whose sons inherited the Valley of Jezreel (Josh. 19:10, 15; 21:34-35; Judges 1:30).*

NAZARETH (*"to blossom," "flower"*), *el Nazirah* (*home town of Jesus*), Kiryat-Natsrat

Nazareth lies in the hills of Galilee, 1,230 feet above sea level, about midway between the Sea of Galilee and the Mediterranean Sea. Today it houses one of Israel's largest Arab communities, with a population of 54,000, a large part of which are Christian. There are also tens of thousands of Jews living in Upper Nazareth, the new suburb, named **KIRYAT-NATSRAT**. Nazareth is the headquarters of the Christian mission movement in Israel, with over 40 churches, convents, monasteries, orphanages, and private parochial schools.

This was the home of Joseph and Mary and for most of 30 years the scene of the Savior's life. Jesus' followers were called Nazarenes.

Nazareth was not an important or significant town at all in Jesus' day; it is not mentioned in the Old Testament, nor by Josephus, nor in the Talmud. "Nazarene" was a derisive term then, as evidenced by Nathaniel's remark, "Can any good thing come out of Nazareth?" (It is interesting that Bethlehem, Nazareth, and Galilee were all small and insignificant, but as Alma wrote, "by small and simple things great things are brought to pass" - Alma 37:6). Jesus took from this environment many lesson-symbols for his teachings: birds of the air, foxes in their holes, lilies in the fields, wine and olive presses, plows, grain, and watchtowers, etc.

POINTS OF INTEREST

GREEK ORTHODOX CHURCH OF THE ANNUNCIATION (Gabriel's Church). This is Nazareth's oldest church. It was originally built in the days of Constantine, and the present church is over 300 years old. The Greek Orthodox members believe Gabriel appeared to Mary here. **MARY'S WELL**, near the church, gets its water from a spring within the church.

GROTTO OF THE ANNUNCIATION. Underneath the **LATIN CHURCH OF THE ANNUNCIATION** is a grotto that is held sacred as the site where the angel Gabriel appeared to Mary to tell her about her future son, Jesus. Two granite pillars, the **COLUMN OF GABRIEL** and the **COLUMN OF MARY**, mark the traditional place where the two persons stood. Byzantines built a church here in the 5th century A.D., Crusaders rebuilt it in 1099, and the Franciscans did the same in 1730. Remains of the original churches are enshrined on the lowest level of the modern one. The Latin Church of the Annunciation is the largest Christian church in the Near East. It was built in the 1960s. Note scenes of Jesus' life on the front doors, the baptismal font in the old chapel beneath the floor of the modern church, and the various nations' artistic portrayal of the Virgin Mary.

SAINT JOSEPH'S WORKSHOP. Under the **CHURCH OF SAINT JOSEPH** are two caves known through tradition as the carpenter shop and storage room of Joseph, husband of the Virgin Mary. This church is just north of the Latin Church of the Annunciation. Next to the Church of Saint Joseph there is a small museum.

OLD SYNAGOGUE. In the western part of the city, on Market Lane, is an ancient synagogue where, according to tradition, Jesus worshiped.

- *Jesus went into the synagogue on the Sabbath day (Luke 4:16).*

MARY'S WELL, or the **VIRGIN FOUNTAIN.** This is the only spring-fed fountain in the city, and thus it is easy to believe that Mary would have drawn water here. It is located by the side of the road to Tiberias, and near the Greek Orthodox Church of the Annunciation, from where it gets its water.

MENSA CHRISTI. This is a small church belonging to the Franciscans. It contains a huge rock called in Latin *Mensa Christi* or the "table of Christ." Tradition indicates that Christ dined here with his disciples after the resurrection. The present church was built in 1861 and is located a small distance west of the old synagogue.

MOUNT OF PRECIPITATION. Known also as the "Leap of the Lord," this is the traditional mount where Jesus was cast out of the city (Luke 4:28-30). It is southeast of the city.

TERRA SANCTA CONVENT. Of particular interest at this convent is a museum containing archaeological finds from the region of Nazareth.

- *At Nazareth the annunciation was made by Gabriel to Mary and Joseph (Isa. 7:14; Luke 1:26-38; Matt. 1:18-25; cf. Mos. 3:8; Al. 7:10; 2 Ne. 17:14).*
- *Joseph and Mary left to go to Bethlehem, where Jesus was to be born (Luke 2:1-7).*
- *Joseph, Mary, and Jesus returned to Nazareth from Egypt (Matt. 2:21-23).*
- *This was the home of Jesus' childhood and youth (Matt. 2:23; Luke 2:39, 51-52).*
- *Jesus left here when he was about thirty to go to the Jordan to be baptized (Mark 1:9).*
- *Here Jesus preached his first recorded sermon, he was rejected, and his life was threatened. The traditional mountain from which the people sought to cast him is today called the Mount of Precipitation (Luke 4:16-30).*
- *Jesus was again rejected; he could perform few miracles because of the people's unbelief (Matt. 13:53-58; Mark 6:1-6).*
- *Nathanael mentioned Nazareth unfavorably, indicating it was rather an obscure village (John 1:46).*

- *Nephi saw a vision of the city of Nazareth and a virgin (1 Ne. 11:13).*

Tsipori, *Sepphoris, Diocaesarea, Saffuriya*

Three miles northwest of Nazareth is the settlement of Tsipori. The name means "bird" and the town perches like a bird on top of a knoll. All roads in Jesus' day ran through Sepphoris, not Nazareth. Sepphoris was the capital of Galilee before Tiberias. Only since Crusader days have main roads intersected at Nazareth. During the first four centuries A.D., Tsipori was the largest and most important city of Galilee. During the Roman period Herod Antipas had rebuilt the city in a grand style. It was, for a time, the seat of the Sanhedrin. It was a great spiritual center and the home of famous talmudic scholars. Rabbi Yehuda Hanassi compiled and edited the Mishna here. After his death in Tsipori he was buried at Beit Shearim. According to one tradition, Anne and Joachim, the parents of Mary, mother of Jesus, lived in Tsipori, and it was here that Mary herself was born. Ruins of a small eighteenth-century **FORT**, a Roman **AMPHITHEATER**, and a second-century **BASILICA** were discovered when the site was excavated by the University of Michigan in 1931. In the 1980s and 90s archaeologists have uncovered a Roman villa, theater, a Jewish ritual bath, reservoir and aqueduct, and buildings with exquisite mosaics. (See *Biblical Archaeology Review* Jan/Feb 1988, 30-33, and May/Jun 1992, 50-62.) Tsipori is a National Parks Authority site.

About 3 miles northwest of Tsipori is a reservoir in the Valley of Beit Netofa. An open canal brings additional water to the reservoir from the Sea of Galilee.

GATH-HEPHER ("*winepress of digging*"), **Tel Gat Hefer**, *Mashhad*

A village about 2 miles northeast of Nazareth, on a height north of the road that goes to Tiberias, is the traditional site of the burial place of Jonah. His tomb is shown here.

- *This was the birthplace of Jonah (2 Kings 14:25; see also the Book of Jonah)*

CANA ("*place of reeds*"), **Kefar Kana**, *Kafr Kanna, Khirbet Qana*

The modern town of Cana is 4 miles northeast of Nazareth. It is believed by some that the **CATHOLIC FRANCISCAN CHURCH** is built over the site of Jesus' first miracle, the changing of water to wine. Stone waterpots, similar to those used in Christ's time, are shown. **A GREEK ORTHODOX CHURCH** with a red dome contains two stone basins, claimed to have been among the six water pots of the miracle. The **SAINT NATHANAEL CHURCH** of the Franciscans is built on the site of the traditional birthplace of Nathanael, a disciple of Jesus. It is located near the Catholic Franciscan Church.

The archaeological site of Cana is actually directly northward across the Beit Netofa Valley from this traditional Cana.

- *This was the home of Nathanael, of whom Jesus said, "Behold an Israelite indeed, in whom is no guile" (John 1:47; 21:2).*
- *Cana was the scene of Jesus' first miracle – the changing of water into wine at the wedding feast (John 2:1-11).*
- *Here Jesus healed – at a distance – the nobleman's son, who was in Capernaum (John 4:46-54).*

Turan, *Merj es-Sunbul* (*"meadow of the ears of corn"*)

Turan is an Arab village about 3½ miles northeast of Cana.

- *According to tradition, the incident of Jesus' disciples plucking grain on the Sabbath took place in the Valley of Turan (Matt. 12:1; Luke 6:1).*

MOUNT TABOR (*"mountain height," Mount of Transfiguration*), *et Tur*

Mount Tabor is a round, symmetrical mountain, 6 miles east of Nazareth on the northeast edge of the Jezreel Valley (Plain of Esdraelon). It is 1,843 feet above sea level. As most mountains and high places were scenes of heathen worship, Tabor is mentioned as the site of ensnaring rituals (Hos. 5:1).

Various ruins of cities are on and around Tabor. Antiochus founded a city here in 218 B.C. As early as the sixth century A.D., three churches had been built here in memory of the three tabernacles that Peter proposed at the time of the Transfiguration, which tradition says occurred here. Franciscan and Greek Orthodox monasteries are located here now, plus the **BASILICA OF THE TRANSFIGURATION** and the **GREEK CHURCH OF SAINT ELIAS** (Elijah). The traditional **CAVE OF MELCHIZEDEK**, where Abraham visited Melchizedek, is near the entrance to the monastery courtyard and the Greek church.

In the Jewish revolt of A.D. 66, Josephus held the top of Tabor as a stronghold (before he defected to the Romans). A wall he built can still be seen. A beautiful view of the valley can be obtained from here. At the foot of the mountain is the Arab village of **DABURIYYA** (from the Hebrew name Deborah), on the site of the ancient town of Dovrat. President Spencer W. Kimball called the Mount of Transfiguration "the highest spot on earth." Peter called it "the holy mount" (2 Peter 1:18). Jesus took with him Peter, James, and John, the three who would become the "First Presidency" after his departure, and all persons involved were transfigured. Peter, James, and John received the keys of the kingdom. They had a vision of the Millennial or paradisiacal earth (D&C 63:20-21), and they apparently received their own endowment (*Doctrines of Salvation*, vol. 2, p. 165) and had their calling and election made sure, that is, they were sealed up to eternal life (2 Peter 1:16-19; D&C 131:5; see also *Doctrinal New Testament Commentary* vol. 1, p. 400).

- *Mount Tabor was a boundary between Issachar and Zebulun (Josh. 19:22-23).*

- *Here Deborah and Barak gathered to defeat Sisera in the Valley of Jezreel (Judg. 4:6-17).*
- *The brothers of Gideon were slain here (Judg. 8:18-21).*
- *It was referred to by the prophets (Jer. 46:18; Hos. 5:1: Ps. 89:12).*
- *Tradition says the transfiguration of Jesus took place here, where Jesus found a spot secluded enough to answer the description, "an high mountain apart by themselves" (Matt. 17:1; Mark 9:2; Luke 9:28). (Others believe this described Mount Hermon, however.)*
- *Tradition says the Greek Church of Saint Elias (Elijah) was built beside the cave where Melchizedek welcomed Abraham (Gen. 14:18-20).*
- *Besides Jesus' transfiguration, the apostles saw a vision of the earth in its paradisiacal or transfigured state (D&C 63:21).*

ENDOR (*"fountain of Dor"*), **Ein Dor**, *H. Safsafot*

Close to Nain on the northeast side of the Valley of Jezreel (Esdraelon) and 3½ miles south of Mount Tabor is the site of Endor. The ancient Endor and the modern Kibbutz Endor are about 2 miles apart.

- *This was the home of the witch Saul visited on the eve of his battle with the Philistines (1 Sam. 28:7-25).*
- *Here the fugitives of Sisera's army perished (Ps. 83:9-10).*

NAIN (*"pleasant"*), **Nein**, *Naim*

Today Nain is an Arab town on the northwest slope of a mountain known as the *Hill of Moreh*, and 4 miles northeast of Afula.

- *The widow's son was raised by Jesus from the dead (Luke 7:11-17).*

SHUNEM (*"uneven"*), **Sulam**, *Solem*

Located 7 miles south-southeast of Nazareth, 2 miles from Nain, and 7 miles south of Mount Tabor is the ancient site of Shunem. The small, still-inhabited town lies at the southwestern foot of the Hill of Moreh (*Moreh* possibly means "former rain," the Hebrew word used in Joel 2:23).

- *The border of Issachar reached to Shunem (Josh. 19:17-18).*
- *Here the Philistines gathered their forces prior to the battle with Saul, whose armies were at Mount Gilboa (1 Sam. 28:4).*
- *It was the birthplace of Abishag, wife of David in his old age (1 Kings 1:1-4).*
- *Here Elisha stayed and here he raised the Shunammite's son to life (2 Kings 4:8-37).*

Afula

This modern city, 8 miles south of Nazareth, is the market center of the Jezreel Valley. It was founded in 1925 by the American Zionist Commonwealth and named after the word *Ofel*, a biblical tower.

- *Elisha was in the area (2 Kings 5:24).*

JEZREEL (*"God sows"*), **Yizre'el**, *Zarin*

Twelve miles south of Nazareth, 4 miles south-southeast of Afula, is Kibbutz Jezreel, founded in 1949. Nearby is the mound of the site of ancient Jezreel. Here, just above sea level, Ahab, king of Samaria, had a winter palace during the ninth century and Jezebel founded an institution for the worship of Baal. Excavations began in the late 1980s by the Institute of Archaeology at Tel Aviv University and the British School of Archaeology in Jerusalem.

- *Elijah ran from Carmel to Jezreel – about 18 miles (1 Kings 18:42, 46).*
- *Here Ahab built one of his palaces (1 Kings 21:1).*
- *It was the place of Naboth's vineyard and cruel murder and the tragic meeting of Ahab and Elijah (1 Kings 21).*
- *Jezebel was eaten by dogs here, and dogs licked up Ahab's blood (1 Kings 21:17-25; 22:37-38; 2 Kings 9:30-37).*
- *Jehu was anointed king and slew Joram and Jezebel (2 Kings 9).*

MOUNT GILBOA (*"bubbling fountain"*), **Jebel Fakua**

A hilly district southeast of the plain of Jezreel, about 10 miles long and 1,696 feet above sea level, is known as Mount Gilboa.

- *It was the place of the last battles and death of Saul and his sons, Jonathan, Abinadab, and Melchishua (1 Sam. 28:4; 31:1-6; 2 Sam. 1:5-10; 1 Chron. 10:1-6).*
- *The death of Saul and Jonathan made David lament, and he prayed that no dew would ever fall on Mount Gilboa (2 Sam. 1:19-27).*

SPRING OF HAROD (*"terror," "trembling"*), **Maayan Harod, Ein Harod**, *Gidona, Aid Jalud*

This spring is located at the northern foothills of Mount Gilboa, near Gidona, and 8 miles southeast of Afula. This is a National Parks Authority site.

- *Gideon gathered here to fight against Midian (Judg. 7:1).*
- *The Midianites were delivered into the hands of the 300 who lapped the water (Judg. 7:4-7).*
- *Perhaps Saul encamped here (1 Sam. 29:1).*

Beit Alpha, *at Kibbutz Beit Alpha*

The best preserved mosaic floor of an ancient synagogue in Israel is found on the grounds of Kibbutz Beit Alpha, at the foot of Mount Gilboa in the southeastern end of the Jezreel Valley. It is one of the most beautiful relics in Israel. The kibbutz was founded in 1922 by pioneers from Poland and Galatia. During their swamp-draining operations in 1928 they found the sixth-century A.D. ruins of a synagogue with an elaborate mosaic floor. The excavation was supervised by the late Prof. E. L. Sukenik, who held the chair in archaeology at the Hebrew University.

The floor is divided into three panels: (1) Abraham's near-sacrifice of Isaac; (2) a zodiac wheel; and (3) a group of religious ornaments, such as the ark of the law and the menorahs.

An Aramaic inscription refers to the emperor Justinus (Justin I) and indicates that the mosaic was laid down during his reign (A.D. 518-27). It is the only dated inscription found in the synagogues of the Holy Land.

This is a National Parks Authority site.

- *The beautiful mosaic at Beit Alpha shows Abraham ready to offer up his son Isaac as a sacrifice (Gen. 22:3-13).*

Gan Ha Shelosha (*"garden of the three"*), *el-Sakhne* (*"the warm" [water]*)

In the southeastern end of the Jezreel Valley, about a mile southeast of Beth Alpha, are beautiful natural warm-water swimming pools set amid the green lawns and trees of Gan Ha Shelosha. Also at the site are an in-door heated pool and an archaeological museum. It is named in memory of three young settlers who were killed by Arabs in 1938. Gentle waterfalls and pleasant surroundings make this a popular and refreshing picnic spot. This is a National Parks Authority site.

BETH-SHEAN (*"house of security"*), *Beit-Shean*, **Tel Bet-Shean**, *Beisan, Scythopolis, Nyssa, Tell el-Husn*

This modern city lies 20 miles south of the Sea of Galilee at a point where the Valley of Jezreel meets the Valley of the Jordan. It was established in 1949. Beth-shean is mentioned in ancient Egyptian documents and inscriptions: Middle Bronze Age Execration Texts, Late Bronze Age El Amarna Tablets, and Thutmose III's lists of conquered cities from 1468 B.C. Beth-shean resisted the Israelite siege (Joshua 17:11; Judges 1:27). Later the bodies of Saul and his sons were hung on the walls of Beth-shean (1 Sam. 31:10, 12); the city then became Philistine. Pharaoh Shishak conquered the city ca. 925 B. C. The ancient city (i.e., the tel) contains 18 levels of settlements. Six temples have been unearthed. The University of Pennsylvania excavated it in 1921-23. Relics are now in the Rockefeller Museum and the University of Pennsylvania Museum. Some of the relics of old Beth-shean include the following:

(1) The **STELA OF SETI I**, pharaoh of Egypt in 1318 B.C. This stone has many hieroglyphs and Egyptian pictures. It tells of the Egyptians and their battle at Beth-Shean. (Rockefeller Museum, Jerusalem)

(2) The **STELA OF THE GODDESS ASHTORETH**. It is Egyptian also, and it speaks of the Temple of Ashtoreth, which is mentioned in the account of Saul's death (1 Sam. 31:10). (Pennsylvania Museum, Philadelphia)

(3) The **STELA TO MEKAL, LORD OF BETH-SHEAN** (1500 B.C.). It has Egyptian hieroglyphs that tell of the king giving offerings to Mekal, god of Beth-Shean. (Rockefeller Museum, Jerusalem)

The massive excavation and restoration project at Beth-shean/Scythopolis has been in progress since 1986. Many millions of dollars have already been spent on the site. Unlike most excavation projects, operating during a few weeks in summertime, at Scythopolis several teams are working year-round. Archaeologists are excavating and restoring at the same time. The ancient Decapolis city promises to be an international tourist attraction comparable to Pompeii or Ephesus.

The name Scythopolis, meaning "City of Scythians," perhaps originated with a unit of Scythian cavalry stationed here from the army of Ptolemy II Philadelphus (285-246 BC). The Scythian empire once extended from the Black Sea to the Volga and Danube rivers.

SCYTHOPOLIS is mentioned by implication three times in the New Testament (Matt. 4:25; Mark 5:20; 7:31). It was the capital and the largest of the ten cities (Decapolis), which included also Damascus and Philadelphia - Josephus *Wars III* 9:7. It is the only city of the Decapolis west of the Jordan, and it is the best preserved Roman and Byzantine city in the country. Beth-shean/Scythopolis is situated at an important crossroads, along Nahal Harod, at 350 feet below sea level. A third century A. D. rabbi said of the city's setting: "If paradise is situated in the Land of Israel, its entrance is Bethshan." A 14th century researcher noted the city's location "amidst a plentiful supply of still waters, a blessed and beautiful land, bearing fruit like the Garden of God, her door leads to the Garden of Eden."

Population during the Byzantine period rose to 35,000-40,000 (twice as many inhabitants as modern Beth-shean). The city was destroyed by a major earthquake in A.D. 747, which is understandable, given its geological position at the intersection of a transverse fault and the great Rift Valley. Strangely, few human remains have been uncovered in the ruins, suggesting that a tremor may have warned inhabitants to flee in advance. One skeleton of a man was found pinned by a column. An archaeologist half jokingly proposed that the man had probably returned to the city for his money and had been trapped in the catastrophe. Sometime later a cache of eleven gold coins was found within a yard of the dead man's hand.

Less than 5% of the city has been uncovered to date.

Remains recently uncovered of Roman-period Scythopolis include the following:

(1) The **AMPHITHEATER** is just off the main road of modern Beth-shean. It probably dates from the second century A. D. It has an unusual shape; it is not oval, but rectangular with the ends rounded off. It was used for gladiatorial combats, games, and various ceremonies. The central arena is two yards lower than seating – to keep lions away from the spectators. Three of twelve or thirteen original rows of seats are still preserved. The amphitheater once accommodated over 6,000 spectators. (The largest amphitheater ever built – the Coliseum in Rome, with a capacity of 50,000 – was constructed by Vespasian and Titus.)

(2) The **COLONNADED STREET** runs from the amphitheater to the tel for over 1500 feet. It dates to about A. D. 500, with a drainage system installed in A. D. 522. Long basalt flagstones were laid diagonally in a herringbone pattern. Sidewalks with curbstones were lined with shops.

(3) The **THEATER** dates from the second century A. D. It is the best preserved and most impressive found in Israel. Seating capacity was around 6,000. A two-story high *scaenae frons*, behind the stage, served as a backdrop for performances. A new wooden stage has been constructed, and performances will be scheduled when restoration is completed.

(4) The **BATHHOUSE** covers 1.5 acres and is the largest in the country. It sported a large paved courtyard with covered porticoes. The porticoes were paved with colored marble and mosaics. The bathhouse was used for baths, swimming, and exercising. It is scheduled for reconstruction.

(5) The **FORUM** was the municipal public square and marketplace. The city's basilica, a civic building, was here. Marble, granite, and limestone columns are lying broken in the same position where they were probably toppled by earthquake.

(6) The **COLONNADED STREET SOUTH OF THE TEL** was over 70 feet wide, with sidewalks. It was paved with basalt stones. One of the columns was preserved to its original height.

(7) **OTHER STRUCTURES** found at Scythopolis include temples to Dionysus (son of Zeus, god of the vine), Nike (Victory), and Nysa (the nurse of Dionysus

who became a city-goddess); hippodrome, circus, monastery, synagogues, nymphaeum, and odeon.

(See *Biblical Archaeology Review* Jul/Aug 1990, 16-31.)

This is a National Parks Authority site.

- *Beth-Shean was a part of Manasseh's inheritance (Josh. 17:11).*
- *Because of the chariots of iron, Manasseh could never subdue it (Judg. 1:27).*
- *Beth-Shean is located at the foot of Mount Gilboa, where Saul and Jonathan were slain. When their bodies were found, the Philistines fastened them to the wall of Beth-Shean, but valiant Israelites gave the bodies a proper burial (1 Sam. 31:8-13; 2 Sam. 21:12-14).*

Neve-Ur (*"abode of Ur"*)

This settlement, near the Jordan River about 7 miles north of Beth-Shean, takes its name from Ur of the Chaldees in Mesopotamia (modern Iraq), birthplace of Abraham. The founders of Neve-Ur came from Baghdad, the capital of Iraq. Interestingly, the empty pipeline that once carried oil from Kirkuk, Iraq, to Haifa is located near Neve-Ur.

Belvoir (*"beautiful view"*), *Kochav Hayarden*

About 8 miles northeast of Ein Harod and 9 miles south of Degania are the remains of a twelfth-century French Crusader fortress, built by the Knights of the Order of the Hospitallers. Its location on a hill gives it a sweeping view of the Jordan Valley and Mountains of Gilead. It may be approached from the Jordan River valley. This is a National Parks Authority site.

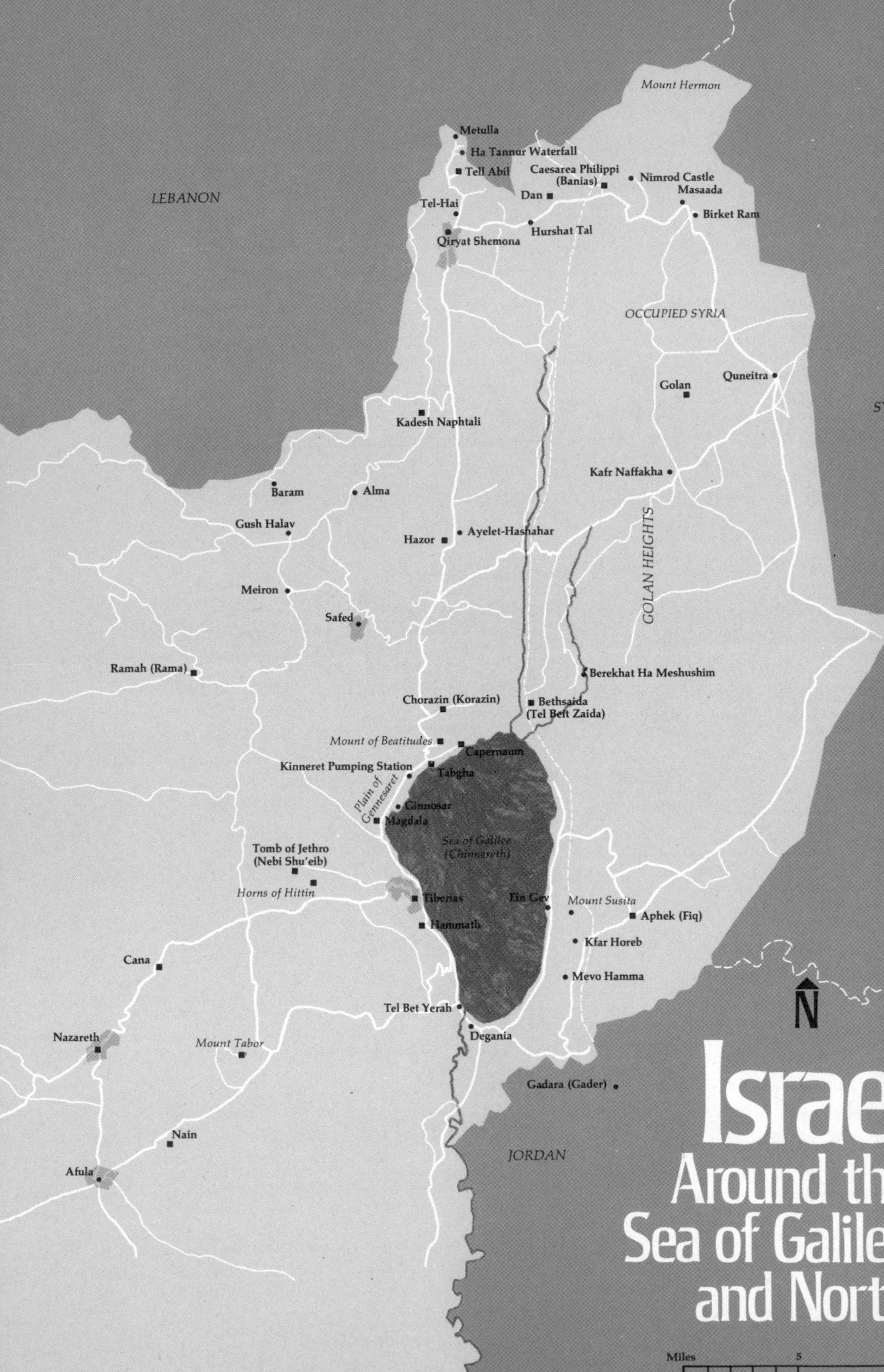
Mount Hermon
LEBANON
Metulla
Ha Tannur Waterfall
Tell Abil
Caesarea Philippi
(Banias)
Nimrod Castle
Masaada
Dan
Tel-Hai
Birket Ram
Hurshat Tal
Qiryat Shemona
OCCUPIED SYRIA
Quneitra
Golan
Kadesh Naphtali
Kafr Naffakha
Baram
Alma
Gush Halav
Ayelet-Hashahar
Hazor
GOLAN HEIGHTS
Meiron
Safed
Ramah (Rama)
Berekhat Ha Meshushim
Chorazin (Korazin)
Bethsaida
(Tel Beit Zaida)
Mount of Beatitudes
Capernaum
Kinneret Pumping Station
Tabgha
Plain of Gennesaret
Ginnosar
Magdala
Sea of Galilee
(Chinnereth)
Tomb of Jethro
(Nebi Shu'eib)
Horns of Hittin
Tiberias
Ein Gev
Mount Susita
Aphek (Fiq)
Hammath
Kfar Horeb
Cana
Mevo Hamma
Tel Bet Yerah
N
Degania
Nazareth
Mount Tabor
Gadara (Gader)
Nain
JORDAN
Afula
Israe
Around th
Sea of Galile
and Nort
Miles
5

AROUND THE SEA OF GALILEE AND NORTH

SEA OF GALILEE, LAKE CHINNERETH, GENNESARET, TIBERIAS, Kinneret, *Gennesar, Behr Tabariyeh*

The Sea of Galilee is 12-13 by 7-8 miles in size, 130-157 feet deep, 686 feet below sea level, and 32 miles in circumference. It is the lowest fresh-water lake in the world. In the King James Version of the Bible the name is spelled *Chinnereth* (Num. 34:11; Josh. 12:3; 13:27). The modern name, *Kinneret*, means "harp," and the sea is shaped like a harp. In New Testament times it was known as *Gennesaret* (Luke 5:1). The lake was named *Tiberias* after Herod Antipas built the city of Tiberias and made it his capital (John 6:1, 23; 21:1). It was also known as the *Sea of Galilee* (Matt. 4:18; 15:29; Mark 1:16; 7:31; John 6:1). Several cities were located on its western and northern shorelines, including Tiberias, Magdala, Tabgha, Capernaum, Chorazin, and Bethsaida. Today there is no city around the lake with a Jewish or Christian name, Tiberias being the only city.

The lake is abundant in fish: carp, sardine, mullet, catfish, and combfish – the same fish caught by the disciples of Jesus. The comb-fish is interesting because the eggs of the fish are hatched in its mouth and the small fish stay there until they are old enough to take care of themselves. Today the fish are caught in nets, the same as in days of old. The modern diesel-powered boats are equipped with sonar devices for hunting out schools of fish.

Owing to the height of the mountains surrounding the lake, different temperatures give rise to sudden and violent storms.

- *Jesus called Peter, Andrew, James, and other apostles (Matt. 4:18-22; 10; Mark 1:16-20; 2:13-14; Luke 5:1-11).*
- *Jesus healed a leper (Matt. 8:1-4).*
- *Jesus spoke to the multitudes from Peter's boat (Mark 3:7-12; Luke 5:1-3).*
- *Galilee yielded two catches of fish in response to Jesus' command (Luke 5:4-11; John 21:6-8).*
- *Jesus stilled the storm (Matt. 8:23-27; Mark 4:35-41; Luke 8:22-25).*
- *Jesus walked on the stormy water (Matt. 14:22-33; Mark 6:45-52; John 6:16-21).*
- *Jesus taught the "parable of the sower" and other parables on or near the sea (Matt. 13:1-52; Mark 4:1-34; Luke 8:4-18).*
- *Jesus taught about the Sabbath day (Mark 2:23-28).*
- *Jesus healed the multitudes (Matt. 15:29-31; Mark 1:29-45).*
- *The Twelve Apostles were ordained in the hills near the Sea of Galilee (Mark 3:13-19).*
- *Jesus appeared here after the resurrection and gave the apostles an endowment (Mark 14:28; 16:7; John 21:1-23; cf. D&C 105:18).*

- *Devils cast from the Gadarene demoniac entered the bodies of 2,000 swine, who ran down a steep place and into the Sea of Galilee on the eastern shore (Matt. 8:28-34; Mark 5:1-21; Luke 8:26-40).*

Degania, *"The Mother of the Kibbutzim"*

Israel's first kibbutz was founded in 1909 on the southern shore of the Sea of Galilee by Russian pioneers – including David Ben-Gurion. The father of Moshe Dayan also lived here, but left to help establish Nahalal. The name *Degania* is taken from the Hebrew *Dagan*, meaning "grain." There are two Deganias, "A" and "B." Degania "A" has a Syrian tank at the gate – a souvenir of the 1948 battles. Degania "B" was settled by the younger Degania kibbutzniks next door to Degania "A." Degania has an excellent natural history museum called **BEIT GORDON**. The book, *Pioneers in Israel*, by Shmuel Dayan (father of Moshe) gives a graphic description of early struggles of the kibbutz. Degania served as an example for other Jewish pioneering experiments.

A **KIBBUTZ** is a collective type of farm, wherein all members live and work on national land leased to them at a nominal rent by the National Fund. There is no privately owned land on the kibbutz.

There are some 270 kibbutzim in Israel and approximately 130,000 kibbutzniks (members). About 2.5 percent of Israel's population live on kibbutzim.

In another kind of agricultural settlement, the **MOSHAV**, each family maintains its own farm and housing. There are approximately 450 moshavim, averaging about 60 families each, and comprising about 3.3 percent of the national population.

Tel Bet Yerah (*"house of the moon"*)

This tel is 6½ miles south of Tiberias, on the grounds of the Ohalo regional school, near Kibbutz Kinneret. Ruins dating from the third millennium B.C., a second-century **SYNAGOGUE**, a fourth-century **BATH HOUSE**, and a sixth-century **BYZANTINE CHURCH** may be seen.

Hammath (*"hot spring"*), **Hammat**, *Hammata*

About a mile south of Tiberias is the site of the biblical city Hammath, famous for its hot baths. Recent archaeological digs reveal what is believed to be the ancient city. A fourth-century A.D. **SYNAGOGUE** found here has a beautiful and well-preserved **MOSAIC FLOOR**, depicting the ark of the covenant set between menorahs. (See *Biblical Archaeology Review* May/Jun 1984, 32-44.) Animals and figures are a part of another one. The **TOMB OF RABBI MEIR BAAL HANESS**, near the hot springs, is considered one of the holiest sanctuaries in Israel.

Hammath is a National Parks Authority site.

Sea of Galilee

▪ *This was one of the fortified cities of Naphtali (Josh. 19:35).*

TIBERIAS, *Tveriah, Tabariyeh*

Tiberias lies on the west side of the Sea of Galilee, about 10 miles south of Capernaum. It was built or rebuilt and named by Herod Antipas (A.D. 18) in honor of the emperor; the city is spelled -*ias* though the emperor was -*ius*. Here Herod built the finest synagogue in Galilee. It was the capital of Galilee under Agrippa I and the Roman procurators. After the fall of Jerusalem in A.D. 70, the Jews settled here and sometime before A.D. 220 codified and wrote down their traditional civil and ritual laws, with the title of *Mishna*, under the direction of Rabbi Yehuda Ha Nassi.

The *Jerusalem Talmud* was compiled in this town in A.D. 400, and the vowel and punctuation grammar was introduced into the Hebrew language by the learned men in Tiberias. (The Jerusalem Talmud was overshadowed by the *Babylonian Talmud*, completed a century later in the academies in Mesopotamia.) The Massoretic text of the Bible, the traditional text upon which our Hebrew Bibles are based, was prepared here by the Ben Asher family during the latter half of the first millennium A.D. Many illustrious Jewish sages are buried at Tiberias, including the intellectual giant of medieval Jewry, Maimonides (the "Ramban"), who died in Egypt in A.D. 1204. **MAIMONIDES' TOMB** is reached from the end of Hagalil Road. Other tombs of famous rabbis are nearby.

In Christian times Tiberias was the seat of a bishop. It fell to the Muslims in A.D. 637. A **JEWISH SCHOOL** of rabbinical theology has been here for a long time. An important **CRUSADER AND TURKISH FORTRESS** is located near the Sea of Galilee in Tiberias.

The modern city is located about 2 miles north of the ancient city. **HOT SPRINGS** have made the city a health resort. They are probably the earliest known thermal baths in the world, having been used for the past 2,500 years. Josephus, Pliny, and other historians have mentioned them.

Public **BEACHES** for swimming are found north and south of the city. Boats transport people to Capernaum and Ein Gev daily.

Other places of interest include the following: the **MUSEUM OF ANTIQUITIES**, the **TOMB OF RABBI AKIVA**, the **CRUSADER WALLS**, and the **WALLS OF HEROD ANTIPAS.**

Tiberias, with a population of 33,000, is the only city of any size on the lake now. It is Israel's leading winter resort. The city was destroyed by an earthquake in 1837 but is now a modern Jewish city.

Although Jesus was in the general area, we have no statement of a particular visit to the city itself.

See *Biblical Archaeology Review* Mar/Apr 1991, 44-51.

- *It was one of the cities given to Naphtali (Josh. 19:35).*
- *It gave its name to the lake (John 6:1; 21:1).*
- *It is referred to (John 6:23).*

Horns of Hittin

A strangely shaped mountain 7½ miles west of Tiberias and southwest of Mount Arbel is called the Horns of Hittin. The hill is shaped like two animal horns. After the Muslims had captured nearly all of Palestine, it was here that the European Crusaders suffered their final and decisive defeat at the hands of Saladin on July 4, 1187. Renaud de Chatillon had violated the peace time and time again and harassed pilgrims en route to Mecca. Saladin trapped the Crusader army in the heat of summer with no water, sweltering under their heavy armor. On July 4th more than 12,000 men were killed or captured. Birds and beasts of prey fed on carrion for weeks, and a year later the stench was still intolerable. The victory at the Horns of Hittin ushered in 700 years of Muslim rule over the Holy Land.

- *Some believe the Sermon on the Mount was given here (Matt. 5-7).*

TOMB OF JETHRO, *Shu'eib*, Nebi Shu'eib

On the edge of the Arbel Valley and at the foot of the Horns of Hittin, overlooking Tiberias, is a tomb of Shu'eib (Jethro, father-in-law of Moses). This is the sacred shrine of Druzes.

Most of the Druzes live in and around Shefaram, a Druze village with men who wear curling moustaches, baggy white trousers, and headgear that is higher than the usual loose Arab *kaffiyehs*. The Druzes speak Arabic but belong to an exclusive religious sect that broke away from Islam 1,000 years ago. Their tenets are secret.

- *Jethro was the father-in-law of Moses (Exod. 3:1; 4:18; 18:1).*
- *He visited Moses at Sinai (Exod. 18).*
- *Hobab, Jethro's son, was a guide to the Israelites (Num. 10:29-32).*
- *Jethro gave the priesthood to Moses (D&C 84:6).*

MAGDALA (*"tower of greatness"*), *Migdal, Dalmanutha, Magadan, Tarichaea ("drying" or "salting")*

Located 4 miles north of Tiberias, Magdala was one of the sites which Josephus fortified when he was governor of Galilee – before his defection to the Romans. When the city fell to Titus in the struggle of the Jews against the Romans, 6,700 Jews were killed; thousands of the strongest were sent to Nero to dig the Corinthian canal (which was not actually accomplished until the 19th century) and 30,400 were auctioned off as slaves.

- *This was the home of Mary Magdalene (Luke 8:2; Mark 16:9).*
- *Jesus came here after feeding the 4,000 (Matt. 15:39; Mark 8:10.)*
- *The Pharisees and Sadducees sought a sign and Jesus told them of the sign of the prophet Jonas (Matt. 15:39-16:4; Mark 8:11-21).*

PLAIN OF GENNESARET

This is a fertile plain on the northwest shore of the Sea of Galilee, 3 miles by 1 mile in size, just north of Magdala.

- *Many diseased were healed by touching the hem of Jesus' garment (Matt. 14:34-36; Mark 6:53-56).*

Ginnosar

This is a kibbutz with a large **GUEST HOUSE** and **BEACH**, on the west side of the Sea of Galilee about 4 miles north of Tiberias. Here, in a new museum, is a 2,000-year-old boat, discovered in January 1986, which dates from the 1st century B.C. It could, therefore, have been in use in Jesus' day (see *Biblical Archaeology Review* Sep/Oct 1988, 18-33).

Kinneret Pumping Station, *Eshed Kinnrot; and* **Minya**

Nestled at the foot of a hill on the northwest shore of the Sea of Galilee, 5½ miles north of Tiberias, is the largest pumping station in Israel, that pumps water out of the lake into a huge pipe 10 feet in diameter. It is piped through the Valley of Beit Netofa to the Yarkon waterworks near Tel Aviv and from there to the Negev. With the completion of the **NATIONAL WATER CARRIER** in 1964, the main water exit from the lake was transferred from the south to its northwest corner. Roughly 60% of consumer's water costs are actually electricity costs, much of the cost originating here with the necessity of pumping the water about 1100 feet higher to the beginnings of the National Water Carrier. The high concentration of sodium chloride in the lake water has been an on-going problem, since much of the water is used for irrigation. The salty waters of the springs at Tabgha were diverted into a specially built canal. It runs southward along the western side carrying the salty waters into the Jordan River south of the lake.

On the sea near here is **MINYA**, a seventh-century ruin of a palace and mosque.

Immediately north of the pumping station is the biblical city of Kinneret, now under excavation.

Tabgha, *Heptapegon* (*"seven springs"*)

Tabgha is 2 miles southwest of Capernaum and 7½ miles north of Tiberias. The **CHURCH OF THE MULTIPLICATION** stands on the site where tradition says Jesus fed the five thousand. (The feeding of the five thousand, however, according to Luke 9:10, was near Bethsaida, to the northeast.) The church has one of the best preserved mosaic tile floors in all of Israel, and dates back to the fourth century A.D. A newer church has been built over the floor of the old Byzantine church, and near the church is the **BENEDICTINE MONASTERY**.

The **CHURCH OF THE ROCK, SAINT PETER'S CHURCH** (Chapel of the Primacy), is located on the seashore. Here, some believe, Peter received the keys of the kingdom from Jesus. The church was erected in 1943 by the Franciscans on ancient ruins.

Across the road northeast of the Church of the Multiplication are the ruins of an **ANCIENT CHURCH**. About a block east of the ruins, on the south side of the road are springs of water.

- *The name Tabgha is not in the Bible.*
- *Jesus fed 5,000 and 4,000 near Bethsaida (Luke 9:10-17; John 6:1-14).*
- *Tradition indicates that Saint Peter's Church is located where Jesus met with his apostles after the resurrection and told Peter to "feed my sheep" (John 21:15-17).*

CAPERNAUM, *Kefar Nahum* (*"town of Nahum"*), *Tell Hum*

This famous city of New Testament times was located about 2½ miles west of where the Jordan River enters the Sea of Galilee and 10 miles from modern Tiberias. Capernaum was near the Via Maris, the international highway; a milestone from Hadrian's day is on display. It was a customs station and place of residence of the high Roman officer. The commander of some Roman soldiers stationed here built a synagogue for the Jews. When Jesus withdrew from Nazareth he went to Capernaum, and this became the center of his activity for 18-20 months. More of Christ's miracles were performed here than in any other city.

Capernaum possibly had a population of 10,000.

Excavations at Capernaum have yielded ruins of **ONE OF THE FINEST LIMESTONE SYNAGOGUES** in the Holy Land. Although some think it might have been the one built by the kindly centurion, experts believe this one was built sometime between the second and fourth centuries A.D. It is built over a basalt synagogue of the 1st century A.D., likely the one in which Jesus taught. A **FRANCISCAN MONASTERY** is near the synagogue. Franciscan Fathers acquired the site in 1894 and have conducted excavations in recent decades; the statue surrounded by a blaze of colorful bougainvillaea near the big building which is their living quarters is of St. Francis of Assisi, who personally established the

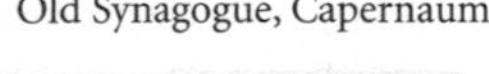

Old Synagogue, Capernaum

Menorah on the stonework of the old synagogue, Capernaum

Franciscan Order in the Holy Land. In the courtyard are **STONE IMPLEMENTS** of ancient inhabitants – flour mills and an oil press. Carved in stone are the **ARK OF THE COVENANT**, the **SHIELD**, or **STAR, OF DAVID** (six-pointed star), a **FIVE-POINTED STAR**, a **MENORAH**, and other designs, including carved representations of the fruits of the land – grapes, dates, olives, figs, pomegranates, etc. The Franciscans (Roman Catholic order) have recently constructed an edifice over the supposed house of St. Peter.

The Byzantine Egeria (ca. 380) wrote that the house of the prince of the apostles in Capernaum had been made into a church, with its original walls still standing. Octagonal-shaped churches were built in those centuries to commemorate special events and places. This could actually be the **SITE OF PETER'S HOUSE**.

(See *Biblical Archaeology Review* Sep/Oct. 1993, 54-61, 90; also previous issues: Nov/Dec 1982, 26-37; Nov/Dec 1983, 24-31.)

- *Jesus made it his home, "his own city" (Matt. 4:13-15; 9:1; Luke 4:31; John 2:12; Mark 1:21).*
- *Here Jesus called Peter, Andrew, James, John, and Matthew and attended Matthew's farewell feast (Matt. 4:13, 18-22; 9:9-13; Mark 2:13-22; Luke 5:27-39).*
- *Peter lived here (Matt. 8:5, 14; Mark 1:21, 29; Luke 4:31, 38).*
- *Jesus taught here in the synagogue (Mark 1:21; Luke 4:31-33).*

- *Jesus delivered a man of an unclean spirit; he also healed Peter's mother-in-law and many others (Matt. 8:14-17; Mark 1:21-34; Luke 4:31-41).*
- *He healed the centurion's servant (Matt. 8:5-13; Luke 7:1-10).*
- *The palsied man was healed when he was let down through the roof (Matt. 9:1-8; Mark 2:1-12; Luke 5:17-26).*
- *Jesus raised Jairus's daughter from the dead (Matt. 9:18-26; Mark 5:22-43; Luke 8:40-56).*
- *Jesus healed the woman who had "an issue of blood" (Matt. 9:20-22; Mark 5:25-34; Luke 8:43-48).*
- *The blind and dumb demoniac was healed (Mat. 9:27-35; 12:22-45; Mark 3:22-30; Luke 11:14-26).*
- *The nobleman's son was healed by Jesus (John 4:46 54).*
- *Jesus healed the withered hand (Matt. 12:9-14; Mark 3:1-6; Luke 6:6-11).*
- *Great multitudes were brought to Jesus and were healed (Matt. 8:16-17; 9:36-38).*
- *Jesus gave a number of discourses here, including the "bread of life" (Matt. 13; 15:1-20; 18:15-35; Mark 2:23-28; 7:1-23; 9:33-50; Luke 6:1-5; John 6:22-71).*
- *Jesus pronounced a curse upon the city (Matt. 11:20-24; Luke 10:15).*
- *Peter caught a fish with a coin in its mouth (Matt. 17:24-27).*
- *Jesus taught that we must be as little children to be saved (Matt. 18:1-6; Mark 9:33-37; Luke 9:46-48).*

Olive Press, Capernaum

Above: Star of David, Capernaum

Below: Ark of the Covenant, Capernaum

BETHSAIDA (*"place of nets"*), Tel Beit Zaida

On the east side of the Jordan River, about 1½ miles north of the point where the Jordan enters the Sea of Galilee, is Tel Beit Zaida. The earlier, New Testament-period site was probably a small fishing village nearer the shore of the lake. The Plain of Bethsaida was the setting for the feeding of 5,000 men (besides women and children – see Matthew's account). Luke calls it a "desert place" (Heb. *midbar*) and John says there was "much grass" here; the two descriptions are quite compatible by a proper definition of "desert" – *midbar* means a *deserted*, or solitary, or uninhabited place, a place for pasturing flocks.

- *Bethsaida was the birthplace of Peter, Andrew, and Philip (John 1:44; 12:21-22).*
- *The feeding of the 5,000 was near here (Matt. 14:13-21; Mark 6:31-44; Luke 9:10-17; John 6:1-14).*
- *The feeding of the 4,000 was near here (Matt. 15:32-38; Mark 8:1-9).*
- *The blind man was healed after Jesus led him out of the town (Mark 8:22-26).*
- *Jesus pronounced a curse on the city (Matt. 11:21-22; Luke 10:13). (The three cities of Bethsaida, Capernaum, and Chorazin were cursed, and none exists today. Tiberias was not cursed, and it still exists.)*

MOUNT OF BEATITUDES

The traditional Mount of Beatitudes is located to the north of the Plain of Gennesaret. It is now the site of an Italian convent and hospice that was a project of Mussolini in 1937.

- *The Sermon on the Mount was delivered here (Matt. 5, 6, 7; Luke 6:12-49; cf. 3 Ne. 12, 13, 14; D&C 58:26-29; 84:81-84).*

CHORAZIN, Korazin, *Khorazin, Kerazeh*

This biblical site lies 3 miles north of Capernaum. It was a Jewish town of the Talmudic era and is represented by ruins of an old third- or fourth-century A.D. synagogue and surrounding town buildings and habitations. A basalt chair, a **"SEAT OF MOSES,"** with an inscription was found, and is displayed in the Israel Museum in Jerusalem. (See *Biblical Archaeology Review* Sep/Oct 1987, 22-36.) Four miles southwest of Chorazin is the gorge of **WADI AMUD**, where in 1925 a Paleolithic skull was found in one of the caves. The skull has been designated as "Galilee Man."

Chorazin is a National Parks Authority site, with on-going excavations.

- *A curse was pronounced upon Chorazin by Jesus (Matt. 11:21-22; Luke 10:13-14).*

Berekhat Ha Meshushim, *Hexagonal Pools*

Hidden within the valleys of the Golan Heights, 6½ miles northeast of Capernaum, the misnamed **HEXAGONAL POOLS** at Berekhat Ha Meshushim

Mount of Beatitudes

are most unusual natural swimming pools. They are surrounded by columns of lava pentagons, the result of an ancient volcanic eruption. The cool, refreshing stream running through the valley and through the pools makes an extraordinary wonder of nature.

Safed, *Safad, Zefat, Tsefat*

Safed is Israel's highest town (2,790 feet – about 300 feet higher than Jerusalem). It was a Jewish stronghold in the war against the Romans and later was the site of a Crusader fort until A.D. 1266. It was the Mameluke capital of Galilee. This is where the Sephardic Jews came when they were persecuted in Spain. These Jewish intellectuals launched into a complex and mystical interpretation of the Old Testament called *Kabala.* Safed became a city of many **SYNAGOGUES** and **UNIVERSITIES**. Now it has become a resort town. Many painters, sculptors, and ceramicists have settled here, and a visit to the **ARTIST'S COLONY** is worthwhile. A **CITADEL** at the top of a hill was built by the Crusaders in the twelfth century. A **MUSEUM** houses sculpture and art.

This city, Jerusalem, Hebron, and Tiberias are the four cities held sacred to the Jews. Safed is the capital of Kabalistic mysticism. The first Hebrew book by Yom Tov was printed here in A.D. 1578 on the first printing press in Asia. In 1738 an earthquake demolished the entire city, and 4,000 persons, mostly Jews, were buried in the ruins.

In 1948 there were 10,000 Arabs and 2,200 Jews in Safed, but when war broke out the Arabs fled.

- *Some believe this was the city Jesus referred to when he said "a city that is set on an hill cannot be hid" (Matt. 5:14).*

Meiron, *Meron*

This is a settlement of orthodox Jews, established in 1949 and located high in the Galilean mountains. Among the famous tombs in the city is that of **HILLEL** the Elder, the famous scholar of the Torah. A second-century Talmudist, Shimon Bar Yochai, defied the Romans and wrote the *Zohar*, the "Book of Splendor," while hiding in a cave here. This is the Bible of the Kabalist sect. In Meiron the members of the sect have a rock they call "Messiah's Chair." They believe that when the Messiah arrives, he will sit there while Elijah blows the trumpet to announce his coming. Many ancient synagogues may also be found here.

Lag Ba'omer holiday occurs on the eighteenth of the month of Iyar, 26 days after Passover (*Pessah*). On the eve of the celebration a great pilgrimage is made from Safed to Meiron. Thousands come to Safed and from thence to Meiron on the afternoon preceding the celebration, to dance and sing during the festival known as *Hilulu de Rashbi*.

RAMAH (*"high"*), **Rama**

This village of Christian-Druze people is located about 6 miles southwest of Meiron. There are several other Ramahs in Israel.

- *It was a city captured by Joshua and allocated to the tribe of Naphtali (Josh. 19:32, 36).*

Gush Halav, *Jish, Gishala*

Located 2½ miles north of Meron is the home of Yohanan of Gishala, commander in the Jewish war against Rome. It was the last Jewish fortress to fall to Vespasian. The tombs of the sages Avtalion and Shemaya are situated here.

Baram

The ancient synagogue of Baram is located in the mountains of Galilee 5 miles directly north of Meron and less than a mile from the Lebanese border. It is the best preserved and one of the earliest synagogues in Israel. It dates back to the end of the second or beginning of the third century A.D., after Galilee became the center of Jewish life. An ornamental lintel has a sculptured garland set between symbols of victory. Baram is the legendary burial site of Queen Esther.

Baram is a National Parks Authority site.

HAZOR (*"enclosed"*), Tel Hazor, *Hatzor, Tell el-Qadeh*

Tell is an Arabic word meaning an artificial mound created by successive layers of habitations superimposed one upon the other, usually implying great antiquity. Hazor is not a natural hill. It is 14 miles due north of the Sea of Galilee, and archaeologists have identified 21 occupational levels on the 25-acre original city site, covering a 3,000-year period extending back to the second millennium B.C. It was once the largest Canaanite city in the country, with a population of 40,000 people. It was one of the few Canaanite cities of antiquity noted in prebiblical literary documents from Egypt, Canaan, and Mesopotamia. The documents indicate it was a major center of commerce in the Fertile Crescent. It was captured by pharaohs Thutmose III, Amenhotep II, and Seti I. Hazor and Laish (later Dan) are the only cities in Canaan mentioned in the Mari archives. In fact, one of the tablets from Mari's royal archive in Mesopotamia notes that Hammurabi, the king of Babylon, had ambassadors residing in Hazor. Archaeologists are still anticipating the discovery of a major cuneiform archive in Hazor itself.

Although the tel was identified as Hazor as early as 1928, it was not until 1955-58 that Professor Yigael Yadin and a team of archaeologists from the Hebrew University excavated Hazor. Nine of the 21 levels were of the Bronze Age or Canaanite period. During the last 5 of these the occupation also extended to an area of about 150 acres to the north of the tel, known as the "Lower City." Upper and lower cities together make this the largest tel in the country – 175-200 acres – ten times larger than most (e.g., Megiddo, Lachish, and Gezer were only 20-40 acres). Canaanite houses in the southwest corner of the lower city belonged to the thirteenth century B.C., and showed signs of violent destruction and abandonment. This fits excellently with the tradition of its burning by Joshua, dated by many scholars to the late thirteenth century B.C. As Mark Twain commented while at the site during his visit over 100 years ago, Joshua never left any chance for newspaper controversy about who won the battle. The level below this corresponded to the fourteenth century B.C. – the period of the Amarna letters. Two of the letters were written by the ruler of Hazor, Abdi-tirshi.

During the summer of 1969, further excavation at Hazor produced the "prize discovery": the **UNDERGROUND WATER SYSTEM** from the Israelite period – the largest of its type and more than twice the size of the one at Megiddo. It dates back to the time of Ahab. (The water tunnels at Megiddo and Gibeon, as well as Hezekiah's Tunnel, were also made in the seventh to ninth centuries B.C.) The Tel Hazor tunnel is 82 feet long, 13 feet high, and 13 feet wide.

Archaeologists found the **STANDARD OF THE SNAKE GODDESS** (a bronze relief of an image of the goddess with a snake in each of her hands) recalling the brass serpent of Moses (Num. 21:8; 2 Kings 18:4). A bone **HANDLE OF A MIRROR OR SCEPTER** has a carving of a winged angel or deity guarding a "tree of life." It dates from the eighth or ninth century B.C. A **STELA** showing two hands raised to an emblem of deity (a sun-disc within a crescent) was found in the holy of holies of a fourteenth-century Canaanite temple. Yadin also believed the city was destroyed by an earthquake during the last days of Jeroboam II (see Amos 1:1). Identification of the city was confirmed by a clay tablet with cuneiform inscription bearing the name Hazor. (See *Biblical Archaeology Review* Mar/Apr 1982, 16-20; Jan/Feb 1983, 16-23; Jan/Feb 1990, 44-45.)

Hazor is a National Parks Authority site and has a lovely, modern **MUSEUM**, located at the entrance of **KIBBUTZ AYELET HASHACHAR**, one of Israel's most beautiful kibbutzim.

- *Joshua fought with Jabin, king of Hazor, and other kings who had united. Joshua took the city and burned it to the ground (Josh. 11:1-14). It had 40,000 people at the time.*
- *The Israelites fell into the hands of another, later Jabin, who controlled Israel from Hazor for 20 years and was noted for his 900 iron chariots. The captain of his army was Sisera. Under the inspiration of Deborah and Barak, the Israelites won a great victory over Sisera in the Jezreel Valley (Judg. 4).*
- *Solomon rebuilt Hazor along with Megiddo and Gezer (1 Kings 9:15).*
- *The city was captured in 732 B.C. by Tiglath-pileser III, king of Assyria (2 Kings 15:29).*
- *A bone handle was found here, showing a young date palm as the Tree of Life, protected by a four-winged seraph and cherubim and a flaming sword (cf. Gen. 3:24).*

Ayelet Hashahar ("*morning star*")

Immediately northeast of the tel of Hazor is a collective settlement that was established originally by young people from Russia in 1915 as a pioneering kibbutz in Upper Galilee. It was shelled and bombed intensively by Syrian forces and suffered many casualties. It has a beautiful guest house.

Alma

Five miles northwest of Hazor is a small village where a third-century inscription was found with these words: "Peace upon this place and upon all the places of his people, Israel."

- *Alma was the name of a descendant of Lehi and Nephi (Mos. 17:2).*

Lake Hula (*Huleh*) *Area, Mei-Merom*

As early as 1883, young Polish Jews settled in the Huleh Lake and swamp area. The Einan Waterworks pump water to the heights of Galilee. In 1957 the drainage of the swampland was completed and the size of Lake Huleh was greatly reduced. Here in the Huleh Valley is a **NATURE RESERVE AND BIRD REFUGE**. The reserve sports 200 acres of **PAPYRUS**, the northernmost place in the world that it grows. There are also many fish ponds in the Huleh Valley. They are fertilized with nitrogenous and phosphate fertilizers, and the fish are fed with cereals and pellets. These ponds have very high yields, actually producing 15% of the total fish production in the country. Carp represents 80% of the fish grown – a good, eating fish, rather than a scavenger trash fish as in the West – and much of the other 20% consists of Saint Peter's Fish.

KADESH NAPHTALI, *Kedesh ("holiness"), Tell Qades, Ramot Naftali*

This ancient Canaanite fortress became a Levitical city of refuge. It was the home of Barak. Heber, whose wife Jael killed Sisera, lived nearby. Kadesh was an important city in Canaan, and its name appears in hieroglyphs on the walls of the temple in Karnak, Egypt. The date of the hieroglyphs is 1310 B.C., the time of Seti I.

- *It was a city of Naphtali (Judges 4:6).*
- *It was the home of Barak, who mustered the tribes of Israel and routed the Canaanites along the Kishon River (Judg. 4:6).*
- *It was captured by Tiglath-pileser (2 Kings 15:29).*

Qiryat Shemona *("city of eight"), Kiryat Shmona*

This town of less than 20,000 people is the urban center of upper Galilee. Because it is near the Upper Galilee and Golan Heights areas, it is a center for tourism. It was named after 8 who fell in defense of nearby Tel Hai in 1920.

Tel Hai *("hill of life")*

A museum of the Hagana underground movement is located 1½ miles north of Qiryat Shemona. Joseph Trumpeldor, founder of the Jewish pioneer (Hekhaluts) movement in Russia and seven others (including two women) were killed trying to defend their Jewish settlement against much bigger Arab forces attacking them shortly after World War I. Trumpeldor is buried in a grave marked by a large lion of Judah statue. An inscription on the statue reads: "It is good to die for our country."

ABEL *("fresh grassy meadows"), Beth-maacha, Abel-Maim, Tell Abil*

Three miles east of Beth-rehob, west of Dan, and north of Lake Huleh is the site of the biblical Abel.

- *Here the rebel Sheba was pursued and killed by Joab (2 Sam. 20:10, 14-15).*

Ha Tannur Waterfall

Located near the main highway and 1 mile north of Tell Abil is a beautiful waterfall of the Iyon River. A 5-minute hike on a footpath brings the visitor to the base of the falls.

Metulla (*Arabic: "overlooking"*)

The village of Metulla, founded in 1896, is the northernmost Israeli settlement. It is on the Lebanese border and has a number of small hotels and restaurants. The broad valley called by the Bible *Iyon* stretches north into Lebanon from Metulla. A beautiful view of the Huleh valley is also obtained from Metulla. To the west of Metulla is the "Good Fence," a semi-open border between Lebanon and Israel. For many years Lebanese citizens have crossed temporarily into northern Israel for medical care and supplies.

Hurshat Tal (*"dew grove"*)

Just east of the settlement of Ha Gosherim is a pleasant camping site with ancient oak trees and natural springs, with waters of the Dan River flowing through the beautifully landscaped forest-park. It is maintained by the National Parks Authority. This region is the closest thing to the Wasatch Front of Northern Utah (and other similar landscapes) with snow melt, rivers, streams, etc. Driving eastward one crosses Nahal Senir (Wadi Hatzbani), then two branches of Nahal Dan (the single biggest water source in the country). On the right (south) note the Hatzbani-Dan hydro-powered turbine, which was inaugurated in June, 1984. The Hermon River (from Caesarea Philippi), the Dan River (from Dan), and the Senir (out of Lebanon) together form **THE JORDAN RIVER**, in the middle of Huleh Valley.

DAN (*"judge"*), *Laish, Leshem, Tell el-Qadi*

Dan marked the northern limit of the land of Israel. It is 3-4 miles west of Banias and identified with a tel (mound) 40 to 80 feet high. The largest of all the springs that make up the sources of the Jordan River rises from the west side of the mound. The Dan produces 220 million cubic meters annually, and is strong and constant year round. The spring is fed by an aquifer carrying cold water, snowmelt from the heights of Mount Hermon; it is the largest karstic spring in the Near East.

Here the Danites captured Laish, which they rebuilt and called Dan (Judg. 18). They established a sanctuary and ritual that persisted as long as the house of God was in Shiloh. The priesthood of this idolatrous shrine continued in the family of Jeroboam until the conquest of Tiglath-pileser.

Professor Avraham Biran of the Hebrew Union College in Jerusalem has been excavating Tel Dan for three decades. **IMPORTANT FINDS** include an inscription "To the god who is in Dan," discovered in digs in 1976, a mud-brick gate from the Bronze Age – the time of Abraham, the cultic high place attributed to kings Jeroboam and Ahab, and most recently an inscription mentioning King David. (See *Biblical Archaeology Review* Mar/Apr 1994, 26-39; Jul/Aug 1994, 54-55; see also previous issues: Sep/Oct 1981, 20-37; Jul/Aug 1987, 12-25.)

Two miles west of Dan is **KIBBUTZ HA GOSHERIM**, a well-known tourist stop with a guest house and swimming pool. (*Gesher* is Hebrew for "Bridge," *Gosherim* is the plural.)

- *Here Abraham rescued Lot from Chedorlaomer (Gen. 14:13-16).*
- *Jeroboam set up a golden calf here, as the Egyptians did (1 Kings 12:26-33).*
- *Dan was subdued by Benhadad, king of Syria (1 Kings 15:20; 2 Chron. 16:4).*
- *It was regained by Jeroboam (2 Kings 14:25).*
- *The city was conquered and its inhabitants were carried captive to Assyria by Tiglath-pileser (2 Kings 15:29).*
- *The expression "from Dan even to Beersheba" is used in the Old Testament to indicate the northern and southern limits of Israelite occupation in the land (Judg. 20:1; 1 Sam. 3:20).*
- *The name Leshem was changed to Dan, the name of the leader of the tribe of Dan (Josh. 19:47).*

CAESAREA PHILIPPI, Banias, *Baniyas, Paneas, Neronica, Neroneus*

Caesarea Philippi is located at the base of Mount Hermon, northeast of the Sea of Galilee. The Greek name was *Paneas,* named after Pan, the Greek god of forests, meadows, flocks, and herds; he is associated with mountain slopes and caves. Pan was half man and half goat, and was wild and unpredictable, striking terror in a moment (hence the origin of our English word "panic;" also in Greek mythology he created of reeds the "panpipe.") At the time of the Arab conquest in the 7th century A.D., Paneas became Banias because in their alphabet the Arabs have no "p" sound.

The city was rebuilt by Philip the tetrarch and named in honor of Augustus and himself to distinguish it from Caesarea on the coast. In 20 B.C. Herod the Great erected a **WHITE MARBLE TEMPLE** here to the god Pan. The site was later called *Neronica* by Agrippa II. The Hermon River branch of the Jordan River rises at the foot of the mountain at the north of the town. Niches of the pagan gods, with accompanying inscriptions, still remain along the cliff face above the water source. A *weli,* or burial place of a Muslim holy man, is also visible above the Shrine to Pan. This is the only place in the country with a river flowing through a city, which is appropriate to what Jesus taught here: revelation is continuous like the river. Revelation is flowing, moving, and progressive like the river. Excavations of Caesarea Philippi in the 1990s have unearthed impressive remains of the once-great border city.

- *It was the northern limit of the Lord's journeys on his second tour to the north (Matt. 16:13; Mark 8:27).*
- *Peter's confession of Jesus' divinity, Jesus' prediction of his own death, and possibly the Transfiguration took place here (Matt. 16:13-20; Mark 8:27-9:10; Luke 9:18-36; cf. D&C 128:9-14, 20).*

Banias Waterfall

About 1 mile southwest of Caesarea Philippi (Banias) is the most massive waterfall in Israel. It is accessible either by footpath from Banias itself, or by path from a nearby parking lot. If approached from Banias care must be taken due to the precipitous drop into the river gorge. It is possible to "swim" in the water, but it is extremely cold.

Nimrod Castle (*fortress*), *Kalat Nimrud, Qalaat Nemrod*

About 1 mile northeast of Banias is a former stronghold of the Assassins. It was conquered first by the Crusaders and then by the Mamelukes. The castle-fortress is one of the best preserved. The visitor can have an excellent view of the Upper Jordan Valley from this point. Near here is Israel's only skiing area.

It is helpful to know the meaning of terms frequently appearing on signs at Nimrod Castle:

A *bailey* is an outer wall of a castle, or wall surrounding the keep. A *barbican* is an outer defensive tower at a gate or bridge. A *fosse* is a ditch, trench, or moat. A *keep* or *donjon* is the strongest, securest part of a castle, a holding cell. A *loophole* is a narrow aperture in a thick wall for shooting arrows out; it gradually widens toward the inside. A *refectory* is a dining hall, and a *turris* or *tour* is a tower.

This is a National Parks Authority site.

Masaada

This Druze town is located just west of Birket Ram. Threshing floors here are like those of Jesus' day. The **DRUZE** are an offshoot from mainstream Islam that occurred in the 11th century. They accept the claim of divinity of Egyptian Caliph El-Hakim Abu Ali el-Mansur. They are known as fierce fighters and are generally loyal to the sovereign where they live. Today, most Druze are in Lebanon and in Jebel Druze in Syria, plus over 70,000 in northern Galilee and on Mount Carmel. They traditionally marry only among their own community. Their religion is mostly secret, even to their own people.

Right: A Druze threshing wheat near Masaada

Below: Winnowing wheat

Birket Ram (*"high pool"*)

At Birket Ram, about 5 miles east of Banias, there is a small village by a lake. The lake is in an old crater.

MOUNT HERMON, *Sirion, Senir, Jebel esh-Sheikh*

Mount Hermon marks the southern terminus of the Anti-Lebanon range. It is 16-20 miles long from north to south and 9,200 feet high. Snow lies on the peak year-long, and the mountain receives up to 72 inches of precipitation annually.

- *Israel conquered all of the Amorite territory to Hermon (Deut. 3:7-9).*
- *This was the northern limit of the territory of the Ten Tribes of Israel (Deut. 4:47-48; Josh. 11:1-3; 12:1-5; 13:5).*
- *Half of the tribe of Manasseh dwelt here (1 Chron. 5:23).*
- *The dew of Hermon was a symbol of religious blessing (Ps. 133:3).*
- *The Transfiguration took place on a "high mountain" (Matt. 17:1-9; Mark 9:2-9; Luke 9:28-36).*
- *The lunatic was healed (Matt. 17:14-21; Mark 9:14-29; Luke 9:37-43).*

GOLAN (*"circle"*), *Jolan, Golan Heights*

The tableland east and northeast of the Sea of Galilee is named Golan. At the end of World War I this area was given to Syria. In Old Testament times it was a part of the inheritance of Manasseh. It had a dense population in the second and third centuries A.D., and Golan was one of its principal cities. Josephus mentioned Golan as a city and Gaulanitis as a district (*Antiquities of the Jews,* XIII:15:3; XVII:8:1). The exact site of the city of Golan is uncertain, but it is perhaps modern Sahen el Jolan, 17 miles east of the Sea of Galilee.

The Syrian bombardment of Ein Gev from the Golan Heights was one of the causes of the six-day war of June 1967. Israel served notice on Syria that she must be prepared to face the consequences and Syria appealed to Egypt and Iraq. Egypt cried for war, turned out the United Nations at Gaza and the Straits of Tiran, and soon the war was on. Taking the Golan Heights was very difficult.

- *Moses assigned Golan to the tribe of Manasseh (Deut. 4:41-43; Josh. 20:8).*
- *It was assigned to the sons of Gershon (Josh. 21:27; 1 Chron. 6:71).*

Gamla

Gamla is located on a towering ridge (or hump, so the name Gamla, which is "camel" in Hebrew) on the Golan 6 miles directly east of the northern shore of the Sea of Galilee. It can be seen from Capernaum and Bethsaida.

Gamla was the site of a dramatic battle during the Great Revolt between Romans and Jews in A. D. 67-68. Three Roman legions, over 25,000 troops, arrived to suppress the revolt. Several sites in Galilee were besieged first, until only

Gamla held out. The Jewish patriots regarded the site as impregnable, situated as it is on a narrow spur of land with deep wadis or ravines on three sides. On the steep slope of this narrow neck of land the houses, synagogue, and other public buildings were constructed. Though at first repulsed and suffering heavy casualties, the Romans regrouped and proceeded to systematically destroy the fortress-city, in a terrible siege in which Josephus tells us that 5,000 Jewish defenders jumped to their deaths rather than submit to the Romans.

For centuries the site of Gamla was forgotten, but since 1967 it has been re-identified and excavated. Finds include broken-down **HOUSES** and the **OLDEST SYNAGOGUE** in the land, plus much evidence of the great battle, including over 1700 rounded **CATAPULT BALLS** flung into Gamla by the Romans. The vivid and awful account is detailed by Josephus in *Wars* 4:1-83. (See also *Biblical Archaeology Review* Jan/Feb 1992, 20-37.)

Gamla is a Nature Reserves Authority site. The hike down into the ruins is fairly difficult, and the return hike back up is long and strenuous.

Quneitra, *Kuneitra, El Kuneitra*

This is a ghost town from which 30,000 Syrians fled the Israeli army in 1967. Before, it was the Syrian army headquarters. It is about 40 miles from Damascus, Syria's capital. The city is in ruins, and near the town a new Jewish kibbutz, **MEROM-GOLAN**, was formed in 1967. In 1968 another village of **EIN ZEVAN** was founded west of Merom-Golan. A number of other Jewish communities have been established on the Golan Heights since the 1967 war.

Somewhere off to the east, on the road to Damascus, Saul (later, Paul) was stopped in his tracks by the Lord Himself, and Paul became a dynamic follower of Jesus and leader in taking the Gospel throughout the Mediterranean world (see Acts 9).

To the west of the Israeli road rises **MOUNT AVITAL**, an extinct volcano, now topped with a lot of sophisticated Israeli military radar and sensing equipment, the eyes and ears of Israel observing its Syrian neighbors.

Qatzrin

Excavations in the 1980s and 90s revealed the important Byzantine/Talmudic-period (3rd-8th century A. D.) village of Qatzrin on the central Golan. Two highlights of the partly restored village are the best-preserved synagogue on the Golan and a reconstructed traditional Jewish house. The two-story house has been reconstructed as well as furnished with interior furniture, decor, and personal possessions. The educational tour includes outdoor and indoor ovens, kitchen utensils, foods, agricultural implements and products, and replicas of lamps and lanterns. A hoard of 9,000 coins from the 4th century A. D. was discovered in the last hour of the last of nine seasons of excavation. See *Biblical Archaeology Review* May/June 1991, 44-56.

APHEK (*"fortress"*), Fiq

This town on the Golan Heights, 4 miles directly east of Ein Gev on the Sea of Galilee, is possibly the location of one of the four Apheks of the Bible.

- *Here Ahab defeated Benhadad (1 Kings 20:26-30; 2 Kings 13:17).*

Mevo Hamma

This new Israeli community, 2 miles south of Kfar Horeb, is built where once the Syrian guns shot down on Kibbutz Ha'on and Kibbutz Ein Gev. Syrian bunkers are located on the edge of the heights and a beautiful panoramic view of the Sea of Galilee can be seen from here.

GERGESA, Kursi

About 4 miles north of Kibbutz Ein Gev, at an intersection of another road leading east onto the Golan, is the site of New Testament Gergesa, the likely candidate for the incident of devils entering swine. Two discrepancies exist in the accounts of evil spirits being cast out in the Decapolis. Matthew indicates two men were possessed with devils while Mark and Luke have only one. Matthew has the incident taking place in Gergesa, whereas Mark and Luke both cite Gadara as the location of the miracle. Other Greek manuscripts have Gergesa and some even claim Gerasa was where the demons were expelled.

The "other side of the sea" and the fact that swine were being herded logically stipulate Gentile country in the Decapolis. The large herd of swine when possessed with the devils ran down a steep place and were drowned in the lake. That alone disqualifies Gerasa (Jerash) as a possible location, as it is over thirty miles from the Sea of Galilee in the hill country of Gilead. Of the other two candidates Gadara (Umm Qeis) seems also to be rather far for a herd to stampede to the shore of Galilee, the slopes of Gadara being several miles distant from the lake with an intervening deep gorge and streambed of the Yarmuk River. Matthew's choice Gergesa (Kursi), now partially excavated and restored, is situated along the eastern shore of the Sea of Galilee less than a mile from the lake. It is the most likely site of this dramatic encounter between the forces of good and evil. A reconstructed **BYZANTINE CHURCH AND CHAPEL** can be seen at the site, along with remains of a **MONASTERY**.

Kursi is a National Parks Authority site.

- *Devils left the bodies of one or two possessed men and entered into a herd of swine (Matt. 8:28-34; Mark 5:1-20; Luke 8:26-39).*

Ein Gev

This kibbutz, founded in 1937 by German and Czechoslovakian pioneers, boasts a 5,000-seat **AMPHITHEATER**, where a musical festival attracts large crowds during Passover time. Visitors can purchase a favorite dish called "Saint Peter's fish" at a restaurant right on the shore of the Sea of Galilee, and also feed the fish here. The settlers of Ein Gev were the first Jewish fishermen of modern times.

Between Ein Gev and Tiberias there is a regular ferry service across the Sea of Galilee, which is 5½ miles wide at this point.

Susita, *Sussita, Hippos*

Immediately east of Ein Gev is Mount Susita, so named because it resembles the back of a horse (Hebrew *Sus*). On the top of the mount are ruins of a Greek Decapolis city and a later Roman fortress.

GADARA, Gader, *Jedur, Hammat Gader*

This was a city of the Decapolis (league of 10 cities east of the Sea of Galilee), on the Yarmuk River 6 miles southeast of the Sea of Galilee. Its territory may have extended to the sea. The site now features extensive excavated Roman-period ruins, especially a complex of hot baths, some once again in operation, along with alligator farms and other attractions. (See the section on Gadara in Jordan).

- *Jesus healed the demoniac and the demons entered into and destroyed the swine (Matt. 8:28-34; Mark 5:1-20; Luke 8:26-39). See above, however, under Gergesa/Kursi, for the more likely site.*

WEST COAST FROM JOPPA TO LEBANON

JOPPA (*"height," "beauty"*), Jaffa, *Yafo*[12]

Joppa is immediately south of Tel Aviv and is a part of "greater" Tel Aviv. It is to Tel Aviv what Old Jerusalem is to the new city of Jerusalem. It is 30 miles south of Caesarea and 40 miles northwest of Jerusalem. It has a recorded history of 3,500 years. Under Solomon, Jaffa became Jerusalem's seaport (though it was never a good port; things had to be unloaded offshore). Under the Romans, 8,000 Jews were killed here. Crusader Richard the Lion-Hearted built a citadel here, but Saladin's brother took it away from him and slaughtered 20,000 Christians in the process. It was razed by Napoleon in 1799 and rebuilt by the Turks.

Janne Sjodahl, a Mormon missionary in the 1880s, baptized two Arab men into the Church, near the place where Peter had his vision extending the Gospel to non-Jews.

The first Zionist pioneers of the nineteenth century entered the Promised Land through Jaffa harbor, but the harbor is scarcely used today.

On the top of a hill near the seashore is the **MONASTERY OF SAINT PETER**, marking the traditional site of Peter's vision of the great sheet; and nearby is a small **MOSQUE** in a little alley close to the lighthouse, built on the traditional site of the **HOUSE OF SIMON THE TANNER**. The **MUSEUM OF JAFFA ANTIQUITIES** houses archaeological findings.

- *Cedars were brought to Joppa en route to Jerusalem for the Temples of Solomon and Zerubbabel (2 Chron. 2:16; also Ezra 3:7).*
- *Jonah embarked from here for Tarshish (Jonah 1:3).*
- *Peter raised Tabitha, or Dorcas, to life (Acts 9:36-43).*
- *Here Peter had his vision of the great sheet, and Cornelius was converted (Acts 9:43-10:48).*
- *Joppa was the home of Simon the tanner (Acts 10:5-6, 32).*
- *Peter told the Church at Jerusalem his experiences (Acts 11:5-21).*

Tel Aviv (*"old-new land," "hill of spring"*)

This is the first city in the world to be built, populated, and administered entirely by Jews in modern times. Its name suggests the *old* and the *new*: a tel is an ancient mound, and aviv is the season spring; Theodor Herzl called this land the *altneuland*, the "old new land." It is the largest completely Jewish city in the world. Although founded in 1909 on the sand dunes, it is now a thoroughly modern city and Israel's second largest (after Jerusalem), with a population of 357,000 (Tel Aviv-Joppa). The entire Tel Aviv conurbation (with suburb cities) comprises approximately 1.5 million people. It is located immediately north of Joppa. Its new hotels on the beach are making it into the Near Eastern "Miami Beach," and to an

LEBANON
Rosh Haniqra
MERITERRANEAN SEA
Tell Achzib
Montfort
Nahariya
Shavei Zion
Yehiam
Lohamei-Hagetaot
Kafr Yasif
Safed
Ramah
Accho
Cabul (Kabul)
Yodefat
Tell Shiqmona
Haifa
Shefaram
Tiberias
Atlit
Nazareth
Dor
Afula
Megiddo
Caesarea
Beth Shean
En-Gannim (Jenin)
Hadera
Kefar Vitkin
Kibbutz Há Ogen
Jordan River
Natanya
Tulkarm
Plain of Sharon
N
Shechem (Nablus)
Tell Arshaf
Kefar Sava
Herzliya
Aphek (Antipatris)
Tell Kasile
Petah-Tikva
Tel Aviv
Joppa (Jaffa)
Miles
5
10
Lod
Ramla
To Jerusalem
Israel
West Coast from
Joppa to Lebanon

idealistic orthodox Jew, the mere mention of its name may conjure up an image of Gomorrah in its worst depravity.

Tel Aviv is the commercial and cultural heart of the country. Crowds throng the streets and beaches, and it seems that the young city reflects the exuberance of youth. Tel Aviv and its neighbor are combined and called *Tel Aviv-Yafo.*

POINTS OF INTEREST

CITY HALL is a beautiful 12-story building in the "Kings of Israel Square" (*Kikar Malkhai Israel*). A view from the top is a treat.

MIGDAL SHALOM is Tel Aviv's tallest building and is in the heart of the financial district. It houses exhibits and has an observatory.

KIKAR DIZENGOFF is like Times Square or Piccadilly Circus. Saturday nights are especially lively.

TEL AVIV UNIVERSITY is in the Ramat Aviv area. It has humanities, science, medicine, business administration, and other faculties. On the campus is the world-class **DIASPORA MUSEUM** (*Beit Hatefutzot*, established 1978), a unique, state-of-the-art museum with several levels of displays, dioramas, replicas, reconstructions, models, and objects, plus interactive video productions and hands-on learning stations, all showing Jewish culture and worship during the Diaspora – the past 2,000 years of Jewish life in countries all over the world.

CARMEL MARKET is Tel Aviv's largest open-air market and has a colorful Oriental flavor. It is located on Rehov Allenby, on the corner of Rehov Nahlat Benjamin.

The **FLEA MARKET** (*Shuk Hapishpishim*) is located in Jaffa, near Kikar Hagana. There are antiques and odd objects here for "bargaining."

The **ZOO** is located at 76 Rehov Keren Kayemet. The **SAFARI PARK** in Ramat Gan is a zoological treat for young and old.

EXPEDITION GARDENS is the site of the biannual Tel Aviv International Fair and Special Exhibits.

The **TEL AVIV MUSEUM** has paintings and sculptures by Israeli and international artists. It is located in the home of Meir Dizengoff, founder and first mayor of Tel Aviv. It was in this home that the State of Israel was declared into existence on May 14, 1948.

BET HAGANA is a museum that shows the development of Israel's defense forces and the War of Independence. It is located at 23 Sderot Rothschild.

At **MUSEUM CENTER** – *Ramat Aviv* – there are museums of glass, money, ceramics, science, ethnography, and folklore.

The **MUSEUM OF ANTIQUITIES** of Tel Aviv-Yafo houses archaeological finds and records illustrating the history of Tel Aviv-Yafo.

OTHER MUSEUMS include the **MUSEUM OF THE HISTORY OF TEL AVIV**, the **ALPHABET MUSEUM, MAN AND HIS WORK**, the **TCHERNICHOVSKY MUSEUM**, the **JABOTINSKY MUSEUM**, and **PERMANENT INDUSTRIAL EXHIBITION, SHALOM ALEICHEM HOUSE**, the **ISRAEL EXPORT INSTITUTE**, and **THE ISRAEL COMPANY FOR FAIRS AND EXHIBITIONS**.

Tel Kassile, *Tel Qasila*

On the northern outskirts of Tel Aviv is the site of an ancient fortress that guarded Yarkon port during the days of Solomon. Tradition indicates that the "cedars of Lebanon" were brought by sea to this point and hauled overland to Jerusalem for Solomon's Temple. Others believe the cedars were brought to the port of Joppa.

- *Hiram, king of Tyre, sent cedar trees to David and Solomon (2 Sam. 5:11; 2 Chron. 2:3-16).*

Petah Tikva (*"door of hope"*) *Petah Tiqva*

Five miles east of Tel Aviv is the oldest Jewish agricultural settlement in Israel, founded in 1878 by Jews from Jerusalem.

APHEK, ANTIPATRIS (*"belonging to Antipater"*)

Two miles northeast of Petah Tikva is the site of ancient Aphek/Antipatris. The Old Testament name of this site was Aphek. Israelites and Philistines squared off in one of their most famous encounters near Aphek, a city shown by recent excavations to be of great importance for many centuries before and after that encounter. Ramses II's governor of Canaan owned a palace at Aphek, and Herod the Great later built a fortress and city here. The geographical importance of Aphek/Antipatris, not only to Israelites but to the entire Near East, lies in its position along the International Highway. The city was situated at the springs which immediately became the Yarkon River, which flows out towards the Mediterranean Sea. All traffic, local and international (the Via Maris), was channelled into the mile-wide corridor between the springs and the hills. Geographical factors had thus given strategic value to the site, so Herod took advantage of it and established a city named for his father Antipater. Because of Jewish threats to kill Paul, he was escorted by 470 soldiers, horsemen, and spearmen, leaving Jerusalem at the third hour of the night (Acts 23:23). En route to Caesarea, Paul and his bodyguard stopped temporarily at Antipatris. Near

Antipatris is **ROSH HA-AYIN**, whose spring water is pumped up to Jerusalem and to the thirsty desert southward.

Aphek/Antipatris is a National Parks Authority site.

- *Here the Philistines captured the ark of the covenant, which had been brought from Shiloh to the battle (1 Sam. 4:1-11).*
- *Here Paul stayed overnight as the soldiers took him from Jerusalem to Caesarea (Acts 23:23, 31).*

PLAIN OF SHARON

This is a strip of comparatively level land between the mountains and the Mediterranean Sea, from 8 to 12 miles wide and 30 miles long (from Mount Carmel to Joppa). In the past it was neglected malarial swampland, now it is fertile and beautiful like the "rose of Sharon," some of the most developed land in the country – full of citrus orchards.

- *David's herds were pastured here (1 Chron. 27:25, 29).*
- *Its excellence was spoken of by Isaiah (Isa. 35:2; 65:10).*

Herzliya

About 4 miles north of Tel Aviv is Herzliya, a city of 77,000 inhabitants. Excellent bathing beaches and hotels make it a holiday resort.

Tel Arshaf, *Rishpon, Apollonia, Arsur*

On the seacoast 1 mile north of Herzliya are ruins of a city known as *Arshaf* in Canaanite times and *Rishpon* in the days of Omri. It was renamed *Apollonia* in the Hellenistic period and later annexed by Alexander Yannai. Near the Crusader castle of Arsur, Richard the Lion-hearted defeated Saladin in 1191.

Natanya (*Hebrew: "Gift of God"*)

This beautiful, clean coastal city is known as the "pearl of Sharon," even though one of the main industries of the city is the cutting of diamonds. The city was founded in 1929, and because of its beautiful **BEACHES** it soon became a popular resort city. During World War II it was the chief rest and recreation center for battle-weary soldiers of the Allied forces in the Near East. The diamond industry was started by Belgian refugees during World War II. Today the export of polished diamonds grosses some $3 billion a year. Citrus groves and tourists help make the livelihood of tens of thousands of citizens.

Kibbutz Ha Ogen

Five miles northeast of Natanya is a beautiful kibbutz that operates a plastic factory. The Jews here are very cordial and will show visitors through the factory.

Crusader Fortress, Caesarea

CAESAREA

Caesarea is an 8,000-acre excavation site, the largest in the land of Israel. The ancient city was a seaport on the Mediterranean about 30 miles north of Joppa and about 70 miles northwest of Jerusalem, built by Herod the Great in 22 B.C. as his summer palace on the site of ancient Strato's Tower. It was the capital of the Roman government in Judea/Palestine for about 500 years. Caesarea was named in honor of Caesar Augustus (Luke 2:1) and had lavish palaces, public buildings, a theater, a hippodrome, and an amphitheater.

The **HARBOR** Herod built was considered a great feat. It was always free from the waves of the sea. The mighty breakwater was constructed by letting down huge stones into twenty fathoms of water. The existing breakwater is small compared to Herod's. A **WALL** and **TOWERS**, a promenade, and dwellings for mariners were also provided.

The **HERODIAN CITY** encompassed about 164 acres, taking about 10-12 years to build. Herod was without question the greatest builder the Holy Land has ever known. He constructed fortresses, like Masada, Machaerus, Herodion, and

Alexandrion, along with cities, like Antipatris, a memorial to his father, Cypros, a memorial to his mother, Phasaelis, a memorial to his brother, and Sebaste (former Samaria), a memorial to Augustus. Caesarea was a much needed port city, also in honor of Caesar Augustus. Herod erected an immense shrine over the Cave of Machpelah in Hebron. Various other construction projects were carried out as gifts to other cities. He built a gymnasium in Ptolemais and Tripoli, a market place and temples in Tyre and Berytus, a theater in Sidon, and a gymnasium and theater in Damascus. He bestowed gifts on Pergamum, Samos, Cilicia, Pamphylia, and Lycia. He rebuilt the Temple of Apollo on the island of Rhodes. He erected buildings in Athens, Sparta, Nicopolis, and other Greek cities. He repaved the main street of Syrian Antioch with marble along the entire length of the city, plus a colonnade. In Jerusalem he built the Antonia Fortress, a royal palace and towers, a theater, amphitheater, and hippodrome, though his greatest building enterprise was the Jerusalem Temple reconstruction. Herod was also a generous contributor to the Olympic games and was given the permanent title "Chairman of the Games," although Augustus, later in Herod's reign, hearing of all his murders, is reputed to have said, "I had rather be Herod's swine than his son."

Caesarea became the home of the Roman praefects and procurators (governors), including Pontius Pilate. Herod Agrippa I died here, being "eaten of worms." He was smitten by the angel of the Lord (Acts 12:19-23).

Terrible cruelties were practiced against the Jews under Felix and Florus. Here Vespasian was hailed emperor by his soldiers, and Titus celebrated the birthday of his brother, Domitian, by setting 2,500 Jews to fight with beasts in the amphitheater. Riots between Gentiles and Jews in Caesarea precipitated the first war between Jews and Romans. The great Jewish war was begun here by the Jews in A.D. 66, and coins "Judaea Capta" were minted here after their defeat. Rabbi Akiva was martyred here by the Romans after Bar Kokhba's abortive rising (the second Jewish revolt - A.D. 132-135), and many a Jew or Christian was thrown to the lions here following the revolt.

In the third century A.D. the Christian scholar Origen established the School of Caesarea. He taught here for 23 years and established a major library. A biographer said he wrote 6,000 works, including a 6-column comparative text of the Old Testament in 50 volumes. Eusebius, a respected historian/theologian, was bishop of Caesarea from A.D. 313 to 340. He was also a friend and advisor of Emperor Constantine. In 548 a massacre of the Christians was organized and carried out by the Jews and Samaritans. The city passed into Muslim hands in 638. In the time of the Crusades it fell to the Christians and then again to the Muslims. It was the scene of a Muslim massacre of many Christians in 1101. It was overthrown by Sultan Baybars I in 1265 but was later regained by the Turks.

Excavations have uncovered along the seashore part of the great second-century **AQUEDUCT** that brought water to the city from the Mount Carmel Springs, some 12 miles away. The first half of this aqueduct is rock-hewn tunnel and the second half is built up on arches. This "high-level aqueduct" actually consists of two aqueducts (as visible in off-set arches): the eastern one is earlier, probably Herod's, and the western one probably dates to Hadrian in the 2nd century A.D. Some dedicatory inscriptions still remain on the west side. One says:

Imperator Traianus
Hadrianus Augustus
a detachment of
Legion X Fretensis

A "low-level aqueduct" brought irrigation water from Nahal Tanninim (Crocodile River) over 4 miles away; this aqueduct carried five times more water than the other. It is possible to see and even enter this aqueduct a little northeast of the parking area.

At Caesarea the first **ARCHAEOLOGICAL EVIDENCE OF PONTIUS PILATE** has been unearthed. It is an inscription bearing the names of Emperor Tiberius and Pontius Pilate, the Roman governor of Judea who ruled between A.D. 26 and 36. He is referred to as "Pontius Pilatus, Praefectus Judaeae" – Pontius Pilate the praefect of Judaea, whose government headquarters were here at Caesarea. The original stone is in the Israel National Museum, and a replica is located on the site.

A famous glass bowl supposedly used by Jesus at the Last Supper was recovered here when the Frank Crusaders reconquered Caesarea. It is now in Genoa, Italy, and is known as the *sacro cantina.* It corresponds to the legendary "Holy Grail."

At a glance you will see vestiges of three civilizations here: the steps leading to Saint Louis's **CRUSADER FORTRESS**, the crumbled **ROMAN COLUMNS** jutting out of the sea, and a **MINARET** from the nineteenth-century **TURKISH OCCUPATION.**

The present ruins include the **WALLS** of the ancient city (the original wall was nearly 3 miles long on the landward side), and within them those of a much smaller town of the twelfth century, whose walls were rebuilt in the thirteenth. The Crusaders built a city only one-tenth the size of Herod's original city. Note the dry moat around the Crusader city to protect against battering rams; note also a gate with hinges, loopholes, and other fortifications. There remain also some of the ruins of the **CATHEDRAL**, which appear to be on the site of the **TEMPLE** raised by Herod to Augustus. A **ROMAN HIPPODROME** 1,500 feet long and 250 feet wide was built in the 2nd century A.D. to accommodate 38,000 people. On the south side of the medieval town are ruins apparently of a large

THEATER close to the shore. Large quantities of building stones have been carried to other towns and used for new building projects. There was a mile-long street, *the Cardo*, between the Forum and the theater during the Byzantine period. A colonnade lined the street, with as many as 700 columns in two rows. (There are hundreds of marble and granite columns lying around – none is native to Israel; the marble was imported from Greece and granite from Upper Egypt). The street was actually a *mosaic sidewalk*, 18 feet wide. Ten feet below the mosaic cardo an elaborate Herodian brick drainage or *sewerage system* has been found, which facilitated the continual, daily flushing of the city by the sea-currents coming from the southwest.

The **GREAT THEATER** at the south end of the city was built by Herod the Great. Although many westerners refer to a semi-circular structure like this as an *amphitheater*, in the Roman period an amphitheater was a structure that went all the way around – fully circular; this is a *theater*. At one time it may later have been converted into an amphitheater, as evidenced by the remains visible to the west. (For more details, including photos, maps, and diagrams, see *Biblical Archaeology Review* May/Jun 1982, 24-47; May/Jun 1983, 10-14; May/Jun 1993, 50-57, 76.)

Caesarea is a National Parks Authority site and has a beautiful golf course, the first in Israel.

- *Philip preached here, lived here, and had four daughters who prophesied (Acts 8:40; 21:8-9).*
- *Peter came here and preached to Cornelius, who was baptized (Acts 10).*
- *Paul visited here three times, and Agabus warned him not to go to Jerusalem (Acts 9:30; 18:22; 21:8-16; 25:3-6).*
- *Peter came here after his deliverance from prison (Acts 12:19).*
- *Paul spent two years in prison here (Acts 23:22-26:32). Note his addresses to Felix, Festus, and Herod Agrippa II. Agrippa replied, "Almost thou persuadest me to be a Christian" (Acts 26:28).*

DOR (*"generation"*), *Dora, Tantura, el-Burj*

A mound near Zikhron Ya'akov, 8 miles north of Caesarea, has been identified as the biblical city of Dor, with its harbor and remains of a fortress and a Byzantine church. King David captured it from the Philistines, and King Solomon gave it to his son-in-law, making it the center of one of the 12 regions responsible for providing the royal household with food for 1 month a year. In Roman times it was called Dora. Dor, in antiquity, was one of the centers for producing the dye known as "Tyrian purple," or "royal purple," for it was so expensive that it was confined to emperors and nobles. The color was actually a purplish red and was extracted from a tiny sac found in a mollusk which abounded along the coast. It was not until the nineteenth century that the Tyrian purple could be matched.

The Jews were famous for dyeing cloth during Roman times. Tel Dor was 75 acres in size, one of the largest ancient cities in the land. The Hellenistic port city had a population of approximately 20,000. The **CENTER FOR NAUTICAL AND REGIONAL ARCHAEOLOGY** at nearby Kibbutz Nahsholim operates a fascinating museum of underwater archaeology. (See *Biblical Archaeology Review* Jan/Feb 1993, 22-31, 76-78; Mar/Apr 1993, 18-36, 84; May/Jun 1993, 38-49.)

- *The king of Dor was killed in battle with Joshua (Josh. 11:2, 8; 12:7, 23).*
- *The city was administered by Ben-Abinadab for Solomon (1 Kings 4:7, 11).*

Atlit, *Athlit, Chateau de Pelerin*

On the Mediterranean seacoast about 9 miles south of Haifa is the ancient Phoenician port of Atlit. The Crusader fortress Chateau de Pelerin at this site was built in 1217 and destroyed by Baybars in 1291.

Tel Shiqmona, *Sycaminium*

On the tip of Cape Carmel, just south of the city of Haifa, was a Jewish settlement and seat of the sages in the Mishnaic period. There was also a Crusader fort here.

Haifa

Haifa was destroyed by Muslim conquerors in the seventh century, conquered by Crusaders in 1100, and destroyed in 1761 by Taher el Amar. Haifa is Israel's shipbuilding center and third largest city with a population of 251,000. It is one of the most beautifully situated cities in the world, in a setting similar to that of San Francisco. Mount Carmel juts into the Mediterranean Sea at this point. Israel's only underground subway, the **CARMELIT** (a mile long), is located here. Little existed here until 1933, when the British built a modern harbor, the main port in Israel. Now the city has the nation's largest heavy industries. There's an Israeli saying: "Jerusalem prays, Tel Aviv plays, Haifa works."

In 1898, Theodor Herzl, father of Zionism, predicted a future large city at Haifa, and thus it has become.

Thousands have come "home" to the promised land through the port of Haifa.

POINTS OF INTEREST

GERMAN TEMPLER AND MILITARY CEMETERY OF HAIFA

A Christian religious group of Germans from the area of Wurttemberg, Germany, formed a "Templer Society" under the direction of Christoph Hoffmann, and moved to Palestine in 1868, where they established nine settlements. The colony in Haifa was the oldest and largest settlement, and when the first Mormon missionary, **JACOB SPORI**, came to Palestine in 1885, he labored in Haifa among the Templers.[13]

About 20 of the Templers became converts of the Church of Jesus Christ of Latter-day Saints, and a branch of the Church was organized in Haifa. As the converts to the LDS Church died in Haifa, they were buried in the German Templer Cemetery, which also became a military cemetery. It is located on Jaffa Street (Derekh Yafo), a block east of the Egged Bus Station, on the north side of the street.

At least six Latter-day Saints are buried in the German Templer Cemetery:

JOHANN GEORG GRAU, the first convert to the LDS Church in Haifa (1885), and the first known convert in the Holy Land since the times of the apostles. His tombstone is in the northwest corner, in the last row of graves (row 10), 15th grave on the left from the center aisle.

MAGDALENE FREY GRAU, wife of Johann Georg Grau. She has the most significantly Mormon tombstone in the cemetery, with a bas-relief of Moroni with the Book of Mormon, and Revelation 14:6 inscribed. Her tombstone is under an olive tree in the center of the cemetery, in row 7, and grave #7 going to the right from the center.

FRED AUGUST KEGEL, LDS member on row 6, grave #10 going right from the center.

CHRISTIANE SAHRA KEGEL, LDS member on row 6, grave #9 going right from the center.

ADOLF HAAG, missionary from Payson, Utah, died Oct. 3, 1892 of typhus fever. His tombstone has a broken marble column, signifying a life cut short, and is located in row 5, grave #2, on the right.

JOHN A. CLARK, missionary from Farmington, Utah, died Feb. 8, 1895, of smallpox. His tombstone also has a broken marble column, and it is located in row 4, grave #4, on the right.

In addition to these six Latter-day Saints buried in Haifa, there are two Saints buried in Jerusalem: LDS former Templer **HEINRICH VOUKENROTH**, buried in the Templer Cemetery in Jerusalem, and **GARABED KAMAJIAN**, an Armenian who died in 1981 and is buried in the Armenian Cemetery on Mt. Zion.

The **DAGON GRAIN SILO** and **ARCHAEOLOGICAL MUSEUM** display both ancient and modern methods of grain storage. The excellent museum has grains over 4,000 years old. (Dagon was a Philistine god of fish and grain.) The grain silo holds 100,000 tons of grain – largest in the Near East.

ARMENIAN LDS MISSION HOME

The new Turkish Mission with Ferdinand F. Hintze as its first president, lasted from 1885-1909, for 25 years, with mission headquarters in Constantinople and Aintab in Turkey, and Aleppo in Syria. There was no mission in the area from 1909-1921, but from 1921-1928, the Armenian Mission functioned with Wilford Booth as president. During Booth's presidency, the Mission headquarters were moved from Aleppo, Syria, to Haifa in 1927, under the direction of **JAMES E. TALMAGE** of the Quorum of the Twelve. While Talmage was in Haifa organizing the mission, he went to Kaiser's Watch on Mt. Carmel and dedicated Palestine for the return of the Jews. The new rented **MISSION HOME** was only used for one year, because Elder Booth died (he was buried in Aleppo in 1928). Between 1928-1933 there was no mission in the area. The mission home in Haifa is still standing on the southeast corner of the intersection of Allenby and Carmel (now David Ben Gurion) streets.

PALESTINE-SYRIAN LDS MISSION HOME

In May of 1933, a new mission, named the Palestine-Syrian Mission, was opened with headquarters in Haifa. A home that is still standing at 25 Garden Street, became the newly rented **MISSION HOME**. It is northwest of the Armenian Mission Home, through one block, and it too is on the southeast corner of an intersection. It served as mission headquarters with Badwagon Piranian as president for two years until 1935, then the headquarters were moved to Beirut, Lebanon. In Beirut, Joseph Jacobs was the president for two years 1937-1939, then Badwagon Piranian again served from 1947-1950. In 1950 the mission was closed and the area was placed under the direction of the Swiss Austrian Mission.

JOHN A. WIDTSOE of the Quorum of the Twelve came to Haifa and organized the Palestine-Syrian Mission in 1933, and while he was in the Mission Home, on May 21, 1933, he dedicated Palestine for the return of the Jews.

The **BAHA'I SHRINE**, **GARDENS**, and **ARCHIVES BUILDING** mark the world center of the Baha'i faith. This complex is one of Haifa's most impressive attractions. The gold-domed shrine (Tomb of the Bab) is covered with 12,000 fishscale, gold-leafed tiles, and the Universal House of Justice is built in classical Greek style, all with exquisite gardens. Baha'is are the fourth world religion to have a center in the Holy Land. The Baha'i faith began in Persia in the mid-nineteenth century, and its leaders were exiled to Palestine. They claim over 5 million followers in more than 140 countries.

Baha'is believe in the brotherhood of all men, a common world language, one world government, and the unity of all religions. They believe that God reveals universal truths through all religions and that all prophets were sent by God to preach the same message. Krishna, Moses, Zoroaster, Gautama Buddha, Jesus Christ, Muhammad, the Bab, and Baha'ullah have all been divine revelators. The most recent of the prophets was Baha'ullah (1817-92), which name means "the glory of God." He was exiled by Muslim and Turkish authorities to Acre, where he wrote his doctrine and died in the Baha'i House, just outside Acre. In the Haifa Persian Gardens, the huge domed temple entombs the remains of El Bab (Mirza Ali Muhammad), the Baha'ullah's herald, who declared himself to be a prophet or herald of the prophet in 1844 and who suffered a martyr's death in 1850. The word/title "Bab" means "the door" or "the gate."

The **CARMELITE MONASTERY** on the Cape of Carmel served as a hospital to Napoleon's army as they laid siege to Turkish Acre in 1799. **ELIJAH'S CAVE** is a sacred Jewish, Christian, and Muslim site. According to tradition, Elijah hid here when he fled from King Ahab, and Jesus, Mary, and Joseph sought shelter here when they returned from Egypt. The site of the cave is marked by the Carmelite **CHURCH OF STELLA MARIS** (= Star of the Sea).

KAISER'S WATCH. An obelisk about six feet high marks a site on Mt. Carmel known as Kaiser's Watch, where Germany's Kaiser Wilhelm was brought for a panoramic view of the city of Haifa and the Bay of Acre on Oct. 25, 1898.

It is located on the south side of Panorama Road and northwest of the Dan Carmel Hotel, at a point directly above David Ben Gurion Street and the Baha'i Shrine. The red-roofed houses straight below are the oldest in the city, the German Templer quarter established in the late 1860s. The obelisk is dedicated to the Kaiser's visit. The Kaiser met Theodor Herzl, and Herzl predicted Haifa would be a great city in a future state of Israel.

The Ottoman Empire at the time of the First World War was called "the sick man of Europe." It was here in September 1918 that the Ottomans made their last stand. General Allenby prevailed over the resistance and ended four centuries of Turkish rule.

In a little grove of young pine trees, about 70 feet east of the obelisk, the land of **PALESTINE WAS DEDICATED** by two apostles of the Church of Jesus Christ of Latter-day Saints. These men were Francis M. Lyman on March 16, 1902, and James E. Talmage on Oct. 18, 1927. The president of the Armenian Mission, Joseph W. Booth, was with Elder Talmage on this occasion, and Pres. Booth read the following scriptures before Elder Talmage gave the dedicatory prayer: Isaiah 35, 2 Nephi 27, and D&C 133. Elder Talmage then dedicated the city of Haifa as a place for the [new] headquarters of the Armenian Mission, and rededicated the land of Palestine and Syria for the preaching of the restored Gospel, and for the gathering of the Jews to their promised land.

Other places of interest include the **MUNICIPAL MUSEUM OF ANCIENT AND MODERN ART**, the **CHAGALL ARTISTS' HOUSE**, the **JAPANESE ART MUSEUM**, and **ETHNOLOGICAL MUSEUM**, the **MUSEUM OF PREHISTORY**, the **MARITIME MUSEUM**, the **ILLEGAL IMMIGRATION AND NAVAL MUSEUM**, the **CARMELITE MONASTERY**, and the campus of the **TECHNION**, Israel's Institute of Technology.

- *According to tradition, Elijah sought shelter in a cave as he fled from Ahab, perhaps on his way to Zarephath (1 Kings 17:10).*
- *Tradition says the Holy Family sought shelter in Elijah's Cave after returning from Egypt (Matt. 2:20-21).*

Shefaram

This was the seat of the Sanhedrin around A.D. 150. It is 12 miles east of Haifa.

CABUL, Kabul (*"dry," "sandy"*)

Nine miles southeast of Akko was the border city of Asher and Galilee. This is the area transferred to King Hiram by Solomon. It was the first town to be conquered by the Romans during the Jewish revolt of A.D. 66.

- *It is mentioned in the Old Testament (Josh. 19:27).*
- *This was the name given by Hiram to twenty cities of Galilee (1 Kings 9:11-13).*

Yodefat, *Jotapata, Yotapata*

About 8 miles northwest of modern Cana are the ruins of a fortress known as Jotapata. (See map: "West Coast from Joppa to Lebanon.") It was in this fortress that the Jews held out against the Romans in A.D. 66 and where the Jewish military commander/priest/historian Josephus surrendered to the Romans.

ACCHO, Akko, Acre, *Acco, Ptolemais, Tell el Fukhkhar*

Akko is a 4,000-year-old Canaanite and Phoenician port city that commanded the approach from the sea and land to the rich Plain of Jezreel. It is 9 miles north of Haifa and 12 miles south of Lebanon. The Egyptians Thutmose III, Seti I, and Ramses II are among the conquerors of Acre. The Assyrians Sennacherib, Esarhaddon, Ashurbanipal, and several of the Ptolemies engaged in its conquest or defense. It played a part in the history of the Maccabees, and Queen Cleopatra of Egypt held it for a time. Here Herod the Great entertained Caesar. When Alexander the Great conquered the country, the Greeks changed the name of Acre to Ptolemais, and this was the name of the city when it was visited by Paul. After the fall of Jerusalem, Acre was the Crusader capital for 100 years (1187-1287). It was the last place held by the Crusaders in the Holy Land, and was taken by the Saracens (Muslim forces) in 1291. Acre has had 17 recorded sieges, and in 1798 it became famous when the Turkish soldiers at Acre withstood Napoleon's famous siege. The city is famous for the remains of **CRUSADER CONSTRUCTION**.

The most ancient site of Acre is believed to have been located on a mound, Tell el-Fukhkhar, 2 miles east of the sea. The present site dates back to the fourth century B.C.

During the Middle Ages Jewish pilgrims, including Maimonides, the Jewish philosopher, landed at Acre on their way to the holy sites.

A **CITADEL** built by the Turks and used as the central prison by the British during the Mandate houses the **ENGLISH HANGING ROOM**, where members of the Jewish underground forces were put to death. On the second floor is a room where Baha'ullah, founder of the Baha'i sect, was imprisoned by the Turks in 1868. The citadel has been turned into a museum of the national struggle for liberation: the **CITADEL MUSEUM OF HEROISM**.

The **MOSQUE OF EL JAZZAR** is claimed by some to be the largest and most splendid mosque in the land. It was built in 1781 on the ruins of a Saint John's Knights monastery church.

The **KHAN EL UMDAN** was built in 1785 as a caravanserai and is open to visitors. The **BURJ ES-SULTAN** is a well-preserved **CRUSADER FORTRESS**. The **CITY WALLS** are preserved in the neighborhood of the Knights' Hall and it is possible to walk on top of the walls. The **CRYPT OF SAINT JOHN**, near the Mosque of El Jazzar, is of special interest, as is the **MUSEUM**.

Accho and the Mosque of El Jazzar

The **BAHA'I HOUSE**, 1 mile north of Acre, is where the Baha'i sect's leader, Baha'ullah, was placed by the Turks in nominal freedom after he had spent 24 years in the Acre jail. His remains are entombed in the main house. Lovely green grounds surround the building. Some Baha'i followers were imprisoned in the Crusader Prison at Acre.

On the north of Acre is a handsome **AQUEDUCT** built in 1780 by Pasha Ahmad Jazzar over one the Romans left. It originally supplied Acre with water from Galilee Springs.

- *The city was assigned to the tribe of Asher but never conquered (Josh. 19:24-31; Judg. 1:31).*
- *It was called Accho (Judg. 1:31).*
- *Paul stopped here briefly on his final trip to Jerusalem (Acts 21:7).*

Kafr Yasif

This traditional home town of the famous Jewish historian, Flavius Josephus, is located 5 miles northeast of Acre.

Lohamei Hagetaot

Three miles north of Acco is a kibbutz founded in 1949 by Jews from Poland and Lithuania. Because of the active part they took in the revolt of the Jewish ghettos during World War II, the **MUSEUM OF THE HOLOCAUST**, with displays of doomed ghettos and Nazi extermination camps, has been built at the kibbutz.

Shavei Zion

Four miles north of Acre, at Shavei Zion, are relics of an early Christian church, with cross ornaments in floor mosaics.

Nahariya (*"river"*)

Lying on both sides of the stream Gaaton, 5 miles south of the Lebanon-Israel border, is a city founded in 1934 by German Jews fleeing the Hitler regime. It was the first settlement in western Galilee. It has beautiful promenades and beaches. The remains of a Canaanite temple, 3,500 years old, were uncovered next to the beach. Molds for statues of the goddess Asherah of the Sea (Astarte, Ashtoreth) were found. The Gaaton Brook, flanked by stately eucalyptus trees, divides the main boulevard of this beautiful city.

TEL ACHZIB, *Ekdippa, Ez-Zib*

About 2 miles north of Nahariya is Tel Achzib. This is the site of an important Phoenician port which became a part of the inheritance of the tribe of Asher.

- *It was a city of Asher (Josh. 19:29-31).*

- *The natives could not be dislodged (Judg. 1:31).*

Rosh Haniqra, *Ladder of Tyre*

Six miles north of Nahariya, on the shores of the Mediterranean Sea and within a mile of the Lebanon border, is *Rosh Haniqra*, "Cape of the Grotto." The cliff of Rosh Haniqra is the southernmost point of a range of hills running along the Mediterranean seashore; the hills are called the **LADDER OF TYRE**. A legend indicates that Abraham said in effect, "This is the place" for the promised land. Rosh Haniqra has been a passageway for the armies of Alexander the Great, for the Crusaders, and for the Allies in 1914 and 1941. Waves have carved labyrinthine grottos out of the rocky cliff and a cable car takes the visitor down to the white grottos.

Yehiam, *Kibbutz Yehiam, Crusader Fort Judin*

A Crusader castle, built by Teutonic knights of the Order of Templars, is located by Kibbutz Yehiam, 8 miles east of Nahariya. It was restored in the eighteenth century by the local emir. It is a good example of an Ottoman ruler's feudal residence. The fortress fell to the Muslim Mamelukes in 1291, when the Crusader rule came to an end in the Holy Land.

This is a National Parks Authority site.

Montfort

Located 12 miles east-southeast of Nahariya is the castle of the Teutonic knights, Montfort. It was built in 1226 by the Crusaders and was the seat of the Teutonic knights. It was destroyed by Sultan Baybars in 1271. The ruins were excavated by the Metropolitan Museum of Art of New York in 1926.

WEST AND SOUTHWEST OF JERUSALEM

MOZAH, *Moza*, Motza

The village of Motza lies on the western outskirts of Jerusalem. *Motza* comes from the Hebrew verb *yatza*, which means to go out – it's a little town on *the way out* of Jerusalem. The brook of Sorek comes in from the north. Beyond it, on a high ridge, is a large building topped with a minaret, the traditional tomb of Samuel the prophet (Nebi Samwil).

- *It was a town of Benjamin (Josh. 18:21, 26).*

Castel

This hill and its surroundings are a national memorial, at the scene of important battles during the War of Independence in 1948. It is a National Parks Authority site.

Aqua Bella (*"beautiful water"*)

About 1 mile south and east of Abu Ghosh are the ruins of a twelfth-century Crusader monastery named Aqua Bella. This is a National Parks Authority site.

KIRJATH-JEARIM, *Emmaus*, Abu Ghosh, *Kiryat-Yearim* (*"city of forests"*)

This is a small town 9 miles west of Jerusalem, in the mountainous terrain. The **CRUSADER CHURCH** is one of the finest remains of Crusader times and dates back to 1142. It was built on Roman fortress foundations over the top of a spring and called Fontenoid. The site of Abinadab's house is marked by a huge statue of Mary carrying the baby Jesus in her arms. A French **MONASTERY OF THE ARK** was built here in 1924. It is called **OUR LADY OF THE ARK OF THE COVENANT** and is served by the Sisters of Saint Joseph. An old church here has a lovely mosaic floor. A beautiful view of Jerusalem can be obtained here, and as pilgrims come from the west they get their first glimpse of the Holy City.

- *Here Abinadab lived and kept the ark of the covenant for twenty years (1 Sam. 7:1-2; 2 Sam. 6:1-16; 1 Chron. 15:25-29).*
- *David took the ark from here to Jerusalem (2 Sam. 6).*
- *The Crusaders believed this was Emmaus (Luke 24:13).*

BETH HORON (*"place of hollows"*), *Beit Ur el-Foqa, Beit Ur et-Tahta*

Because of its important position guarding the approach to the Jerusalem Corridor, Beth Horon was the scene of many battles. Whoever controlled the Ajalon Valley and the Beth Horon Pass controlled the first line of defense for the

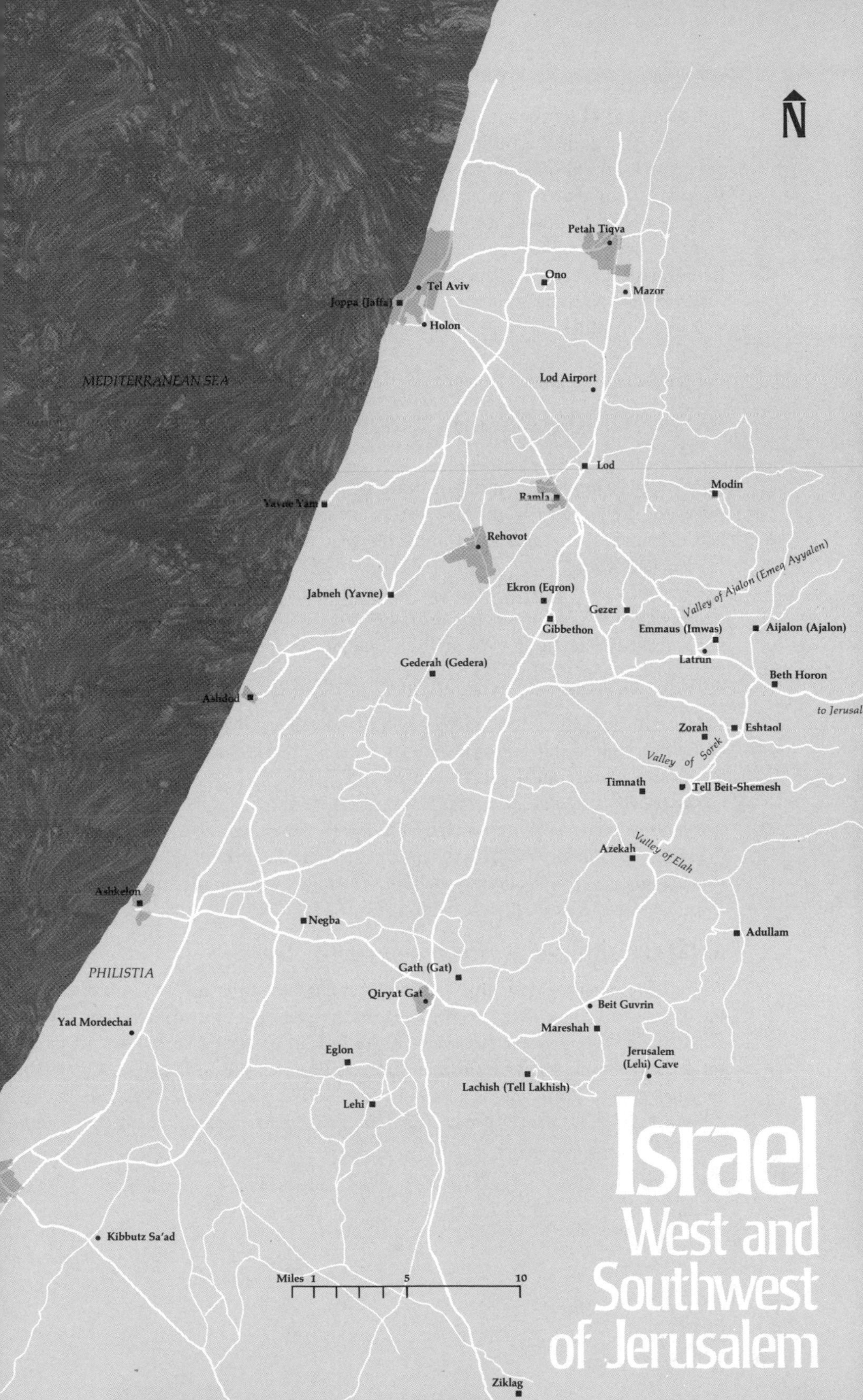

Israel
West and
Southwest
of Jerusalem
N
MEDITERRANEAN SEA
Petah Tiqva
Ono
Mazor
Tel Aviv
Joppa (Jaffa)
Holon
Lod Airport
Lod
Modin
Ramla
Yavne Yam
Rehovot
Valley of Ajalon (Emeq Ayyalen)
Ekron (Eqron)
Jabneh (Yavne)
Gezer
Gibbethon
Emmaus (Imwas)
Aijalon (Ajalon)
Latrun
Gederah (Gedera)
Beth Horon
Ashdod
to Jerusale
Zorah
Eshtaol
Valley of Sorek
Timnath
Tell Beit-Shemesh
Azekah
Valley of Elah
Ashkelon
Negba
Adullam
PHILISTIA
Gath (Gat)
Qiryat Gat
Beit Guvrin
Yad Mordechai
Mareshah
Eglon
Jerusalem (Lehi) Cave
Lachish (Tell Lakhish)
Lehi
Kibbutz Sa'ad
Miles 1 5 10
Ziklag

hill country and Jerusalem. The **BETH HORON PASS** was also Jerusalem's link with her port, Jaffa. It is difficult to over-emphasize the importance of this strategic pass! It is one of history's most important war paths, over which trod the Egyptians, Philistines, Romans, Crusaders, and others. Hellenists were repulsed here by Judah the Maccabee. In A.D. 66 Romans invaded via Beth Horon. The First Crusade marched on Jerusalem via Beth Horon. In 1917 British troops fought hard in stormy weather here.

- *Solomon fortified Beth Horon (2 Chron. 8:5; 1 Kings 9:17).*
- *It was located on the frontier between Benjamin and Ephraim (Josh. 16:3-5; 18:11, 13).*
- *Here Judas Maccabaeus defeated the Syrians (1 Macc. 3:13-24).*

VALLEY OF AJALON, AIJALON, Emeq Ayyalon, *Ayalon* (*Hebrew: "deer"*)

This valley is about 2½ miles northeast of Latrun. It is the widest, gentlest, and easiest of the passages from the coast up into the hill-country. It has served as a battleground for the Israelites, Philistines, Maccabees, Romans, Arabs, Crusaders, British, and Jews.

- *Here Joshua defeated the Amorites; great hailstones killed many, and the sun stood still while the battle was won (Josh. 10:6-27).*
- *In this valley Saul won a victory over the Philistines (1 Sam. 14:31).*

AIJALON, Ajalon (*"place of deer"*), *Yalo, Elon-beth-hanam*

This was an ancient city of Israel located in the Valley of Ajalon 20 miles southeast of Tel Aviv and 14 miles west of Jerusalem. It is mentioned in the Tell el Amarna letters and was occupied as early as 2000 B.C.

- *The tribes of Joseph subdued it (Judg. 1:35).*
- *It later became an Ephraimite city of refuge (1 Chron. 6:67, 69).*
- *Beriah and Shama, who defeated the men of Gath, came from here (1 Chron. 8:13).*
- *It was fortified by Rehoboam (2 Chron. 11:5, 10). It was captured by the Philistines in the time of Ahaz (2 Chron. 28:16, 18).*

EMMAUS, Imwas, *Ammaous, Nicopolis, Amwas*

One mile northeast of Latrun and about 15 miles west of Jerusalem is a traditional site of Jesus' appearance to two travelers on the evening of the resurrection. There are actually three possible locations of the Judean village of Emmaus, and most agree that this one, known in Roman times as Emmaus Nicopolis, since it is about 20 miles west of Jerusalem, is a little far for the disciples to walk to and return in the same day. The name comes from *Hamma*, which means "warm well," and there are several warm wells in the area. Next to a monastery are the ruins of a Byzantine Crusader church.

- *Jesus appeared to two disciples (Luke 24:13-35).*
- *This was the scene of an engagement between Judas Maccabaeus and Gorgias (1 Macc. 3:40, 57; 4:3-27).*
- *It was fortified by Bacchides (1 Macc. 9:50).*

Latrun

Latrun is about 15 miles east of Ramla on the Jerusalem Road. The name Latrun comes from the Latin *Latronis*, which means "thief," from the tradition that the "good thief" crucified with Jesus was from here, and the Crusaders built a castle here based on that tradition. It is a strategic fortress captured by the Israelis in the 1948 war with a loss of over 1,000 soldiers. This fortress guarded the entrance to the Jerusalem Corridor. The battle-cry was "whoever controls Latrun, controls the road to Jerusalem." Since the Jews could not take terrain east of Latrun, the border remained here from 1948 to 1967. From here to the east begins what has been known as the "West Bank." A trappist monastery (with monks that don't speak) is the only other structure that now stands at Latrun. When travelling through the Jerusalem Corridor (Hebrew: *Sha'ar HaGai*; Arabic: *Bab el Wad* – meaning "gate of the wadi"), one should note the overturned tanks and trucks that are now **WAR MEMORIALS** in honor of the men who lost their lives to open the corridor. On the Jerusalem Road note that the mountains are covered with pine and carob (or locust) trees. These are part of an extensive reclamation project, in which over 200,000,000 trees have been planted in recent decades. Note the **TABOR OAKS** in the middle of the highway. They are among the oldest trees in Israel. The Turks destroyed most of the trees in Israel, but because of a weli (Muslim holy place) at this location they preserved these trees.

- *Reforestation is felt to be in fulfillment of Ezekiel's prophecy (Ezek. 36:8).*

GEZER (*"a precipice"*), Tel Gezer

Gezer was a Canaanite stronghold which withstood Joshua's onslaught. Later it was one of Solomon's fortified cities, along with Megiddo and Hazor.

In 1908 at Tel Gezer, 20 miles west-northwest of Jerusalem and 2 miles south of the main road, the British Palestine Exploration Fund, headed by R.A.S. Macalister, discovered a small 4½-by-2¾-inch inscribed limestone tablet now called the **GEZER CALENDAR**. It is dated to the tenth century B.C. and is the most ancient inscription in early Hebrew writing – dating back to the time of Saul or David. The inscription is an agriculture calendar telling what crops were harvested during certain months. The Gezer Calendar is located in the Archaeological Museum in Istanbul.

Standing at a Canaanite high place at Gezer are **CULT PILLARS**, representing pagan deities. A great **WATER TUNNEL** at Gezer dates back to about 1500 B.C. The late Nelson Glueck, one-time president of Hebrew Union College in Jerusalem, did archaeological work at the site, and more recently William Dever has been directing the archaeological work here. A relief was found at Nimrod showing Gezer being besieged by Assyrian troops about 732 B.C.

(See *Biblical Archaeology Review* Jul/Aug 1983, 30-42; May/Jun 1994, 66-69.)

- *Joshua defeated Horam, king of Gezer, but failed to capture the city itself (Josh. 10:33).*
- *An Egyptian pharaoh gave the city as a dowry for his daughter, one of King Solomon's wives (1 Kings 9:16).*
- *Solomon rebuilt the city as one of his fortified cities, like Megiddo and Hazor (1 Kings 9:15-19).*
- *Cult pillars were perhaps the graven images spoken of by Micah (Micah 5:13).*
- *Gezer was occupied, cleansed, and fortified by Simon the Maccabaean in 142 B.C. (1 Macc. 13:43-48).*

EKRON, Eqron, TEL MIQNE, *Akir, Khirbet el-Muqanna*

This was the most northerly of 5 principal Philistine cities – located 15 miles southeast of Joppa. The Philistines brought the captured ark of the covenant to Ekron, and from here it was sent back. Ekron was destroyed in 711 B.C. by the Assyrians. (See *Biblical Archaeology Review* Jan/Feb 1990, 20-36; Mar/Apr 1990, 32-42, 59.)

- *When Joshua was old, Ekron still remained to be subdued (Josh. 13:3); it was allotted to Judah (Josh. 15:11-12, 21, 45-46) and then to Dan (Josh. 19:40-43).*
- *It was prominent in connection with Philistine suffering on account of the ark (1 Sam. 5-6).*
- *Israel pursued the Philistines to Ekron after David killed Goliath (1 Sam. 17:52).*
- *Beelzebub was worshiped here (2 Kings 1).*
- *It was denounced by the prophets (Jer. 25:15-17, 20; Amos 1:8; Zeph. 2:4; Zech. 9:5-7).*

GIBBETHON (*"mound"*), Tel Malot, *Tell el-Melat*

This was a town that belonged to Dan. It is a mile southeast of Ekron.

- *It was located in territory of Dan (Josh. 19:40, 44).*
- *It was appointed as a Levitical city (Josh. 21:20, 23).*
- *While Nadab was besieging the city he was assassinated by Baasha (1 Kings 15:25-27).*
- *Omri was besieging it when Zimri assassinated Elah (1 Kings 16:15-16).*

MODI'IN, *Modim*

This was the place of origin of the Maccabees, with whom 18 tombs cut into the rocks are associated. It is near Aphek and 6 miles east of Lod. Each year at Hanukkah, the Feast of Lights, a torch is kindled at this spot and carried by relay runners to Mount Herzl, Jerusalem, where it is used to light a great menorah symbolizing that which was relit by Judas Maccabaeus in the Temple in 165 B.C.

- *The Maccabees lived at Modi'in (1 Macc. 2).*

Neot Kedumim

Located midway between Tel Aviv and Jerusalem, in the Ben-Shemen Forest of the Modi'in Region, is the world's only **BIBLICAL LANDSCAPE RESERVE**, with 625 acres of gardens and three major trails taking hikers back to their biblical roots. Tens of thousands of trees, shrubs, and flowers have been planted in recent decades to study the flora of the Bible and Talmud. The vast network of gardens includes the "Oaks of Abraham and Sarah," "Jordan River thickets," "Valley of Jericho," "Forest of Milk and Honey," "Vineyard of Isaiah," "Hill of Jeremiah," "Garden of Choice Products," "Seven Varieties," "Four Species of Sukkot," "Wisdom Literature," "Dale of the Song of Songs," "Carmel Forest," "Ascent of the Spices," "Hill of the Menorah," "The Desert and the Wilderness," and "The Garden of the Sages."

Ramla (*"sand"*)

This "newest" of the old cities of Israel lies 2 miles southwest of Lod and 10 miles southeast of Tel Aviv. It is the only city built by conquering Muslims in Palestine. A clock-faced tower marks the **HOSPICE OF SAINT NICODEMUS AND SAINT JOSEPH OF ARIMATHEA** on the main street, Herzl Avenue. The Crusaders believed that Joseph of Arimathea lived here, and it is also believed that Napoleon "slept here" when he attempted in vain to conquer Palestine from the Turks. The **POOL OF SAINT HELENA**, near the police station and Main Street, is an eighth-century reservoir or underground cistern. It was built by the legendary caliph Harun al-Rashid of *A Thousand and One Nights* fame and is named after Saint Helena, mother of Constantine. Visitors can ride a gondola on its waters. The **GREAT MOSQUE** in Ramla is one of Israel's best examples of Crusader architecture. The **WHITE TOWER** was built in the fourteenth century as a minaret of the white mosque which had been built earlier. A view from its top is desirable.

- *One tradition says this was Joseph of Arimathea's home (John 19:38).*

LOD, *Lydda, Diospolis*

Eleven miles southeast of Joppa is the city of Lod, twin of Ramla. According to tradition, Lod was a fortified town in the days of Joshua and was rebuilt by descendants of the tribe of Benjamin. The Greeks changed the name to Lydda. In A.D. 70 the Romans burned the town.

During the second and third centuries Lod was famous as a seat of Jewish learning and housed an academy.

Lod is the legendary city of Saint George, who, according to tradition, was buried here in A.D. 303 after he was martyred by the Romans for tearing down the anti-Christian edicts of the Roman emperor. The **SAINT GEORGE CHURCH** is named in his honor, and after his death the name of the city was changed to *Georgeospolis.*

Lod is the location of Israel's International **BEN-GURION AIRPORT**. (The airport is actually 3 miles north of the city.) This airport is the home of El Al Airlines and is 32 miles from Jerusalem.

- *It was founded by Shemed, a Benjaminite (1 Chron. 8:1, 12; Neh. 11:31-35).*
- *Some natives settled here after their captivity in Babylon (Ezra 2:1, 33; Neh. 7:6, 37).*
- *Peter healed Aeneas (Acts 9:32-35).*

Mazor

Ten miles east of the seacoast and Tel Aviv is this Roman mausoleum of the second or third century A.D.

ONO (*"strong"*)

This was an ancient fortified town built by the "sons of Elpaal." It was located about 5 miles east of the seacoast, east of Tel Aviv.

- *It was a Benjaminite city (1 Chron. 8:1, 12).*
- *Nehemiah was invited to a treacherous conference here (Neh. 6:2).*
- *It was reoccupied after the exile (Neh. 7:6, 37; 11:35).*

Note: From this point the biblical sites and places of interest are listed in an order from the Valley of Sorek south to Lehi, west to Gaza, and north to Joppa.

VALLEY OF SOREK (*"vineyard"*), *Nahal Kesloh, Wadi es-Sarar*

The name Sorek comes from Isaiah 5:2 - "choicest vine." This was the valley in which Delilah lived, and is 14 miles west of Jerusalem.

East of the Sorek Valley and the city of Beth-shemesh is the recently discovered **SOREK CAVE**, with an impressive display of natural stalagmites and stalactites.

- *Eshtaol and Zorah were in or near the Sorek Valley (Judg. 13:25; 14:1-2).*
- *Here Samson and his parents lived and here he met and succumbed to the enticements of Delilah (Judg. 16:4-21).*

ESHTAOL (*"hollow way"*), *Eshwa*

This was a lowland city of Judah, 13 miles west of Jerusalem and 2½ miles south of the main road from Jerusalem to Tel Aviv. It was inherited by the tribe of Dan in biblical days and was reestablished in 1949.

- *It was a city of the lowland (Shephelah) of Judah (Josh. 15:21, 33).*
- *It was near here that Samson was buried (Judg. 16:30-31).*
- *It was the home of some of the Danites who attacked Laish (Judg. 18:2, 11, 27).*

ZORAH (*"prominent," "wasp"*)

This was a town on the top of a high hill on the north side of the Valley of Sorek, 14 miles southwest of Jerusalem and just west of Eshtaol.

- *It was allotted to Judah (Josh. 15:21, 33).*
- *It was the birthplace of Samson (Judg. 13:2, 25).*
- *Samson was buried between Zorah and Eshtaol (Judg 16:31).*
- *Zorah was fortified by Rehoboam (2 Chron. 11:5, 10).*
- *It was repopulated after the exile (Neh. 11:29).*

BETH-SHEMESH (*"temple of the sun"*), *Ain Shems*, **Tel Beit-Shemesh**

This was a Canaanite town dedicated to the worship of the sun-god. Later it was a town of Judah called *Ir-Shemesh* and allotted to the children of Aaron. It was located on the south slope of the Sorek Valley, 15 miles west of Jerusalem. Excavation by the British Palestine Exploration Fund (1911-12) and Haverford College in Pennsylvania (1928-33) have shown evidence of occupation from 3000 B.C. until its destruction by Nebuchadnezzar in the sixth century B.C. Casemate walls of the early iron age probably indicate David's fortifications against the Philistines.

- *The ark was returned here from the Philistines by the men of Ekron (1 Sam. 6:7-21).*
- *Amaziah of Judah was defeated and captured by Jehoash, king of Israel (2 Kings 14:11-14; 2 Chron. 25:17-24).*
- *It was one of the cities of Judah taken by the Philistines in the time of Ahaz (2 Chron. 28:16, 18).*

TIMNATH, *Khirbet Timna, Khirbet Tibneh, Tel Batash*

This was a city on the northern frontier of the tribe of Judah, between Beth-shemesh and Ekron to the west, or 2 miles southwest of Beth-shemesh. (See *Biblical Archaeology Review* Jan/Feb 1989, 36-49.)

- *Its location is given in the Bible (Josh. 15:10).*

- *Here Samson celebrated his marriage, which seems to have been the beginning of his downfall; he also killed a lion here (Judg. 14:1-15:6).*
- *The town was held by Israelites in the reign of Uzziah but was lost to the Philistines by Ahaz (2 Chron. 28:16, 18).*

AZEKAH (*"breach"*), **Kefar-Zekharia**, *Tell Zakariyeh*

This was a city in the lowland of Judah (Shephelah), overlooking the Valley of Elah. It stood on the high hill opposite Kefar Zekharia. With the exception of Lachish, it was the last stronghold to be captured by Nebuchadnezzar before the fall of Jerusalem in 586 B.C. In the Lachish letter number 4, reference is made to the cessation of fire signals from Azekah, presumably an indication of its fall while Lachish still held out.

- *It was located in Judah, overlooking the Valley of Elah (Josh. 15:21, 35; 1 Sam. 17:1-3).*
- *Joshua defeated Canaanite kings here (Josh. 10:5, 10).*
- *It was fortified by Rehoboam (2 Chron. 11:5, 9).*

VALLEY OF ELAH (*"oak trees"*), *Wadi es-Sant*

This is a valley in the Shephelah, the scene of the battle between David and Goliath. It lies 20 miles southwest of Jerusalem and just east of Azekah. The valley gets its name from elah trees in the area. The stream bed stretches eastward toward Bethlehem. It is dry except in the winter. David *had* to challenge the giant bully because if the Elah Valley fell to the Philistines, their next objective would be Bethlehem, his home town, or Hebron, where he would soon reign as king, or Gibeah, the capital of the country. If he didn't stop the Philistines right then and there, he might have no country to rule. The Philistine incursion into the Elah Valley represented a real threat to David's homeland – they had to be stopped. Skill and faith combined to overcome.

A few minutes' drive south of the Elah Valley, on the west side of the road, some Roman-period **MILESTONES** have been set up together. The Romans built about 1,500 kilometers of major roads in Judea. The largest group of milestones which has survived (about 25) dates from the reign of Marcus Aurelius. Other milestones and portions of the Roman Road may be seen on the east side of the valley while traveling toward Beit Guvrin.

- *Here in the Elah Valley, David killed Goliath (1 Sam. 17; 21:9).*

ADULLAM (*"resting place"*), *Tell esh-Sheikh Madhkur*

This was a city in the Shephelah assigned to Judah (Josh. 15:35). It was 16 miles southwest of Jerusalem.

- *Judah's friend, Hirah, came from here (Gen. 38:1, 12, 20).*

- *It was formerly a Canaanite city (Josh. 12:8, 15).*
- *Rehoboam fortified it (2 Chron. 11:5, 7).*
- *The children of Israel returned to it after the Exile (Neh. 11:30).*
- *The cave of Adullam, where David hid, must have been in an adjoining valley (1 Sam. 22:1; 2 Sam. 23:13).*
- *Micah predicted that the glory of Israel would seek refuge here (Mic. 1:15).*

Khirbet Midras

Located about 8 km. north of Beit Guvrin/Eleutheropolis (between 5 and 6 km. markers), a dirt road turns eastward up to a fence; a few steps beyond the fence are paths leading to the right, to a tomb. Flashlights are helpful. Here is a 1st century B. C. tomb with a large, heavy **ROLLING STONE** in front; the best example in the country of what Jesus' tomb could have been like. Note the antechamber with burial niches (Heb. *kokhim*) and inner chamber with sarcophagi still on shelves – elements of both 1st and 2nd Temple-period tombs. *Sarcophagus* means "flesh eater;" flesh decays off bones in the stone casket. *Ossuary* means "bone eater;" after the flesh decays away, bones are reinterred in a smaller casket (space is precious in this land.)

After visiting the tomb, visitors may walk one minute to the north and a short distance down the slope and enter a **COLUMBARIUM**. According to Israeli archaeologist Amos Kloner, columbaria were used either for cultic sacrifice, the worship of Aphrodite at Ashkelon, or production of manure from the doves, or for meat of the doves for food. According to Kloner, they were not used by people for refuge.

Beit Guvrin, "Bell Caves," *Eleutheropolis, Gibelin, Beit Jibril*

One mile north of Tel Maresha, ½ mile southeast of the modern settlement of Beit Guvrin, and 7 miles east of Qiryat Gat was a large important Roman town. In A.D. 200 Emperor Septimius Severus visited Beit Guvrin and granted the inhabitants special privileges. He established a Roman Colony and gave it the largest area of any city in Palestine: from En Gedi to Gerar. It was the most important city in Idumea. Its name was changed to *Eleutheropolis* ("city of liberty"). Eleutheropolis was used as a reference point for Eusebius' and Jerome's *Onomastikon*, a 4th century A.D. list of biblical toponyms. The Crusaders named the city Gibelin, and in the Middle Ages it was called *Beit Jibril* ("house of Gabriel"). Third-century **JEWISH RUINS**, beautiful **MOSAICS**, and **CRUSADER RUINS** have been found. The mosaics are in the Israel National Museum.

In the area are some 800 **CAVES** dating back to the Roman and Byzantine periods. The purpose of the man-made caves is uncertain. They are shaped like a bell or beehive and have round holes at the top. Chisel marks and Christian

Bell Cave, Beit Guvrin

crosses are plainly seen on some of the walls. It is believed by some that clay was taken from these caves to build the walls around Ashkelon. Most of the quarrying was done between the 7-10 centuries A.D., apparently by Christian Arabs. This is a National Parks Authority site.

MARESHAH (*"possession"*), Tel Maresha, *Marissa, Tell es-Sandahannah*

This ancient biblical site is located 1 mile south of Beit Guvrin, 3½ miles northeast of Tel Lachish, and 7 miles east of Qiryat Gat. It was excavated by Bliss, and pottery found here dated back to 800 B.C. It served as a base for Seleucid operations against Judas Maccabaeus and his family. (See 1 Macc. 5:66, in which *Maresha* should be read for *Samaria.*) It was finally destroyed by the Parthians in 40 B.C.

West and south of Tel Maresha is an intricate network of **CAVES** and subterranean houses, baths, agricultural facilities, and water cisterns, most dating from the 2nd and 3rd centuries B.C. There are also at least 60 **COLUMBARIA**. The

Latin word *columbarium* means "dovecote," or place for raising pigeons. Pigeons were raised for food and religious rituals and their droppings were used as fertilizer. One large columbarium has over 2,000 nesting coves. Twenty underground oil presses have been found, and some have been restored. To the east of the tel of Maresha/Marissa are the Sidonian Burial Caves, with paintings, drawings, and inscriptions. The burial caves have the typical 2nd Temple period niches (*kokhim*) common in Roman Judea. Bodies were placed inside each one – until with decomposition only bones remain, and bones could then be placed in a repository and the niche reused for generations. Maresha and vicinity are included in the Beit Guvrin National Parks Authority site.

- *This was a town in the lowland of Judah (Shephelah) fortified by Rehoboam (Josh. 15:21, 44; 2 Chron. 11:5, 8).*
- *Asa conquered a million Ethiopians (2 Chron. 14:9-13).*
- *Micah prophesied: "Yet will I bring an heir unto thee" (Mic. 1:15).*

LACHISH (*"height"*), Tel Lakhish, *Lakhish, Tell ed-Duweir*

The biblical city of Lachish lies 20 miles inland from Ashkelon and 6 miles southeast of Qiryat Gat. Excavations show that the Late Bronze Age city was destroyed by fire, as described in the Old Testament. After Joshua conquered the city it became a city of Judah on the border of Philistia (Josh. 15:21, 39). Lachish was important because it guarded the approaches to the Judean hills and Jerusalem to the north and Egypt to the south. This whole region called the Shephelah ("low

Tell Lakhish

hills") served as a buffer zone/battle ground for the ancient Judahites living in the hill country. The Shephelah was Judah's first line of defense; important fortress cities like Lachish guarded the hills from incursions by foreign enemies. Today Lachish is merely a tel. The town of Lachish is referred to several times in the Tell el Amarna letters.

During the Judean Monarchy, Lachish featured a **PALACE-FORTRESS** atop the city mound which is the largest, most massive, and most impressive structure of the Israelite period yet known in the Holy Land. This building must have been a central governmental or royal palace-fortress in the kingdom of Judah. It was possibly founded by Rehoboam, who fortified Lachish (see 2 Chron. 11:9), and likely continued in use until its destruction by Sennacherib in 701 B. C. It may be associated with a biblical event: in about 769 B.C. King Amaziah fled to Lachish when a revolt against him erupted in Jerusalem. The rebels "sent after him to Lachish and slew him there" (2 Kings 14:19; 2 Chron. 25:27). The king probably took refuge in the palace-fortress and was murdered here.

In 701 B.C. the Assyrian king Sennacherib personally led an attack against Lachish and conquered it on his way to besiege Jerusalem during Hezekiah's reign. During the siege of Lachish Sennacherib sent his emissaries to harass Hezekiah and the Jews at Jerusalem. **RELIEFS** on the walls of Sennacherib's palace at Nineveh carefully depicted his method of conquering Lachish. The bas-reliefs, portraying archers, spearmen, slingers, chariots, and horsemen, are now housed in the British Museum in London. Copies of Sennacherib's reliefs are located in the Israel Museum in Jerusalem.

The *Taylor Prism*, found at Nineveh, also tells of Sennacherib's sieges of 46 walled cities and fortified positions in Canaan in this campaign.

From the Prism the following account of his view of the campaign is excerpted: "As to Hezekiah, the Jew, he did not submit to my yoke, I laid siege to 46 of his strong cities, walled forts and to the countless small villages in their vicinity, and conquered (them) by means of well-stamped (earth-)ramps, and battering-rams brought (thus) near (to the walls)(combined with) the attack by foot soldiers, (using) mines, breeches as well as sapper work. I drove out (of them) 200,150 people, young and old, male and female, horses, mules, donkeys, camels, big and small cattle beyond counting, and considered (them) booty. Himself I made a prisoner in Jerusalem, his royal residence, like a bird in a cage. I surrounded him with earthwork in order to molest those who were leaving his city's gate." (*Ancient Near Eastern Texts Relating to the Old Testament* p. 288, translation by W. F. Albright; cf. D. Winton Thomas, *Documents from Old Testament Times*, 64-69.)

The tel was excavated in the 1930's by an American archaeologist, J. L. Starkey. Near the entrance he found objects from the Assyrian assault, such as iron arrowheads, scale armor, and an Assyrian helmet with a crest of bronze. At the gate (the largest and most massive city gate from the Israelite period yet found in the Holy Land), he also found some inscribed potsherds (18 ostraca) known as the *Lachish Letters* (ca. 588 B.C.) – military correspondence exchanged between the cities of Lachish, Azekah, and Jerusalem as they were being besieged by Nebuchadnezzar. The letters corroborate the Bible story. Lachish was one of the last cities to hold out against Nebuchadnezzar but was finally defeated and destroyed.

Starkey was killed by Arab robbers on his way to Jerusalem shortly after his discoveries, and the digging on this site was not resumed until 1973. Under the direction of Prof. David Ussishkin of the Institute of Archaeology at Tel Aviv University, excavations continued through 1987, and renovation and reconstruction work continues. Among other things, Ussishkin's team cleared the southwest corner of the mound, exposing the **ASSYRIAN SIEGE RAMP** (the most ancient siege ramp found in the Near East, and the only archaeologically attested Assyrian siege ramp).

The Lachish Letters were written during Jeremiah's time. The ostraca provide one of the earliest external Israelite witnesses for the full form of the tetragrammaton, *YHWH* (Jehovah or Yahweh).

(See *Biblical Archaeology Review* Jan/Feb 1987, 18-39; Mar/Apr 1988, 42-47.)

- *Joshua completely destroyed the inhabitants of Lachish (Josh. 10:31-33).*
- *Rehoboam strengthened its defenses about 921 B.C. (2 Chron. 11:5-12).*
- *The Judahite king Amaziah was murdered here (2 Kings 14:17, 19).*
- *The Assyrian king Sennacherib attacked Lachish and sent emissaries to parley with Hezekiah (2 Kings 18:13-17).*
- *The reconstructed city was one of the last cities of Judah to hold out against Babylon, but it was destroyed by Nebuchadnezzar ca. 588 B.C. (Jer. 34:7; cf. Lachish Letters).*
- *Lachish was resettled by Jews after the captivity in Babylon (Neh. 11:30).*
- *Micah denounced Lachish as "the beginning of the sin to the daughter of Zion" (Mic. 1:13).*

The Hazan Caverns

Two kilometers south of Moshav Amaziah are the Hazan Caverns, a fantastic array of underground hiding places from the 2nd Temple period, at the time of the Bar Kokhba rebellion. They were discovered in 1980 and are composed of 35 hollowed-out areas connected by caves and passages, carved at different levels, and extending more than 220 meters in length.

The Hazan Caverns date to the 1st century A. D. and were used for storing over 10,000 liters of olive oil. In preparation for the Bar Kokhba revolt, the site was reorganized to serve as an underground hiding place. During the Byzantine period production of oil was renewed.

Jerusalem Cave, *Khirbet Beit Lei (Bayt Layy)*

Near Amazia, at the western foot of the Judean range of mountains, 22 miles southwest of Jerusalem, 10 miles west of Hebron, 5 miles east of Tel Lachish, on the eastern slope of the hill of Khirbet Beit Lei, is an ancient rock-cut burial cave called the Jerusalem Cave. It is located on what was anciently the border between Judah and the Philistines.

The cave was uncovered in 1961 during road construction operations. Excavations were carried out in June of 1961 under the direction of Dr. Joseph Naveh of the Israel Department of Antiquities.

The cave is named the *Jerusalem Cave* because it featured the earliest mention of Jerusalem in a Hebrew inscription.

In the soft limestone cave were three chambers, two of which had three benches in each. On the benches were found human bones and jewelry. The entrance to the cave was blocked by large stones.

Of particular interest in the cave are the drawings on the walls: three human figures, two ships, circles, and Hebrew inscriptions. One of the figures is of a man apparently holding a lyre, and the other man is shown raising his hands as though in prayer. One of the Hebrew inscriptions reads as follows, according to Dr. Naveh:

> *Yahveh (is) the God of the whole earth; the mountains of Judah belong to him, to the God of Jerusalem.*

Frank Cross, Jr., has interpreted the Hebrew letters a little differently. It is especially important to note that it is written in the first person:

> *I am Yahweh thy God: I will accept the cities of Judah and will redeem Jerusalem.*

The other two inscriptions read:

> *Exalt us, O merciful God!*
> *Deliver us, Lord!*

The form or style of this burial cave dates back to the pre-Babylonian exile period in Jewish history, and through archaeology, paleography, and history it has been suggested by some that the sixth century B.C. is the date of the drawings and writings on the walls.

Frank Cross, Jr., feels that the Hebrew inscriptions are not funerary in nature but were placed here by chance visitors, refugees, or travelers who took shelter in the cave. One inscription is a petition for deliverance, another is a plea to be spared from guilt or punishment, and the third is in the form of a prophetic oracle in which Yahweh speaks in the first person in poetic form. The couplet is reminiscent of Jeremiah. Cross indicates that it is difficult to avoid speculation that one inscription is the citation of a lost prophecy and that the companion inscriptions were written by a refugee fleeing the Babylonians who conquered Judah and destroyed Jerusalem in 586 B.C. Cross suggested that we should suppress the temptation to consider the oracle and the petitions the work of a prophet or his scribe fleeing Jerusalem.

The Israel Department of Antiquities preserved the portions of the walls of the cave that contain the inscriptions, and they are presently exhibited in the National Museum in Jerusalem.

Some Latter-day Saints and non-Latter-day Saints have wondered, since the figure of a man appears to have arms extended toward heaven and an inscription speaks of the God of Judah in Jerusalem, and because the graffiti are so hastily scrawled on the cave walls, and there is even the semblance of a ship, that perhaps this could have been the work of the Prophet Lehi and company fleeing Jerusalem on their way to the Red Sea in the year 600 B. C. Some rather elaborate "evidences" have been devised to support claims about this supposed "Lehi Cave." However, (1) There is no evidence that the cave's incisions date to 600 B.C. Some scholars have suggested that the cave's temporary tenants could have been refugees from the Babylonians during the war atmosphere of the late seventh century B.C., but others have proposed that the refugees were fleeing the Assyrians a century earlier. (2) There is no evidence that Lehi or anyone else heading toward the Red Sea would have traveled *southwest* instead of southeast; indeed, *The Book of Mormon* specifies that they abandoned their home in the land of Jerusalem and fled *into the wilderness*, in a route southeast. (3) There is no evidence that Lehi and group knew anything about the future prospect of building a ship; that was yet eight years away. (For more information about the moribund controversies over this cave and its graffiti, see LaMar C. Berrett, "The So-called Lehi Cave," unpublished manuscript circulated by the Foundation for Ancient Research and Mormon Studies.)

GATH ("*wine press*"), Gat, *Tell es-Safi*

This ancient city of the Philistine Pentapolis ("five cities") is believed to have been over a mile west of the city of Azekah, near the mouth of the Valley of Elah.

- *Here Anakim took refuge (Josh. 11:22).*
- *The ark was brought here from Ashdod (1 Sam. 5:8).*
- *It was the home of Goliath (1 Sam. 17:4; 2 Sam. 21:19).*
- *David took refuge here when persecuted by Saul (1 Sam. 21:10).*
- *It was captured by David (1 Chron. 18:1).*
- *It was rebuilt by Rehoboam (2 Chron. 11:5-12).*
- *It was destroyed by Uzziah (2 Chron. 26:1-6).*

- *It was captured by Hazael of Damascus, Syria (2 Kings 12:17).*
- *It was referred to by Amos and Micah (Amos 6:2; Mic. 1:10).*

EGLON, Khirbet Egla, *Tell el-Hessi (Hasi)*

This conical mound on the bank of Nahal Shikma – Sycomore Brook – was probably the Eglon of biblical days. It was an important fortified city.

In 1892 the British Palestine Exploration Fund excavated the hill. This was the first archaeological research to be done outside the limits of Jerusalem in Palestine. Clay tablets with cuneiform writing dating back to 1450 B.C. were found at Eglon.

- *It is mentioned in connection with Joshua's campaigns (Josh. 10:3-5; 12:12).*
- *King Debir of Eglon joined forces with five other kings against the Gibeonites (Josh. 10:3).*

ZIKLAG, Ziglag (*"winding"*), *Tell Tsiglag, Tel Sera*

This site is about 40 miles southwest of Jerusalem, directly south of Tell el-Hessi, and just east of Tel Haror.

- *It was given by Achish, the Philistine king, to David for a residence (1 Sam. 27:6-12; 1 Chron. 12:1, 20).*
- *It was raided by the Amalekites, on whom David took vengeance (1 Sam. 30:14-26).*
- *The messenger that announced the death of Saul was slain here (2 Sam. 1:1-16; 4:10).*
- *It is mentioned in a list of the postexiles (Neh. 11:28).*

Urim (*"lights"*)

About 8 miles southwest of the Gilat crossroads, on the main road between Gaza and Beersheba, is Urim, a communal settlement founded in 1948. Many Jewish pioneers of this settlement are from the United States.

- *The scriptures mention the Urim along with the Thummim as being in the high priest's breastplate and giving an oracular response (Exod. 28:30; Lev. 8:8; Num. 27:21; Deut. 33:8; 1 Sam. 28:6; Ezra 2:63; Neh. 7:65).*
- *The Urim and Thummim were used by Joseph Smith to help him translate the Book of Mormon (D&C 10:1; see also 17:1).*

BETH-PHELET, Tel Sharuhen, *Saruhen, Tell Fara - South*

Five miles southwest of Urim and 12 miles southeast of Khan Yunis is the site of the ancient Sharuhen, a town in the area of the tribe of Simeon, but later assimilated into Judah. In ancient Egyptian records this city is named as the scene of a great victory of the Egyptians over the Hyksos. Flinders Petrie excavated here in

1930 and felt it was the ancient biblical site of Beth-Phelet. This conclusion is questioned, however. Carvings on ivory found at the site date back to 1200 B.C.

- *It was a town of Judah (Josh. 15:21, 27; Neh. 11:25-26).*

Rafa, *Rafah*

Five miles southwest of Khan Yunis is Rafa, the starting-point for the Assyrian conquest of Egypt by Esarhaddon in 671 B.C. It was here that Cleopatra married Mark Antony.

Khan Yunis

This town, 15 miles southwest of Gaza, dates back to a Mameluke settlement but was built on foundations of an older settlement.

GERAR, Tel Haror

Gerar is believed to be located at the site on Israeli maps called Tel Haror Migdal, the site which has been known for centuries as Tel Abu Hureireh, and recently supposed to be the site of biblical Gerar.

- *Here Abraham met the king of Gerar, Abimelech (Gen. 20).*
- *It was here that Abraham reported that his wife was his sister (Gen. 20).*
- *Here Isaac reported that his wife, Rebekah, was his sister (Gen. 26:6-16).*
- *Here wells were dug by Abraham and reopened by Isaac (Gen. 26:17-22).*
- *Part of David's army remained at the brook Besor while he attacked the Amalekites (1 Sam. 30:9-10).*

Kibbutz Sa'ad

This is a religion-centered kibbutz, with a new synagogue, a beautiful lawn, and flowers. It is 4 miles southeast of Gaza, on the road to Beersheba.

PHILISTIA (*"migration"*)

This southern coastal region of Canaan was occupied by the Philistines, who were non-Semitic.

- *During the time of Eli the Philistines conquered the Israelites and captured the ark (1 Sam. 4).*
- *A plague forced them to return the ark (1 Sam. 6).*
- *Here the Philistines worked iron (1 Sam. 13:19).*
- *Sargon marched against Philistia and captured Ashdod (Isa. 20:1).*
- *Later Hezekiah smote the Philistines (2 Kings 18:8).*

GAZA (*"the strong place"*), *Ghezzeh, Azzah*

Gaza, an Arab town, is probably the oldest and most important of the 5 principal Philistine cities. It is 40 miles south of Joppa and is the last important city on the seacoast as the traveler goes south and west toward Cairo. George Adam Smith called Gaza "the outpost of Africa, the door of Asia." It was controlled by Egypt, Assyria, and then Alexander the Great, who captured it in 332 B.C. and killed all of its men and sold the women and children into slavery. It has been the scene of the martyrdom of many Christians. During World War I it was the main base of the Turks. The British lost about 10,000 men in capturing the city. In the six-day war of 1967 it was the scene of much bloodshed among Egyptians, Arab Palestinians, and Israelis.

- *It was a prominent city of Canaan in early times (Gen. 10:19).*
- *Joshua reached but did not conquer it (Josh. 10:41; 11:22).*
- *It was given to Judah and captured by them (Josh. 15:47; Judg. 1:18).*
- *The Bible tells of Samson's exploits here. He took the city gates to Hebron – 40 miles away. He was imprisoned in Gaza, was blinded, and met his death here (Judg. 16).*
- *The Philistines presented a trespass offering to Jehovah (1 Sam. 6:17).*
- *Hezekiah defeated the Philistines at Gaza (2 Kings 18:8).*
- *It was occupied by Pharaoh Necho (Jer. 47:1).*
- *It was prophesied against (Amos 1:7; Zeph. 2:4).*
- *Philip went toward Gaza. On the way he met and baptized the Ethiopian eunuch (Acts 8:26-27).*

Yad Mordechai

About 7½ miles south of Ashkelon is Yad Mordechai, a kibbutz established in 1943 and known for its resistance to Egyptian armored divisions in 1948. A reconstructed **BATTLEFIELD**, with tanks and men, is realistically displayed. A beautiful, modern **MUSEUM** is worth visiting.

This is a National Parks Authority site.

ASHKELON (*"holm oak"*), *Khirbet Asqalan*

One of the oldest known Canaanite cities in the world (2000 B.C.) became the Philistine city of Ashkelon, the only Philistine city built on the coast with a harbor. The Tell el Amarna letters (fourteenth century B.C.) mention Ashkelon as a rich but rebellious city. Pharaoh Ramses II recorded the capture of this city on a thirteenth-century B.C. bas-relief at Karnak, in upper Egypt. The carved picture shows Egyptian soldiers storming the fortified city with the help of ladders, while the bearded Ashkelonite defenders man the walls.

Under Roman rule many beautiful buildings were constructed in Ashkelon. It was the seat of the worship of the Syrian goddess Derketo, who, like Dagon, was in the form of a fish. Herod the Great was born here and later embellished the city. The Crusaders fought many battles here, until it was taken by Baldwin III in 1153. It was finally destroyed in 1270, and it never recovered. The Crusaders didn't get much out of Israel but onions. Latin *ascaliona* was anglicized to "scallion."

Some scholars of Greek legend claim that Ashkelon, and not Crete, may have been the original home of Aphrodite, goddess of love. An ancient burial cave in Ashkelon has beautiful **PAINTINGS** on the ceiling. The **WALL** around the city protrudes through the sands, and remnants of the ancient **HARBOR** may be seen along the beach. There is also a **SCULPTURE PARK** here, with sections of columns and other archaeological finds. The British Palestine Exploration Fund excavated here in 1920-21, and excavations have continued in the 1980s and 90s by Lawrence Stager of Harvard University. Finds include the world's oldest arched gateway, Canaanite ramparts and monumental buildings, and remains of the Philistine city, destroyed by Nebuchadnezzar in 604 B.C. (See further in *Biblical Archaeology Review* Mar/Apr 1991, 24-43.)

Ashkelon is a resort town now with a population over 75,000, and it is a National Parks Authority site. Opposite Ashkelon is Israel's main **OIL FIELD**, at **HELETZ.** The first oil discovery was made in 1955, and oil wells can now be seen among the orange trees. They produce only a small percentage of the country's oil consumption.

- *Ashkelon was captured by Judah (Josh. 13:3; Judg. 1:18).*
- *Here Samson slew 30 men (Judg. 14:19).*
- *The ark was returned with a trespass offering (1 Sam. 6:17).*
- *"Publish it not in the streets of Ashkelon" (2 Sam. 1:17-20).*
- *The prophets spoke against it (Amos 1:8; Zeph. 2:4, 7 [there is a Zephaniah Boulevard]; Jer. 25:20; 47:6-7).*

Negba

Negba is a kibbutz 7 miles east of Ashkelon, founded in 1939. At that time it was the southernmost Jewish colony. During the 1948 war the Jews in this kibbutz were completely surrounded by Egyptian forces, and were about to be overwhelmed; but they held out and were never taken. Note the **BRITISH POLICE POST**, the **EGYPTIAN TANK, BARBED WIRE**, and **WATER TANK** for evidence of the heavy fighting.

ASHDOD (*"fortress," "castle"*), *Azotus, Esdud*

This was an ancient Hyksos town and later a Philistine city, about 3 miles south of the present new city of the same name. The old city was a center of worship of the god Dagon, and a temple was erected in his honor. The modern city, established in 1957, has been developed into one of Israel's largest seaports, with a population over 90,000. The largest industry in the city is the Leyland bus factory.

- *Anakim prevented Joshua from taking it (Josh. 11:22).*
- *It was allotted to Judah but was not taken (Josh. 13:1-3; 15:46-47).*
- *It was the chief seat of the worship of Dagon – where the ark was carried by the Philistines when they defeated Israel (1 Sam. 5).*
- *It was possessed by Judah in the time of Uzziah (2 Chron. 26:6-7).*
- *It was captured by Sargon, king of Assyria (Isa. 20:1).*
- *Jews intermarried with its inhabitants, arousing Nehemiah's indignation (Neh. 13:23-24).*
- *It was prophesied against (Amos 1:8; Zeph. 2:4).*
- *Philip came here after baptizing the eunuch (Acts 8:26-40).*

GEDERAH ("*sheepfold*"), Gedera

This Zionist settlement, 7 miles northeast of Ashdod, was begun in 1884 by Russian students. The founders were persistent in conquering brackish water, isolation, hostility, poor housing, and poor food.

- *It was a town of Judah in the lowlands (Josh. 15:21-63).*

JABNEH, Yavne, *Yabneel, Yavniel, Kerem Yavne, Yavneh*

Four miles southwest of Rehovot is the site of Yavne. When the Temple was destroyed in A.D. 70, Rabbi Johanan ben Zakkai asked Titus to give Yavne as a safe place for himself and his fellow sages. This request was granted, and a great school of learning was established here, called *Kerem Yavne*. It was here that the sages established the canon (authorized version) of the Old Testament. The Mishna was also begun here and finally completed in Galilee. Tradition maintains that Johanan's school was on top of a hill where today a mosque has been built on the remains of a Crusader castle. To the west of the village is an ancient mausoleum capped with two domes. Jews have believed this to be the **TOMB OF GAMALIEL**.

- *Uzziah fought the Philistines here (2 Chron. 26:6).*
- *Gamaliel was a member of the Sanhedrin (Acts 5:34-40).*
- *Paul studied under Gamaliel (Acts 22:3).*

Rehovot

This city, 13 miles south of Tel Aviv, was founded by Polish Jews in 1890. Its chief pride is the **WEIZMANN INSTITUTE OF SCIENCE**, Israel's foremost scientific establishment. It contains 50 acres of beautiful buildings and green gardens. It was dedicated in 1949 in honor of Israel's first president, Dr. Chaim Weizmann, a distinguished chemist who did vital research for the Allies in World War I. He died in 1952 and is buried in a beautiful garden at the Institute. Hundreds of students and scientists do research at the Institute in such areas as nuclear physics, electronics, biophysics, chemistry, plant genetics, and mathematics.

The **WIX CENTRAL LIBRARY** houses 100,000 books and subscribes to more than 1,750 scientific journals from all over the world.

YAVNE YAM (*Yavne on the Sea*), JAMNIA, *Yamnia*

This was the ancient Greek port of Jamnia, where Judas Maccabaeus fought and vanquished the Greeks in 156 B.C. It was a Jewish spiritual center erected with Vespasian's permission by Johanan ben Zakkai after the fall of Jerusalem. It was also a Crusader stronghold. All that is left are crumbling pieces of masonry sticking out of the water, remains of a harbor and ancient walls.

- *Here Judas Maccabaeus fought the Greeks (2 Macc. 12:9).*

Holon

About 2 miles southeast of Joppa is the Jewish city of Holon, established in 1935. A Samaritan colony originally from Nablus is located now at Holon.

SOUTH OF JERUSALEM

VALLEY OF REPHAIM (*"strong"*), Emeq Refaim

Running west out of south Jerusalem is the Valley of Rephaim. This was the scene of one of David's great victories over the Philistines.

- *David battled the Philistines here (2 Sam. 5:17-25).*

Ramat Rahel (*"Rachel's heights"*), *Ramat Rachel*

Ramat Rahel, in the southeastern part of Jerusalem, is Israel's only kibbutz within the municipal bounds of a city. It was founded in 1925. Many battles were fought here in the War of Independence. Excavations near Ramat Rahel have uncovered ancient ruins, and an excellent view of the surrounding country may be seen from the kibbutz. (See also site no. 111, in the section on Jerusalem, above.)

CHURCH OF ELIJAH, *"My God is Yah" (Jehovah), Mar Elias Monastery*

Along the highway just southwest of Ramat Rahel is a Greek Orthodox sixth- and eleventh-century monastery, built where, according to tradition, Elijah rested when he fled from the wicked Jezebel. It is inhabited by a few Greek Orthodox monks.

- *Elijah may have rested here when he fled from Jezebel (1 Kings 19:1-4).*

Israel
South of
Jerusalem
N
Miles
5
10
15
20
25
MEDITERRANEAN SEA
Tel Aviv
Ashdod
Beit Shemesh
Valley of Rephaim
Jerusalem
Ramat-Rahel
Rachel's Tomb
Bethlehem
Qumran
Solomon's Pools
Ashkelon
Negba
Herodion
Tekoa
Valley of Berachah
Qiryat Gat
Bell Caves
Beth-Zur (Beit Zur)
Spring of Philip
Seir
Yad Mordechai
Tel Lachish
Valley of Eshcol
Halhul
Gaza
Hebron
SALT SEA
(DEAD SEA)
Saad
Adoraim (Dura)
Ziph
En-Gedi (Ein Gedi)
Dahahiriya
Maon
Eshtemoa (Es Sammui)
Masada
Urim
Beth-Phelet (Tell Sharuhen)
Arad (Tell Arad)
JORI
Beersheba (Beer-sheva)
Ein Bokek
Zohar
Flour Cave
Dimonah (Dimona)
Sodom and Gomorrah (Sedo
(Lot's Wife)
Salt Works
Oron
Nitsana
Shivta
Sde Boker
ARABAH (ARAVA)
Tell Avdat
NEGEV
Mitspe Ramon

RACHEL'S TOMB

Along the highway at the northern entrance to Bethlehem is a 23-foot square tomb where, according to tradition, Rachel, wife of Jacob and mother of Joseph, is buried. She died on her way to Bethlehem while giving birth to her last son, Benjamin. This is a sacred place to Jews, Christians, and Muslims. Men and women in the area frequently visit the tomb, weep, and pray. Women often pray for fertility and successful childbirth. The tomb dates back to the fifteenth century. Near the tomb are first-century remains of a Roman aqueduct.

- *Jacob went form Beersheba to Haran, where he worked twenty years, seven of them for Rachel (Gen. 29; 31:38).*
- *This was Rachel's burial place (Gen. 35:10-20; 48:7; 1 Sam. 10:2).*

BETHLEHEM (*"house of bread," "place of food"*) *Ephrathah, Ephrath, Beit Lahm*

Bethlehem is located on the hills 5 miles south of Jerusalem, 2,350 feet above sea level. Constantine built a church over the cave stable which is pointed out as being the scene of Christ's birth, and since that time many convents, monasteries, churches, and shrines have been built in the area.

It was from Bethlehem that Elimelech and Naomi went to Moab with their two sons at the time of the famine (Ruth 1:1). After the death of her husband and sons, Naomi, with Ruth, her daughter-in-law, returned to Bethlehem (Ruth 1:19-22), and Ruth's marriage to Boaz is a fitting climax to the inspiring story. She became the great-grandmother of David, king of Israel (Ruth 4:17, 1 Sam. 17:12). Thus Bethlehem is the original home of the Davidic family, and for this reason Joseph and Mary came here to pay taxes. The phrase "City of David" always refers to Jerusalem, except in one instance, in the Nativity story, where Bethlehem, the birthplace and hometown of David, is referred to (see Luke 2:11). No mention is made of Bethlehem after Jesus' Birth; there is no specific evidence of further ministry here, though we suppose there must have been.

POINTS OF INTEREST

The **CHURCH OF THE NATIVITY**, in Manger Square, is the oldest church in Christendom. It was built over the cave where it is believed Jesus was born. It was originally constructed by Constantine about A.D. 326 after his mother, Helena, determined the site. The present large church was built originally during the reign of Justinian (527-565) but was completely altered by the Crusaders. It is owned jointly by the Greek Orthodox, Roman Catholic, and Armenian churches. The doorway to the church is so low you have to bend to enter it. Legend has it that the doorway was made that small to prevent the unbelievers from riding into the church on horseback.

Below the church is the **GROTTO OF THE NATIVITY**, the traditional birthplace of Jesus. In this cave Joseph and Mary sought shelter when there was no room for them in the inn. Note the trappings, embellishments, and centuries of worship paraphernalia, but actual limestone cave walls are behind it all. Marking the traditional birthplace is a silver star inscribed in Latin: "Here of the Virgin Mary, Christ was born." The star has 14 points, representing the 14 stations of the cross. It was placed by the Roman church in 1717 and removed by the Greeks in 1847. The removal of the star, along with its subsequent restoration by the Turkish government in 1853, was one of the contributing factors of the Crimean War (1853-1856). Of the Church of the Nativity, Elder Harold B. Lee said, "Presently, we were as it seemed with the shepherds at the mouth of the cave hewn out of the rock now to be found in the basement of the Church of the Nativity. There seemed to be in this place a kind of spiritual assurance that this was indeed a hallowed spot although marred by centuries of, shall I say, unhallowed embellishment [called by Mark Twain "gewgaws, and tawdry ornamentation" - *The Innocents Abroad*, p. 377]. Down in the basement is the cave hewn out of the rock that seemed to us to mark a sacred place" (LDSSA Fireside Address, Oct. 10, 1971).

Across from the Grotto is a small **CHAPEL OF THE MANGER**, where, according to tradition, Mary placed the baby Jesus in a manger. Boards of the manger are, according to tradition, located in the Basilica of Santa Maria Magiore in Rome. Some bones in the **CAVE OF THE INNOCENT CHILDREN** are supposed to be bones of babies killed by the order of King Herod. Under the northern side of the church, the Roman Catholic side, is "Jerome's Grotto," a **ROOM WHERE JEROME WORKED ON THE LATIN VULGATE BIBLE**. Jerome, a church father in the 4th century A. D., wanted to have a quiet, holy place in order to do a translation of the Bible as commissioned by the Latin church (similar to Elder Talmage, who worked on his near-scriptural volume *Jesus the Christ* in a room prepared for him in the Salt Lake Temple). Here in this room, near where Jesus was born, Jerome produced the Latin Vulgate Version of the Bible. He translated and revised the old Latin 2nd century-version of the New Testament, and with the help of Jewish scholars and ancient Hebrew manuscripts, produced a revised translation of the Old Testament. Jerome's complete new version of the Bible took twenty years to complete (A.D. 382-402), and became the basic text for the 1610 English Douay Version of the Catholic Church. Flanking the basilica of the Church of the Nativity is the **CHURCH OF SAINT CATHERINE**.

About a block east and a little south of the Church of the Nativity is the Franciscan **CHURCH OF THE MILK GROTTO**. According to tradition, it was here that Mary, while nursing Jesus, dropped some milk on a stone. This promptly turned the rocks of the cavern chalky white. Visits are made here by nursing mothers who believe this will help their lactation. Round cakes made from the powdered stone are sold as souvenirs. In the grotto is a most beautiful carving of **JESUS' FLIGHT INTO EGYPT**.

KING DAVID'S WELLS are located on a hill to the north of the Church of the Nativity on King David Street. Traditionally, this was where David wanted a drink while fighting the Philistines (2 Sam. 23).

Near Beit Sahur (Arabic: "place of the shepherds"), a village east of Bethlehem, is one of the **FIELDS OF THE SHEPHERDS**, and nearby is the Roman Catholic **GROTTO OF THE SHEPHERDS**, a subterranean chapel. Tradition indicates that this is where the shepherds were visited by the angels (Luke 2:8-14). Other churches have their own "Fields of the Shepherds."

Bethlehem is one of the more prosperous cities; the soil is productive, and there are small manufacturing concerns producing furniture, olivewood statues, mother-of-pearl beads, and ornaments. The colorful **MARKET** is located a block west of Manger Square.

- *Bethlehem was the home and burial place of Ibzan, the judge (Judg. 12:8-10).*
- *Micah hired a Levite from Bethlehem as priest (Judg. 17:7-13).*
- *The Levite's concubine who was abused at Gibeah was from Bethlehem (Judg. 19).*
- *The story of Ruth and Boaz centers here (Book of Ruth).*
- *It was the place of David's birth and his anointing as king of Israel in Saul's place (1 Sam. 16:1-14; 17:12).*
- *David was a herdsman here (1 Sam. 17:15; 34-37).*
- *David went from here to Saul's army and slew Goliath (1 Sam. 17:12-58).*
- *It was claimed that David came here when he fled from Saul (1 Sam. 20:6, 28).*
- *David obtained water from the well by the gate (2 Sam. 23:14-17; 1 Chron. 11:15-19).*
- *Bethlehem became insignificant after David; it was fortified by Rehoboam (2 Chron. 11:5-6).*
- *Micah foretold Christ's birth at Bethlehem (Mic. 5:2; Matt. 2:4-6; John 7:42).*
- *Matthew and Luke told of Jesus' birth (Matt. 1:18-25; Luke 2:1-7).*
- *Here the shepherds visited the infant Jesus (Luke 2:8-20).*
- *The wise men later visited and worshiped (Matt. 2:1-12).*
- *The angel appeared to Joseph, he fled with Mary and Jesus to Egypt, and Herod had the children killed (Matt. 2:13-23; Jer. 31:15; 40:1).*
- *Alma prophesied in 83 B.C. that Jesus would be born of Mary at Jerusalem (Alma 7:10). (Bethlehem was in that same part of the world, as seen from Alma's view-point in America, and Bethlehem is – as stated in Alma – in the land of Jerusalem.)*

Mar Saba

Eight miles east of Bethlehem is Mar Saba, founded by Saint Sabas in A.D. 483. This is the oldest center of Christian monasticism in the Holy Land.

Above: Bethlehem and Shepherd's Field

Below: Church of the Nativity, Bethlehem

The Herodion

Three or four miles southeast of Bethlehem is a fortified palace built by Herod the Great at the end of the first century B.C. The top third of this volcano-shaped hill was artificially built up by Herod's engineers; material was taken from the (now) flat hill to the east. It is the only building project of Herod's in all the land that is named after him. (Either spelling of the name is correct: the Greek form has -ion and the Latin has -ium.) At its foot were palaces, terraced gardens, and pools, and 200 white marble steps led to the citadel on top. During the Roman and Jewish wars of A.D. 66-70 and 132-35, the fortress played an important part. Josephus described these wars. During the Byzantine period Christian monks inhabited the site. According to Josephus, Herod died in Jericho but was buried here – not far from where he ordered the slaying of the infants.

Recent excavations by Hebrew University archaeologist, Ehud Netzer, feature the following:

The **SYNAGOGUE** room was originally a *triclinium*, a dining hall, but Jewish rebels and their families converted it into a synagogue about A. D. 66.

The Roman **BATH-HOUSE** has the usual frigidarium, tepidarium, and caldarium. The tepidarium is almost completely preserved, perhaps the oldest such construction in the country.

The whole round **PALACE-FORTRESS** was built 90 feet above bedrock (about seven stories).

The **EASTERN ROUND TOWER** was once over 75 feet higher than the solid foundation that remains today, towering to a height of about 140 feet (15 stories). According to Josephus the tower had palatial rooms and baths inside.

LOWER HERODION was serviced by a Herodian aqueduct 4 miles long bringing water from the west, from a spring near "Solomon's Pools."

The **POOL** was nearly 10 feet deep and could hold about 10,000 cubic meters of water; some kind of round structure, probably a pavilion, stood in the center. (See *Biblical Archaeology Review* May/Jun 1983, 30-51; Jul/Aug 1988, 18-33.)

This is a National Parks Authority site.

- *Herod was the king of Judea when Jesus was born (Matt. 2:3).*
- *Herod ordered all babies under two years of age to be slain (Matt. 2:16).*

TEKOA (*"firm," "settlement"*), Tell Tequ'a

This ancient village, 2,800 feet above sea level and 10-12 miles south of Jerusalem, overlooks the desolate hills on the east toward the Dead Sea. Some ruins are still visible here. Amos, the prophet who lived here, was a "herdman, and gatherer of sycomore fruit [a small fig]" (Amos 7:14). None of these trees are found in the area now. Josephus wrote that the tomb of Amos was located here.

- *This was one of the fortified cities of Rehoboam (2 Chron. 11:6).*

- *From here came the "wise woman" brought by Joab to make a reconciliation between David and Absalom after Absalom had slain his brother, Amnon, because of the latter's wrong to Tamar, their sister (2 Sam. 14:1-24).*
- *It was the native city and burial place of Amos, the herdsman prophet (Amos 1:1; 7:14).*

"SOLOMON'S POOLS"

Eight miles south of Jerusalem and 2 miles south of Bethlehem are 3 large rock-built reservoirs, near a small Turkish fortress dating back to A.D. 1540. Water is supplied by springs south of here. In the past, water ran by gravity to Bethlehem, to the Herodion, and to Jerusalem's Temple Mount via conduit from these reservoirs. They are probably misnamed, since two of them were built by Herod or Pontius Pilate and the third pool was built in the fifteenth century. About a mile beyond the pools to the east is the **MONASTERY OF HORTUS CONCLUSUS**.

- *Solomon's pools are mentioned (Eccles. 2:4-6).*

VALLEY OF BERACHAH (*"blessing"*), Berakha

About 7 miles southwest of Bethlehem is the Valley of Berakha.

- *King Jehoshaphat and the children of Israel went forth to meet the enemy here. The Lord destroyed the enemy, and in the Valley of Berachah Israel blessed the Lord (2 Chron. 20:26).*

BETH ZUR (*"house of the rock"*), Beit Zur, *Khirbet et-Tubeiqah*

Close by the Spring of Philip, on the mountainside west of the spring, are the ruins of Beth Zur, an important city of Judah. Here the Hasmoneans defeated Antiochus' army decisively in 165 B.C.

- *It was a city in Judah (Josh. 15:1, 58).*
- *It was fortified by Rehoboam (2 Chron. 11:5, 7).*
- *Simon fought against and ruled over it (1 Macc. 11:65; 14:7).*

SPRING OF PHILIP, Ein Dirwa

On the road to Hebron, near Beit Zur and near a house and Muslim "praying place," are traces of an ancient church and two rock tomb chambers. A spring provides water for the villagers and perhaps provided water for Philip's baptism of the eunuch.

- *This is traditionally where Philip baptized the eunuch (Acts 8:26-40).*

HALHUL (*"full of hollows"*)

Three miles north of Hebron and east of the main highway between Hebron and Bethlehem is Halhul, the ancient site of a Canaanite town of that name. It is the highest village in the country. In the Middle Ages the sacred tombs of Gad the seer and Nathan the prophet were shown in the village. Now it is said that the tomb is that of the prophet Jonah.

- *It was a city of Judah (Josh. 15:1, 58).*

SEIR, Siir, *Siair*

According to tradition, this small village is where the tomb of Esau is located. The village is 2 miles east of Halhul.

- *This is where Esau is supposed to have settled permanently (Gen. 35:29; 36:6; Deut. 2:4-5; Josh. 24:4).*

VALLEY OF ESHCOL (*"cluster of grapes"*), Eshkol

Located 2½ miles north of Hebron is the Valley of Eshkol, from whence Moses' spies returned carrying clusters of grapes. This event portrayed in picture has become the official tourist emblem of the modern State of Israel. The valley still produces grapes in abundance.

- *The spies brought back grapes, pomegranates, and figs from the brook Eshcol (Num. 13:22-24).*

HEBRON (*Hebrew: "the friend"*), *Kiriath-Arba, El Khalil* (*Arabic: "the friend"*), *Kirjath-Arba, Ramat el-Khalil*

Hebron, David's capital for seven years, is 20 miles south of Jerusalem and 30 miles north of Beersheba, and 3,042 feet above sea level. It was named after Arba, the father of Anak (Josh. 15:13-15; 21:11; Kirjath or Kiriath means "town of"). The ancient town stood a mile northwest of the present city, where a large oak called the **OAK OF MAMRE** has purportedly been standing since the twelfth century. Nearby is a cistern called the **BATH OF SARAH**, and also a **RUSSIAN MONASTERY**. There are 38 springs in the area, and northeast of the city is **ABRAHAM'S WELL**, where Abraham pitched his tent. This site is designated today as *Mamre*. The Hebrew text of Gen. 23:19 suggests the place called Mamre is west of the Cave of Machpelah. The "plains of Mamre" should be the "oaks [or terebinths] of Mamre."

The **POOL OF SOLOMON** is supposed to be one of the authentic sites in Hebron.

The **TOMB OF THE PATRIARCHS** is the **CAVE OF MACHPELAH**, located beneath a huge shrine dating back to Herod's time. This was a sacred site where people visited as tourists in the days of Jesus. (See *Biblical Archaeology Review* May/Jun 1985, 26-43.)

Because Abraham is important to three great religions the building was never destroyed. It is one of the few buildings built by Herod that is standing fairly complete. It has similar architectural features to Jerusalem's Temple Mount walls: pilasters to create vertical breakup of massive walls, and huge ashlars with Herodian borders. **CENOTAPHS** in the Mosque commemorate those who are buried below. The cenotaphs are supposed to be directly over the actual tombs in the cave. (A *cenotaph* [Gr. *kenos* = empty; *taphos* = tomb] is a monument in honor of a person buried elsewhere.) A limited view of the cave may be had through a small opening under a small dome supported by four pillars and located near the cenotaphs of Isaac and Rebecca. No one is allowed to enter the cave. The cenotaphs are elaborately decorated with gold-embroidered velvet. The locations of the cenotaphs are as follows: **ISAAC** and **REBEKAH** are in the large room on the south, Isaac to the west and Rebekah to the east; **ABRAHAM** and **SARAH** are just north of the open courtyard, with Abraham on the west; **JACOB** and **LEAH** are in rooms farthest north, with Jacob on the west; **JOSEPH'S CENOTAPH** is in a room to the west, just before the tombs of Jacob and Leah. Some believe that **ADAM** and **EVE** are also buried in the Cave at Machpelah. One legend has Adam being created out of the dust at Hebron. In the western portion of the courtyard is a long hall called the **WOMEN'S MOSQUE**. In the corner near Abraham's cenotaph is a small window, inside which is a stone that tradition indicates has the impression of Adam's foot on it.

Mosque over the Tomb of the Patriarchs, Hebron

To the Jews, Abraham was the first Jew, and thus Hebron is one of the four sacred cities of the Jews. The others are Jerusalem, Tiberias, and Safed. Three parcels of ground, Hebron and the sites of the Jerusalem Temple and the Tomb of Joseph, are claimed by the Jews because the property was purchased by their ancestors.

Hebron was burned by Titus during the first Jewish revolt and has passed through several conquerors' hands over the years. In modern times, Hebron was a center of Jewish learning until the riots and massacres of 1929 and 1939. Since then it has been entirely Arab Palestinian.

The city, with an Arab Palestinian population of over 65,000, has interesting shops in the marketplaces, veiled women, and dirty streets. A stop in Hebron is worthwhile. Hebron is famous for its handblown glass, pottery-making, and leather products.

During the years 1964-67 members of an American expedition excavated in Hebron under the direction of Dr. Philip C. Hammond of the University of Utah. They dug on the slope just west of the Mosque of Abraham and recovered 160,000 pieces of ceramic material. They found a 36-foot-thick wall built in 1728 B.C. and a house dating back to a period of time before the pyramids of Egypt were built (3500 B.C.). According to Dr. Hammond, Hebron is the oldest continuously occupied unwalled city in the world, although portions of it were walled at one time. Hundreds of different levels of major human occupation have been uncovered, dating back to the beginning of agriculture for man.

Hebron is mentioned 69 times in the Old Testament, from Genesis to Jeremiah.

- *The place was named Hebron (Josh. 14:15; 20:7).*
- *Abraham built an altar here after he and Lot separated (Gen. 13:18).*
- *From here Abraham went to rescue Lot (Gen. 14:13-24).*
- *Here Ishmael was born (Gen. 16). The Arabs believe Ishmael, father of all Arabs, is also buried here.*
- *Abraham entertained three holy men and made intercession for Sodom and Gomorrah (Gen. 17:1; 18:16-33).*
- *Abraham, Isaac, and Jacob dwelt here (Gen. 35:27, 37:1).*
- *Abraham, Sarah, Isaac, Rebekah, Jacob, and Leah were buried in Machpelah (Gen. 23; 25:7-11; 49:29-31; 50:13).*
- *Isaac and Jacob spent much time here (Gen. 35-37).*
- *Joseph left Hebron to go to Dothan in search of his brothers (Gen. 37:3-19).*
- *Jacob and his sons went from here to Egypt (Gen. 46:1).*
- *Moses' spies visited it and gathered grapes, pomegranates, and figs. This was where Anak and the giants lived (Num. 13:22-33).*
- *Hoham, its king, was overcome by Joshua (Josh. 10:3-27).*
- *Hebron was taken by Joshua and given to Caleb (Josh. 10:36-37; 14:6-15; 15:14-19).*

- *It was made a Levite city of Judah (Josh. 15:54; 20:7; 21:13).*
- *It was a city of refuge (Josh. 20:7).*
- *David was anointed the first king of Judah, then of all Israel, and Hebron became the first capital of David (2 Sam. 2:1-4, 10-11; 5:1-5; 1 Kings 2:11).*
- *Abner was slain by Joab (2 Sam. 3:6-39).*
- *David slew the murderers of Ishbosheth (2 Sam. 4:5-12).*
- *Absalom organized his revolt against his father, David, and made Hebron his headquarters (2 Sam. 15:7-12).*
- *It was fortified by Rehoboam (2 Chron. 11:5-12).*
- *It was colonized by Jews returning from Babylon (Neh. 11:25).*
- *Abraham, Isaac, Jacob and wives are already exalted with their resurrected bodies (D&C 132:37).*

ADORAIM, Dura, *Adora*

Four miles southwest of Hebron is the village of Dura, where some believe Noah was buried.

- *Genesis records the story of Noah and the flood (Gen. 5:29-8:22) and the death of Noah (Gen. 9:29).*
- *The city was fortified by Rehoboam (2 Chron. 11:9).*
- *It was called by the Maccabees Adora (1 Macc. 13:20).*

ZIPH (*"refining place"*)

Ziph is 4 miles southeast of Hebron. David spent some time here while fleeing from Saul and escaped when Ziphites tried to betray him into Saul's hands.

- *David fled from Saul (1 Sam. 23, 26).*

MAON (*"habitation"*), *Tell Main, Wilderness of Maon*

Seven miles southeast of Hebron was the biblical town of Maon. It was the home of Abigail, the wife of Nabal, who later became David's wife.

- *Nabal dwelt in the wilderness of Maon (1 Sam. 25:2).*
- *David sojourned in this area while in hiding (1 Sam. 23:24-36; 25:2-7).*

YUTTAH, Yatta

Five miles directly south of Hebron is the Arab village of Yatta, the biblical town called Juttah – pronounced in Hebrew exactly as we pronounce the western American state, Utah. The early church father Eusebius concluded that Juttah was the birthplace of John the Baptist.

- *It was a town in the tribe of Judah (Josh. 15:55).*

ESHTEMOA, Es Sammui, *Eshtamoah, Samu, Samua*

This town, 7 miles south of Hebron, was a town in Judah assigned to the Levites.

- *It was a town of Judah (Josh. 15:50; 21:14; 1 Sam. 30:28; 1 Chron. 6:57).*

NEGEV, *Negeb ("the dry land")*

The Negev is an ill-defined tract of desert land south of the hill country of Judah. It is bounded on the east by the Dead Sea and Arabah (Arava), while on the west it fades into the maritime plain. Although comprising about half of the country's land area, the Negev has only 7% of the current population. The area was settled by the Nabataeans in the early Christian period and again in Byzantine times, when it was a frontier area. There are many traces of Nabataean methods of obtaining water for their crops: channeling of hillsides, building cisterns for collection and storage of water, damming of wadis, and terracing of slopes against erosion of soil. The State of Israel is developing the Negev into a farming area, with water piped in from the north. In the Negev rainfall diminishes rapidly, approx. 5-8 inches average per year. The northwest Negev doesn't have great amounts of winter rainfall, but it does have 250 dew-nights a year. Today the Negev is still home to tens of thousands of Bedouin (Arabic *badu* means "desert;" a *badui* is a desert man). They are divided into tribes, and each tribe is governed by a sheikh and has its own grazing territory. Once a week the Bedouin go to Beersheba to market their animals and produce. The Bedouin in many ways live as the patriarchs of Israel did over 3,000 years ago. They are quite hospitable.

- *This was an arid area in Canaan (Deut. 1:7, 34:3; Josh. 15:19; Judg. 1:15).*

Ein Gedi, David's hideout near the Dead Sea

- *Abraham lived in the Negev (Gen. 12:9; 13:1).*
- *Here Hagar was succored by an angel (Gen. 16:7, 14).*
- *Isaac (Gen. 24:62) and Jacob (Gen. 37:1; 46:5) both dwelt here.*
- *Its dry winds were dreaded (Isa. 21:1).*
- *It was filled with many wild beasts (Isa. 30:6).*

BEERSHEBA (*"well of the seven," "well of the oath"*), Beer-sheva, *Tell es Seba, Shibah*

Beersheba is 35 miles west of the south end of the Dead Sea and 50 miles south of Jerusalem. It marked the southern border of Judah (Josh. 15:28; Judg. 20:1; 1 Sam. 3:20) and was the southern limit of the cultivated land. Seven ancient wells existed here to provide water, and one of them is reported to have been the **WELL OF ABRAHAM**. The well at the entrance to the tel, at the Israelite city gate, is 120 feet deep (BYU faculty and students helped dig it in an archaeological project started by Professors Yohanan Aharoni and A. F. Rainey.). Beersheba is 950 feet above sea level, which is over 2,000 feet lower than Hebron.

In 1917, during the First World War, Beersheba was the first town captured from the Turks by General Allenby. When Israel captured it from the Egyptians in 1948 it had 3,000 people. Today it has over 140,000 Jewish inhabitants and is the capital of the Negev.

A **MUNICIPAL MOSQUE**, a **MUSEUM**, and the **ARID ZONE RESEARCH CENTER** are also of interest in Beersheba. The **RAILWAY STATION** is worth visiting. It was along the Beersheba line running to Egypt that Lawrence of Arabia blew up trains.

The Beersheba of the Patriarchs and the period of the Judges was likely to the west of the tel, where the modern city is. The archaeological excavation site of Beersheba east of the modern city was first established by Solomon as a fortified position in the Iron Age. It is a planned, fortified, Israelite city. Remains include the city gate, drainage channel, storehouse and family dwellings.

- *An angel spoke to Hagar (Gen. 21:14-21).*
- *Abraham and Abimelech, the Philistine king, made a covenant concerning Abraham's well (Gen. 21:29-33).*
- *Abraham lived here (Gen. 22:19).*
- *Isaac and Abimelech made a covenant (Gen. 26:26-33).*
- *God appeared to Isaac (Gen. 26:23-25) and to Jacob (Gen. 46:1-7).*
- *A well was dug by Isaac (Gen. 26:32-33).*
- *Jacob fled from Esau toward Haran (Gen. 28:10).*
- *Jacob offered sacrifices to God as he journeyed to Egypt to live with Joseph (Gen. 46:1-5).*
- *Samuel's two unworthy sons were judges here (1 Sam. 8:1-3).*

- *An angel appeared to Elijah here and served him food (1 Kings 19:1-8).*
- *It was the birthplace of Zibiah, the mother of king Joash (2 Kings 12:1; 2 Chron. 24:1).*
- *The proverbial expression "from Dan to Beersheba" describes the limits of Israelite settlement in the land (2 Sam. 17:11; 1 Chron. 21:2; 2 Chron. 30:5; 2 Kings 23:8).*
- *Some Jews lived here after the captivity (Neh. 11:27, 30).*
- *Amos classified it with Gilgal and Bethel and prophesied its destruction because of idolatry (Amos 5:5; 8:14).*

Dimonah, *Dimona*

About 22 miles southeast of Beersheba is the urban settlement Dimona, founded in 1955 and named after a town of Judah. Several hundred black "Hebrews" live among the white Jews here. There is no claim that this is the site of the ancient Dimonah.

- *Dimonah was a city in the south of Judah (Josh. 15:21-22).*

Mamshit, *Kurnub*

Mamshit, or Mampsis, is a Nabataean site southeast of Dimonah and is a National Parks Authority site. The city was conquered by Romans and flourished during the Byzantine period. In 636 it fell to invading Muslims, and was destroyed and abandoned. Excavations reveal residential quarters, public buildings, bath houses, mosaics, and frescoes.

Sde Boker (*"field of the herdsman"*), *Sede Boqer*

Sde Boker is the famous kibbutz where Israel's first prime minister, David Ben-Gurion, a wise, genteel, hospitable person, lived. He became an example to his people by moving onto this kibbutz in the middle of the desert.

Sde Boker was established by 16 young men and 3 young women in 1952. It was a daring exploit, and during the first year one of the girls, a university graduate from Jerusalem, was murdered by Arab marauders while out with the sheep. There are now over 500 persons living at the kibbutz. David Ben-Gurion and his wife, Paula, joined the group in 1954 after Mr. Ben-Gurion served 3 terms as prime minister (1948-53). He later served as minister of defense and then prime minister again. He died at age 87 on Dec. 1 and was buried on Dec. 3, 1973.

The **SDE BOKER INSTITUTE FOR DESERT RESEARCH** is 1½ miles south of the kibbutz. This first "desert" university in the world is the fulfillment of BenGurion's dream. Its dormitories accommodate 100 students. On these grounds is the national memorial where the Ben-Gurions are buried. The gravesite is located on the edge of a deep chasm featuring a magnificent panorama of the biblical Wilderness of Zin.

Ein Avdat

Two or three miles south of Sde Boker are the springs and beautiful pools of Wadi Ein Avdat. The natural water pools and canyon make swimming and hiking a favorite pastime for visitors in the area. This is a National Parks Authority site.

David Ben-Gurion

Tel Avdat, *Abda*

Avdat is an ancient tel 15 miles south of Sde Boker. It is surrounded by green fields that were once farmed by the Nabataeans. Ruins of the numerous Nabataean, Roman, and Byzantine settlements lie on the top and sides of the tel. They date from the first to the seventh century A.D. The Nabataeans used Avdat as an important station for caravans carrying precious cargos from Arabia to the Mediterranean seacoast. The Nabataeans lived east of the Byzantine ruins that remain on the tel. They preserved water by (1) digging holes or caves, (2) clearing triangular areas to divert the water, (3) building dams, and (4) building canals and channels.

In A.D. 105 the emperor Trajan captured Avdat and made it a Roman province. There are still some Roman ruins outside the walls.

Byzantine Christians were next to occupy the site, building two churches on the acropolis (with baptismal fonts).

In 1959 students of the Institute of Desert Research began using Nabataean methods of preserving water by the "runoff" water system in order to raise crops in fields near Tel Avdat. A great deal of agricultural experimentation has been done here during recent decades.

The ruins include a **WINE PRESS, SAINT THEODORIUS'S CHURCH**, a **BYZANTINE MONASTERY**, a **POTTERY HOUSE, CAVES, HOUSES**, a **BATH HOUSE**, and an eighth-century **BAPTISMAL FONT**.

This is a National Parks Authority site.

Shivta, *Subeita*

About 13 miles west-northwest of Sde Boker and 28 miles southwest of Beersheba are the ruins of Shivta, one of the best-preserved ruins of the Byzantines in the Negev. It dates back to the fifth or sixth century and was excavated by the British Colt archaeological expedition in 1934.

Among the most important ruins are the **NORTH CHURCH**, the **SOUTH CHURCH**, the **CENTER CHURCH**, the **MUNICIPALITY HOUSE, DWELLING HOUSES, RESERVOIRS, WINE-PRESSES, WORKSHOPS**, a **BAKERY OVEN**, and a **POTTERY KILN**. The South Church has a **BAPTISTRY** with a stone font that suggests baptism by immersion.

This is a National Parks Authority site.

Nitsana

Located 46 miles southwest of Beersheba and 18 miles west-southwest of Shivta are the ruins of an ancient Nabataean city. The city is near a major crossroads. One highway leads west to El Arish, on the Mediterranean Sea, and one leads southwest to the Suez Canal.

Mitspe Ramon, *Makhtesh Ramon, Wadi Ramun*

Makhtesh Ramon is the **LARGEST NATURE RESERVE** in Israel, totaling 250,000 acres. It is about 14 miles southeast of Avdat and is a great oblong depression in the earth's crust, about 25 miles long, 5 miles wide, and 1200 feet deep. It is the **LARGEST CRATER IN THE WORLD**, a volcanic-type geological formation, from which rare fossils dating back to the Triassic period have been found. The fossil of the Tanystropheus, with a lizard-like body over 16 feet long, was found here, along with other strange fossils. There are 1200 different kinds of desert vegetation, and the crater is inhabited by ibex, gazelles, wolves, foxes, leopards, and birds of prey. It is a "picture window" into the earth's geological strata.

BROOK OF PARAN, *Wadi Jirafi*

About 22 miles south of Mitspe Ramon and 5 miles north of Tsomet Tsihor is the dry bed of the Brook of Paran, which begins in the central part of Sinai where Israel camped while being led by Moses. It is the longest watercourse that drains the southern Negev.

- *Spies were sent into Canaan from the wilderness of Paran (Num. 13:1-3).*

ARABAH, Arava

The *Arava* is the name given by the Hebrews to the whole of the great depression (rift zone) that goes from Mount Hermon to the Gulf of Aqaba. The east branch of the Red Sea is an extension of the same rift. The rift is a meeting place of two tectonic plates. Jerusalem and Amman, Jordan, though only about 50 miles from each other, are on two different plates of the earth's surface! Though Jerusalem has historically and geographically been associated with Asia, geologically it is situated on the African plate. In modern times the Arava generally refers to the valley area between the Dead Sea and the Red Sea. It is about 10-20 miles wide and about 110 miles long. According to tradition, the Israelites traversed the Arava when they went to Kadesh-Barnea, and again when they returned to the south in their detour past Edom (Num. 20:21; 21:4; Deut. 2:8). The southern part of the Arava was an important trade route, and copper was mined there.

- *It is spoken of in the Scriptures (Deut. 3:17; 4:49; 11:30; Josh. 8:14; 1 Sam. 23:24; 2 Kings 25:4; Jer. 39:4; Ezek. 47:8).*
- *It is sometimes translated "wilderness," or "desert," or "steppe" (Job 24:5; 39:6; Isa. 33:9; 35:1, 6; Jer. 2:6).*

Beer Menuha, *and* SELAH, SELA, *Petra ("rock")*

A workers' camp is located at Beer Menuha, at the forks of the road. Directly east of this point, in the tops of the mountains of Edom, is Sela of the Bible (Petra of the Greeks). The traditional tomb of Aaron on Mount Hor, the highest peak, can be seen on a clear day. It is marked by a mosque.

- *King Amaziah of Jerusalem took Selah by war (2 Kings 14:1, 7).*
- *The Bible tells of the death of Aaron (Num. 20:28-29).*

Hai Bar - National Biblical Wildlife Reserve

Twenty miles north of Eilat hundreds of acres of land are home to many animals known from Bible times. Today ibex, oryx, addax, gazelles, wild asses, ostriches, and other biblical fauna run free within the reserve.

TIMNA, *Copper Mines and Smelters*

Timna is 16 miles north of Eilat. Here are the **OLDEST COPPER MINES IN THE WORLD**. At this site a large, copper-mining plant was set up in 1948. Copper was mined here anciently, and then the mine was worked again after 2,000 years.

Dr. Nelson Glueck, an American archaeologist, found the mines, furnaces, slag heaps, and the ruins of the enclosure Solomon built to keep his slave labor from escaping. The ruins date back to the tenth and ninth centuries B.C. Prof. Beno Rothenberg, of the Hebrew University, and other experts believe that the so-called "King Solomon's Mines" were in operation centuries before Solomon's time, and that the mines were inactive during his reign. The ancient copper mines are 2 miles northwest from the modern mining and smelting operation. Near the mines the visitor may see russet-colored projections of rock, called **SOLOMON'S PILLARS**.

Pharaonic mines were operated from Seti I to Ramses V, during the 18th and 19th dynasties (14th and 13th centuries B.C.). Ramesside mining featured a complex system of vertical and horizontal tunnels, over 10,000 saucer-shaped clearings with vertical shafts. One shaft was over 100 feet deep and there intersected with a horizontal tunnel! A Temple of Hathor (the Egyptian mining goddess with cow or bull-like appearance) was found with over 11,000 votive objects. See *Biblical Archaeology Review* June 1978, p. 19. Midianites and Kenites operated the mines for the Egyptians. Mine shafts, cisterns, smelting ovens, and workshops associated with ancient mining works have been discovered. In 1955 Israelis resumed copper-mining, but halted operations in 1976 when it became unprofitable.

- *This area would have been on the Israelites' route as they journeyed to Canaan (Num. 33:35; Deut. 2:8).*
- *Copper was used by Moses to make a bronze serpent in the wilderness [copper + zinc = brass; copper + tin – bronze] (Num. 21:9; 2 Kgs. 18:4).*
- *Copper was also used in Solomon's Temple (1 Kgs. 7:14; 1 Chron. 18:8).*

Solomon's Pillars, near Timna

EZION-GEBER, ELATH, Eilat, *Elat, Berenice, Tell el-Kheleifeh*

To Israelis, Eilat is the end of their world – a 3-hour drive from Beersheba. Eilat is a port city, settled in 1950 on the Israeli, or west, side of the head of the Gulf of Aqaba, a branch of the Red Sea. Aqaba is a Jordanian port on the opposite side, and 15 miles southward, is Saudi Arabia. The biblical Elath was a little east of the modern Eilat.

Today Eilat vies with Tiberias as Israel's leading winter tourist resort. Its native population stands around 26,000. It boasts fine **BEACHES** and 360 days of sun each year. It is a combination port, military installation, and vacation land. There are also **GRANITE QUARRIES** in the area. **GLASS-BOTTOMED BOATS** give the tourist a look at the wonderful marine world, including beautiful corals that thrive below the surface of the Red Sea. There is also a wonderful **MARITIME MUSEUM AND OBSERVATORY** in the city. Jewelry made of copper stones can be purchased in Eilat. Two big desalination plants make it possible to drink the sea water. The temperature gets up to 120 degrees here, but the dry air is not oppressive. Israel's Red Sea shoreline is only a few miles long and provides a strategic port for Israel's back door.

The *Ezion-geber* of the Bible is a mound that lies less than a mile east of the Jordan-Israel border, directly east of Eilat. It was excavated by Nelson Glueck. Remains of a copper smelting and refining plant were found here.

- *This was a stopping place during the Israelites' wanderings in the wilderness (Num. 33:35; Deut. 2:8).*
- *This was King Solomon's port (1 Kings 9:26-38; 2 Chron. 8:17). Copper and salt were shipped to Africa and gold and spices brought to Israel in return.*
- *Phoenician sailors brought gold to Solomon from Ophir (1 Kings 9:26-28; 10:22-24; 2 Chron. 8:17; 9:10-11, 21-22).*
- *Solomon had a "navy of Tharshish" (1 Kings 10:22).*
- *The Queen of Sheba must have landed here (1 Kings 10:1-13).*
- *Elath was later built up again by Uzziah, king of Judah, in the eighth century B.C. (2 Kings 14:22).*
- *Ships of Jehoshaphat were broken at Ezion-geber (1 Kings 22:48).*
- *The Israelites crossed the Red Sea (Exod. 14).*
- *The Book of Mormon also refers to the crossing of the Red Sea (Al. 29:12; 36:28; Hel. 8:11).*
- *Perhaps near here on the Red Sea was the Valley of Lemuel (1 Ne. 2:14; 9:1; 10:16; 16:6).*

SODOM *and* GOMORRAH; Sedom, *Sdom*

South of the Dead Sea was the Valley of Siddim (Gen. 14:10), where once stood the cities of Sodom and Gomorrah, believed to be now entirely submerged in water.

Scriptures describe this region with such terms as brimstone, salt, burning, nothing grows, nettles, salt pits, perpetual desolation, never again to be inhabited, no shepherds, no Arabs to pitch a tent here! The area now has a potash and bromide business that is part of a billion-dollar mineral extraction industry. North of the chemical plant about 3 miles, above one of the many salt caves in the area, is a natural stone outcropping that supposedly (with much imagination) has the form of a woman. It is known as **LOT'S WIFE.**

- *Five wicked cities were in the valley: Sodom, Gomorrah, Admah, Bela (Zoar), and Zeboiim (Gen. 10:19; 13:10; 14:2-11).*
- *They were destroyed (except for Bela), but Lot was saved (Gen. 19; Deut. 29:23; Isa. 13:19; Jer. 50:40; Matt. 10:15; 2 Pet. 2:6; Jude 7; cf. 2 Ne. 23:19).*
- *Lot's wife turned into a pillar of salt (Gen. 19:26; Luke 17:32).*
- *They were used as a warning by Moses (Deut. 29:23; 32:32); by Isaiah (1:1-10; 13:19); by Jeremiah (23:14; 49:18; 50:40); by Amos (4:11); by Zephaniah (2:9); by Jesus (Matt. 10:15; 11:24); by Paul (Rom. 9:29); by Peter (2 Pet. 2:6); and by Jude (4, 7).*
- *They were cited as types, or symbols (Rev. 11:8).*

Peratsim Canyon, Flour Cave, and the Chimney Cave

About 1/7 of a mile north of the Mifale Sdom Salt Works is a road running northwest into the desert. At a point 3½ miles from the main road is Peratsim Canyon, which is carved in the beautiful white clay. A hike down the shallow canyon about ⅓ of a mile will place the visitor at the opening of a cave known as *Flour Cave* because of its white flour appearance. The cave is approximately 300 feet long and very dark inside. Israeli youth enjoy hiking through this marvel of nature.

One kilometer south of the junction of Zohar, and north of the so-called Lot's Wife, is another unusual cave called the *Arubotaim* ("The Chimney Cave"), formed from salt and water action.

Ein Zohar

This is a hot mineral spring near the Dead Sea and just north of the road between Sodom and Arad.

Citadel of Zohar ("*nobility,*" "*distinction*")

The remains of the second- or third-century Roman fortress of Zohar are located about 2 miles west of the Dead Sea along Wadi Zohar, a dry riverbed, and near the road from Arad to Neve Zohar, on the shore of the Dead Sea. In ancient times it was on the "Road of the Salt" and was used to defend the road.

ARAD (*"a court"*), **Tel Arad**

In the early 1960s a new city of Arad was built by the Israelis in the Negev, 5 miles east of the ancient city and about 17 miles south of Hebron. Here are underground reservoirs of natural gas.

The **ARCHAEOLOGICAL SITE** of Tel Arad represents two distinct phases of occupation: a 25-acre city from the Early Bronze Age and a ¾-acre citadel with a series of fortresses from the Iron Age (Israelite settlement). The original inhabitants must have selected the site for defensive and topographical reasons, the configuration of the terrain allowing maximum rainfall collection into a natural depression near the city-center. The city was dependent on rain storage and ground water. Arad was settled in the early Israelite period by Kenites, descendants of Moses' father-in-law Jethro. The tel's highest point features six successive Israelite fortresses. Prof. Benjamin Mazar suggests that the **TEMPLE** discovered here was operated by these descendants of Jethro (a man who had held the Melchizedek Priesthood), not Levites; it is the only Israelite temple ever discovered in an excavation in the Holy Land. The inner sanctum of the sanctuary follows the layout of the Holy of Holies in Solomon's Temple as described in the Bible. The Arad temple dates from the 10th to 7th centuries B. C. Original steps leading up to it, and its floor, and two stone altars are on display in the Israel Museum in Jerusalem.

The Hebrew University and Department of Antiquities excavated Tel Arad from 1962 to 1967. During the 1965 excavations a number of ostraca were uncovered. In 1967 an ostracon of particular importance was discovered. Its writing was a combination of Hebrew and hieratic scripts, dating back to about 600 B.C. The person who wrote the ostracon knew how to use both the Egyptian hieratic and the Hebrew systems of writing. There are two major historical implications of the Tel Arad finds: (1) there were close ties between Judah and Egypt in the seventh century B.C.; (2) there were in Judah, in the late seventh century B.C., persons who made use of both the Hebrew script and the Egyptian hieratic systems of writing.[14]

Tel Arad is a National Parks Authority site.

- *As the Israelites penetrated into the Promised Land from the south, the men of Arad took some of the children of Israel prisoners, whereupon Israel vowed to destroy the city and Joshua killed the king (Num. 21:1-2; 33:40; Josh. 12:14; Judg. 1:16).*
- *In its vicinity the Kenites settled (Judg. 1:16).*
- *King Solomon had a fortress here.*
- *Shishak I of Egypt captured Arad.*

Ein Bokek

At Ein Bokek, about 3½ miles north of Neve Zohar, there is a health resort featuring mineral water from the hot springs of Hamei Zohar. Above the resort are the ruins of the Bokek Fort, built to guard the sweet-water spring.

MASADA, *Metsada* (*"fortress"*)

About 2½ miles from the western shore of the Dead Sea and 15 miles north of Sodom, in the wilderness of Judah, is a rock fortress ½ mile long, 220 yards wide, and nearly 1,500 feet above the level of the Dead Sea. It is located opposite the white peninsula of Halashon ("the tongue"), which projects into the Dead Sea from the Jordan shore.

Herod the Great (37-4 B.C.) built his winter palaces here. Around his fortress he built a **WALL** 18 feet high and 38 **TOWERS** 75 feet high. When Rome marched on the Jews in A.D. 66, a band of Jewish patriots, Zealots, led by Menachem Ben Yehuda of Galilee, fled to Masada and captured it from a Roman garrison. The Romans had captured Jerusalem, and Masada was one of the last strongholds to resist the Romans. This small band of Jewish patriots was a "thorn in the flesh" of the Romans. Under the leadership of Flavius Silva, the Romans built a 3-mile wall around Masada. The entire siege force probably totalled 15,000 (when Zealots

Masada

Storehouses, Masada

rolled big boulders off on Roman soldiers building a siege ramp, the Romans brought in Jewish slaves to get the job done – Zealots were less inclined to kill their own countrymen). The collapsed stone outline of Silva's main camp is visible to the northwest of Masada. Others of the 8 Roman camps around the mountain are also visible. After a 3-year siege and the construction of an earthen ramp, the Romans broke into the fortress and found that all had killed each other and themselves, except 2 women and 5 children. On that April 15, A.D. 73, 960 persons perished.

Eleazar gave a long oration to the Jews to help prepare them for the mass "murder-suicide." This speech is recorded by Josephus in his *Wars of the Jews*, VII:8:6-7.

Among the important finds are the **ROMAN WALL**, the **WATER SYSTEM** with giant cisterns (the largest held 80,000 gallons of water), **NORTHERN AND WESTERN PALACES, THE OLDEST MOSAICS IN THE COUNTRY, ROMAN BATHS, STOREROOMS, COINS, POTS, SWIMMING POOLS, IMMERSION POOLS, A SYNAGOGUE, A BYZANTINE CHURCH**, and fourteen **SCROLLS**, including *Deuteronomy, Ezekiel, Leviticus, Psalms*, and nonbiblical texts: *Sabbath Sacrifices, Book of Jubilees*, and *Ecclesiasticus*. These scrolls are especially impor-

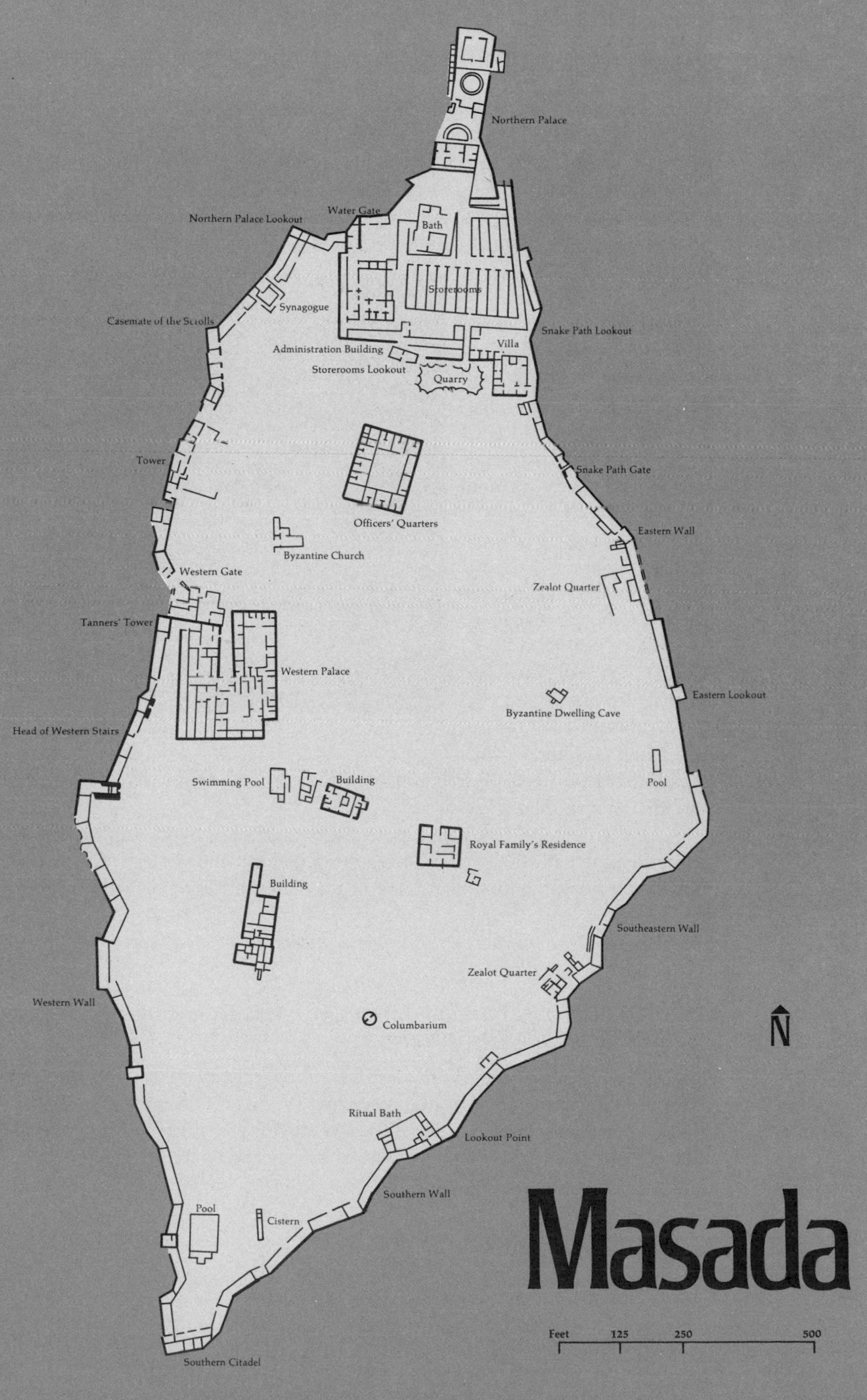
Northern Palace
Water Gate
Northern Palace Lookout
Bath
Storerooms
Synagogue
Casemate of the Scrolls
Snake Path Lookout
Villa
Administration Building
Storerooms Lookout
Quarry
Tower
Snake Path Gate
Officers' Quarters
Eastern Wall
Byzantine Church
Western Gate
Zealot Quarter
Tanners' Tower
Western Palace
Eastern Lookout
Byzantine Dwelling Cave
Head of Western Stairs
Swimming Pool
Building
Pool
Royal Family's Residence
Building
Southeastern Wall
Zealot Quarter
Western Wall
Columbarium
N
Ritual Bath
Lookout Point
Southern Wall
Pool
Cistern
Masada
Feet
125
250
500
Southern Citadel

tant because of the exact dating and the important scroll *Songs of the Sabbath Sacrifices*, which is identical to a Qumran scroll.

Yigael Yadin was the archaeologist responsible for the excavation of Masada during eleven months of digging and reconstruction (2 seasons), from Oct. 1963 to May 1964 and Nov. 1964 to Apr. 1965. Over 5,000 applications were received, and volunteers came from 28 countries. Ninety-seven percent of the built-on area of Masada has been excavated.

Old Synagogue, Masada

Masada has become a shrine and symbol to the nation of Israel. "Masada shall not fall again!" was an oath of many cadets who graduated from Israel's military academy. Nearly every school child has climbed Masada. It is a national tradition. Masada represents (1) the stand of a few against the many, (2) the weak against the strong (like David and Goliath), (3) religious and spiritual freedom, and (4) men of different sects and beliefs living together. They were united in a struggle for freedom. Some were Essenes, some were Zealots, and some are not identified.

Ascent to the top of Masada is possible by gondola or by foot up the 2-mile-long serpentine path or by the shorter ramp path on the western side. A road from Arad leads to the foot of the ramp path. This is a National Parks Authority site.

- *Some believe Masada was the "stronghold" where David's followers joined him (2 Sam. 24:23; 1 Chron. 12:1-16).*

EN GEDI (*"spring of the kid"*), **Ein Gedi**, *Hazazon-tamar* (*"pruning of the date palm"*), *Tell el-Jurn*

Ein Gedi has been an oasis in the desert for thousands of years, with immense fountains of water emerging from underground springs. It is on the west shore of the Dead Sea, about midway, at Ein David Wadi. It is 10½ miles north of Masada and has a kibbutz nearby which was settled in 1949 and named Ein Gedi. Here is one of Israel's few waterfalls that run year-round. The water drops nearly 300 feet. One can splash around in beautiful natural pools. There are many caves in the area. The "wild goats" referred to in the Bible (1 Sam. 24:1-3; Ps. 104:18) are the **IBEX** which still live in this canyon, and biblical "conies" (Ps. 104:18; Prov. 30:26) are the little rock-badgers now called **HYRAX**.

There have been inhabitants at Ein Gedi since pre-Israelite times. North of here the Dead Sea scrolls were found, and near here the Bar Kokhba Scrolls were found by Yigael Yadin.

Ezekiel prophesied (47:1, 10) that the waters of the Dead Sea will be healed and that fish will abound here.

- *It was occupied by Amorites (Gen. 14:7).*
- *It was in the territory of Judah (Josh. 15:20, 62).*
- *Here David took refuge and cut off part of Saul's garment (1 Sam. 23:29-24:22).*
- *Here Jehoshaphat defeated his enemies (2 Chron. 20).*
- *It was a fruitful area (Song of Sol. 1:14).*
- *The acacia tree, from which the ark of the covenant, table, staves, etc. were built, grows in this area, as well as in other desert areas (Exod. 25:5, 10, 13, 23, 28).*

HEVENU SHALOM ALEICHEM*

*"We Bring You Peace." This is a popular Israeli song.

NOTES

1 Note also 2 Ne. 24:29, 31, where this prophecy of Isaiah's is quoted.

2 The prophet Lehi lived and preached in the city of Jerusalem. He was forced to flee for his life. He journeyed into the wilderness and came by boat to the land of America. The story of Lehi's descendants is found in the Book of Mormon.

3 Travelers conversant with the Book of Revelation will be interested in a reference to an event which is apparently to transpire on the streets of Jerusalem. As many Christians understand it, two prophets are to be raised up among the Jews to testify to Judah for 3½ years concerning the mission of Jesus, as part of the "wind-up" scene in the last days. They will have power to hold the army of 200 million in check while they prophesy (Rev. 9:16). They will finally be killed during the last great battles and their bodies will lie in the streets of Jerusalem for 3½ days and then be resurrected (Rev. 11:3-11; Zech. 4:3, 11, 14). To these references Latter-day Saints add Doctrine and Covenants 77:15.

4 Also, 1 Ne. 11:33; 19:10; 3 Ne. 27:14; Eth. 4:1; Moses 7:55; D&C 6:37; 45:51-52.

5 Also, Eth. 12:7; 2 Ne. 25:13; D&C 20:23; 35:2; 45:52; 46:13; 76:41.

6 Note also D&C 107:53; 116.

7 Many Christians anticipate that the Mount of Olives will have a definite part in the final "wind-up" scenes of the last days: Armageddon, the two witnesses, the appearance of Jesus on the Mount of Olives, the "touching down" scene, and the beginning of the Messiah's reign. They believe that the Mount of Olives will cleave in the midst when Jesus comes (Zech. 14:4-5) and that all believers will come into the valley and the Jews will feel his wounds and accept him as their Messiah (Mal. 3:2; D&C 45:51-53; 3 Ne. 20:29).

A Prayer on the Mount of Olives

The Church of Jesus Christ of Latter-day Saints has long been interested in the dispersion and subsequent gathering of Israel. In 1831, in Kirtland, Ohio, a revelation was given concerning a special call to Orson Hyde, who in 1835 became an apostle in the Church. He was to preach the gospel from "land to land" (D&C 68:1-7). In the fall of 1840 he left Nauvoo, Illinois, on a mission that took him 20,000 miles. Visiting the principal cities of Europe, he told them about the gospel and his commission to dedicate Palestine for the return of the Jews. As he neared the port of Joppa, a miraculous vision reassured him of his mission.

On October 24, 1841, Hyde ascended the Mount of Olives all alone, built an altar to the Lord, and offered a dedicatory prayer that was to inaugurate a miraculous movement – the gathering of the Jews from the four quarters of the earth. The following excerpts are from that prayer:

Thy servant...has safely arrived in this place to dedicate and consecrate this land unto Thee, for the gathering together of Judah's scattered remnants, according to the predictions of the holy Prophets – for the building up of Jerusalem after it has been trodden down by the Gentiles so long, and for rearing a Temple in honor of Thy name....

O Thou, Who didst covenant with Abraham, Thy friend, and Who didst renew that covenant with Isaac, and confirm the same with Jacob with an oath, that Thou wouldst not only give them this land for an everlasting inheritance, but that Thou wouldst also remember their seed forever. Abraham, Isaac, and Jacob have long since closed their eyes in death, and made the grave their mansion. Their children are scattered and dispersed abroad among the nations of the Gentiles like sheep that have no shepherd, and are still looking forward for the fulfillment of those promises which Thou didst make concerning them....

Let the land become abundantly fruitful when possessed by its rightful heirs; let it again flow with plenty to feed the returning prodigals.... Incline them to gather in upon this land according to Thy word. Let them come like clouds and like doves to their windows. Let the large ships of the nations bring them from the distant isles; and let kings become their nursing fathers, and queens with motherly fondness wipe the tear of sorrow from their eye.

...Let them know that it is Thy good pleasure to restore the kingdom unto Israel – raise up Jerusalem as its capital, and constitute her people a distinct nation and government, with David Thy servant, even a descendant from the loins of ancient David to be their king [History of the Church 4:456-457, emphasis added].

In 1845 the Quorum of Twelve Apostles, of which Orson Hyde was a member, issued a "Proclamation of the Twelve to the World," in which they said:

And we further testify that the Jews among all nations are hereby commanded, in the name of the Messiah to prepare to return to Jerusalem in Palestine, and to rebuild that city and temple unto the Lord.

And also to organize and establish their own political government, under their own rulers, judges, and governors, in that country.

For be it known unto them that we now hold the keys of the Priesthood and kingdom which are soon to be restored unto them [Parker Pratt Robison, *Writings of Parley Parker Pratt* (Salt Lake City, 1952), p. 3].

Elder Orson Hyde served on the first High Council in this dispensation. He served at least six or seven missions, including several times to England, to Palestine, and was even called to Russia. He journeyed to Washington, D. C., visiting twice with President Tyler. He knew the Bible in English, German, and Hebrew. Orson Hyde served as a member of the Utah Bar and Territorial Legislature and as president of the Senate. He had 32 children. He was president of the Quorum of the Twelve (next in line to be prophet) longer than any other in this dispensation, 31 years.

8 This is similar in many respects to Lehi's dream of the iron rod (1 Ne. 8, 11, 15).

9 Jesus said concerning Isaiah: "Search these things diligently; for great are the words of Isaiah" (3 Ne. 23:1).

10 As the Book of Moses also does (Moses 6:64; note also D&C 91:1-3).

11 This star of David is like one that has recently been found in America and is located in the National Museum in Mexico City. The star was found on a Mayan stela, an upright stone carved in relief. The figure on the stela is that of a man with the star of David in the center of what appears to be an ear plug. This evidence, along with much more, has caused American scholar Cyrus H. Gordon to believe that Mediterranean people discovered America at least a thousand years before Columbus.

12 At this harbor Orson Hyde debarked in 1841 as he came to Jerusalem to dedicate the land for the "return of the Jews." On his way by ship to Joppa from Beirut, he had a unique experience. At 1:00 A.M. he beheld a bright sword in the heavens, grasped by an extended arm and hand, while the Arabs on board kept saying, "Allah! Allah! Allah!" Hyde, a member of the Quorum of the Twelve Apostles of The Church of Jesus Christ of Latter-day Saints, saw this as one of the "signs of heaven" that had been promised him.

At this same harbor other apostles later arrived also. In Feb. 1873 three apostles, Pres. George A. Smith, Elders Lorenzo Snow and Albert Carrington, along with Lorenzo's sister, Eliza R. Snow, and Bro. and Sis. Feramorz Little, and others, landed at Joppa to begin an extended tour of the Holy Land.

13 Jacob Spori, a Swiss university professor living in Bern, was given a copy of The Book of Mormon by a friend named Karl G. Maeser, who told him, "read this book and your life will be changed." Spori read the book and was converted to the Church of Jesus Christ of Latter-day Saints. But the price he paid for his belief was heavy – his wife left him and went to her father who closed the door on Jacob. Even the city of Bern ejected him because of his new Mormon faith. With a broken heart he left Switzerland, emigrated to Utah, and made his home in Logan.

In October 1884 he was called by President John Taylor on a mission to his native country of Switzerland. From there he was called to do missionary work in Istanbul.

In the Spring of 1886 Francis M. Lyman, Jr. came to Constantinople, and with Joseph M. Tanner traveled through the Near East and Palestine. While in Haifa they visited the German colonies, established here about 1870 by devout Templers who entered the Holy Land to await the second advent of the Lord. By their thrift, orderliness, and observance of law, they made Haifa an oasis of civilization in a desert of semi-barbarism.

Elder Tanner wrote to Daniel H. Wells, president of the European Mission, telling him about the German colonies and encouraging some work be done here. It was decided that Tanner and Spori would go, but since they had only enough money for one of them, and Spori was Swiss and knew German and French, he was selected to go. After a prayerful night, Elder Tanner asked Elder Spori how he felt about the hardships he would encounter. Smiling, Elder Spori replied, "I had a vision in the night and was told to begin my labors in the town of Haifa. In this vision I saw a man with a short coal black beard. He was a blacksmith, and as I passed his shop he came out to meet me. I was further told that he would be notified of my coming and that he and his family should be prepared to receive me and the message I had for them." Confidently he said, "I shall know the man if I ever see him."

In the afternoon of July 29, 1886, Elder Spori boarded a ship for the Holy Land. Upon reaching Haifa he made his way to the street he had seen in his vision. After walking a short distance up the street, he heard the ring of the anvil. Walking in the middle of the street, as he had been told in his vision, he walked towards the blacksmith shop. The blacksmith, with the coal black beard, upon seeing Elder Spori, dropped his hammer, tongs, and iron and ran out into the street calling to the Elder. He introduced himself as Johann Georg Grau, and declared that he had seen this stranger in a dream the night before and that the stranger had a divine message for him. Elder Spori was invited into the house of the blacksmith and treated most kindly. Grau's family was called together and Elder Spori delivered his message. The Grau family was converted, and on August 29, 1886, in the Bay of Acco, Johann Georg Grau was baptized. Less than a month later Georg, having been ordained an elder, baptized his wife Magdalena.

Jacob Spori was a man of linguistic attainments, speaking German, French, English, Turkish, Italian, Russian, and Arabic, yet he was humble enough to be led by the Spirit of the Lord and boldly defended the truth before all opposition. He felt discouraged at times because he didn't baptize more people. On his way to Utah he stopped in Switzerland where his wife and family joined him on his voyage to the land of Zion in America. Spori was later one of the founders of Ricks College in Rexburg, Idaho. The old administration building there is named in his honor.

14 See 1 Ne. 1:2; Mos. 1:4; Morm. 9:32-34. See also *Biblical Archaeology Review* Mar/Apr 1987, 16-35.

Egypt

Egypt, also named Mizraim (Gen. 10:6, 13; 1 Chron. 1:8, 11), occupies the northeast corner of Africa. Its land area is over 386,000 square miles and with the Sinai peninsula, 465,000 square miles. Ninety-seven percent is arid desert, swamp, or barren mountains. Less than 3% of the country is under cultivation. Since most of the land is desert it should not be surprising that Egypt is one of the driest countries in the world. Cairo *is* the world's driest capital, averaging only one inch of rain per year. Egypt is 892 miles long and 758 miles wide.

HISTORY

From earliest times the Nile River valley has been settled by man. Historical man in Egypt dates back to approximately 3200 B.C. When one compares the history of this 5,000-year-old civilization with the 200-year history of the United States of America, one begins to see a new concept of time.

The world's first "united nation" was formed when upper and lower Egypt became one in 3100 B.C. and formed the first of thirty dynasties of pharaohs. For 2,000 years Egypt enjoyed a magnificent civilization. A united government, a 365-day year, a system of writing for keeping records, a method of calculating, a firm belief in life after death, medical science, the science of astronomy, material wealth, sea trade, and knowledge of art and architecture were a part of the Egyptian genius that was to inspire the Greek, Roman, and western civilizations thereafter.

For 2,000 years the secrets of the Egyptians were hidden in the unreadable hieroglyphs. Only since the nineteenth century and the discovery and deciphering of the Rosetta Stone has man been able to understand the written records of this ancient civilization.

During the Eighteenth Dynasty (1567-1320 B.C.), under the rule of Thutmose III, Egypt expanded her borders to the Euphrates River and reached the zenith of her power. But after Pharaoh Amenhotep IV, who changed his name to Akhenaton (Ikhnaton), Egypt was never the same. Following the reign of Ramses III (1195-1164 B.C.), the last of the great pharaohs, the grandeur ended. Wave after wave of invaders overran the country. In the seventh century B.C. the prophet Isaiah predicted that "the spirit of Egypt shall fail in the midst thereof.... And the Egyptians will I give over into the hand of a cruel lord" (Isa. 19:3-4). His prophecy was fulfilled many times – by the Assyrians, by the Persians, and finally in 332 B.C. by Alexander the Great, whose Ptolemaic period kindled a final flare of cultured glory. The library at Alexandria became the universal center of learning; all eyes turned toward the learning of Egypt. In the year 30 B.C., however, the glory ended when Cleopatra and Antony lifted the asp to their breasts and died. With their

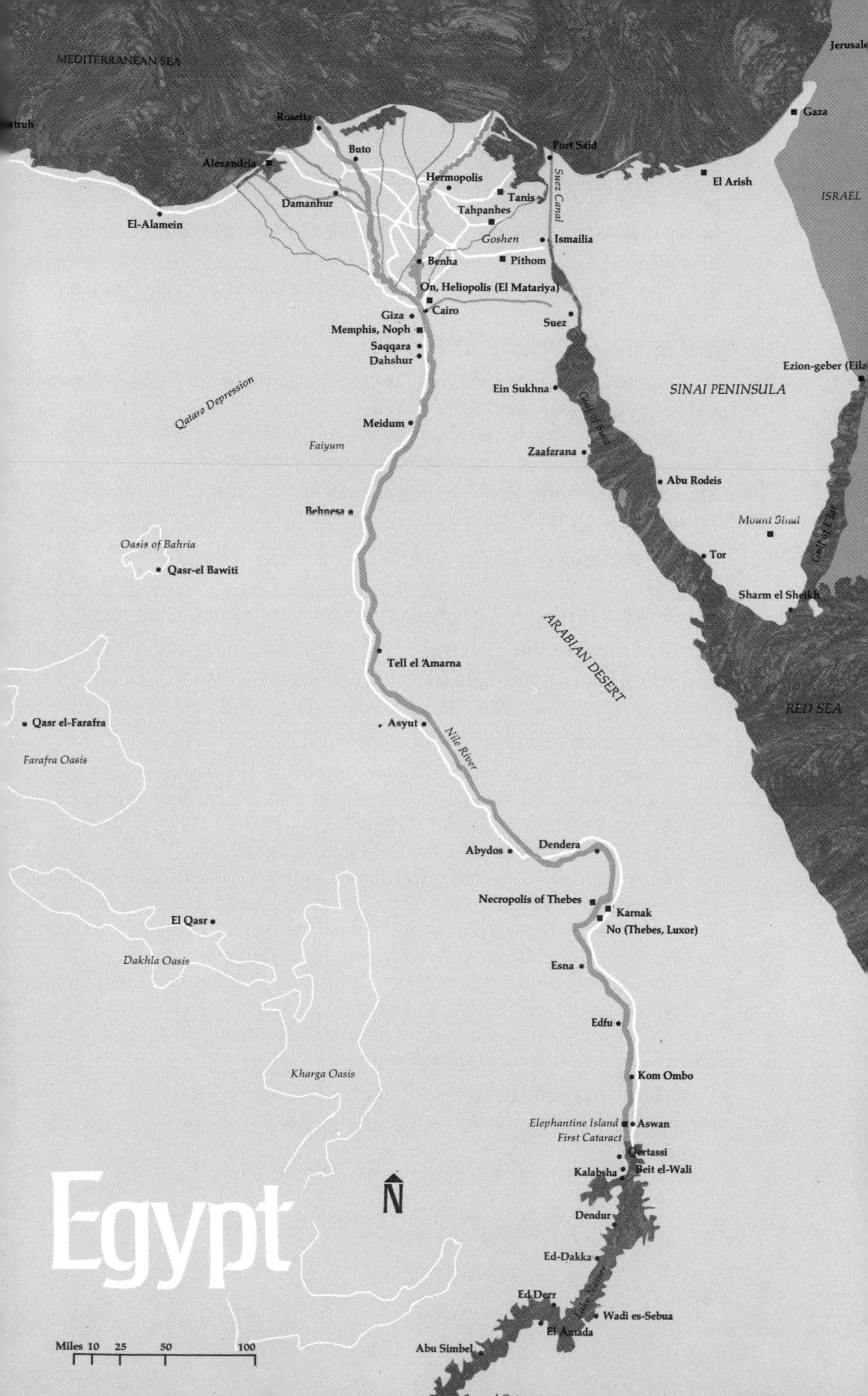

MEDITERRANEAN SEA
Jerusalem
Gaza
atruh
Rosetta
Port Said
Buto
Alexandria
Hermopolis
Suez Canal
El Arish
ISRAEL
Tanis
Damanhur
Tahpanhes
El-Alamein
Goshen
Ismailia
Benha
Pithom
On, Heliopolis (El Matariya)
Giza
Cairo
Suez
Memphis, Noph
Saqqara
Dahshur
Ezion-geber (Eila
Ein Sukhna
SINAI PENINSULA
Qatara Depression
Gulf of Suez
Meidum
Faiyum
Zaafarana
Abu Rodeis
Behnesa
Mount Sinai
Oasis of Bahria
Tor
Gulf of Elat
Qasr-el Bawiti
Sharm el Sheikh
ARABIAN DESERT
Tell el 'Amarna
RED SEA
Qasr el-Farafra
Asyut
Nile River
Farafra Oasis
Abydos
Dendera
Necropolis of Thebes
Karnak
El Qasr
No (Thebes, Luxor)
Dakhla Oasis
Esna
Edfu
Kharga Oasis
Kom Ombo
Elephantine Island
Aswan
First Cataract
Qertassi
Kalabsha
Beit el-Wali
Egypt
N
Dendur
Ed-Dakka
Ed Derr
Lake Nasser
Wadi es-Sebua
El Amada
Miles 10 25 50 100
Abu Simbel
Second Cataract

deaths, Egypt became a Roman province and lost her independent power in the ancient world.

OUTLINE OF EGYPT'S HISTORY

Early Dynastic Period *(3100-2686 B.C.). Dynasties I-II*

King Menes established the first capital at Memphis after upper and lower Egypt were united in 3100 B.C. This was the biblical Noph (Isa. 19:13; Jer. 2:16; 46:14, 19; Ezek. 30:13, 16).

Old Kingdom *(2686-2181 B.C.). Dynasties III-VI*

Djoser (Zoser), the outstanding pharaoh of the period, built the Step Pyramid, and King Snefru built the Bent Pyramid.

During the Fourth Dynasty the great pyramids of Cheops (Khufu), Chephren (Khafre), and Mycerinus (Menkure) were built.

First Intermediate Period *(2181-2060 B.C.). Dynasties VII-X*

This was a period of decline. Princes ruled the provinces with frequent civil wars.

Middle Kingdom *(2060-1786 B.C.) Dynasties XI-XII*

This was the classical period, in which art and architecture flourished. The capital was moved to Thebes, the biblical No (Jer. 46:25; Ezek. 30:14-16; Nah. 3:8).

Second Intermediate Period *(1786-1567 B.C.) Dynasties XIII-XVII*

The Hyksos from Asia, who controlled Egypt about 1674-1567 B.C., had their capital at Avaris in the Nile delta. They introduced horses and chariots into Egypt.

New Kingdom *(1567-1085 B.C.). Dynasties XVIII-XX*

After the Hyksos were driven from Egypt, this became the age of Egypt's supreme power, expansion, and wealth. It was a period of temple building at Luxor, Karnak, Abu-Simbel, Abydos, and Memphis.

In 1468 B.C. Thutmose III conquered Canaan at Megiddo.

Famous pharaohs reigned: Hatshepsut, Amenhotep III, Amenhotep IV (Akhenaton, who married Nefertiti). (Greek authors render *Amenhotep* as *Amenophis.*) Other famous pharaohs of the period were Tutankhamon, Ramses I, and Ramses II. The children of Israel were in Egypt during this time.

During the period 1370-1352 B.C., Akhenaton believed in a revolutionary doctrine of monotheism and moved his headquarters to Tell el Amarna, in middle Egypt. During this period elaborate tombs were hewn in the Valley of the Kings, and the *Book of the Dead* was written on papyrus.

Post-Empire Period *(1085-341 B.C.). Dynasties XXI-XXX*

Shishak ruled during the Twenty-second Dynasty (1 Kings 11:40; 14:25-26; 2 Chron. 12:2-9).

Necho, who ruled during the Twenty-sixth Dynasty, conquered Judah at Megiddo in 609 B.C. (2 Kings 23:29-30, 33-35; 2 Chron. 35:20-24; 36:4; Jer. 46:2).

The Persians ruled in Egypt from 525 to 398 B.C. and again between 378 and 341 B.C.

Greek Rule, Ptolemaic Period *(332-30 B.C.)*

Alexander the Great, who conquered Egypt at age 24, founded and built Alexandria. After his death, the Ptolemaic dynasty ruled for 300 years.

Egypt was the cultural hub of the old world, and the great minds flocked to Alexandria.

Cleopatra reigned (51-30 B.C.) until she and Antony committed suicide with the asp.

Roman Rule *(30 B.C.-A.D. 323)*

As early as the first century, Christianity was established in Egypt, with Alexandria as the center of activity. Tradition says that Saint Mark, the apostle, was responsible.

It was in Egypt that the monastic hermit style of Christianity originated.

In the middle of the fourth century A.D. the Coptic translations of the Bible were made.

Byzantine Rule *(A.D. 323-640)*

During this period, Egyptian temples were destroyed or converted into Christian monasteries and churches.

By 451, part of the Copts had decided to stop giving allegiance to the Pope, and they became known as the Orthodox Copts. The Uniate Catholic Copts, however, still recognize the papacy.

Arab Rule *(A.D. 640-1517)*

570. Muhammad was born at Mecca.

640. The second Muslim caliph, Omar I, invaded Egypt. The people of Egypt became Muslims, and Egyptian temples and Christian churches were converted into mosques.

1250-1390. The Bahri Mamelukes reigned.

1390-1517. The Circassian sultans reigned. This was a period of frequent revolts and disturbances.

Modern Period

1517-1798. Egypt was a Turkish province of the Ottoman Empire.

1798-1801. Napoleon conquered Egypt in 1798, but France was forced by the British to withdraw in 1801.

1801-1805. Egypt was under British control.

1805-1952. This was the dynasty of the Albanian Muhammad (or Mehemet) Ali and the last dynasty of Egypt.

1882-1936. The British occupied Egypt.

1952. King Farouk, the last of Muhammad Ali's dynasty, abdicated.

1953. Egypt became a republic after being ruled by foreign masters for 2,800 years.

1954-1970. Gamal Abdel Nasser, the president of Egypt, was the moving force behind the creation of the United Arab Republic in *1958*. He died September 28, 1970.

1956. The Suez Canal was nationalized by Egypt.

1970. After the death of Nasser, the vice-president, Anwar El Sadat, became president of Egypt, and the Aswan High Dam was dedicated.

1973. October (Yom Kippur) War with Israel.

1979. Peace treaty with Israel.

1981. Sadat assassinated; Vice-President Hosni Mubarak succeeded him.

EGYPT IN THE SCRIPTURES

- ***Abraham*** *went to Egypt because of famine (Gen. 12:10-20).*
- *Hagar was an Egyptian who mothered Ishmael, Abraham's firstborn (Gen. 16:1).*
- *Ishmael married an Egyptian. The Ishmaelites were three-quarters Egyptian (Gen. 21:21).*
- ***Joseph*** *was sold to Ishmaelites and carried to Egypt, where he was sold to an Egyptian officer, Potiphar, as a slave (Gen. 37:26-28, 36; 39:1-20). He was imprisoned (Gen. 39:21-41:40). He was exalted as a ruler (Gen. 41; Acts 7:9-10). He was reunited with his family (Gen. 42-45).*
- *Jacob and his family came to Egypt when the famine struck them in Canaan. He spent the last 17 years of his life in Goshen, the southeast part of the Nile delta (Gen. 42-50).*
- *The children of Israel were oppressed as slaves in Egypt, perhaps under Ramses II (Gen. 15:13; Exod. 1, 2; Acts 7:6).*
- ***Moses*** *was born in Egypt during the oppression and was reared in the house of royalty (Exod. 2).*
- *Moses accomplished the deliverance of Israel (Exod. 3-14).*
- *Joseph's bones were carried out of Egypt (Gen. 50:25-26; Exod. 13:19; Josh. 24:32; Heb. 11:22).*
- *Hadad fled to Egypt, married a sister of the queen of Egypt, and came back as the king of Edom and an enemy of Solomon (1 Kings 11:14-22).*
- *Jeroboam fled to Egypt until Solomon died (1 Kings 11:26-40), and then Jeroboam returned and at Shechem he became king over ten tribes (1 Kings 12:1-25).*
- *Shishak, king of Egypt, invaded and subdued Judah (1 Kings 14:25-26).*
- *Zerah, king of Egypt, unsuccessfully invaded Judah (2 Chron. 14:9-15; 16:8).*

- *Hoshea, king of Israel, and Hezekiah, king of Judah, sought the help of the Ethiopian kings of Egypt against Assyria (2 Kings 17:4; 19:9).*
- *Remnants to return from Egypt. Isaiah's lament over Egypt (Isa. 11:11; 27:13).*
- *Necho, king of Egypt, slew Josiah (2 Kings 23:29-30; 2 Chron. 35:20-24).*
- *A remnant of the Jews fled to Egypt and settled (2 Kings 25:25-26; Jer. 42-44).*
- ***Jeremiah** was carried to Egypt, where he was located at Tahpanhes (Jer. 43:8).*
- *Jeremiah predicted woes against Egypt (Jer. 43:9-46:28), and tradition has Jeremiah beaten to death for uttering them.*
- *Ezekiel's explanation of Egypt's desolation and his lamentation over Egypt (Ezek. 29-32; esp. 29:13-26; also 30:14-16).*
- *"When Israel was a child, then I . . . called my son out of Egypt" (Hosea 11:1).*
- *After being warned by an angel, Joseph and Mary took **Jesus** to Egypt to escape the death decree of Herod (Matt. 2:13-15, 19-21).*
- *Abraham was nearly sacrificed by the priests in Ur of Chaldea "after the manner of the Egyptians" (Abr. 1:1-20).*
- *The king of Egypt was a descendant of Ham (Abr. 1:21-22).*
- *Egypt was first discovered by a woman while flood waters still covered it (Abr. 1:23-24).*
- *The first government of Egypt was patriarchal (Abr. 1:24-28).*
- *Abraham went to Egypt because of famine (Abr. 2:21-25; Josephus, Antiquities of the Jews, 1:8:1). (The Ras Shamra Tablets, dating to 1400 B.C., contain, among other things, the Keret Legend, which scholars see as evidence for the story of Abraham's journey to the south of Canaan. The Genesis Apocryphon, part of the Dead Sea Scrolls, also verifies the story.)*
- *Abraham taught the Egyptians astronomy (Abr. 3:1-15; Josephus, Antiquities of the Jews, 1:8:2).*
- *Joseph was sold by his brothers and carried captive into Egypt (1 Ne. 5:14; 2 Ne. 3:4; 4:1; Al. 10:3; also Eth. 13:7).*
- *The Lord, through Moses, accomplished the deliverance of Israel from Egypt (1 Ne. 5:15; 17:40; 19:10; 2 Ne. 3:9-10; 25:20; Mos. 12:34; 7:19; D&C 8:3).*
- *The Book of Mormon was said to be written in "reformed Egyptian" characters (Mormon. 9:32; 1 Ne. 1:2; Mosiah 1:4).*

EGYPTIAN WRITING

HIEROGLYPHIC: sacred inscriptions of the pharaohs, consisting of small, carefully drawn figures or pictures.

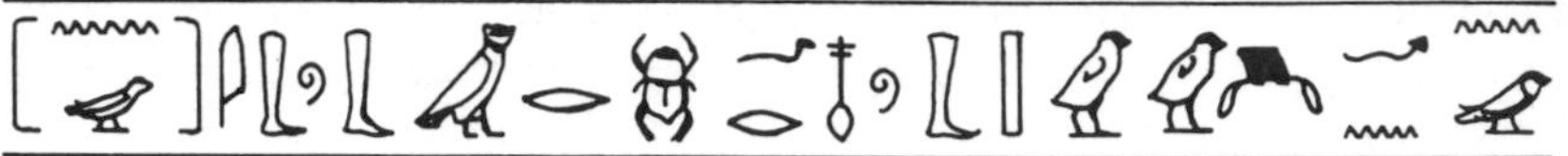

HIERATIC: the cursive form of hieroglyphs, usually found on papyrus and dating from 1300 B.C.

DEMOTIC: the popular writing of the Egyptians during the years 400-100 B.C.; a simplification of the hieratic.

COPTIC: a form of Egyptian writing which uses a Greek alphabet; spoken only by the Copts in the churches and monasteries

ARABIC: used since the seventh century, and now the national language

تعتبر الجيزة من أهم احياء القاهرة الفخمة على الشاطئ الغربي

*Adapted from Kurt Schroeder, *Guide to Egypt* (Cairo, 1965), by permission.

Egyptian Alphabet

The ancient Egyptian alphabet consisted of the following 24 consonants. The vowels were not written.

	Sign	Conventional Reading		Sign	Conventional Reading
1		*a*	13		*kh*
2		*i-j*	14		"line *kh*"
3		*ajin, a*	15		s (z)
4		*w* or *u*	16		s
5		*b*	17		*sh*
6		*p*	18		*k*
7		*f*	19		*k*
8		*m*	20		*g*
9		*n*	21		*t*
10		*r*	22		*th*
11		"soft *h*"	23		*d*
12		"hard *h*"	24		*dj* or *z*

*Adapted from Kurt Schroeder, *Guide to Egypt* (Cairo, 1965), by permission.

Ancient Egyptian Signs

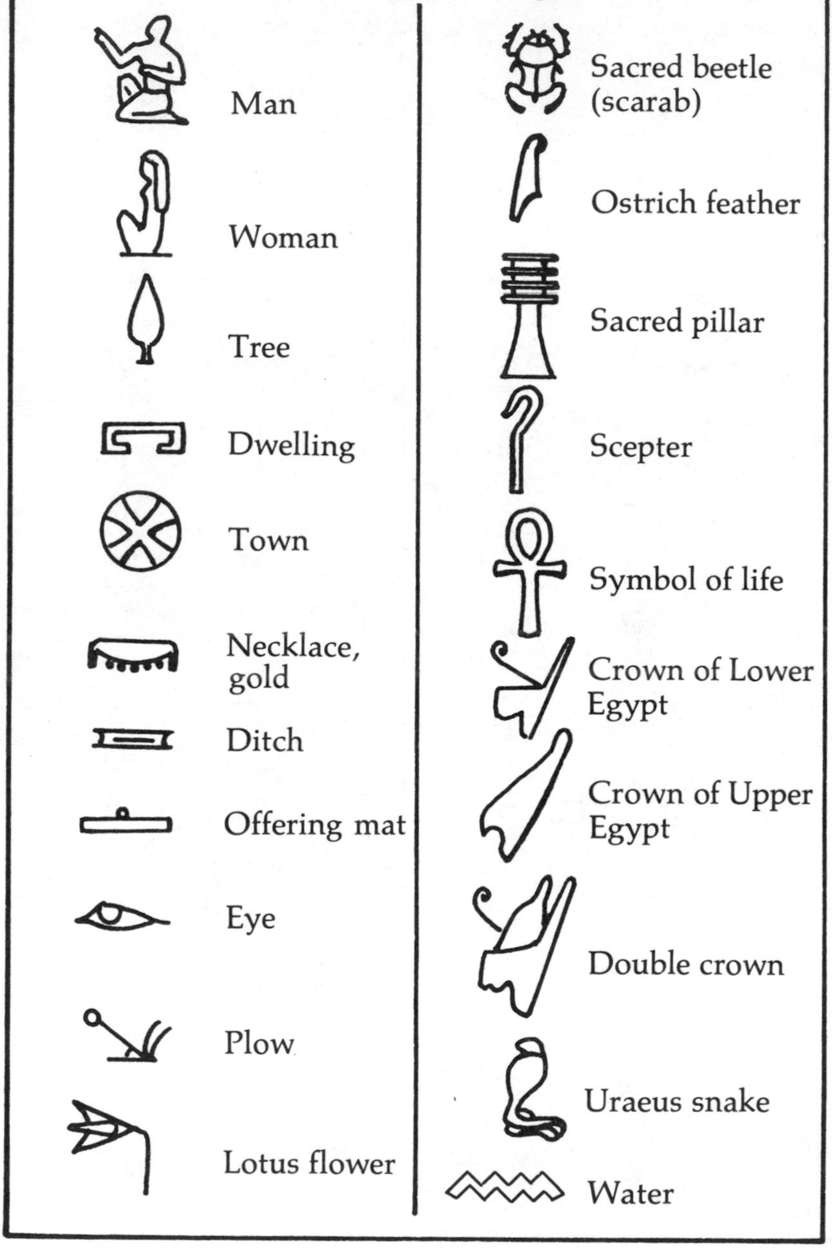

Man	Sacred beetle (scarab)
Woman	Ostrich feather
Tree	Sacred pillar
Dwelling	Scepter
Town	Symbol of life
Necklace, gold	Crown of Lower Egypt
Ditch	Crown of Upper Egypt
Offering mat	Double crown
Eye	Uraeus snake
Plow	Water
Lotus flower	

*Adapted from Kurt Schroeder, *Guide to Egypt* (Cairo, 1965), by permission.

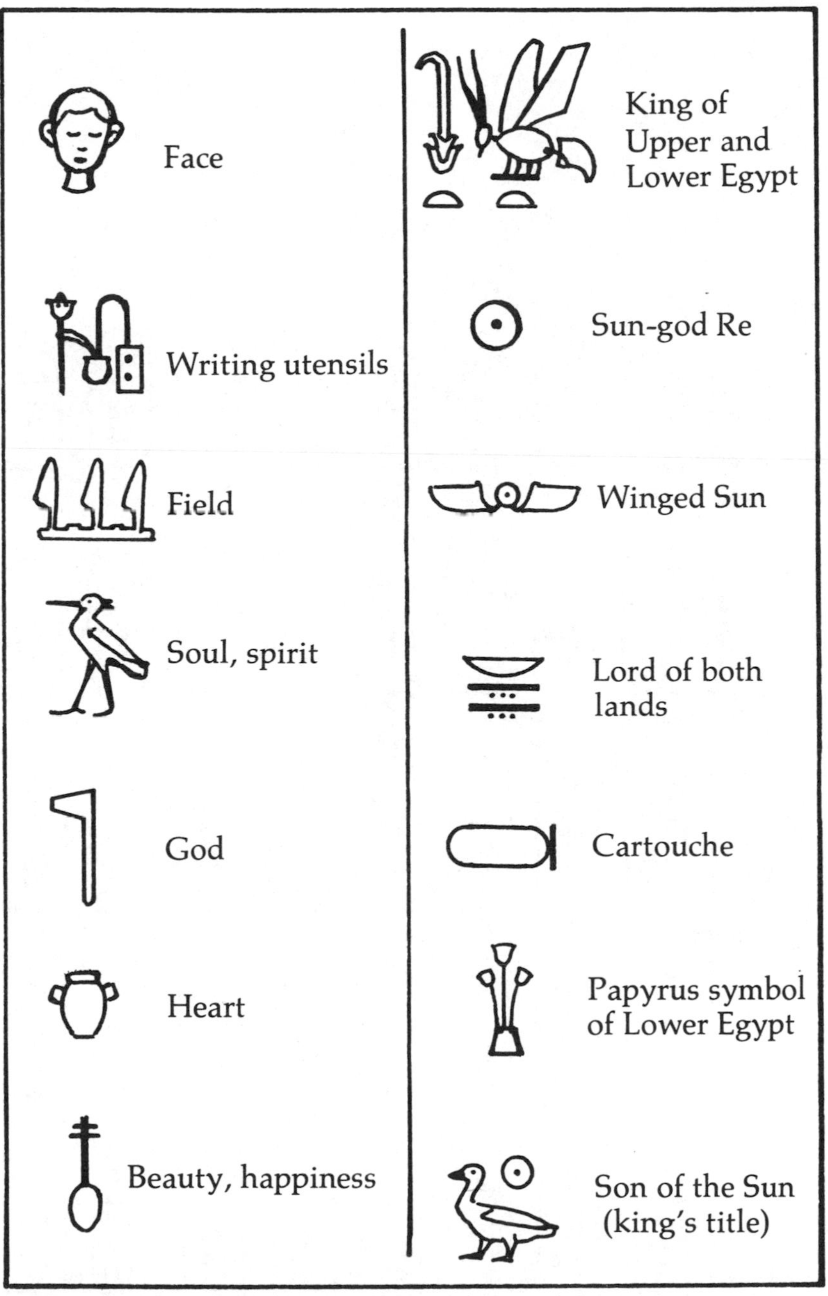

*Adapted from Kurt Schroeder, Guide to Egypt (Cairo, 1965), by permission.

THE MOST IMPORTANT KINGS' CARTOUCHES

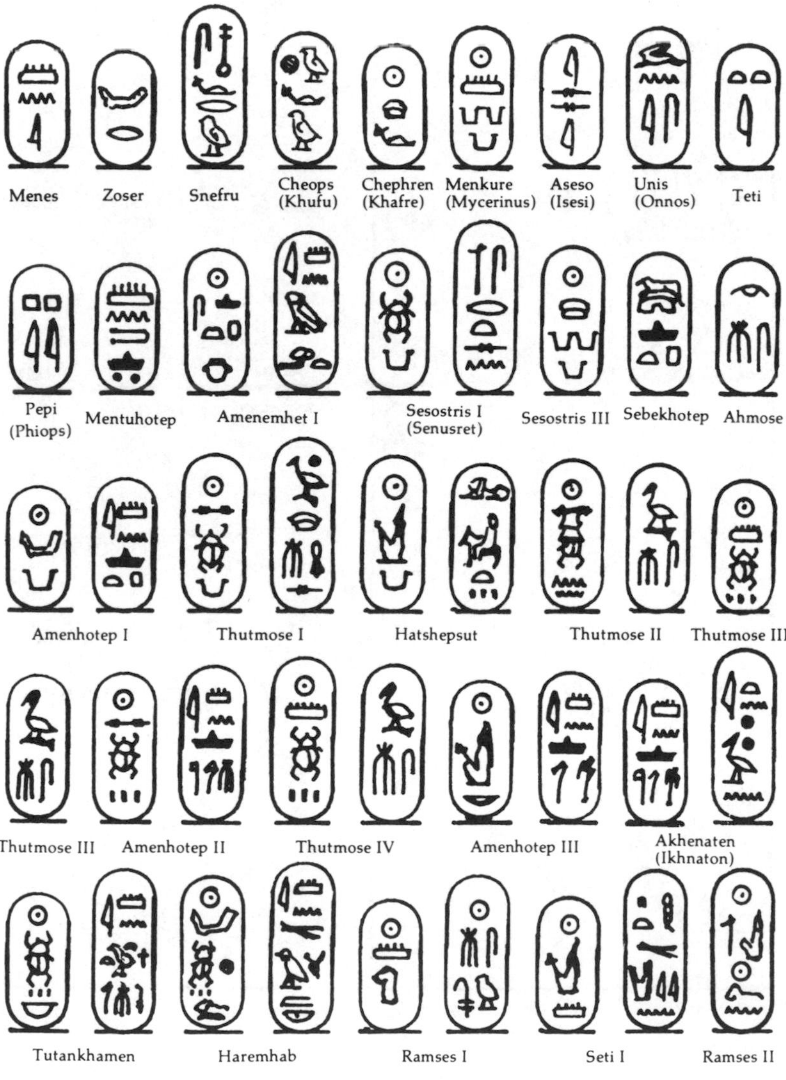

*Adapted from Kurt Schroeder, Guide to Egypt (Cairo, 1965), by permission.

RELIGION

Egyptian Gods

The Egyptians showed reverence to many animals, the sun and moon, the Nile River, and man. The concept of an anthropomorphic god had come even before the First Dynasty, but because of ancient prior practices of worshiping animals, the Egyptians fused three ideas: nature, animal, and man. An example of this type of fusion is the goddess of love, Hathor, who might appear as a human or a cow. When she was given a human body, she still retained the element of a cow with horns over her head. The god Thoth had the head of an ibis, and Anubis the head of a jackal.

Each village and community usually had its local deities, and temples were built for them. Sometimes a universal god, such as Amon, became incarnate in the pharaoh, whose name included the god's name. *Amenhotep (Amenophis)* and *Tutankhamon* are examples of this practice.

Amon (Amen, Amun) was the Theban universal god of all Egyptian gods. He is shown with plumes and sometimes with a sun-disc between the plumes, symbolizing celestial origin. Amon, whose name means "hidden one," is represented as a ram-headed deity; in the Roman period he was identified with Jupiter.

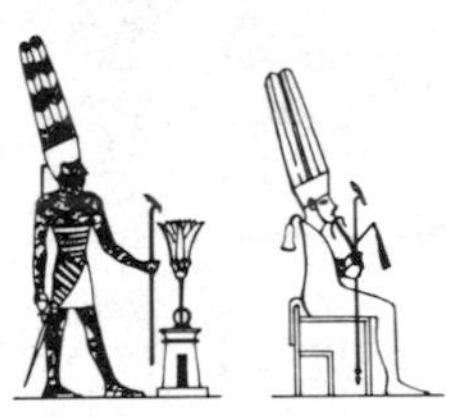

Mut, mother of gods, sky goddess, and wife of Amon, was represented as a vulture or painted green with a vulture's head and a double crown. She was one of the great triad of Thebes, along with Amon and Khons.

Khons, the moon god of Thebes, was the son of Amon and Mut, the three forming the Theban family triad.

Ra (Re-Harakhte) was the sun-god, a form of the sun-god Horus. He is usually represented as a hawk with a solar disc over his head, or sometimes as a divine eye, ram, or man. He was the son of Nut, the sky goddess, and was venerated at Heliopolis.

Osiris was the judge of the dead and the god of vegetation (green human face). He carried a crook and flail, insignia of kingship. His wife was Isis.

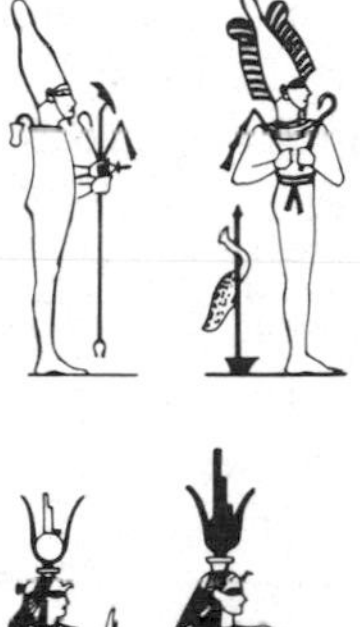

Iris was the goddess of mothers and love. She was a daughter of Geb and Nut, the wife of Osiris, and mother of Horus. She is sometimes represented as a cow-headed being.

Horus, the sun-god, or god of the day, was the son of Osiris and Isis. He is portrayed as a winged sun-disc or as a falcon head with a double crown.

Anubis, as god of the heavens and god of the cemetery, supervised the passage of the soul to the judgment hall in Amenti, the region of the dead in the West. There the hearts of the dead were weighed against the feather of truth. He presided over the tombs and is portrayed as a jackal-headed god. He is called the son of Osiris.

Ptah was the local god of Memphis and the creator of all things. He is represented by the sacred bull, Apis.

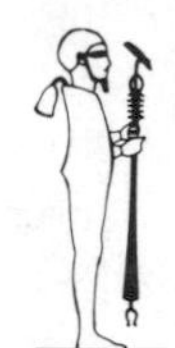

Hathor, the goddess of love, joy, and sky, is portrayed as a woman wearing a headdress with horns and a red disc between the horns. At Deir el-Bahri she is portrayed as a cow nursing Pharaoh Amenhotep II. She is sometimes represented with cow's ears. She was regarded by the Greeks as Aphrodite.

Thoth was the moon god of Hermopolis and the god of writing. As the scribe of the gods, he measured time and invented numbers, and at the judgment he recorded the results of the weighing of the heart. He is portrayed as a man with an ibis head or as a baboon.

Seshet was the goddess of writing.

Khnum, a ram head, was a god of Upper Egypt and husband of Anuket.

Sobk (Sebek) was a crocodile-headed god.

Maat was the goddess of truth and justice. Her symbol was the ostrich feather.

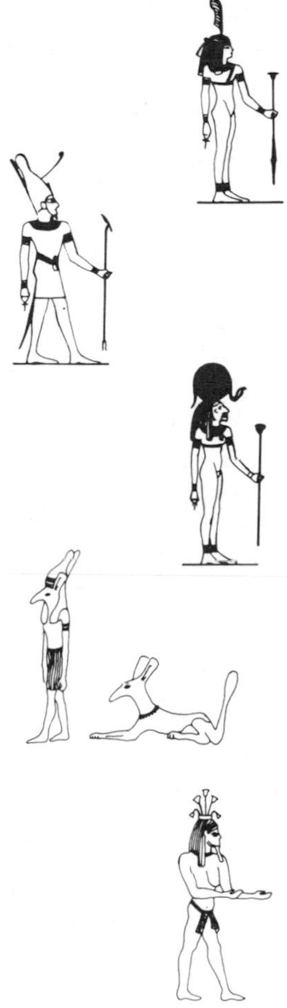

Atum, a god of Heliopolis, is represented by the form of a human, a snake, or a lion.

Sekhmet, the war goddess of Memphis and wife of Ptah, is usually shown with the head of a lion.

Seth, a god of Upper Egypt, was the god of the desert and storms and was portrayed as a human with the head of a large-eared (mulelike) animal. He was the brother of Osiris, whom he murdered.

Hapi was the god of the Nile River.

Nut, a sky goddess, or goddess of the lower heavens, was the wife of Geb and mother of Ra. As goddess of the dawn she daily gave birth to the sun. She is shown sometimes with an elongated body and sometimes as a cow.

Shu, the god of air, is sometimes shown standing beneath Nut, as if supporting her with his outstretched arms.

Geb, the earth god, was the husband of Nut, the sky goddess. He is sometimes portrayed reclining beneath the arched body of Nut.

Bast (Bastet) was a cat-headed goddess of joy.

Mont (Month) was the Theban falcon-headed god of war.

Khepri (Khepre), the sun-god Ra, is represented by the dung beetle (scarab, *Scarabeus sacer*).

Buto (Uazet, Wadjet) was the serpent goddess of the Delta. From earliest times to the present day the cobra serpent has been considered sacred. Three goddesses appear in serpent form: (1) Uazet, the Delta goddess of Buto; (2) Mert-Seger, the goddess of the Necropolis at Thebes; and (3) Rannut, the harvest goddess. Uraeus is the representation of the sacred serpent which appears on the headdress of rulers, often just over the forehead, as a symbol of sovereignty.

Nekhbet was the vulture goddess of Upper Egypt.

Mnevis, a sacred bull, was worshiped at Heliopolis.

Apis, the sacred bull of Ptah, was worshiped at Memphis and is considered by some to be the reincarnation of Osiris. When a new Apis was chosen, it had to have a white, square spot on its forehead, a figure of an eagle on its back, and a knot like a beetle under its tongue. Tombs of these sacred bulls (the Serapeum) are found at Saqqara. There seems to be a relationship between the god Apis and the golden calf made in the wilderness by the Israelites (Exod. 32).

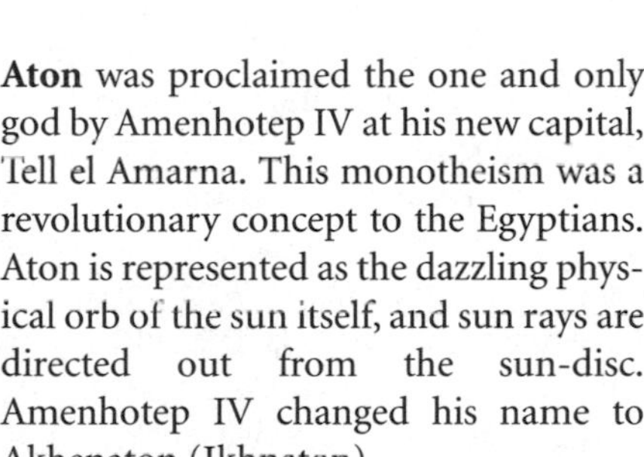

Aton was proclaimed the one and only god by Amenhotep IV at his new capital, Tell el Amarna. This monotheism was a revolutionary concept to the Egyptians. Aton is represented as the dazzling physical orb of the sun itself, and sun rays are directed out from the sun-disc. Amenhotep IV changed his name to Akhenaton (Ikhnaton).

Religious Life in Egypt

From earliest times the sun and the river were the two main Egyptian deities. The sun, like the river, was the giver of life. Ra, the god of the sun, was the god of creation, the father of the pharaohs, and author of the cosmic order. Akhenaton worshiped one god, Aton, the source of all energy and power, a formless intelligence that permeated the universe. Another concept of deity was a divine triad of father, mother, and son.

The Egyptians were firm believers in a life after death, and they felt that the *Book of the Dead*, their guidebook for the deceased, contained the requirements for entrance into the realm of Osiris. They believed that man is accountable for his actions in this life and that he must stand judgment and testify that he is moral. Then his heart is weighed against a feather on a balance to see if he has proved his worthiness to have eternal life.

At Heliopolis a temple cult arose, with an organized priesthood of sun worshipers. The temple was the "house of God," and in addition to its holy place and outer court it had a holy of holies, in which was a symbol called the *benben*, a pyramid-shaped stone representing the sun-god. This was perhaps the forerunner of the pyramids. Only the priest could go into the holy of holies, where the bark and the golden cult image that represented the god were kept. Each day the god was fed, dressed, and adorned; even cosmetics were applied. The god appeared in public only on festivals, and was usually taken in a procession on the avenue of the sphinxes. False doors provided a way for the god to enter the temple. During the New Kingdom the god served as a divine oracle, as at Delphi in Greece. Sacrificing of animals and vegetables, as well as circumcising, is graphically portrayed on the walls of temple and tomb.

The Egyptians believed blessings would be bestowed upon them if they sacrificed to the gods. They also believed in a loving God, who stressed the joy of living on the earth, and in a life concerned with eternal values. In the creation story found in the *Pyramid Texts, maat* (the divine order of nature) replaced chaos; order and law replaced disorder. It was the pharaoh's responsibility to maintain maat in all his doings. This meant honesty, respect, virtue, honor, moderation, self-restraint, humility, integrity, benevolence, and kindness.

The oldest religious documents are the *Pyramid Texts*, consisting of prayers and incantations written by the priests of Heliopolis. The *Coffin Texts* are a collection of spells used for the protection of Egyptians as they made their way to the realm of Osiris, and the *Book of the Dead*, written on papyrus, is nearly the same thing, only more elaborate. The *Book of Breathings* deals with the rituals of the temples and the tombs, which are designed with one main objective: eternal exaltation.

The temples and the tombs were intended to help either the living or the dead Egyptian on his way as an initiate into a new form of life. He was examined for purity, stood judgment, and demonstrated knowledge by answering certain questions and giving certain code words at various gates or doors. Indeed, the Egyptian word for "burial" means to initiate one into the mysteries. The ultimate objective of the dead was to receive permission to enter into the holy of holies of the temple at Heliopolis, on the grounds that as an elder he had been initiated into the deepest secrets of the temple.

Egyptian temples generally have three different parts: a courtyard, a hypostyle hall, and a holy of holies. One cannot help but notice the likeness of Moses' Tabernacle and Solomon's Temple to that of the Egyptian temples. Moses' Tabernacle had a courtyard, a holy place, and a holy of holies. Both Egyptians and Israelites allowed the priests only to go into certain parts of the temple (Exod. 25-27). Both had altars upon which animals were sacrificed. Both practiced circumcision. These similarities would cause one to believe the remark of the Egyptian guide at Luxor when he said, "There is nothing new under the sun." Surely there are eternal principles or concepts involved. It should come as no surprise to Latter-day Saints to see parallels or similarities in ancient Egyptian beliefs and practices to truths revealed to God's ancient and modern covenant peoples. Egyptian religion included false imitation of Priesthood, worship practices, and Temple ordinances (Abraham 1:25-27). We may expect to see some fragments of the truth, some "doctrinal debris," coming down through the centuries, especially knowing that "the learning of the Egyptians, and their knowledge of astronomy was no doubt taught them by Abraham and Joseph, as their records testify, who received it from the Lord" (*Teachings of the Prophet Joseph Smith*, p. 251; see also Abr. 3:15).

Embalming

Not all the secrets of Egyptian embalming are known, but apparently the following steps were taken to prepare the bodies of royalty for the afterlife. Most of the brain was drawn out through the nostrils, and the part left was dissolved with aromatic lotions. The viscera were then removed through an incision in the side of the body, and the body washed out with palm wine. The lungs, stomach, liver, and intestines were embalmed and placed in separate urns, the heart was replaced in the body, and the abdomen was filled with crushed myrrh and cassia. The body was shaved and soaked in a bath of dry natron (a natural form of sodium carbonate), which absorbed all its remaining moisture. It was then washed, laid to dry on a funerary bed, and wrapped in linen. As prayers were recited, liquids were used to make the bandages stick together. This treatment would take up to seventy days for a person of royalty. Thus the body was prepared for eternity. After a complex funeral liturgy, it was placed in a coffin and was then ready for the return of the spirit.

In second-class embalming, for the less royal Egyptians, the viscera were not removed and embalmed separately, but were dissolved by means of cedar oil or oil of turpentine injected into the body cavity.

A third method, for the peasant class of people, consisted of simply desiccating the body without attempting to remove the internal organs. The corpse was then wrapped and buried.

EGYPT TODAY

Population

In recent decades Egypt has experienced a 3% annual increase, one of the highest in the world. It is now the second largest African state population-wise (after Nigeria). Total population in the early 1990's rose to 56,000,000. The population divides into 82% Sunni Muslim, 17.5% Christians, and .5% others. Nubians constitute the second largest minority after Christians. Jews, though an important minority throughout history, are now almost extinct in Egypt.

A new Egyptian is born every 26 seconds; each month there are 100,000 more mouths to feed – a serious challenge to a nation already importing 50% of its annual food requirement. Nearly half of the total population lives in the Delta. Ninety-five per cent of the people live within a dozen miles of the Nile; that is, 97% of the people live on 4% of the land. Excluding uninhabitable lands, Egypt is one of the most densely populated countries on earth (12,000 sq. mi. of fertile land divided by 56,000,000 people)!

Despite campaigns to limit family size, Egypt's population is doubling every twenty-five years. Half the nation's population is urbanized; there are twenty-six cities with over 100,000 population.

Cairo is the capital of Egypt and the largest urban center in Africa and the Near East; it is one of the ten largest in the world. Population of Cairo-Giza is over 14 million, with another million workers entering from the countryside each day.

The Nile

The most famous remark ever made about the land of Egypt is the classic statement by Greek historian Herodotus in the 5th century B.C., "Egypt is the gift of the Nile." This is literally true. Egypt is a belt of soil deposited annually by Nile inundations, which amounted to over 20 million tons annually. Egypt is actually the gift of Abyssinia (the ancient name of Ethiopia), where water collected from high mountain ranges and flowed west and then northward to supply Egypt.

The Nile is the world's longest river (4,160 miles), and its drainage area is the fourth largest in the world, draining nearly one-tenth of the land area of Africa. It is one of the few rivers in the world that run north. No other river crosses so many different climatic zones as the Nile. The "White Nile" begins at Lake Victoria (a broad, shallow lake, second largest in area in the world) and the Rift Valley lakes in central Africa. The "Blue Nile" originates in the high mountains of Ethiopia. The two Niles become one at Khartoum, the capital of Sudan. Arabic poetry calls the union of the two great rivers "the longest kiss in history." At that point the Nile still has a journey of 1850 miles to the Mediterranean. The Nile in Egypt has no tributaries, and there is hardly any rain, so no water is added through all of Egypt. No other river on earth flows so far without receiving any perennial tributaries. The river is half a mile wide at Luxor and a full mile wide at Cairo. Today modern pumping stations spill the waters of the Nile into a network of canals, from which the Egyptians, by ancient methods, lift the water onto their fields. *Shadufs* (water lifts), *saqiyas* (water wheels), and *tambours* (screws) may be seen frequently in the country.

About 84 billion cubic meters of water flows into Egypt annually. The quantity of water carried in the Nile is as much as all of Turkey's rivers together. It carries twice as much water as the combined Tigris and Euphrates; but it carries only 1/6th of the Mississippi's flow and only 1/14th of the Zaire River. Its total discharge is less than fifty others in the world (including the Susquehanna River in Pennsylvania). Instead of a major river the Nile at present is merely a "managed ditch." For millennia, until the early 1970s, the annual floods of the Nile reached Aswan in Upper Egypt about mid-June and raised the level of the river 23 feet higher! From six to twelve days later the annual flood waters would reach Cairo, with twenty times the normal flow. All of the fertile silt once carried down the river is no longer carried because of the Aswan Dam.

Aswan High Dam

After years of research and planning Egypt embarked on one of the most massive construction projects in history. Despite some potential problems, Egypt and Sudan both concluded that a major dam on the river could serve to put millions of additional acres under cultivation, which would in turn increase food production, and also provide hydroelectric power on a wide scale. Indeed, all 4,000 villages in Egypt now have electricity (eight billion kilowatt hours are now generated annually).

Aswan, nearly 600 miles south of Cairo, was chosen as the ideal location. The dam was dedicated in 1971, having cost a total of one and a half billion dollars (with most of that financed by the Soviet Union).

Seventeen times more building material went into the building of the Aswan High Dam than the Great Pyramid of Giza! It is two and a half miles wide, 364 feet high, and ugly, yet functional. It has twelve giant turbines. The dam created Lake Nasser, the largest artificial lake in the world, inundating over 300 miles of the river's valley in Egypt and Sudan. That 300 miles of water backed up behind the dam totals approximately 170 billion cubic meters of water, enough to supply the whole country's needs for about three years.

In retrospect some have wondered if it would not have been wiser to build several smaller dams along the course of the Nile. A number of serious problems have surfaced because of the project. (1) Since Lake Nasser lies in the heart of the desert much water is lost from massive surface evaporation. (2) By trapping millions of tons of silt behind the dam annually, farmers along the banks of the Nile and in the Delta are experiencing soil degradation plus the necessity of purchasing expensive fertilizers. (3) Water quality has also deteriorated. (4) Schistosomiasis (bilharzia), a dangerous parasitic disease transmitted by snails in the slower moving waters, is increasing. (5) Without the tons of alluvium deposited by the Nile over the centuries, the Delta coastline is eroding – already up to a mile in some places – and seawater incursion into the coastal aquifers is on the rise. And (6) the water table under cultivated fields of the floodplain has risen, resulting in poor drainage and threatening salination of productive soils and even threatening damage to world-famous antiquities such as the Sphinx on the Giza plateau. The major goal of the Dam, improvement of agriculture, has not been attained (and agricultural production accounts for 80% of export income).

The Delta

Looking down on the Nile Valley with its Delta from the air looks like a lotus flower, which is the symbol of Upper Egypt. Papyrus is the symbol of Lower Egypt. The Greek word papyrus, or Biblical *bulrush*, is the origin of our English word "paper." It grows plentifully in the Nile Delta.

The Delta (as the Greek letter, delta) is a fan shaped region 100 miles long and 150 miles wide. Half of the Egyptian population lives in the region. Just north of Cairo the Nile divides into two main branches, Damietta on the east and Rosetta on the west, with thousands of canals spreading out to create one of the most intensively cultivated regions on earth. Fewer ancient remains are noticeable than south of Cairo because of the annual floods and alluvial deposits over the centuries. Alexandria is the chief city. It was founded by Alexander the Great in 332 B.C. and has since served not only as the Roman Empire's second greatest provincial capital, but also as capital of Egypt for centuries.

Suez Canal

Until modern times, navigators longed for the day when shipping distance could be greatly reduced by cutting through the Red Sea to the Mediterranean instead of circumnavigating the whole of Africa. Finally in modern times the advantage was realized. The Canal shortens the trip from the Persian Gulf to Western Europe by about 5,600 miles. The 100-mile (160 km) Suez Canal, built by French capital and technicians, was opened in 1869. Depth of the Canal is about 65 feet. From 1875 to 1956 it was operated by France and Britain, with profits to them. Nasser nationalized the Canal in 1956, repulsing a French and British attack from Sinai. In 1967 the Canal was taken by Israel, who kept it closed until 1975. Annual profits accruing to Egypt from Canal tariffs and fees amounted to over $1.25 billion in the early 1980s.

Economics

Egypt's import expenses are often double the export income. The country imports 50% of its annual food requirement, including 70% of wheat needed.

The country's chief mineral resource is oil, and one recent year brought over $3. billion profit to Egypt.

Agricultural exports include: cotton (one-third of the high-quality, long-stemmed cotton produced worldwide is from Egypt); also rice, onions, sugar, sesame, lemons, dates, grapes, and oranges.

Industrial products include: textiles (using the cotton), tobacco, cement, and steel works.

Tourism is another of Egypt's main foreign currency earners. It brings in billions of dollars annually, unless terrorism and other factors discourage the tourists.

It is estimated that two and a half million Egyptians are living and working outside Egypt; in a recent year they remitted back to their homeland over $1.8 billion.

Egypt's major suppliers and customers during recent decades have been USA, USSR, Germany, Italy, France, United Kingdom, Greece and Czechoslovakia.

Per capita income in the mid-1980s was only $690.

Literacy in Egypt is now up to 50% and increasing.

Life expectancy for males is 56 years and for females, 58 years.

Infant mortality is 113 per 1,000 births.

The *fellaheen* are the common farmers of Egypt and are considered to be more or less "pure" Egyptian. They make up about 80 percent of the population. Over the centuries they have changed very little in religion, language, dress, and customs.

Another group of "pure" Egyptians are the 6-7 million *Copts*, or Coptic Christians – the tradesmen and artisans of Egypt. When the Arabs conquered Egypt, the Copts remained faithful to Christianity while most of the Egyptians converted to Islam.

A third group of people are the *Bedouins*, the wandering shepherds.

Among the most used Arabic expressions are *salam aleikum* ("good day"), *ahlan wa sahlan* ("welcome"), *shukran* ("thank you"), *baksheesh* ("tip"), *bikam* ("how much"), *la* ("no"), *aywa* ("yes"), and *men fadlak* ("please").

Today the Egyptian *pound* is divided into 100 *piasters*. There are many westernized stores with fixed prices, but merchants in the Khan el-Khalili bazaar are ready to bargain. Vendors often quote prices double what they expect buyers to pay. Hotels and restaurants expect a 10-percent tip, but for small services a few piasters is sufficient.

Flora and Fauna

Flowers and forests and grasslands are almost completely absent from the landscape of Egypt. The camel, donkey, horse, and gamus (water buffalo) are readily seen, but little wildlife exists. Pigeons are raised to use their dung for fertilizer.

CITIES AND SITES

Cairo, (*Arabic: "the victorious"*), *El Kahera, Masr*

Egypt's current capital city was founded in A.D. 969 by invading Arabs, and is perhaps one of the most rationally situated capitals in the world. It links the pop-

1. Al Qubba Palace
2. Ain Shams University
3. Main Railway station and Ramses Square
4. Gezira Island
5. Agricultural Museum
6. Cairo University
7. Zoology Gardens and Botanical Gardens
8. Giza
9. Roda Island and the Nilometer
10. Old Cairo
11. Coptic Museum, El-Moallaka Church, St. Sergius's Church, Saint George's Church
12. Ibn Tulun Mosque, Beit el Kretelia, Anderson Museum
13. Sultan Hassan Mosque
14. Citadel, Alabaster Mosque, and Museums
15. Muqattam Hills, Bektashi Monastery
16. Tombs of the Caliphs and Mamelukes
17. Al Hussein Mosque
18. Al-Azhar Mosque and Islamic University
19. Khan Khalili Bazaar
20. Museum of Islamic Art
21. Abin Palace Museum
22. American University
23. Geological Museum
24. American Embassy
25. Egyptian Museum

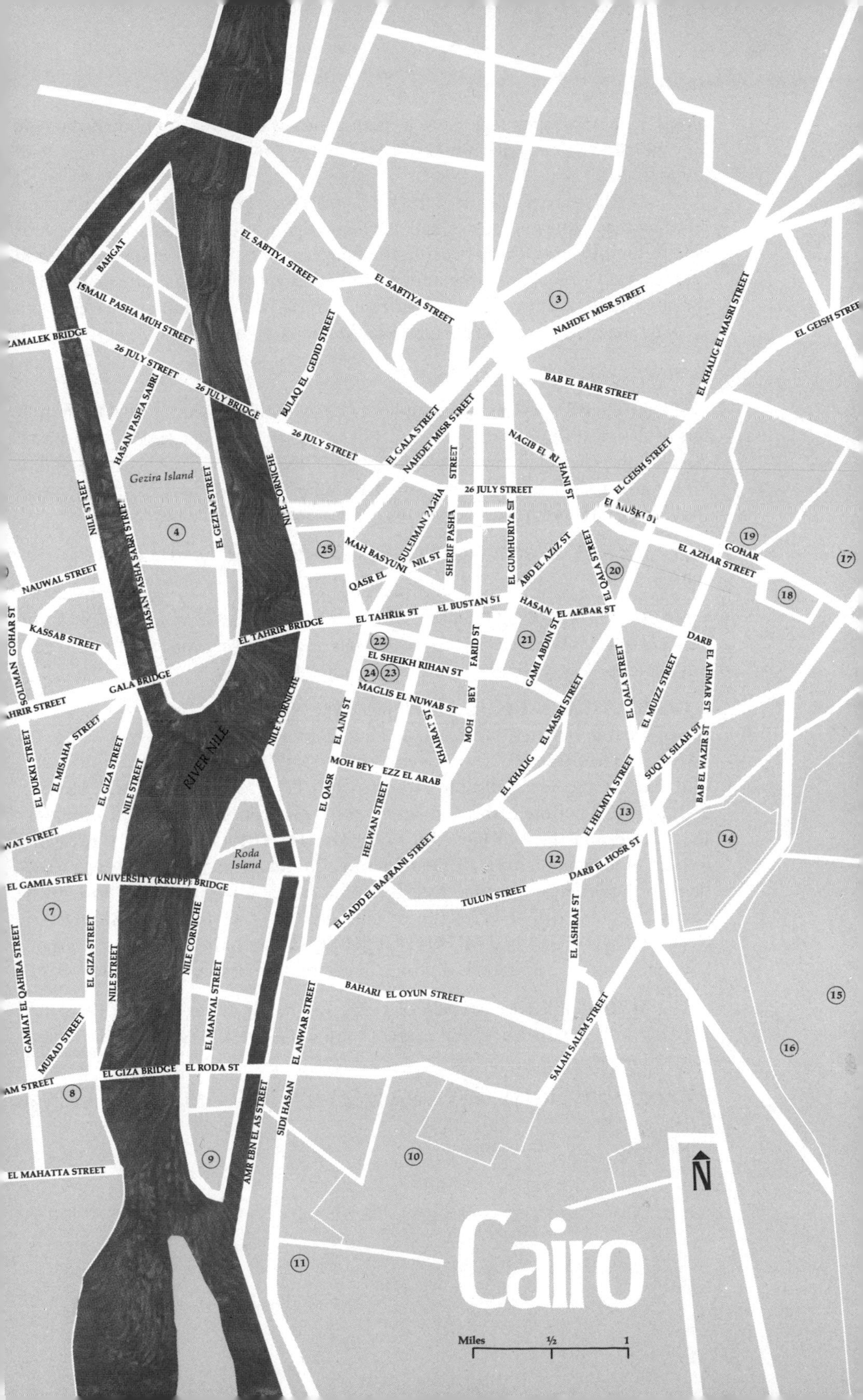
Cairo
Miles
½
1
N
EL SABTIYA STREET
EL SABTIYA STREET
NAHDET MISR STREET
EL GEISH STREET
EL KHALIG EL MASRI STREET
BAB EL BAHR STREET
BAHGAT
ISMAIL PASHA MUH STREET
ZAMALEK BRIDGE
26 JULY STREET
26 JULY BRIDGE
26 JULY STREET
26 JULY STREET
BULAQ EL GEDID STREET
EL GALA STREET
NAHDET MISR STREET
SHERIF PASHA STREET
SULEIMAN PASHA
NAGIB EL RI HANI ST
EL GEISH STREET
EL MUSKI ST
HASAN PASHA SABRI
HASAN PASHA SABRI STREET
Gezira Island
EL GEZIRA STREET
NILE STREET
NILE CORNICHE
MAH BASYUNI
QASR EL NIL ST
EL GUMHURIYA ST
ABD EL AZIZ ST
EL QALA STREET
GOHAR
EL AZHAR STREET
NAUWAL STREET
KASSAB STREET
SOLIMAN GOHAR ST
EL TAHRIR BRIDGE
EL TAHRIR ST
EL BUSTAN ST
HASAN EL AKBAR ST
DARB EL AHMAR ST
EL SHEIKH RIHAN ST
FARID ST
GAMI ABDIN ST
GALA BRIDGE
TAHRIR STREET
MAGLIS EL NUWAB ST
MOH BEY
EL QALA STREET
EL MUIZZ STREET
EL MISAHA STREET
EL DUKKI STREET
EL GIZA STREET
NILE STREET
RIVER NILE
NILE CORNICHE
EL QASR EL AINI ST
KHAIRAT ST
EL KHALIG EL MASRI STREET
SUQ EL SILAH ST
BAB EL WAZIR ST
MOH BEY EZZ EL ARAB
HELWAN STREET
EL HELMIYA STREET
Roda Island
EL SADD EL BARRANI STREET
EL GAMIA STREET
UNIVERSITY (KRUPP) BRIDGE
DARB EL HOSR ST
TULUN STREET
EL ASHRAF ST
GAMIAT EL QAHIRA STREET
EL GIZA STREET
NILE STREET
NILE CORNICHE
EL MANYAL STREET
EL ANWAR STREET
BAHARI EL OYUN STREET
SALAH SALEM STREET
MURAD STREET
EL GIZA BRIDGE
EL RODA ST
AMR EBN EL AS STREET
SIDI HASAN
EL MAHATTA STREET
3
4
7
8
9
10
11
12
13
14
15
16
17
18
19
20
21
22
23
24
25

ulous Delta and valley regions at a natural east-west crossing point of the Nile and the natural focus of river traffic and north-south communication by road and rail.

Located on the east bank of the Nile, it was built because Memphis, the capital when they came into power, had an alien religion and was therefore objectionable to the Muslims. Cairo became the new capital of Egypt under the Fatimid caliphs in A.D. 969. When England controlled Egypt (1882-1922), the new part of the city was modernized. The old Cairo is oriental in design and has bazaars and crooked streets. The city boasts a population of 14-15 million people.

POINTS OF INTEREST

1. The **AL QUBBA PALACE**, a couple of miles south and west of El Matariya, is one of the most important palaces that belonged to the Muhammad Ali dynasty. Named after the small town Qubba nearby, it was built by the khedive Ismail in 1863. Since 1955 it has been the official seat of the president of the Egyptian Republic. The buildings cover nearly 70 acres, and a garden covers 125 acres.

2. The **AIN SHAMS UNIVERSITY** is located between El Matariya and the railway station.

3. **MAIN RAILWAY STATION** and **RAMSES SQUARE**. The main railway station houses the **RAILWAY MUSEUM**, which has an interesting collection of old railway vehicles. Ramses Square has a large statue of Ramses.

4. **GEZIRA ISLAND**. The largest island of the Nile in Cairo (3 by ½ miles), and site of a battle between the Egyptians and Napoleon on July 21, 1798, is the **ISLAND OF GEZIRA**. On the north end of the island is **ZAMALIK**, the most beautiful residential quarters of Cairo. In the **GROTTO GARDEN** is an **AQUARIUM**, and the middle of the island is covered with a golf course, the **GEZIRA SPORTING CLUB** and the **NATIONAL CLUB**. The **TOWER OF CAIRO**, a revolving restaurant located on a needlelike structure, is one of the highest concrete structures in the orient – over 600 feet. It is built in the form of a lotus flower. The panoramic view from the restaurant is lovely. The **EXHIBITION GROUNDS, COTTON MUSEUM**, and **MUKHTAR MUSEUM**, with the works of the famous Egyptian sculptor Mahmoud Mukhtar, are all on the southern end of the island.

5. The **AGRICULTURAL MUSEUM** is located in the center of an area named *Madinet al Awqaf*, which is west of the Island of Gezira and southwest of an area named *Embaba*.

6. **CAIRO UNIVERSITY**, west of the Island of Roda, is the largest university in Egypt.

7. **ZOOLOGICAL GARDENS** and **BOTANICAL GARDENS.** Not far from the Nile River and west of the Island of Roda are the large **ZOOLOGICAL GARDENS**, covering an area of 52 acres. Housed here are 600 animals, 3,000 birds, 300 reptiles, and 150 kinds of fish. The **BOTANICAL GARDENS** are also nearby, on the north.

8. **GIZA.** The residential area of Giza is located along the Nile just south of the Zoological Gardens.

9. **RODA ISLAND** and the **NILOMETER.** West of Old Cairo is **RODA ISLAND**, in the Nile River. On the southern tip of the island is the **MENESTERLI GARDEN**, and at the southern end of the garden is the old **NILOMETER** dating back to A.D. 716. This gauge measured the official level of the Nile River. Since taxes were computed in the olden days according to the height of the flood and its consequences to agricultural crops, the Nilometer was important. The modern Nilometer is located nearby.

- *The Muslims claim that Moses was found by the pharaoh's daughter in the bulrushes on the island (Exod. 2:1-6).*

10. **OLD CAIRO.** On the east bank of the Nile, and south of the center of the city, is Old Cairo. It includes the old Roman **FORTRESS BABYLON**, the **COPTS' QUARTER**, and the first Arab settlement in Egypt: **AL-FUSTÂT** (A.D. 642). The **OLD CAIRO SYNAGOGUE** and **MOSQUE OF AMR** are nearby. In the Old Ben Ezra Synagogue may be seen some of the most ancient manuscripts of parts of the Old Testament. In the Geniza (Heb. "storage"), in 1894, thousands of biblical and biblical-related documents were discovered, written in Hebrew, Aramaic, Greek, Arabic, and Samaritan.

11. **COPTIC MUSEUM, EL-MOALLAKA CHURCH, SAINT SERGIUS'S CHURCH, SAINT GEORGE'S CHURCH.** The **COPTIC MUSEUM**, built in 1908 and located within the Fortress Babylon, houses the largest collection of Christian Coptic treasures in the world. Besides paintings, carvings, metalwork, early Christian vestments, and medieval glass and pottery, the library has a collection of Coptic manuscripts and religious works from the Coptic churches and monasteries of Egypt.

The **COPTIC CHURCH EL-MOALLAKA** (Holy Virgin's Church) is built on top of the gateway of the Fortress Babylon. It dates back to the fourth century A.D. and was the seat of the Coptic patriarchate. It has been rebuilt several times. According to legend, the Virgin Mary appeared here in A.D. 968.

SAINT SERGIUS'S COPTIC CHURCH (*Abu Serga*) dates back to the tenth century A.D. Joseph, Mary and Jesus are said to have stayed here for thirty days during their flight into Egypt. Under the altar is a cave where the Holy Family is supposed to have lived. From here, according to tradition, the angel sent them back to Nazareth (Matt. 2:13-23).

SAINT GEORGE'S CHURCH (*Mary Gurguis*), which belongs to the Greek Orthodox Church, was built upon a bastion of the fortress of Babylon in the sixth century and houses a **BYZANTINE ICON MUSEUM**. A splendid view of the city may be obtained here.

12. **IBN TULUN MOSQUE, BEIT EL KRETELIA, ANDERSON MUSEUM.** The oldest Arab structure preserved in Cairo, the Ibn Tulun Mosque, was built by Ibn Tulun in A.D. 868. The minaret is unique because it has an exterior staircase. Next to his mosque is Beit el Kretelia, an annex of the Islamic Art Museum. It is a house furnished in the cosmopolitan Oriental spirit of the eighteenth century. The Anderson Museum is also located at Beit el Kretelia.

13. The **SULTAN HASSAN MOSQUE** is considered by many to be the most important piece of Arab architecture in Egypt. Built in A.D. 1356-63, it is 495 feet long.

14. **CITADEL, ALABASTER MOSQUE**, and **MUSEUMS**. On the southeast edge of the city is the **CITADEL OF SALADIN**, a former fortress built in A.D. 1176. Of the early fortress, only the eastern outer wall remains. This was the site of the massacre of 480 Mamelukes in 1811 by order of Muhammad Ali.

The **MOSQUE OF SULTAN AL-NASIR** may be seen through the main gate on the left. Legend has it that the prison in which Joseph of old was confined (Gen. 39:21-41:40) was located on the site of the Citadel. Southwest of the Nasir Mosque is the **WELL OF JOSEPH**, said to have been dug by that same Joseph.

The **MUHAMMAD ALI MOSQUE** (Alabaster Mosque) is located straight ahead after one enters the main gate. This mosque, the symbol of Cairo, was completed in 1857 under the supervision of a Turkish architect. As you enter the mosque, you can see **MUHAMMAD ALI'S TOMB** on the right. The walls and pillars, made of alabaster from Beni Snel in Egypt, make this the most costly and beautiful mosque in the city.

The **MILITARY MUSEUM** is located in the old Palace of Hareen on the north end of the Citadel; **EL GAWHARA PALACE MUSEUM** is located on the south end. Also nearby is the **MUSTAFA KAMAL MUSEUM**.

15. **MUQATTAM HILLS, BEKTASHI MONASTERY**, and **GUYUSHI MOSQUE**. Behind the Citadel is a limestone range of hills, 660 feet high – the **MUQATTAM HILLS**. From the top of the hills the panoramic view is delightful. The road goes through the **LIMESTONE QUARRIES** from which the stone blocks for the pyramids were quarried.

Halfway up the mountain is the **BEKTASHI MONASTERY**, which belongs to a Muslim sect. The Janissaries were also members of this sect, and after the order was dissolved in Turkey in 1924, the monks fled to Egypt.

The **GUYUSHI MOSQUE**, one of the oldest mosques in Cairo, was built on top of the hills in A.D. 1085.

16. **TOMBS OF THE CALIPHS AND MAMELUKES.** At the foot of the Muqattam hills are numerous tombs of the Caliphs and Mamelukes. These huge mausoleums, dating back as far as the thirteenth century A.D., are designed with domes, minarets, chambers, halls, marble floors, and sarcophagi. Near the tombs are modern cemeteries. The largest of thc tombs, the **MOSQUE OF SULTAN INAL**, covers an area measuring 346 by 187 feet.

This "**CITY OF THE DEAD**" – miles of cemeteries, tombs, and mausoleums – has, as of the early 1990's, over 500,000 poor, *living* people residing inside also.

17. The **AL HUSSEIN MOSQUE** houses sacred Islamic relics, such as pieces of Muhammad's clothes. Al Hussein was a grandchild of the prophet Muhammad.

18. **AL-AZHAR MOSQUE** and **ISLAMIC UNIVERSITY.** The six-minaret Al-Azhar Mosque, a part of the complex of the oldest and most notable Islamic university, dates from A.D. 972 and is called *The Splendid.* At first it was a placc of worship only; however, from A.D. 988 it became a school of religion. The full period of study is from 15 to 22 years. Pupils begin their studies when they are 12-16 years of age, and a requirement of admission is to know the whole Koran by heart. Seven different degrees are offered, the highest being *Scholar.* Since most students are too poor to support themselves, the school and students are supported by endowments. Approximately 12,000 students are enrolled.

19. The **KHAN KHALILI BAZAAR**, established in 1292 by Prince Asraf Khalili, is now the popular shopping place for the tourist. Artisans are at work, and bargaining is in order.

20. **MUSEUM OF ISLAMIC ART**. Founded in 1880, this museum houses the world's largest collection of Islamic ceramics, carpets, textiles, marble, weapons, inscriptions, furniture, and so forth. It is located in Ahmed Maher Square, in the same building that houses the **NATIONAL PUBLIC LIBRARY**.

21. The **ABIN PALACE MUSEUM** is in Al Gomhuriya Square. Built during the years 1863-73, this palace became the official royal residence for King Farouk and his predecessors from 1874 until 1952. It has 500 rooms, gorgeously decorated and furnished in Islamic Italian style.

22. The **AMERICAN UNIVERSITY** is situated southeast of El Tahrir Square.

23. The **GEOLOGICAL MUSEUM** is east of the American Embassy, near Tahrir Square at El Sheikh Rihan Street.

24. The **AMERICAN EMBASSY** is on El Zahra Street, southeast of the Hilton Hotel.

Egyptian Museum

25. **THE EGYPTIAN MUSEUM**, on the north side of El Tahrir Square, near the Hilton Hotel, houses the world's most complete collection of Egyptian antiquities. The museum was built in the form of a rectangle in 1902. In the middle of the south side is the main entrance. If the visitor turns directly to the left after entering (after the shops) and makes the complete tour of the rectangle, while at the same time inspecting the side rooms of the main galleries, he will follow in chronological order the history of Egypt. It is interesting to the student of art to follow progressively the development of Egyptian art. Gallery 48, under the rotunda just inside the main entrance, has the most recent acquisitions.

OLD KINGDOM

OLD KINGDOM antiquities, dating from 2800 to 2200 B.C., are displayed to the left of the entrance, in galleries and rooms numbered 47, 46, 41, 42, 31, and 32. They contain statuettes, sarcophagi, stelae, false doors, and painted reliefs.

Room 47 contains three statues of **MENKURE** (Mycerinus) between the goddess Hathor and a local deity (nos. 180, 158, 149).

Room 42 houses a diorite statue of **KING KHAFRE** (Chephren) (no. 138), builder of the second of the three famous pyramids; a limestone statue of **PHARAOH ZOSER**, from the Third Dynasty (no. 6008); and a painted limestone statue of the **SQUATTING SCRIBE** from Saqqara with a roll of papyrus, dating from the Fifth Dynasty (no. 141).

In room 32 are two limestone statues of **PRINCE RA-HOTEP** and his wife, **NOFRET**, from the Fourth Dynasty ("Clark Gable and Elizabeth Taylor" – the moustache is a rare feature in ancient Egypt.) Numbers 230-31 are statues of **KING PEPI I** and his son, **MER-EN-RA**. They are the oldest life-size metal statues of ancient Egyptian workmanship and date back to the Sixth Dynasty. In the gallery leading to the next room are large fragments of **INSCRIBED RED SANDSTONE** from Serbit el Khadem and Wadi Maghara in the Sinai Peninsula, about midway between the Suez and the Monastery of Saint Catherine. They tell of Egyptian expeditions against desert Bedouins who were interrupting mining operations for malachite and turquoise.

MIDDLE KINGDOM

MIDDLE KINGDOM artifacts are housed in galleries and rooms numbering 26, 21, 22, and 16. Burial chambers, reliefs, and royal statues are just a few of the contents. Pharaohs with small heads and big ears represent Hyksos.

Item number 300, in room 22, is a **BURIAL CHAMBER** with a sarcophagus from Deir el-Bahri at Thebes, dating from the Eleventh Dynasty. A wooden statuette of **SENWOSRET I** from Lisht is also displayed.

NEW KINGDOM

NEW KINGDOM galleries and rooms are numbered 11, 12, 6, 7, and 8. Near the entrance is a statue of **THUTMOSE III**, who was the hero of the Battle of Megiddo of 1468 B.C. and who extended the borders of Egypt. Note the bas-relief horsebreakers. Before the date of this statue, no horses appeared on reliefs or paintings, as horses had not been known in Egypt until they were introduced by the Hyksos in the seventeenth century B.C.

Gallery 11 has a colored limestone **SPHINX OF QUEEN HATSHEPSUT** from Thebes (no. 6139) and a schist statue of **THUTMOSE III** (no. 400) from Karnak – both beautiful pieces of art.

In gallery 12 the famous **HATHOR COW** from Deir el-Bahri (Temple of Hatshepsut) is shown with Thutmose III standing under her head and feeding from her udder. Behind the cow is the chapel in which the holy cow once stood.

In the center of the north gallery, room 3 is totally devoted to **AMENHOTEP IV** (Akhenaton, Ikhnaton), who adopted a monotheistic religious belief and had the solar disc represent his god, Aton. This room shows a new art developed by Tell el Amarna artists, who sought to introduce grace and elegance in accordance with the aesthetics of that day. It is interesting to see their exaggeration of the king's deformities: his pointed skull, emaciated cheeks, protruding chin, almond-shaped eyes, swollen belly, and effeminate thighs. Amarna art is noted for its family-oriented and sentimental scenes. In case F is a huge stone statue of **AKHENATON** (no. 472) and a very beautiful head of his wife, **QUEEN NEFERTITI** (no. 6206). Case C has a colored relief of Akhenaton and Nefertiti worshiping the sun-god Aton. Some of the original El Amarna tablets with diplomatic correspondence are also displayed here.

From room 3, visitors who, like the mummies, are "pressed for time" should go up the northwest stairs to view the **TUTANKHAMON COLLECTION**.

Galleries 8, 9, 10, and 15 and room 14, on the northeast, have monuments from the Nineteenth and Twentieth Dynasties. The remainder of the rooms on the east are devoted to later periods, from the Twentieth Dynasty down to and including the Greek, Roman, Ptolemaic, and Byzantine periods. A copy of the **ROSETTA STONE** is included.

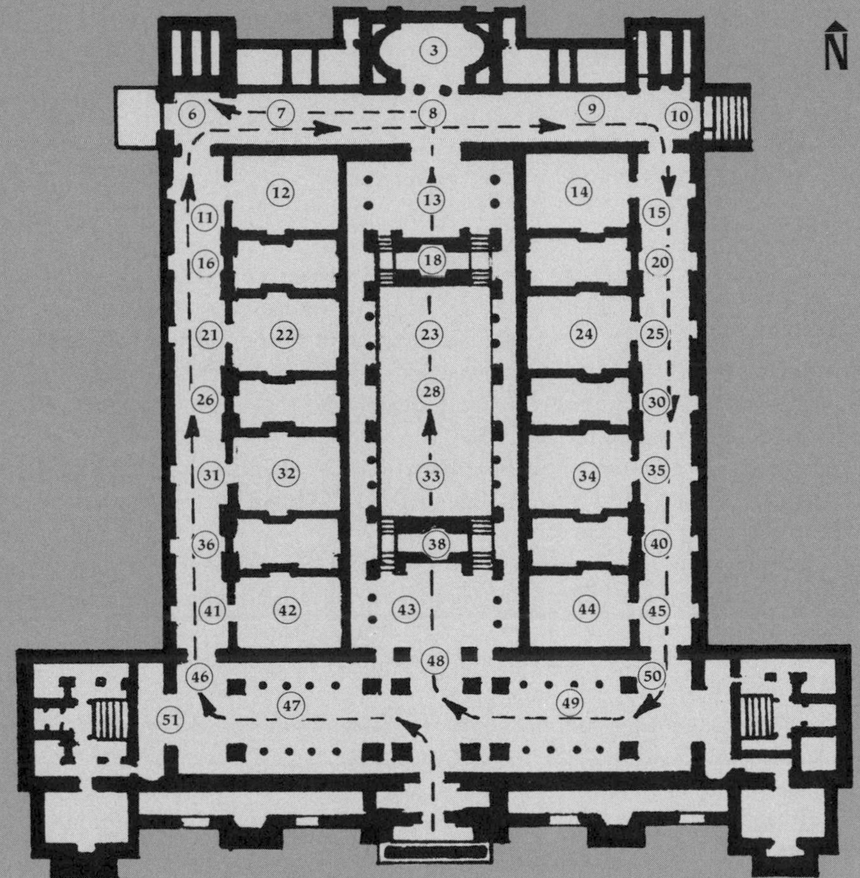

Egyptian Museum: First Floor

47, 46, 41, 42, 31, 32. Old Kingdom
26, 21, 22. Middle Kingdom
6, 7, 8, 9, 10, 15. New Kingdom
3. Akhenaten
25, 24. Late period
35, 34. Greco-Roman period
45, 44. Nubian collection
50, 49. Ptolemaic sarcophagi
43, 38, 33, 28, 23, 18. Atrium

*Adapted from Kurt Schroeder, *Guide to Egypt* (Cairo, 1965), by permission.

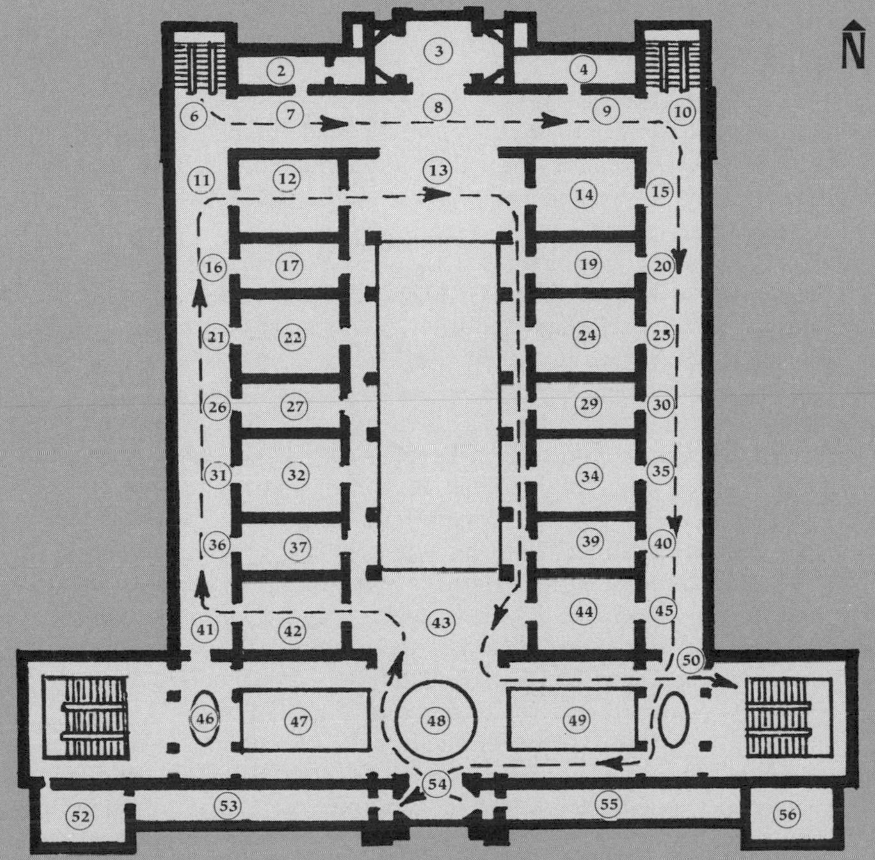

Egyptian Museum: Second Floor

6. Scarabs
2. Hetepheres
2A. Tanite kings
3. Ornaments
7, 8, 13, 9, 4, 10, 15, 20, 25, 30, 35, 40, 45. Tutankhamen
54, 55. Weapons
43, 42. Archaic period
41, 36, 26, 21, 16, 11. Coffins
32, 27, 22, 17, 12. Funerary pomp
13. Chariots and finds from tombs
14. Roman coffins and portraits
19. Deities and sacred animals
24, 29. Drawings and manuscripts
34. Tools, weapons, and musical instruments
49. Furniture

*Adapted from Kurt Schroeder, *Guide to Egypt* (Cairo, 1965), by permission.

In Galleries 49 and 50 in the front of the museum are **GRANITE SARCOPHAGI** of the Ptolemaic period.

ATRIUM

The **ATRIUM, GALLERY 13**, and the **ISRAEL STONE**. The visitor should now proceed north through the **ATRIUM**, in the center of the building. The Atrium houses antiquities from various periods, including two **WOODEN BOATS** of the dead found at Dahshur and dating back to the Twelfth Dynasty.

GALLERY 13, on the north of the Atrium, houses war chariots and tomb artifacts. One of the most important Jewish and Christian antiquities located in Gallery 13 is the **ISRAEL STELA OF MERNEPTAH**, son of Ramses II. Called the "Israel Stone," this black granite stone was originally set up in 1490 B.C. by Amenhotep III, but was appropriated by Merneptah in 1224 B.C. and stood in his funerary temple at Thebes. It was discovered in western Luxor in 1896. It is 8 feet high, 4 feet wide, and 2 feet thick. Artwork decorates the top, and a text of Merneptah's hymns of victory, in Egyptian hieroglyphs, covers the rest of the stone. The relief above the inscription is divided into two almost identical scenes. In the center, the god Amon stands under the winged sun-disc, giving Merneptah the sickle-sword with his right hand and holding the scepter of the gods in his left. Mut is on the far left and Horus on the far right. In line 27 of the text, the word *Israel* appears in hieroglyphics. As this is the only mention of Israel in any Egyptian text, it helps to date the period. When the stone was set up in Merneptah's mortuary temple, a duplicate was carved on the great temple at Karnak. The latter now survives only in fragments, however.

The inscription of the stela is dated the third day of the third month of summer in the fifth year of the pharaoh's reign. The stone tells of the defeat of various peoples, including the Philistines. It says: "In Egypt there is great rejoicing; her cities shout for joy.... All men speak of Merneptah's conquests.... The devastated, the Hittites, are pacified. Canaan is conquered and all her wickedness. Ashkelon is captive, Gezer is fallen, Israel is ravaged and has no offspring. Palestine is widowed."

UPPER FLOOR

UPPER FLOOR. Gallery 6, at the head of the northwest stairway, has a collection of **SCARABS**.

On the left, room 2 houses the treasures from the tomb of **QUEEN HETEPHERES**, mother of Cheops (Khufu) (2700 B.C.), and room 2A houses the collection of the **TANITE KINGS**.

Galleries and rooms 7, 8, 13, 9, 4, 10, 15, 20, 25, 30, 35, 40, and 45 have the huge collection from the **TOMB OF TUTANKHAMON**. After the death of Akhenaton and the brief reign of Smenkhkara, Tutankhamon ("King Tut") became the pharaoh. He had been a follower of Akhenaton and monotheism, but when he came to the throne he moved to Thebes and apparently gave up his belief in monotheism. Discovered in 1922 by Howard Carter, King Tut's tomb shows the influence of both Amarna and Theban art, and its contents cover a quarter of the upper floor of the Egyptian Museum. The north gallery, with items from Tut's tomb, is the finest area in the whole museum. Here is displayed the most complete set of burial objects in existence.

Galleries 7, 8, and 9 have four **FUNERARY CHAMBERS** in huge glass cases. They are made of wood and covered with beautifully engraved gold leaf. The largest is 10 feet 10 inches by 16 feet 5 inches by 9 feet. Tutankhamon was buried in three gold mummiform coffins resting in a stone sarcophagus, which, in turn, lay in the four funerary chambers. A **MINIATURE BUILDING** – housing the **ALABASTER CANOPIC BOX**, which, in turn, housed four **CANOPIC URNS** – is adorned with a frieze of uraeus serpents, erected and crowned with the solar disc. Goddesses sculptured in high relief with arms outstretched seem to be guarding the building. The alabaster canopic box on a sledge is beautifully decorated with hieroglyphs and other art work. The four canopic urns have lids that portray Tutankhamon's head wearing the "nemset." These urns housed miniature coffins 15 inches long, in the shape of the innermost gold coffin of Tutankhamon. These miniature coffins were used to preserve the mummified viscera: stomach, intestines, lungs, and liver. Only the heart remained in King Tut's mummy.

Israel Stela of Merneptah

Tutankhamon's alabaster canopic box

Two of the **MUMMIFORM SARCOPHAGI** of King Tutankhamon are located in the museum. The number 2 (middle) sarcophagus, in case 36, is inlaid in multicolored glass paste, and at the soles of his feet the goddess Isis, in gold bas-relief, mourns the death of the king. The number 1 (innermost) sarcophagus is in the number 29 case, and the number 3 (outside) one is in the tomb at Thebes, with the body in it. Case 33 contains the solid gold mask which covered the head of the royal mummy. The stripes of the headdress are of blue glass. On the forehead of King Tut are two goddesses: Wadjit of the North, a serpent goddess; and Nekhbet of the South, a vulture goddess. The king's beard makes him similar to Osiris, as do the scepter and flail in his hands on the mummiform coffins. Toward the east end of the north gallery there are **FUNERARY COUCHES**.[1]

Room 3 contains miscellaneous **JEWELRY** dating from the First Dynasty to the Byzantine period.

Room 4 has the **JEWELRY** that came from **TUTANKHAMON'S TOMB**.

The east galleries are filled with the Tutankhamon collection. Proceed through the gallery without entering the side rooms. Of particular interest is the famous **THRONE** in case 21, a **PAINTED WOODEN CHEST** in case 20, **ALABASTER VASES, BOOMERANGS, FANS, TRUMPETS, COFFERS, BOATS, GAMES**, and two **WOODEN GUARDS** of the tomb and so on. The throne in case 21 is carved in wood and decorated with faience, glass paste, semiprecious stones, and silver. The Amarna influence is clearer here than elsewhere. Note the solar disc. The chair must have been made at Amarna, because a cartouche on a side of the throne is inscribed with the name Tut-ankh-*Aton*, "living image of Aton" – Tut's name before he left Amarna. When he returned to Thebes he changed his name to Tut-ankh-*Amon*.

After visiting the east gallery, continue by going west through the south gallery. Note the two **WATER CLOCKS** near the head of the stairs.

Room 55 has an interesting set of **PHOTOGRAPHS** taken from the air.

Room 54 displays **WEAPONS**.

Rooms 43 and 42 have archaic-period funerary exhibits. In room 42 are the fragments of the famous **PALERMO STONE** and the slate **PALETTE OF KING NARMER**, which dates back to 3100 B.C. It is 25 inches high and shows King Narmer celebrating a victory over Lower Egypt. Those interested in art should notice the sense of order in the horizontal bands. The Egyptian artist was faced with the fact that the standing human figure, unlike that of an animal, does not have a single main profile, but rather two competing profiles. For the sake of clarity he had to combine these two views, and his method survived unchanged for 2,500 years. In the large figure of Narmer, the eye and shoulders are a frontal view, but the head and eyes are in profile. This shows the pharaoh in as complete a way as possible. The underlings (the two animal trainers and four men carrying standards) do not have to have their dignity preserved; hence they are shown in strict profile throughout – except for their eyes.

Room 37 contains wooden **SARCOPHAGI.**

Room 32 has funerary objects of the **OLD** and **MIDDLE KINGDOMS**. The rest of the rooms off the West Gallery have sarcophagi and funerary objects.

Room 22, upper level, back right corner, has a display of *hypocephali* – similar to Facsimile No. 2 in *The Pearl of Great Price.*

Crossing east through gallery 13, where the **CHARIOTS** are located, the visitor should go through the side rooms along the east corridor, beginning with number 14, which has Greco-Roman **COFFINS.** In the glass cases are shown complete **MUMMIES.** These artists broke with Egyptian tradition and painted the portraits in full face. Ancient Egyptians presented a profile, never a full face.

Room 19 is the room of the **DEITIES.**

Room 24, the **OSTRACON ROOM**, contains literary writings and drawings.

Room 29 is the **PAPYRUS ROOM**, with the soul-weighing scenes that are a part of the Book of the Dead. Examples of Egyptian writing from different periods are shown.

Room 34 shows the **MANNERS AND CUSTOMS** of daily life. In the last room is a collection of architectural models. Pyramids and their accompanying temples are shown in relief.

Those who desire to see the special **MUMMY ROOM** may do so for an extra fee. Those interested should inquire about it.

ON, *Heliopolis*, El Matariya

The site of this ancient city is in the northern suburbs of El Matariya, about 7 miles from the center of Cairo. From the Fifth Dynasty, this was the principal center of sun worship (*Heliopolis*= "city of the sun"). The god was Ra (Re-Harakhte), who replaced the older god Atum. The living manifestation of Ra-Atum was the Mnevis bull.

Here was a great university, especially for the training of the priesthood. It is said that men like Plato, Pythagoras, Euclid, Solon, and Thales came here to learn from the priests of Heliopolis, that Manetho wrote his history of Egypt from the archives of the temple at On, and that Plato wrote his works here. Solon supposedly wrote his laws here. Strabo, the geographer, who was in Heliopolis twenty years before the birth of Christ, described the worship of the Mnevis bull at On and the Apis bull at Memphis.

Here possibly Joseph ruled as the prime minister of Egypt. Moses perhaps received his education here, becoming learned in all the wisdom of the Egyptians (Acts 7:22).

On has been almost deserted since the Roman period. The only remains of the city are parts of the **ENCLOSURE WALL** that surrounds the temple and an **OBELISK** of Aswan granite 68½ feet high, with hieroglyphics on all four sides. This is the oldest obelisk in all Egypt. On it is the cartouche of King Usertesen, who lived in 2760 B.C. The obelisk is known by some as the *Matariya Obelisk, Sesostris Obelisk*, or *Pharaoh's Needle.* These obelisks, connected with sun worship, represented the bright rays of the sun. Two other obelisks were once located here and were seen by the Israelites; one now stands in London and the other in Central Park in New York City. They were moved to Alexandria by Augustus Caesar in A.D. 23, and from there they were removed to their present locations.

- *Joseph married Asenath, daughter of Potipherah, the priest of On (Gen. 41:45, 50; 46:20). As his wife's home, On was undoubtedly familiar to Joseph.*
- *Asenath bore Joseph two sons, Manasseh and Ephraim (Gen. 41:50-52).*
- *Jeremiah called the area Beth-shemesh (City of the Sun) and said it would be destroyed (Jer. 43:13).*
- *Ezekiel spoke of the overthrow of On, called Aven (Ezek. 30:17).*
- *On is thought to be one of the five cities referred to by Isaiah (Isa. 19:18).*

EL MATARIYA and **the Virgin's Tree**

South of the Matariya Obelisk is the city of El Matariya, the traditional site of a resting place of Joseph, Mary, and Jesus when they fled to Egypt after Herod issued his edict to kill the babies in Bethlehem (Matt. 2:14). The **VIRGIN'S TREE** at Matariya stands in a garden on the right side of the main street, just before the Church of Our Lady at Matariya. It is a sycamore tree, planted in 1672 as a shoot of a fourteenth-century tree that stood in this same spot and supposedly gave shade to the Holy Family. The present tree looks dead. According to tradition, Mary washed Jesus' swaddling clothes in a spring 25 yards west of the tree. Many pilgrims still visit this site. The tree is believed by many to have supernatural qualities.

GOSHEN (*"place of pasture"*), *the land of Ramses*

The home of the Israelites during their sojourn in Egypt, Goshen was located on the east side of the Nile River, from the Mediterranean Sea to the Red Sea. Goshen contained about 900 square miles of level and rich alluvial lands, and was called by Moses the "land of Rameses [Ramses]" (Gen. 47:11). It was the best of the land.

- *Joseph promised Goshen to his brethren (Gen. 45:10).*
- *Israel and his family entered Goshen and were met and instructed by Joseph (Gen. 46:28-34).*
- *At their request, the children of Israel were assigned Goshen for a home, where they prospered and multiplied (Gen. 47:1-12, 27).*

- *Jacob was carried from here to Canaan for burial (Gen. 50:1-14).*
- *The plagues did not come here as they did in the rest of Egypt (Exod. 8:22; 9:26).*
- *The children of Israel dwelt here for centuries (Exod. 12:40-41; Gal. 3:17).*
- *The Israelites went from Goshen to Succoth, where they were freed from Pharaoh (Exod. 12:37; Num. 33:3, 5).*

TANIS, *Ramses*

Tanis, identified as Ramses, was built as a store city by the Israelites while in Egypt, and was the starting point of the Exodus. After the Twentieth Dynasty, the royal necropolis was moved to Tanis from Thebes. The site is approximately 40 miles southwest of Port Said. With the establishment of the 19th dynasty (at the beginning of the 13th century B.C.), the Egyptians renewed their efforts to dominate Canaan and parts of Syria. To that end, they transferred their capital to Zoan, the old Hyksos headquarters in the northern Delta, and renamed the town Pi-Ramses (after Ramses II). This is the Ramses the Israelites helped to build (Exod. 1:11). From here the Israelites journeyed eastward and crossed a branch of the Red Sea, possibly at modern Qantara (Arabic "bridge").

- *Ramses was the store city of the Israelites (Exod. 1:11).*
- *The Exodus began at Ramses (Exod. 12:37; Num. 33:3, 5).*

TAHPANHES (*"the Negro"*), *Tahapanes*, Tel Defneh

The name of this Egyptian city is the same as the Greek *Daphnae* and most probably identified with the modern Tell Defneh which lies on the Pelusiac branch of the Nile about 20 miles southeast of Tanis. Tel Defneh was excavated by Petrie at the end of the nineteenth century.

- *Tahpanhes is mentioned in the Old Testament (Jer. 2:16; 44:1; 46:14; Ezek. 30:18).*
- *After the destruction of Jerusalem by Nebuchadnezzar in 586 B.C., many Jews fled to Tahpanhes (Jer. 43:7; also 2 Kings 25:26).*
- *Jeremiah apparently lived here toward the end of his life (Jer. 43:8).*
- *Jeremiah foretold many woes against the Egyptians (Jer. 43:9-13; 46:28).*

PITHOM (*"narrow pass"*), *Tell er-Retabeh*

This site has been identified as Tell er-Retabeh, and in biblical times it was located in the land of Goshen.

- *Pithom was one of two "treasure cities" said to have been built for the pharaoh who oppressed the Hebrews (Exod. 1:11). (The other was Rameses.)*

Giza

The **PYRAMIDS OF GIZA**. About 7½ miles southwest of Tahrir Square and 6 miles southwest of Giza are the pyramids of Giza. They were built for and by

Pyramids of Giza

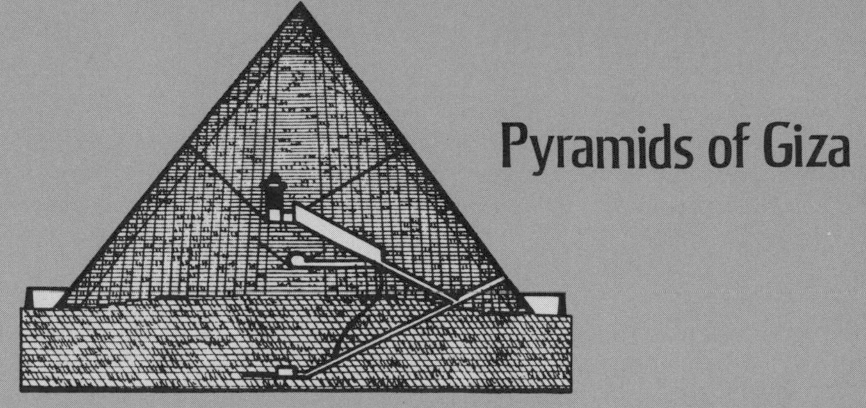

South-north longitudinal section of the Cheops pyramid

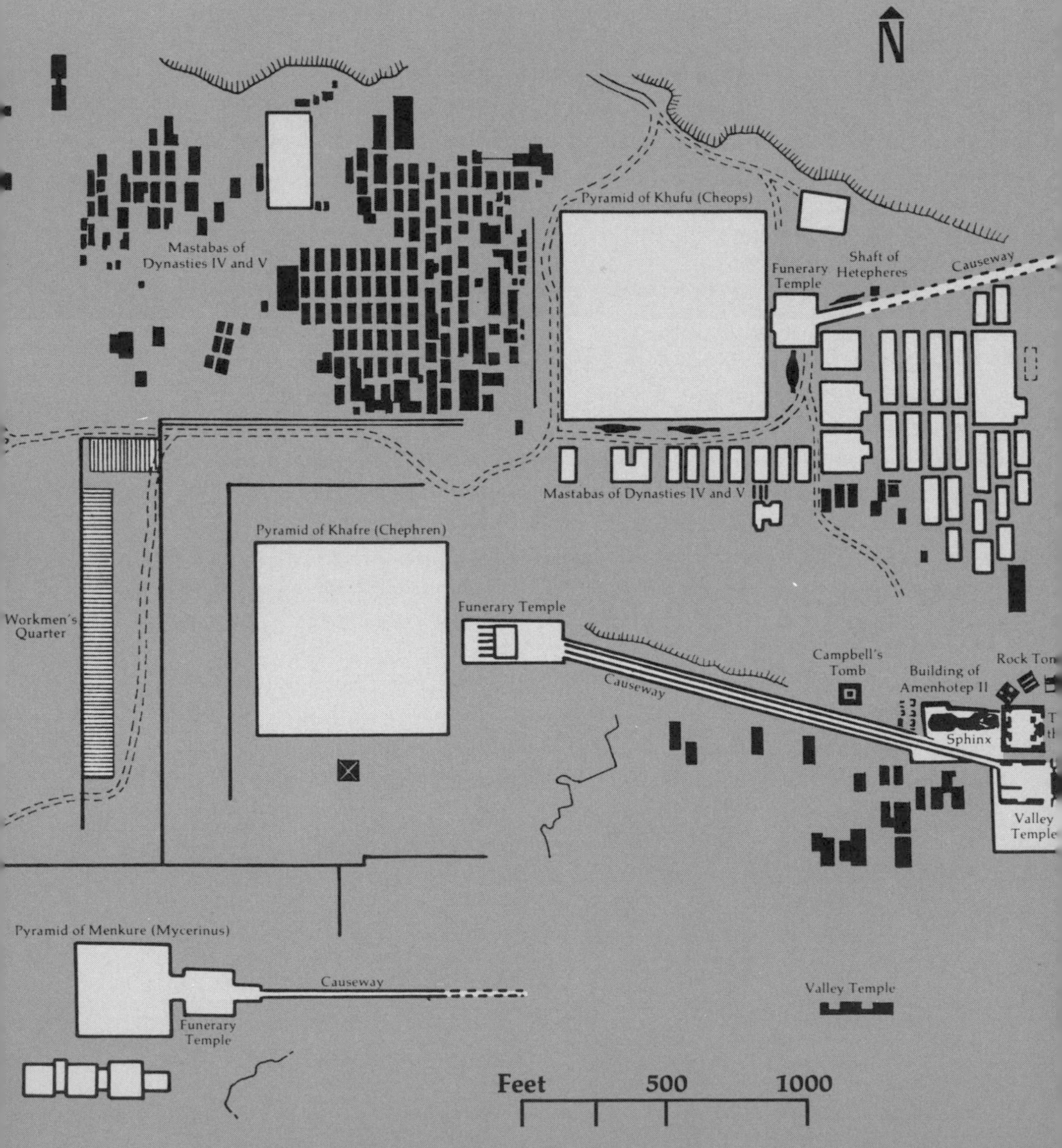

*Adapted from K. Lange and M. Hirmer, *Egypt: Architecture, Sculpture, Painting*, 4th ed. (Hirmer Verlag München, 1968), by permission.

Pyramids of Giza

Khufu (Cheops), Khafre (Chephren), and Menkure (Mycerinus). (*Cheops* and *Chephren* are the Greek names; *Mycerinus* is Latin.) An old Arab saying reveals the timeless regard for the great pyramids: "The world fears time, but time fears the pyramids!" The largest one, **CHEOPS**, is the lone survivor of the Seven Wonders of the Ancient World (the other six were: the Lighthouse at Alexandria, the Hanging Gardens of Babylon, the Colossus of Rhodes, the Temple of Diana/Artemis at Ephesus, the Mausoleum of Mausolus at Halicarnassus, and the Statue of Zeus at Olympia). It is 450 feet high (originally 481.4 feet – cf. the Church Office Building in Salt Lake City at 444 ft.) and 750 feet long on each side and covers 12-13 acres of ground (eight football fields). Each of the 2,300,000 stones weighs an average of 2½ tons. Only a few of the white limestone facing blocks remain. It is estimated that the pyramid was built in 20 years (working four months a year) by 100,000 slaves as a burial site for Khufu. It is the largest tomb ever built for one man. These three pyramids date from about 2700 B.C. The pyramid of **KHAFRE** is 447½ feet high; the pyramid of **MENKURE** is 204 feet high. Each builder respected his father by making his pyramid shorter.

The three large pyramids are offset from each other at a 45-degree angle, so that each faces the four cardinal points of the compass without any obstruction.

The visitor should walk around the Great Pyramid of Cheops if he wants to get an impression of size. Whereas for centuries tourist-visitors climbed the great pyramid, now it is dangerous and forbidden. However, it is still possible to go inside one of the two large pyramids. The entrance to the pyramid of Cheops – on the north side, 55 feet above the base – is a passage 3 feet 11 inches high and about 3½ feet wide. It slopes into the interior at an angle of 26 degrees for 320 feet, and at the end is a small chamber with the stone sarcophagus. On the south side of Cheops' Pyramid is a museum housing his **SOLAR BARK**, the oldest and best preserved wooden boat ever found. It was part of the funerary equipment for the king to use in the other world. The bark, discovered in May, 1954, was found dismantled in 650 parts, including 1,224 pieces of worked cedar wood meticulously arranged inside a rectangular pit, which was sealed by 41 limestone blocks of up to 18 tons. Nearby is another pit, with another bark.

A **CAMEL RIDE** is a tourist attraction at the pyramids, and if time will allow, a ride into the desert is worthwhile. Around the pyramids are **MASTABAS** (tombs of the nobles) and **FUNERARY TEMPLES**. Of the 9 pyramids in the Giza area, 6 are small.

The **GREAT SPHINX**. Near the pyramids of Giza, the Great Sphinx has been staring across the desert for nearly 5,000 years. It is 240 feet long and 66 feet high. The face is 13 feet by 8 feet, and the ear is 4½ feet long. Carved out of the natural cliff, it has been covered by sand during much of its history. It represents the Pharaoh Khafre (Chephren), who built the sphinx, or the god Horus, who guarded temples and tombs.

The head of an Egyptian sphinx might be a man or a beast; if a man, then the face usually represented the pharaoh of the time. Egyptian sphinxes with human heads and lion bodies symbolize power and intelligence. The other two types of sphinxes in Egypt are ram-headed and hawk-headed lions.

The body of the sphinx of Giza is a lion. Between the sphinx's legs is a stone, placed there by Thutmose IV, who cleared the sand from the sphinx in the 1400s B.C. It was also cleaned during Roman times and again in 1818, 1886, and 1925. In A.D. 1380 the face of the sphinx was damaged by an iconoclastic sheikh and later by the Mamelukes, who apparently used it as a target.

The **VALLEY TEMPLE OF KHAFRE**, near the sphinx, is a granite temple with alabaster floors. This was a part of the temple complex that accompanied the pyramid of Khafre.

MEMPHIS, NOPH, *Mit-Rahina*

Fifteen miles up the Nile River south of Cairo, on the west bank, is the ancient capital of Egypt, Memphis. It was built by Menes, who first united the two kingdoms of Upper and Lower Egypt in 3100 B.C.

Memphis was the white-walled capital city of Egypt at the time of Abraham, Jacob, Joseph and Moses. Moses was possibly reared here in the palace of the Pharaoh.

After Alexander the Great built Alexandria in the fourth century B.C., Memphis ceased to be the chief city. Following the Arab conquest, its population rapidly declined, and the temple was destroyed in the fourth century A.D. The old city has long been buried.

POINTS OF INTEREST

There are few ruins for a one-time "greatest city on earth." Jeremiah 46:19 says "O thou daughter dwelling in Egypt, furnish thyself to go into captivity; for Noph shall be waste and desolate without an inhabitant." More than 200 sphinxes found in and around the city have been moved away, most of them to museums. However, one **ALABASTER SPHINX** is still here. Measuring 26 feet long by 13 feet 2 inches high and weighing 80 tons, it dates back to 1600 B.C.

A few minutes' walk southwest from the sphinx is a fine red granite **STATUE OF RAMSES II**, located in a mud room. The visitor must climb wooden steps to reach it.

A gigantic limestone **STATUE OF RAMSES II** is housed in a new building. It is 42 feet long and dates to the Nineteenth Dynasty – about 1250 B.C. About 550 yards north of the building lie the remains of the **TEMPLE OF PTAH**, where the huge statue once stood. One minute's walk to the west, alabaster embalming tables for Apis bulls constructed by Shishak may be seen. The bull was considered the physical manifestation of the creator god, Ptah, worshipped at Memphis. Note the lion bedstead similar to that in Facsimile No. 1, Book of Abraham.

- *Memphis (Noph) is mentioned repeatedly in the Old Testament (Isa. 19:13; Jer. 2:16; 44:1; 46:14, 19; Ezek. 30:13, 16; Hos. 9:6).*

Saqqara

Just west of Memphis is the modern village of Saqqara. Immediately west of the village is a complex of burial sites for more than twenty pharaohs and hundreds of nobles, dating back as far as the Third Dynasty (ca. 2686 B.C.). The oldest of all pyramids is here. Saqqara was the necropolis of Memphis.

Pyramids between Cairo and Dahshur

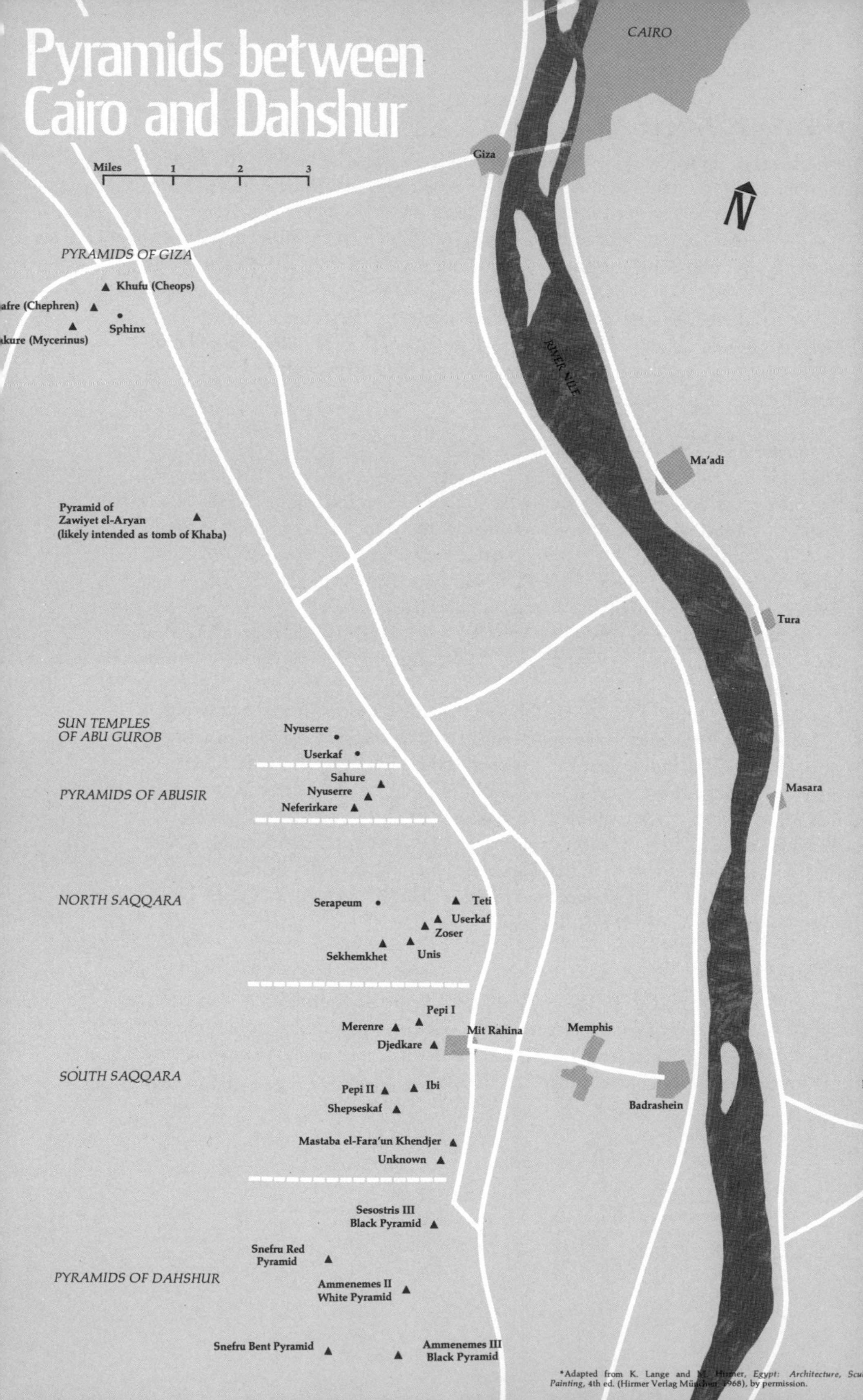

*Adapted from K. Lange and M. Hirmer, *Egypt: Architecture, Scul Painting*, 4th ed. (Hirmer Verlag München 1968), by permission.

POINTS OF INTEREST

The **STEP PYRAMID OF ZOSER** (Djoser) is the oldest known pyramid and the oldest free-standing cut-stone structure in the world. It is the first of about 80 pyramids built on the west bank of the Nile and constructed over a span of 1,500 years. It was actually a Step *Tomb*; the architect Imhotep's purpose was not to build a pyramid. Built about 2778-2723 B.C., the Step Pyramid is 204 feet high, and the base measures 411 feet from west to east and 358 feet from north to south. A wall once surrounded the 37-acre complex. King Zoser is the first artist whose name is recorded in history. He was a genius in architecture, medicine, and other fields, and after his death he was deified. The Greeks equated him with Aesculapius (Asclepias), the patron-god of medicine.

MUSEUM. By the Pyramid of Zoser is a museum housing a collection of alabaster vases from the Fifth Dynasty. Hieroglyphic inscriptions on some vases are known as the oldest religious documents in the world.

The **PYRAMID OF UNIS** (Onnos), dating back to 2450 B.C., is 385 yards southwest of the Step Pyramid of Zoser. The interior has the granitc sarcophagus of the king and a roof of the burial chamber that tapers upward. The chamber walls are completely covered with hieroglyphics dealing with the hereafter. They consist of spells and prayers, and the entire collection of such spells, known as *The Book of the Dead*, has about 700 spells, found in the various pyramids of Egypt.

The **MASTABA OF MERERUKA** is situated northeast of the Step Pyramid. Mereruka was Grand Chamberlain of the Pharaoh. The tomb, 133 feet by 79 feet, was built about 2400-2200 B.C. and consists of 32 chambers and passages. The walls are covered with beautiful paintings.

The **MASTABA OF TI**, northeast of the Mariette House, is the largest and most beautiful of the private tombs at Saqqara. Ti was an "architectural overseer" about 2563-2429 B.C. The walls of the tomb, famous for their painted limestone relief of everyday life in ancient Egypt, have scenes of weaving, hunting, sculpturing, harvesting, boating, sacrificing, shipbuilding, fishing, papyrus gathering, flogging, plowing, treading in the seed, eating, and the birth of a calf. Note the expression on the cow and calf in a scene that shows a calf being carried across the stream on the back of an Egyptian.

The **SERAPEUM**, 650 yards west of the Mastaba of Ti, is an underground burial site for the sacred Apis bulls that were worshiped at Memphis. The Apis bull, a manifestation of the creator god Ptah, was embalmed after death and buried with great ceremony in a special sarcophagus. This burial site is 35 feet underground and nearly 1,200 feet long. The main gallery is 660 feet long and houses 24 granite

Above: Painting from the mastaba of Ti, Saqqara

Below: Sarcophagus of an Apis bull, Saqqara

sarcophagi that average about 10 feet high, 13½ feet long, and 6½ feet wide. The lids are 3 feet thick and each weighs about 15 tons. Each sarcophagus weighs about 60 tons, and the heavy granite pieces were transported from Aswan, 450 miles away.

The oldest tomb of the bulls dates back to 1600 B.C.; the one at Saqqara dates from 650 B.C. The Serapeum gets its name from the fact that Apis assimilated with Osiris after death and was then called *Osiris-Apis,* or *Oserapis.* In the Ptolemaic period, Oserapis was equated with the Greek god of the underworld, Serapis, and hence the name *Serapeum.*

Some bull burials date from the 18th and 19th dynasties, which may partly explain why we find Israelites making a golden bull to worship in Sinai; and later, Jeroboam saw this kind of worship in Egypt and took it back to Israel (1 Kgs. 11:40; 12:27-29).

- *There seems to be a correspondence here to the children of Israel's golden calf episode under the direction of Aaron (Exod. 32).*

The **MASTABA OF PTAH-HOTEP** is located a short distance south of the Mariette House. Ptah-Hotep was a judge of the High Court during the Fifth Dynasty. The walls are covered with beautiful, well-preserved reliefs and paintings of daily life.

Dahshur

About 5 miles south of Saqqara and 27 miles south of Cairo are the five pyramids of Dahshur.

The **BENT PYRAMID** of King Snefru still has the original smooth stone that once covered all the pyramids. Snefru, an early Fourth Dynasty (2600 B.C.) king, was the father of Khufu (Cheops), the builder of the Great Pyramid at Giza. The base is 620 feet wide. The Bent Pyramid is the predecessor of the first true pyramid, also built at Dahshur.

It has been suggested that perhaps the second pyramid, named the *Meidum Pyramid,* 35 miles south of Saqqara, was being converted from a step pyramid into a true pyramid at the same time that the Bent Pyramid was being built, but when the new sides collapsed into piles of rubble all the builders of the Bent Pyramid observed this disaster and decided to change the angle of their pyramid from 52 degrees to 43 l/3 degrees.

The **BLACK PYRAMID OF AMMENEMES III**, in the south end of Dahshur, is made of brick.

The **WHITE PYRAMID OF AMMENEMES II** is located in the center of Dahshur.

The **RED PYRAMID**, 325 feet high and 702 feet at the base, was built by Snefru. Its base is the same size as the pyramid of Khufu, but the pyramid is shorter because the angle of the sides is 43 ⅓ degrees instead of 52 degrees.

The **BLACK PYRAMID OF SESOSTRIS III** is 100 feet high and 345 feet wide and is made of brick.

ALEXANDRIA

Alexander the Great established this city in 332 B.C. It is located on the Mediterranean coast near the mouth of the west branch of the Nile River and approximately 130 miles north of Cairo.

For centuries it was one of the most magnificent and renowned cities in the ancient world. It was the center of Hellenistic culture during the Ptolemaic dynasty (332 B.C.-30 B.C.) During Cleopatra's reign 50,000-100,000 Greeks, Egyptians, and Jews lived in the city. After the destruction of Jerusalem in Jeremiah's day, Jews fled to Alexandria in large numbers (Jer. 42:14). It was the largest city of the Roman Empire outside of Rome itself, and it boasted a library of 700,000 manuscripts.

Between 250 and 132 B.C. the Hebrew Scriptures were first translated into the Greek tongue in Alexandria. This volume was known as the *Septuagint* and is the only authorized version of the Old Testament in the Greek Orthodox church.

Alexandria became a center of Christianity very early. The apostle Paul seems to have refrained from coming here because the gospel had already reached the city (Rom. 15:20). Eusebius says the apostle Mark brought Christianity to Egypt. During the second and third centuries Alexandria was the intellectual capital of Christendom. Here Clement and Origen taught in a theological school against the Gnostic philosophy, and Athanasius defended the doctrine of the deity of Christ in the Nicene controversy.

The Jewish philosopher Philo lived in Alexandria. He was a contemporary of Jesus and took it upon himself to interpret the scriptures allegorically in order to make Jewish theology compatible with Greek philosophy. Philo's theory that mind or spirit was a product of the Deity led to his conception of the Deity as having complete absence of all qualities.

Philo was one of the many philosophers who helped to pave the way for a written definition of God that appeared later in Christian creeds. He indicated that God, being better than virtue, knowledge, good, and beauty, transcends all qualities. God is not in space, he said, because he contains it. He is without body, parts or passions: without feet, for whither should he walk who fills all things; without eyes, for why does he need eyes who made the light? He is invisible, for how can eyes that are too weak to gaze upon the sun be strong enough to gaze upon its maker? It is incomprehensible, says Philo; we know *that* he is, but we cannot know *what* he is.

When the Arabs made Cairo the capital of Egypt in A.D. 642, Alexandria began to decline. For nearly 1,000 years it had been the center of culture and commerce, but it soon became a fishing village. Muhammad Ali, however, saw the importance of Alexandria and gave the city the needed impetus to bring the population from 7,000 in 1805 to over six million in the 1990s. Today it is the second largest city in Egypt. With the exception of the Arab quarters and bazaars, the city is European in nature. It is a vital commercial center to Egypt and is the principal port of Egypt. Exports include cotton, grain, beans, sugar, and rice. White sandy beaches and a wonderful climate make Alexandria a major summer resort.

- *Alexandrians opposed Stephen (Acts 6:9).*
- *Alexandria was the birthplace of Apollos (Acts 18:24).*
- *Paul embarked on an Alexandrian ship when he left Myra and Malta (Acts 27:6; 28:11).*

POINTS OF INTEREST

Antiquities of the past are not prevalent in Alexandria, but the following are possible points to visit:

POMPEY'S PILLAR (*Amoud el Sawari*), a red Aswan rose granite column, dates from the Ptolemaic period and was erected in honor of Diocletian. It is southwest of the city, near the Arab cemetery. It is nearly 90 feet high, has a 9-foot diameter at the base, and tapers to 6½ feet at the top. A Corinthian capital graces the top. The column received its name from Pompey whose tomb was believed to be on that spot. At this site the Serapeum, a temple to the god Serapis (god of the underworld), once stood during the Ptolemaic period.

CATACOMBS OF KOM EL SHUQAFA. A couple of blocks north of Pompey's Pillar are the Catacombs of Kom el Shuqafa, ancient burial tombs dating from approximately A.D. 200-300. They are built on three levels and show decorations of Egyptian, Roman, and Greek influence. The lowest level, 100 feet below the surface and usually under water, is believed to be a sanctuary for the bull god Apis.

The **ANFOUSHY NECROPOLIS** (*Anfushi*), a second-century Greek burial site, is smaller and less important than the Catacombs of Kom el Shuqafa, but paintings on the walls, as well as the tombs themselves, make a visit worthwhile. It is located nearly 2 miles east of the Ras el Tin Palace.

The **RAS EL TIN PALACE**, at the West Harbor, is a palace to which King Farouk went into exile on July 26, 1952. The 300 rooms may now be viewed by the public.

AQUARIUM. Different forms of sea life from the Red Sea, the Mediterranean, and the Nile are on display at the Aquarium, in the western part of the city near Fort Qaitbai.

PHAROS (lighthouse) and **KAIT BEY FORT**. In 280 B.C. Ptolemy II built a huge lighthouse on the east end of Pharos Island. It stood nearly 500 feet tall. It was adorned with marble columns, balustrades, and statues, and was known as one of the Seven Wonders of the World. From this first Pharos, the idea of a lighthouse spread throughout the world. An earthquake destroyed the lighthouse in the fourteenth century A.D., and Fort Kait Bey was built on the site. Pharos Island is connected to the mainland with fill.

The **ALEXANDRIA LIGHTHOUSE** is located near Fort Kait Bey.

MONTAZA PALACE, the royal summer palace, stands at the eastern end of the Corniche, and houses mementos of the last kings of the Muhammad Ali dynasty. The palace, flowers, and grounds are beautiful.

The **GRECO-ROMAN MUSEUM** was founded in 1891 and houses 40,000 items dating back to Greek and Roman periods, including a collection of 50,000 coins and Egyptian antiquities.

The **CENTRAL MUSEUM FOR FINE ARTS** is an art gallery featuring paintings by modern and other artists.

Rosetta, *Rashid*

Forty-five miles east of Alexandria, where the western branch of the Nile flows into the Mediterranean Sea, is the city of Rosetta. Northeast of Rosetta, at Fort Saint Julian, the Rosetta Stone was discovered by Bouchard, a French officer of the Engineers, in 1799. This black basalt stone slab was responsible for the breakthrough in the interpretation of Egyptian hieroglyphs. The stone is 3 feet 9 inches in length, 2 feet 4½ inches in width, and 11 inches in thickness. It is believed that originally the entire stone was 5-6 feet in height.

It has three inscriptions or versions of the same decree that was passed by the general council of Egyptian priests assembled at Memphis to celebrate the first commemoration of the coronation of Ptolemy V, Epiphanes, king of all Egypt. It is dated April 4, 196 B.C. Among other things in the decree are the benefits which Ptolemy V had conferred upon Egypt: remission of taxes; restoration of temple services; forgiveness of debts; endowments to temples; gifts of money and corn to temples; restoration of the temples of Apis and Mnevis Bulls and of other sacred animals. The inscription is written in two languages, Egyptian and Greek. The Egyptian is in two portions: (1) *hieroglyphic*, a type of picture writing; and (2) *de-*

motic, a cursive form of hieroglyphic writing, used in the Ptolemaic period (323 B.C.-30 B.C.).

In 1822 a 32-year-old French scholar, Jean Francois Champollion, began to decipher the hieroglyphs. During the next ten years, until his death in 1832, he correctly deciphered the hieroglyphic forms of the names and titles of most of the Roman emperors, drew up a classified list of Egyptian hieroglyphs, and formulated a system of grammar and general decipherment that is the foundation upon which all later Egyptologists have worked. The Rosetta Stone is now housed in the British Museum.

UPPER EGYPT

Luxor, Egypt, is 416 miles south of Cairo and can be visited by car (two days' journey one way), train (8-11 hours), boat (several days), or plane (1-2 hours). On the way are several places of interest:

Deir Mawas, Tell el Amarna

At a point 190 miles south of Cairo are the ruins of Tell el Amarna, near the town of Deir Mawas, on the east bank.

Tell el Amarna was the residence of Pharaoh Amenhotep IV (Akhenaton), who lived about 1400-1360 B.C. When he was born the Egyptians believed in many gods – polytheism – with some gods more prominent than others. But Akhenaton launched a heretical revolt against the great god Amon and other gods and sought to impose upon Egypt a new god, Aton, and do away with other gods – a new monotheism. Aton was represented by a sun-disc with celestial rays penetrating the universe and bestowing life on all living things. Many modern scholars believe this is where Moses received his concept of one god. The name *Moses* is Egyptian, being a variation of the word for "child." *Thutmose* means "child of the god Thoth." There is no evidence of a direct connection between Moses' and Akhenaton's monotheism, but there were certainly Egyptian influences on Moses and the Israelites.

After ruling for five years at Thebes, Amenhotep IV changed his name to Akhenaton, carried out a reformation not only in religion but also in Egyptian art, and moved his capital from Thebes (Luxor) to Tell el Amarna, halfway between Thebes and Cairo. The 17-year reign of this "heretical pharaoh" (about 1375-1358 B.C.) is an interesting chapter in the history of Egypt. His statues exaggerate his physical imperfections: pot belly, stumpy legs, and camel legs. He cannot be mistaken.

Akhenaton's wife was the beautiful Nefertiti. The famous bust of Queen Nefertiti shows her in a royal headdress with a brightly painted face under a crown. *Nefer* means "good and beautiful."

Akhenaton fought against Amon Ra and had the god's name erased from all Egyptian monuments. But forces were at work against Akhenaton. One of these forces was Queen Ty, Akhenaton's mother. When she came to Amarna, trouble brewed. Nefertiti, a strong believer in Aton, was banished to a separate part of the city and was stripped of her royal titles. Akhenaton took one of his daughters as his chief wife and made no further moves against Amon Ra. The spirit of rebellion went out of Amarna, and five years later Akhenaton died.

Soon young Tutankhaton became pharaoh and changed the ending of his name to *-amon.* Young Tut went back to Thebes and Amon was restored for another 1,000 years.

Only a few traces remain of the **TEMPLE TO ATON**. It was 2,409 feet long and 907 feet wide – evidently a huge complex. In a hillside, there are 24 rock **TOMBS**, on whose walls remarkable intimate and familiar domestic scenes show a freedom of artistic expression that was hitherto unknown.

In addition to the bust of Nefertiti – a very important find – the *Tell el Amarna Tablets* (now located in the Berlin Museum, the British Museum, and other museums) are also very important. They are letters written on some 400 clay tablets in Akkadian cuneiform, and are part of the diplomatic correspondence between rulers and officials in Western Asia to the pharaohs Amenhotep III and Amenhotep IV (Akhenaton) about 1400-1360 B.C., before the Hebrew exodus. Those from Canaan and Syria include six from Abdi-Heba, governor of Jerusalem, who described Canaan as being gravely disturbed by "Habiru" invaders. The governor was seeking aid from the Pharaoh against the Habiru.

The question is, who were the Habiru? Were they Israelites? Some scholars feel that the letters tell of the Israelite invasion of Canaan and others believe that the Habiru are simply lawless gangs within Canaan. Part of letter no. 287 says: "Behold, this land of Jerusalem, neither my father nor my mother gave it to me...and the deed of the sons of Labaya who have given the land of the king to the Habiru...I fall at thy feet." Letters 47 and 48 are from Abdi-tirshi, the ruler of Hazor to the pharaoh of Egypt assuring him that he will guard the cities. Other letters are from Gezer, Ashkelon, Gaza, Joppa, Shechem, Lachish, Hebron, and Megiddo.

Asyut (*Assiout*), *Lycopolis*

This is the largest city in Upper Egypt, with about 300,000 people. It is 232 miles from Cairo and is the center of an important Coptic community. Here Plotinus, the Greek philosopher and founder of Neoplatonism, was born in 205 B.C. At age 20 he went to Alexandria to study philosophy under the great teachers there, and in 244 B.C. he settled in Rome. He developed his own philosophy and believed that material things represented evil. Men, he felt, should reject material things and purify their souls by communion with God. His ideas had an influence on early Christian thought.

Rock tombs in the area have been rifled by the natives and are not very impressive. The city is famous, however, for its beautiful silver shawls, carpetmaking, and ebony and ivory work.

Abydos, *This, Thinis*

Located 322 miles from Cairo and 7½ miles southwest of the el-Baliana railway station are the ruins of Abydos – some of the oldest in Egypt, dating from the First and Second Dynasties. **TOMBS OF THE FIRST PHARAOHS** (3100-2686 B.C.) are here. One of the pharaohs, Djer, was accompanied into death by 587 human victims.

The **TEMPLES OF SETI I AND RAMSES II** still stand. Osiris seems to have been the main god of these temples, but there are chapels to many other gods. Reliefs and colored paintings are well preserved, and many tombs of the New Kingdom are located at Abydos.

To celebrate the "resurrection" of Osiris, an annual "passion play" was held at Abydos. Osiris was symbolically buried, and then as stones were removed from the tomb the people shouted, "The Lord is risen!" In this rebirth of Osiris the Egyptians saw their own triumph over death.

Dendera, *Ant*

These ruins are located near Qena, 37 miles north of Luxor on the east bank of the Nile. A train takes one hour to reach Qena from Luxor. A ferry must be taken to the west bank, and then the ruins can be found 3 miles from the Nile.

Dendera was a religious center for the worship of Hathor, goddess of love and joy, like the Roman Venus and the Greek Aphrodite. The **TEMPLE** dates from the first century B.C. but there are older ruins from as far back as the Fourth Dynasty. On the walls of the temple are many scenes, including some showing the Roman emperors Caligula, Tiberius, Nero, and Claudius, representing pharaohs worshiping the gods. On the south wall is a relief of Caesar and Cleopatra and their son. Six beautiful Hathor-columns form the facade of the temple, and 24 support the roof.

NO, *Thebes*, Luxor

The city of Luxor (from Arabic *el-Uqsur*, meaning "the castles") 416 miles south of Cairo, bears the Egyptian name *Weset* ("middle"), the biblical name *No*, and the Greek name *Thebes*. It is possible that ancient Thebes had a million inhabitants. In *The Iliad* Homer referred to "Thebes, city where rich are the houses in treasure, a hundred has she of gates..." – the richest and mightiest city in the

world. It reached its glory about 1500 B.C., and names such as Tutankhamon, Hatshepsut, Amenhotep III, Akhenaton, and Ramses II are household words in Luxor. For hundreds of years temples, statues, obelisks, columns, and sphinxes were built to make this area the central place of worship of the Egyptians – a most important religious center of the god Amon, the first universal god in Egypt.

After 1000 B.C., however, Thebes was well on the way of decline. In 661 B.C. the city was sacked of what riches were left, and her wealth was carried off by Ashurbanipal (Nah. 3:8). But her temples, built to last through eternity, still remain.

The ancient city of Thebes consisted of three areas that are known today as *Luxor, Karnak,* and the *West Bank.*

- *Thebes is mentioned as No in the scriptures (Jer. 46:25; Ezek. 30:14-16).*
- *The fate of Thebes was that which Nahum predicted for the hated Assyrian city of Nineveh (Nah. 3:7-8).*
- *Upper Egypt was called Pathros by Isaiah and Jeremiah (Isa. 11:11; Jer. 44:1).*

Modern Luxor

The narrow streets, open-fronted shops, primitive houses, street sweepers, donkeys, city smells, and the people of Luxor are a sight the Westerner will never forget. Carriages can be hired to take a traveler through the back alleys.

Temple of Luxor

On the edge of the Nile is the ancient temple of Luxor, built between 1400 and 1100 B.C. by the Pharaohs Amenhotep III, Tutankhamon, Hatshepsut, and Ramses II. It was dedicated to the god Amon, his wife Mut, and their son, the moon god Khons. The temple complex is 857 feet long and 182 feet wide.

In front of the pylons were six **STATUES OF RAMSES.** Only three remain now, and the two seated figures are 76 feet high. Only one of the rose-colored Aswan granite **OBELISKS** is still standing at the temple site. The other was given to France in 1833 because of Champollion's work in deciphering the Rosetta Stone. It is now located in the Place de la Concorde in Paris.

The two obelisks were placed in front of the temple by Ramses II, who had a real flair for the superlative. He reigned for 66 years (ca. 1290-1224 B.C.), lived past the age of 90, sired 92 sons and 106 daughters – many of whom he married – and bestrewed the Nile valley with countless monuments, obelisks, pylons, temples, and colossal statues commemorating his deeds. At Karnak he built the largest columned hall ever reared by man. Many believe that Ramses II was the king who "knew not Joseph" (Exod. 1:8) and put the children of Israel in bitter bondage. As is attested by nine succeeding pharaohs bearing his name, no pharaoh of Egypt had greater influence than Ramses II.

Running north from the Luxor temple is the **AVENUE OF RAM-HEADED SPHINXES**. There were approximately 1,500 sphinxes lining the two-mile avenue between the Luxor and Karnak temples. During the great festival of Amon at Thebes a splendid procession moved along the avenue carrying the sacred bark of Amon. This was a 27-day religious festival, filled with the banging of tambourines, chanting of priests, and burning of incense. It is only recently that the avenue was excavated, but the temple itself was excavated beginning in 1884. Before that time the temple was buried under a hill of rubbish and native houses. It was discovered when a drainage shaft was being sunk from a house.

Entering the main entrance of the temple from the north, one comes to the **COURT OF RAMSES II**. On the southwest wall is a relief showing the Nile god Hapi tying together the lotus and papyrus plants, symbols of Upper and Lower Egypt. This was the uniting that took place in 3100 B.C., making Egypt the first united civilization. The female breasts on the male god Hapi symbolize the fertility and nourishment of the Nile.

The corridor decorated by Tutankhamon, the **COLONNADE OF HARMHAB**, is the next columned area, followed by the very beautiful **COURT OF AMENHOTEP III** (about 1411-1375 B.C.). The court is surrounded by 99 excellently preserved papyrus capital columns. This was the hypostyle hall of the temple, like the holy place in the temple of Solomon.

Other miscellaneous sanctuaries make up the temple complex, with beautiful bas-reliefs on the walls, outside and inside. Parts of the temple have been used by Christians and Muslims, and they remodeled and painted to suit their own needs.

Karnak

Nearly 2 miles north of the Luxor temple is the largest temple complex in the world. It covers over 60 acres and took about 2,000 years to build (2133-100 B.C.). The temples are dedicated to Amon Ra, Mut (wife of Amon Ra), and Khons, their son (the divine triad). In fact, Karnak is a whole city of temples, the largest of which is the **TEMPLE OF AMON**. The magnificence of the god Amon may be measured by his properties: he had over 5,000 statues; 81,000 slaves/vassals/ servants/ priests; 421,000 cattle; 433 gardens and orchards; 691,000 acres of land; 83 ships; 46 building yards; and 63 cities and towns.

An **AVENUE OF SPHINXES**, constructed by Ramses in 1292 B.C., connects the Luxor and Karnak temples. There are several pylons or entrances to the various temples, but the following list of antiquities will begin at the largest of the pylons – those located on the west side of the complex.

The **PYLONS** forming the chief entrance are the largest at Karnak. They are 429 feet wide, 50 feet thick, and 144 feet high. Stairs ascend to the top, which offers

an excellent view. These pylons were started in 304 B.C. and were never completed.

The **COURT** behind the pylons is the largest of all Egyptian temple courts – 340 by 277 feet. It dates back to the sixth century B.C. On the left as you enter the courtyard is the **TEMPLE OF SETI II** (1209 B.C.). The single **LOTUS-CAPITAL COLUMN** in the court was erected by the Ethiopian pharaoh Taharka in 688 B.C.

On the south side of the court is a small **TEMPLE OF AMON**, built by Ramses III in 1198 B.C. It measures 172 feet in length. Large statues of Ramses III line the outer court of the temple. The three small chapels at the south end are to the gods Amon (middle), Mut (right), and Khons (left).

The **GREAT HYPOSTYLE HALL** is entered through a second set of pylons. This "Hall of Columns" is the largest columnar structure ever built by man. It consists of 134 sandstone columns arranged in 16 rows and covering an area of 56,000 square feet. The central avenue consists of 12 columns with open papyrus capitals. The columns are 69 feet tall and 33 feet in circumference, and 100 persons could stand on top of each. The other columns, with closed papyrus-bud capitals, are 42½ feet tall and 27½ feet in circumference. All of the columns are made of stones stacked like pancakes, engraved, and originally painted.

The hypostyle hall was begun perhaps by Harmhab in 1350-1315 B.C. and finished by Ramses I about 1315 B.C. Reliefs were added as late as 1230 B.C. by Ramses II. The outside walls of the hall have beautiful **BATTLE SCENES**: the victories of Seti I over the Libyans on the north wall and the victories of Ramses II over the Hittites (or actually, the peace treaty of Ramses with the Hittites) on the south wall. Also on the outside south wall are the giant figure of Sheshonk (Biblical Shishak) and the cartouches of those enemies subdued in Canaan (on the incursion where he raided the treasures of Solomon's Temple in Jerusalem – the subject of the film "Raiders of the Lost Ark" – 1 Kgs. 14:25-26; 2 Chron. 12:2-9). Karnak owes its special fame to this hall. From ancient times it was considered one of the wonders of the world. Because of its columns and aisles, the hall is a prototype of the later Christian basilicas. Each column matches the size of Trajan's Column in Rome.

The third set of **PYLONS OF AMENHOTEP III** (1411 B.C.) forms the entrance to an early temple dating back to 1580-1350 B.C. A 76-foot **OBELISK OF THUTMOSE I** is still standing in the court between the two pylons. There were originally four obelisks, dating from 1535 B.C.

A fourth set of **PYLONS BUILT BY THUTMOSE I** is badly damaged. On the left, in a columned hall, is a polished red Aswan granite **OBELISK OF QUEEN HATSHEPSUT**. Standing 97 feet tall, it is the tallest obelisk still standing on Egyptian soil. It dates from 1485 B.C. A fragment of a companion obelisk lies near the sacred lake. Hatshepsut said she made two obelisks to the god Amon at

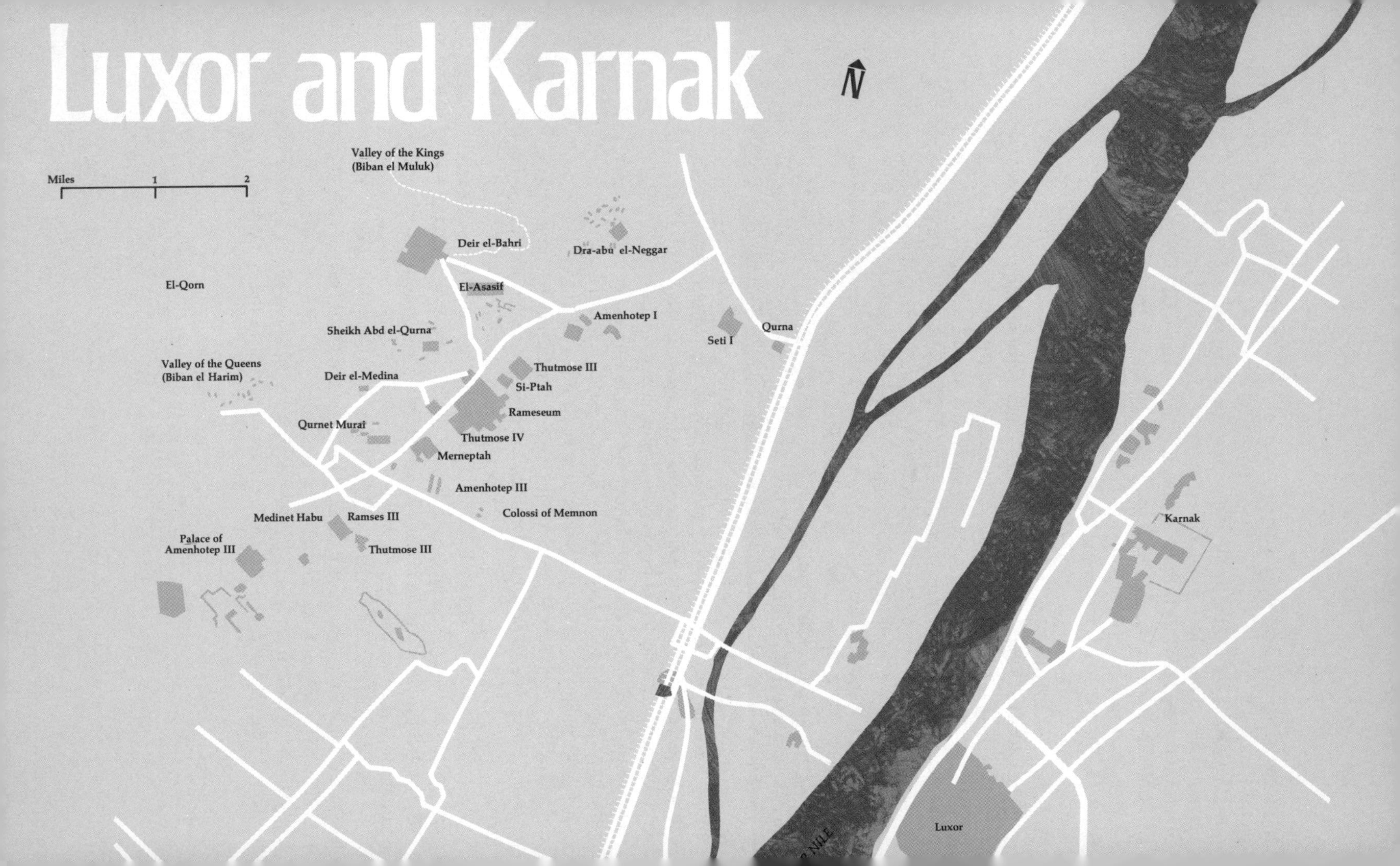

Luxor and Karnak

N

Miles 1 2

Valley of the Kings
(Biban el Muluk)
Deir el-Bahri
Dra-abu el-Neggar
El-Qorn
El-Asasif
Amenhotep I
Qurna
Seti I
Sheikh Abd el-Qurna
Valley of the Queens
(Biban el Harim)
Deir el-Medina
Thutmose III
Si-Ptah
Rameseum
Qurnet Murai
Thutmose IV
Merneptah
Amenhotep III
Colossi of Memnon
Medinet Habu
Ramses III
Palace of
Amenhotep III
Thutmose III
Karnak
Luxor
NILE

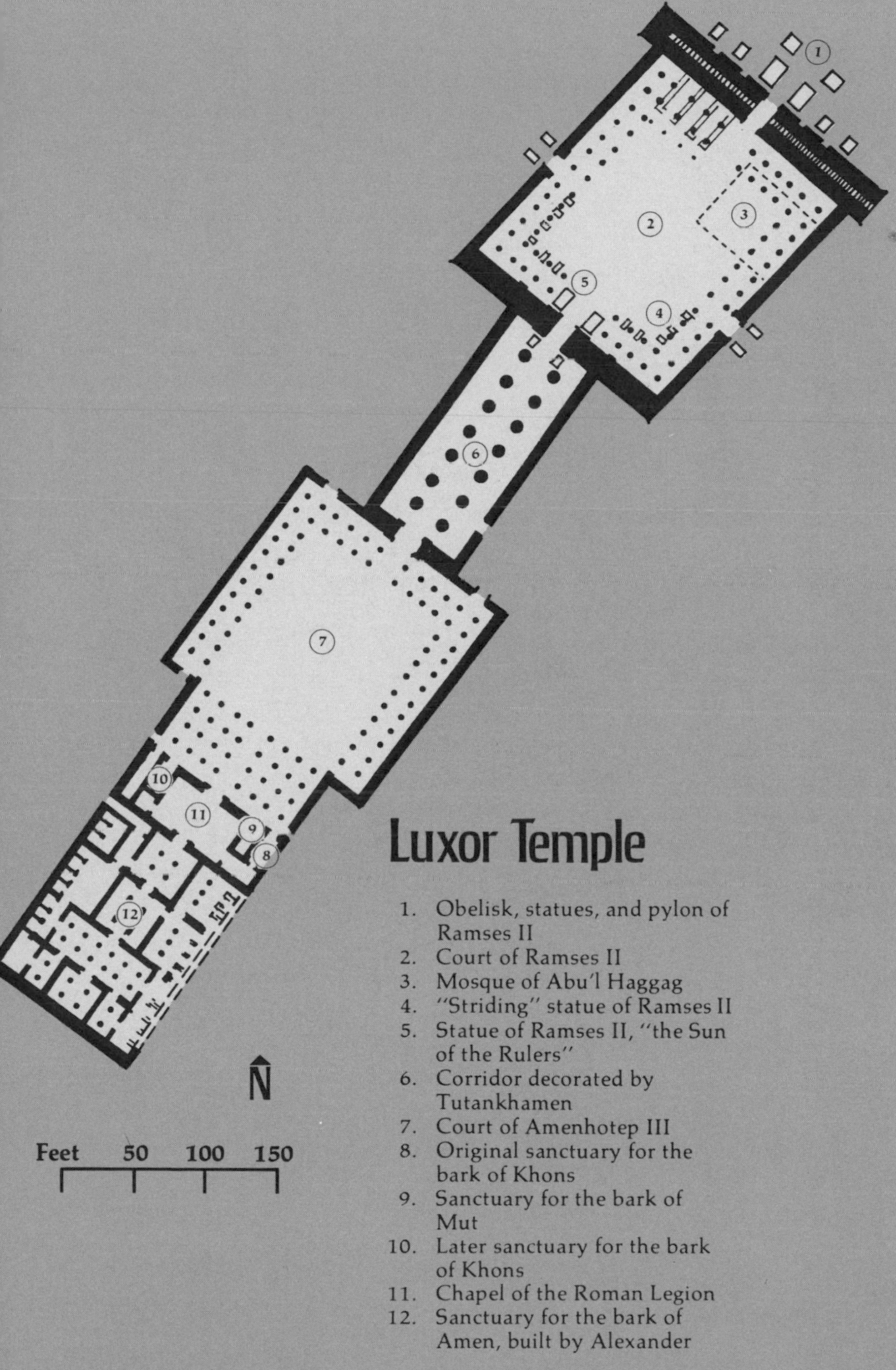

*Adapted from K. Lange and M. Hirmer, *Egypt: Architecture, Sculpture, Painting*, 4th ed. (Hirmer Verlag München, 1968), by permission.

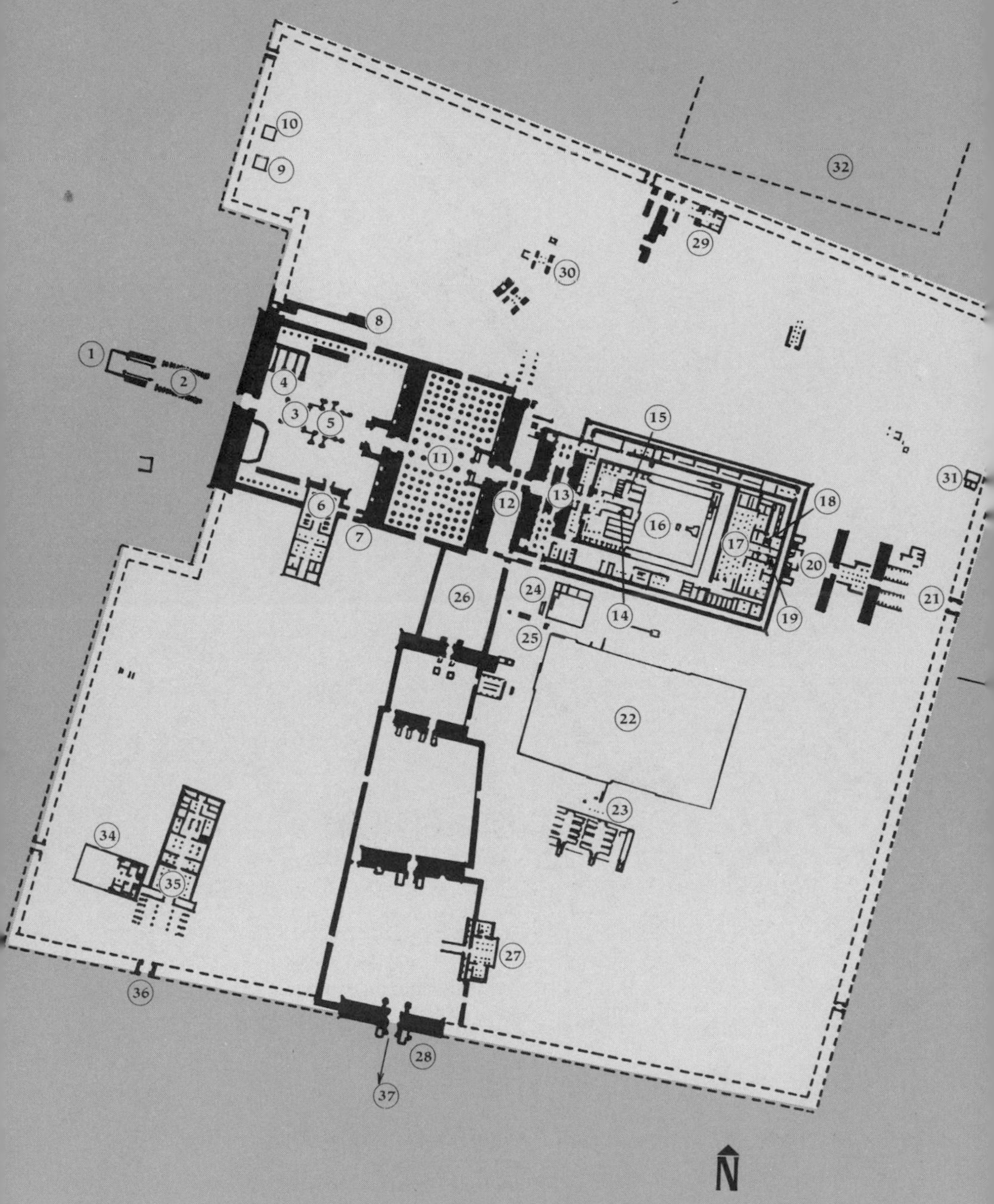

Temenos of Amen, Karnak

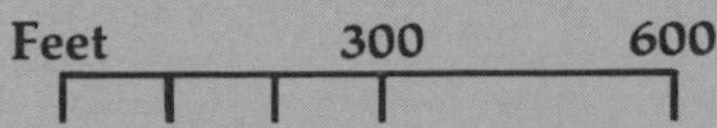

1. Quay
2. Sphinx-lined dromos
3. The First Court
4. Way station of Seti II
5. Kiosk of Taharka
6. Way station of Ramses III
7. Triumphal inscription of Sheshonk I
8. Modern stairs to top of first pylon
9. Reconstructed chapel of Senusret I
10. Reconstructed alabaster chapel of Amenhotep I
11. The great hypostyle hall
12. Obelisk of Thutmose I
13. Hall of Thutmose I and obelisks of Hatshepsut
14. Sanctuary for the bark of Amon, built by Phillip Arrhidaeus
15. Rooms of Hatshepsut
16. Middle Kingdom remains
17. Festival Hall of Thutmose III
18. Room of botanical pictures
19. Chapel of Alexander
20. The "Hearing Ear," a chapel for public prayers of Thutmose III, Ramses II, and later Rulers
21. East gateway of Nekhtnebef
22. Temple lake
23. Fowl yard and store rooms
24. Top of fallen obelisk of Hatshepsut
25. Scarab-topped monument of Amenhotep III
26. Court of the cache
27. Festival Hall of Amenhotep II
28. Base of standing colossus of Amenhotep III
29. Temple of Ptah
30. Late chapels
31. Chapel dedicated to Osiris, "Ruler of Eternity"
32. Temenos of Montu, southern edge
33. Approximate position of temple of Akhenaten
34. Temple of Ipet
35. Temple of Khons
36. Gateway of Ptolemy III and Euergetes I
37. Avenue of the Temenos of Mut

Adapted from K. Lange and M. Hirmer, Egypt: Architecture, Sculpture, Painting, 4th ed. (Hirmer Verlag, München, 1968), by permission.

Karnak. She had intended to make them of solid gold, but because this was not possible she gold-plated them. One can still discern near the corners the grooves in which Hatshepsut's craftsmen set the sheets of electrum (gold alloy).

Hatshepsut's successor, Thutmose III, suggested in his inscription that he made two obelisks entirely of gold alloy. They represented perhaps the vital rays of the sun-god Ra. These were probably the two obelisks mentioned in the Louvre cylinder as weighing 1,250 talents (83,325 pounds) each, which stood in the sanctuary at Karnak, and which the priests of Thebes gave to Ashurbanipal to avert the sack of the city. When the Egyptian dynasties were on the decline, Greeks

Nile god Hapi tying together the lotus and papyrus plants, Luxor

Above: Drying adobe bricks, Luxor

Below: Tomb 33, of Pentamenopet, with the temple of Queen Hatshepsut in the background, Valley of the Nobles

made fun of the sacred "tall pillars dedicated to god with a pyramid-shaped top" and dubbed them "obelisks," or "spits."

The **FIFTH SET OF PYLONS** leads to two small **ANTECHAMBERS BY THUTMOSE III.** From here the visitor passes through the last and smallest pylons into the **FIRST HALL OF ANNALS**, where two beautiful, highly polished **ROSE GRANITE SHAFTS** of Thutmose III show heraldic lotus and papyrus flowers, symbols of Upper and Lower Egypt. They are nearly 3,500 years old. Past the shafts is a two-roomed **GRANITE CHAPEL**, in which was kept the sacred bark (boat) of the god Amon. This room was the holy of holies of the temple and contained not only the bark but a closed shrine which was located on the bark. It contained a golden image of Amon. The image was considered not the god himself but a portrait of him. Once a year, on the fifteenth day of the second month, the "Luxor Festival" began. For this festive occasion the bark with the image was carried by the priests to the Nile and taken to the Temple of Luxor until a return journey.

The **SECOND HALL OF ANNALS** is located northeast of the **SANCTUARY.** The famous Annals of Thutmose III have, among other things, an account of the Egyptian battle at Megiddo in Israel.

The **FESTIVAL HALL OF THUTMOSE III** is next in line. It was built in 1500 B.C. over the site of an earlier temple dating back to 2000 B.C.

The last site on the east, within the walls, is the large **HALL OF STATE** with its 20 columns and 32 pillars in rows.

South and east of the Temple of Amon is the **SACRED LAKE**, dating back at least to 1292 B.C. Near its northwest corner is a large **GRANITE SCARAB OF AMENHOTEP III** and the **TOP OF A FALLEN OBELISK OF HATSHEPSUT**.

North of the Temple of Amon is the **TEMPLE OF PTAH**, and southwest of the Temple of Amon is the **TEMPLE OF KHONS**, built within the outer walls of the temple complex.

South of the temple complex is the **TEMPLE OF MUT**, a **SACRED LAKE**, and a small **TEMPLE OF RAMSES III**, all at the north end of the Avenue of Sphinxes. Mut's temple dates from 1411 B.C.

There is a huge adobe wall around the Karnak Temple complex. Our word *adobe* comes from the Egyptian word *tobe*, meaning "brick."

In 1954 there was found at Karnak a stone slab with 38 lines of hieroglyphics, telling of the expulsion of the Hyksos from Egypt.

Coptic Monastery

A 1½-hour ride north from Luxor brings one to the famous fifteenth-century Coptic Christian **MONASTERY OF DEIR EL SHAYEB**, or "the gray-haired

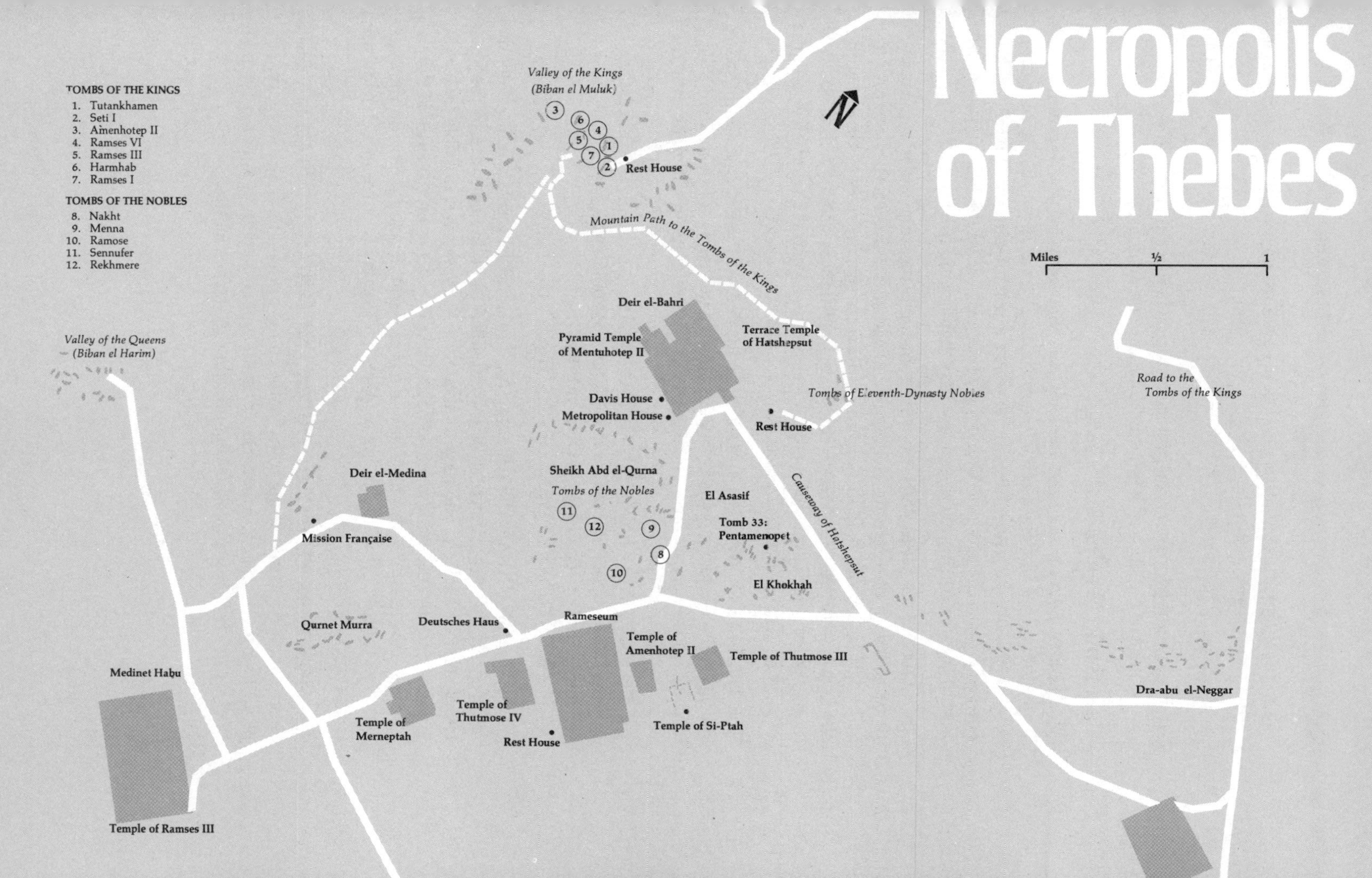
Necropolis of Thebes
TOMBS OF THE KINGS
1. Tutankhamen
2. Seti I
3. Amenhotep II
4. Ramses VI
5. Ramses III
6. Harmhab
7. Ramses I
TOMBS OF THE NOBLES
8. Nakht
9. Menna
10. Ramose
11. Sennufer
12. Rekhmere
Valley of the Kings
(Biban el Muluk)
Rest House
Mountain Path to the Tombs of the Kings
Miles
½
1
Deir el-Bahri
Pyramid Temple of Mentuhotep II
Terrace Temple of Hatshepsut
Tombs of Eleventh-Dynasty Nobles
Road to the Tombs of the Kings
Valley of the Queens
(Biban el Harim)
Davis House
Metropolitan House
Rest House
Deir el-Medina
Sheikh Abd el-Qurna
Tombs of the Nobles
El Asasif
Causeway of Hatshepsut
Tomb 33: Pentamenopet
El Khokhah
Mission Française
Qurnet Murra
Deutsches Haus
Rameseum
Temple of Amenhotep II
Temple of Thutmose III
Medinet Habu
Temple of Merneptah
Temple of Thutmose IV
Rest House
Temple of Si-Ptah
Dra-abu el-Neggar
Temple of Ramses III

saint." It contains three chapels plus rooms used for baptismal purposes. Coptic writing and crosses adorn the walls.

Pottery Factory

Near the Coptic Monastery is a pottery factory, where Egyptians fashion pots and jars by ancient methods of hand- and foot-wheel machines.

West Bank, *Necropolis of Thebes*

The Theban hills on the west bank of the Nile River are the location of the Necropolis – "city of the dead." Entire hillsides have networks of connecting tombs. It is like an immense anthill, where a person can travel freely without emerging above the ground. After a ferry boat ride across the Nile and a bus ride toward the west, the traveler usually visits the following sites:

The **COLOSSI OF MEMNON**, two 52½-foot-high sandstone seated figures, seem to be guarding the gigantic Necropolis. Originally, however, they guarded the mortuary temple of Pharaoh Amenhotep III (1411-1375 B.C.). In Hellenistic times the figures were thought to represent Memnon, who was slain by Achilles at Troy. The figure on the right used to emit a weird moan when the wind blew, and the noise was called "Memnon's voice."

The **TEMPLES OF MEDINET HABU** are located on the extreme south end of the Theban Necropolis. *Medinet* means "town" and refers to a Christian village that developed here in the fifth century A.D. There are four different constructions at Medinet Habu:

(1) the **MORTUARY PAVILION OF RAMSES III**;
(2) the **MORTUARY TEMPLE OF QUEEN AMENERTAIS**;
(3) the **MORTUARY TEMPLE OF RAMSES III**;
(4) the **MORTUARY TEMPLE OF THUTMOSE III**.

The **PAVILION OF RAMSES III** (1198 B.C.) is a castlelike fortress, built under the influence of Syrian architecture. It was intended to be the entrance to the great temple further back. As one passes through the gateway it is possible to see the grooves made by the chariots in the flagstones. The scenes on the sides of the entrance are the most deeply cut of any in Egypt, and the battle scenes on the walls are very beautiful. (It is interesting to note that Joseph also rode in a chariot. See Gen. 41:43.)

The **MORTUARY TEMPLE OF QUEEN AMENERTAIS** (700 B.C.) is a small temple on the west side of the court, between the pavilion and the mortuary temple of Ramses III. Queen Amenertais was the wife of the Ethiopian king Piankhi. Wall scenes show the queen making offerings to various deities.

The mortuary temples were built for the purpose of performing ceremonies in memory of the king or queen.

The **MORTUARY TEMPLE OF RAMSES III** is one of the best preserved and most colorful monuments in Thebes. Its pylons are almost perfect, and they are very beautiful, with scenes of Ramses III's victories especially the unique depiction of Philistines on the 2nd pylon, east side. A perfect stairway in the right pylon leads to the top, and the visitor should not miss a view from this summit.

In the first court is a row of eight papyrus columns with open capitals. On the right is a row of pillars on which the statues of Osiris once stood. The deeply cut scenes on the walls show victories of Ramses III in Libya and Syria.

A causeway surrounded by colonnades and scenes leads through the second doorway into the second court. On the west is a terrace, then the hypostyle hall, which is now almost in ruins. It once had 24 pillars supporting the ceiling. Other chambers, chapels, and treasuries are located in the west end.

The **MORTUARY TEMPLE OF THUTMOSE III** (1557 B.C.) is located northwest of the pavilion of Ramses III. It was begun by Queen Hatshepsut and finished by Thutmose III. After Akhenaton's destruction, Harmhab and Seti I restored the temple.

VALLEY OF THE QUEENS (*Biban el Harim*). During the Seventeenth Dynasty the queens were buried in small tombs in the Valley of the Kings near the pharaohs' tombs. The wife of Amenhotep III was the first queen who had a large tomb of her own in the Valley of the Kings (1400 B.C.) When Ramses I buried his wife Seta in 1315 B.C. he chose a new valley, now known as the Valley of the Queens. From that date until 1090 B.C. the valley was used to bury queens and princes. It is located in the southern end of the Necropolis and close to the Theban Hills, and there are about 70 tombs here, of which 4 are recommended for visitors:

(1) **QUEEN NEFERTARI**, wife of Ramses II (no. 66);
(2) **QUEEN TITI**, wife of one of the Ramessides (no. 52);
(3) **PRINCE AMUNKHOPESHFU**, who died at the age of 12, son of Ramses III (no. 55);
(4) **PRINCE KHAEMWAS**, son of Ramses III (no. 44).

The **TEMPLE OF DEIR EL-MEDINA** was built by Ptolemy IV, called Ptolemy Philopator, in 210 B.C. and was dedicated to the goddesses Hathor and Maat. It is 1,000 yards directly west of the Rameseum, and has a delicate construction. After viewing the open court, the visitor sees 3 chapels. Above the entrance of the Hathor chapel are 7 Hathor heads, and in the right-hand chamber is a well-preserved scene of judgment, presided over by Osiris, god of the underworld. Horus and Anubis are seen weighing the heart against an ostrich feather, while the god Thoth writes down the sentence of the court. To the right is a monster of the underworld waiting to carry off the soul of the deceased should the judgment of the scales be unfavorable. Above are the 42 judges of the dead. During early Christian times, this temple was used as a monastery.

MORTUARY TEMPLE OF MERNEPTAH. Located southwest of the Rameseum is the Temple of Merneptah. It is not visited as a part of most guided tours, but is of interest because of the "Israel Stela" of Merneptah. (See the section on the Egyptian Museum, in Cairo, above.)

The **RAMESEUM** (the mortuary temple of Ramses II) was built by Ramses II (1298-1232 B.C.) and dedicated to the god Amon. (Ramses is actually "Ra-mses", the prefix Ra being that of the god Amon-Ra.) At one time the temple measured 890 feet in length, and although today it is a vast heap of ruins there is still much of interest to see here. The inner sides of the ruined pylons are war scenes of Ramses II against the Hittites.

In the first court there is a broken statue of Ramses that was once the **LARGEST STATUE IN ALL OF EGYPT.** It weighs over 1,000 tons and is 59 feet high. The index finger and ear are 3½ feet in length, and the shoulders are 23 feet wide. The statue was hewn from one piece of Aswan granite. Legend says that the Persian king Cambyses ordered the statue to be broken.

The second court has a fine sculptured black granite **HEAD OF RAMSES II.** In the second hypostyle hall parts of the roof remain, with finely decorated astrological figures. At the far end of this hall, on the right-hand wall, is a scene showing the three gods writing the king's name on the tree of life.

Ruins of other temples are located both north and south of the Rameseum.

TOMBS OF THE NOBLES at Sheikh Abd el-Gournah. Although these structures are called "tombs," the nobles who excavated them were not buried here. They were really "mortuary chapels," serving for the worship of the repose of the souls of the dead. About 75 of the known 120 preserved chapels are located in the vicinity of Sheikh Abd el-Gournah. The walls are covered with beautiful paintings depicting the daily manners and customs of the Egyptians 3,000 years ago. Most of the "tombs" date back to the Twenty-eighth Dynasty. In most cases a chapel contains a broad hall and then a passage leading to a niche, in which a statue of the dead was placed. The most interesting chapels are the following:

(1) **NAKHT** (no. 52), overseer of the royal granaries. It has beautiful paintings of agricultural life and a famous scene of "The Dancers."

(2) **MENNA** (no. 69), chief of the king's estates.

(3) **SENNUFER** (no. 96), prince and chief overseer of the granaries. It has beautiful orchard scenes.

(4) **RAMOSE** (no. 55), vizier of Egypt under Amenhotep and Akhenaton. This chapel has a well-known funeral scene, with mourning women.
(5) **KHAEMHAT** (no. 57), superintendent of the granaries.
Also **USERHAT** (no. 56), **ENNE** (no. 81), **REKH-MERE** (no. 100), **NEFERHOTEP** (no. 50), **AMENEMHAB** (no. 85), and **HARMHAB** (no. 78).

TOMB 33: PENTAMENOPET. Located at El Asasif, near the Arab village of Gournah and approximately one-half mile east of the Temple of Queen Hatshepsut, is perhaps the largest "pit tomb" in the Necropolis. A painted sign at the entrance identifies it: "33 PENTAMENOPET XXVIth DYN." The nobleman Pentamenopet lived between 664 and 525 B.C. and was a contemporary of the third king of the dynasty, Necho (Neco, Nechoh) II, who ruled from 609 to 593 B.C.

Necho is a biblical figure. He marched into Canaan to assist Ashuruballit (2 Kings 23:29-30). He defeated Josiah of Judah, who had allied himself with Babylon at Megiddo. When Josiah was killed and his son Jehoahaz reigned in his stead, the prophet Jeremiah, a contemporary of Necho, lamented for Josiah. Necho deposed Jehoahaz and sent him to Egypt and made Jehoahaz's elder brother, Eliakim, king, changing the new monarch's name to *Jehoiakim* (2 Kings 23:33-34; 2 Chron. 35:20-25; 36:1-4).[2]

At the present time the "outer court" and "forecourt" are in ruins, and the entrance to the tomb is on the west side of the former "forecourt."

The walls on the inside have been blackened with smoke and damaged by souvenir hunters, but there are some paintings and figures still discernible. It had been painted beautifully like the other important tombs on the West Bank. Since it houses millions of dollars' worth of antiquities, the tomb is presently locked, sealed, and heavily guarded. Mummies are laid out on the floor, with barely enough room to walk down a narrow path between them. Statues, boxes, beds, jars, sarcophagi, and mummies fill the tomb. These antiquities are temporarily stored in tomb 33 because of its large size until they are placed in a new museum being built in Luxor. The tomb has no electric lights, and because of this, and the fact that the antiquities are so valuable and are scattered all over the floor of the tomb, it is little wonder that the Egyptian Department of Antiquities is not anxious to allow tourists into tomb 33.

TEMPLE OF QUEEN HATSHEPSUT. The magnificent funerary temple of Queen Hatshepsut is located at Deir el-Bahri, an Arabic title for "the northern monastery," so called because of a seventh-century monastery built here. The temple is at the base of majestic cliffs of the Theban Mountains.

Hatshepsut was one of the most famous of all women rulers in Egypt. Some believe she was the queen who reared Moses (Exod. 2:5-10), and some feel that

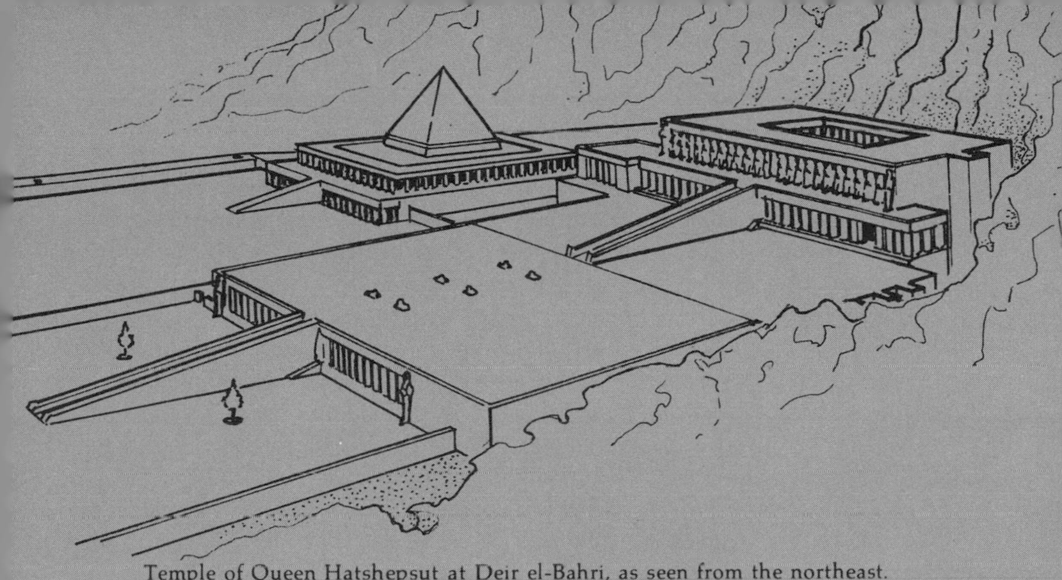

Temple of Queen Hatshepsut at Deir el-Bahri, as seen from the northeast. In the background is the funerary temple of King Mentuhotep Nebhapetre.

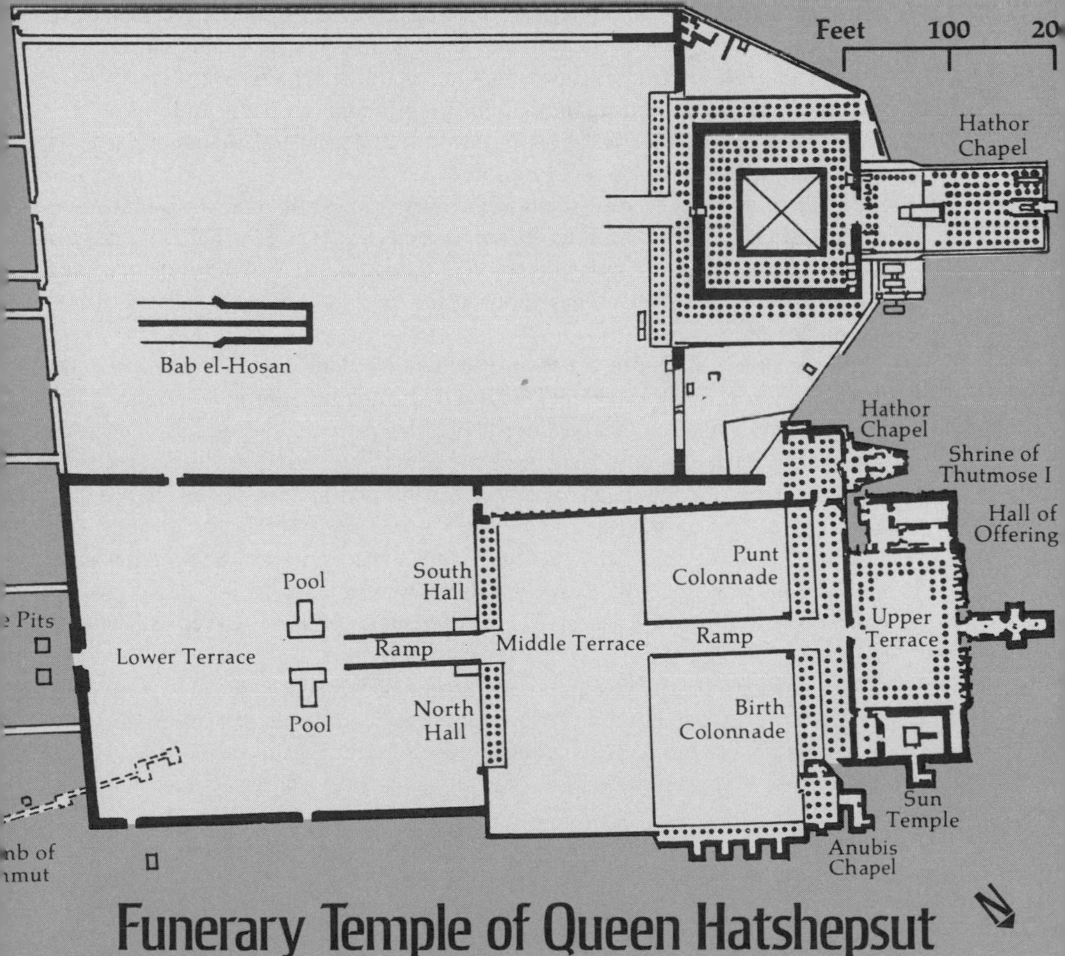

Feet 100 20

Hathor Chapel

Bab el-Hosan

Hathor Chapel

Shrine of Thutmose I

Hall of Offering

Punt Colonnade

Pool

South Hall

e Pits

Lower Terrace

Ramp

Middle Terrace

Ramp

Upper Terrace

Pool

North Hall

Birth Colonnade

Sun Temple

nb of
mut

Anubis Chapel

Funerary Temple of Queen Hatshepsut

*Adapted from K. Lange and M. Hirmer, *Egypt: Architecture, Sculpture, Painting*, 4th ed. (Hirmer Verlag München, 1968), by permission.

Hatshepsut may have lived several centuries after Moses and may have been the Queen of Sheba, who visited Solomon (1 Kings 10:1-13). With the exception of the women in the biblical account, she is the first great woman recorded in history.

Because of the Egyptian desire to concentrate royal blood, Hatshepsut had married her brother Thutmose II, and when he died in 1493 B.C. she became regent. Thutmose III was then only 10-12 years old. He was the son of Thutmose II by a harem girl, hence both stepson and nephew of the queen. To reinforce her regency, Hatshepsut appropriated male titles and attributes, including the symbolic beard of authority, and became "king." Twice before in Egypt's earlier history a queen had usurped the kingship, but it was a new departure for a female to pose and dress as a man.

Queen Hatshepsut was a very successful ruler. She fostered vast public works, restored old temples, and built new ones. She also exploited the copper mines of Sinai. She firmly dominated the nation.

Hatshepsut's nephew, stepson, and husband, Thutmose III, wanted the kingdom, but because he could not get it from his aunt, step-mother, and wife he became jealous and angry. Then, in the seventeenth year of her reign, the great queen died, and Thutmose III became king. His first act after Hatshepsut's death was to overthrow the statues in her temple and erase her name and image wherever they appeared. He bricked entirely around the beautiful obelisk at Karnak, in order that her works would not be adored.

Thutmose III then conquered the Canaan-Syria-Lebanon region. The siege at Megiddo lasted seven months. When he died in 1447 B.C. he left as his creation the world's first great organized empire. It lasted for 300 years. But the temple of his stepmother, Hatshepsut, has endured for over 3,000 years as a work of everlasting beauty.

The temple of Queen Hatshepsut differs in plan, style of architecture, and decoration from all other temples in Egypt. The architect Senmut designed a temple that is graceful, free, and beautifully blended into the Theban hills. The ramps and the colonnades echo the shape of the cliffs. The temple was dedicated to the god Amon, but it contained chapels for Anubis and Hathor. It was intended as a mortuary temple for the worship of Hatshepsut's soul after death. Royal funerary temples served the cult of the dead, and were as necessary for the dead man's resurrection as was his tomb. Here the offerings were made which would give him nourishment in the next world. The mortuary temples also served as homes for the gods.

Hatshepsut's temple is composed of three widely spaced terraces. At one time sphinxes led up to the bottom terrace, but hardly any traces remain of the sphinxes or the bottom terrace. An incline connects each of the terraces. Ascending the ramp to the second terrace, one comes upon a most impressive scene. On both sides of the ramp are colonnades of sixteen-sided pillars. That on the right is called the Birth Colonnade because the wall scenes depict the supposed miraculous origin of the queen. The preliminaries to the act of procreation are discreetly indicated by the figure of the queen sitting on a couch opposite the god Amon. The next scene shows the infant.

Colonnades, well-preserved colored scenes, chapels to the goddess Hathor, the sanctuary, and effaced figures of Queen Hatshepsut make a visit to this religious sanctuary a memorable experience.

The **MORTUARY TEMPLE OF MENTUHOTEP** lies just south of Queen Hatshepsut's temple. It is the oldest temple in Thebes, dating from 2060-1800 B.C. It is in such a ruinous state that it is seldom visited.

HIKING FROM DEIR EL-BAHRI TO THE VALLEY OF THE KINGS. From the mortuary temple of Queen Hatshepsut, it is a 30-40-minute hike to the Valley of the Kings. A path marks the way over the top of the hills, and it is a most impressive and beautiful view. The path begins on the north side of the causeway of Hatshepsut.

Valley of the Kings

On the West Bank, over the tops of the cliffs behind the Temple of Queen Hatshepsut, is a valley in which over 60 royal tombs have been found. The valley is called the "Valley of the Kings," *Dra-abu el-Neggar, Biban el Muluk,* and the "Tombs of the Kings." It is probably the most impressive of all the sites in Thebes. It is dominated by the natural rock pyramid of the summit of El-Qorn.

The pharaohs and rulers who were buried in the Valley of the Kings reigned during the Eighteenth, Nineteenth, and Twentieth Dynasties – from 1580 to 1085 B.C. and during the time when the Israelites were in Egypt.

Most of the tombs follow a similar plan: three corridors in a line leading to the burial chamber. Some have small chambers on the sides of the first corridor, and some have rooms by the second and third corridors, used to store furniture, jewelry, and other items that were buried with the pharaoh. The walls are usually painted with scenes of pharaohs, gods, stars, hieroglyphs, and so forth, that generally have a religious theme. The most extensive tombs on the West Bank are more than 650 feet long. (Queen Hatshepsut's [no. 20] is 693 feet long.)

Only 17 of the known 64 tombs can be visited by the unprofessional tourist. Most of the tombs are either in ruins or are not accessible. The great majority of the tombs housed the bodies of kings, but among them is the tomb of Queen Ty, wife of Amenhotep III and mother of Akhenaton. The principal tombs are described as follows:

TOMB OF TUTANKHAMON (no. 62). On November 25, 1922, the first stone was removed from the wall enclosing the entrance of Tutankhamon's tomb, allowing archaeologist Howard Carter and his group a glimpse of the first royal sepulcher ever to be found intact in the Valley of the Kings. Carter had worked in the area for twenty years before he found this 3,265-year-old burial place, and even after he found it he spent almost six full years emptying the tomb and restoring on the spot every piece of the most complete set of burial objects known to man. Even though it appeared that grave robbers had been in part of the tomb twice, they had apparently taken only a few small gold objects and sixty percent of the jewels.

Lord Carnarvon supplied the money for the expedition. He saw the tomb, but died before he saw the mummy.

The first room of the tomb contained 170 different objects and pieces of furniture. Many of the latter were trunks filled with such materials as alabaster, ebony, gold, turquoise, and ivory, used as funerary objects. For two months the archaeologists worked on the materials in the first room (antechamber); then on February 17, 1923, they pulled down the wall to the burial chamber. After opening shrines, a stone sarcophagus, and mummiform coffins, they finally viewed the mummified body of Tutankhamon.

Although well protected from the elements, his body was in a bad state of deterioration. Besides the usual embalming materials, plus linen and 143 gold jewels distributed over his body, his head was covered by a solid gold mask and then he was sealed in a solid gold mummiform coffin weighing 2,448 pounds. On the headdress are small golden heads of Nekhbet, the vulture goddess of Upper Egypt, and Wadjet, the serpent goddess of Lower Egypt. The lines on the headdress are all the same gold color. The hands of the figure are folded on his breast, as in the representations of the god Osiris. The flail and the crook – emblems of royalty – are in his hands, and the beard is on his chin.

The innermost solid gold (91.85 percent pure gold) coffin was enclosed in a second mummiform coffin, made of Lebanon cedar wood covered with 22-carat gold leaf, with blue and red glass paste laid in a featherlike pattern. It was also made in the form of Osiris. The headdress has alternating blue glass paste lines on it. The footplate is covered with beautifully engraved gold foil, on which the goddess Isis is shown kneeling on the hieroglyph sign for "gold." It is similar to the footplate of the inner coffin.

A third mummiform coffin, made of Lebanon cedar wood and covered with 22-carat gold leaf, contained the other two. It also was made in the form of Osiris and has blue and red glass paste laid in the gold. This outside mummiform coffin is still in the original burial chamber and houses the mummified body of Tutankhamon.

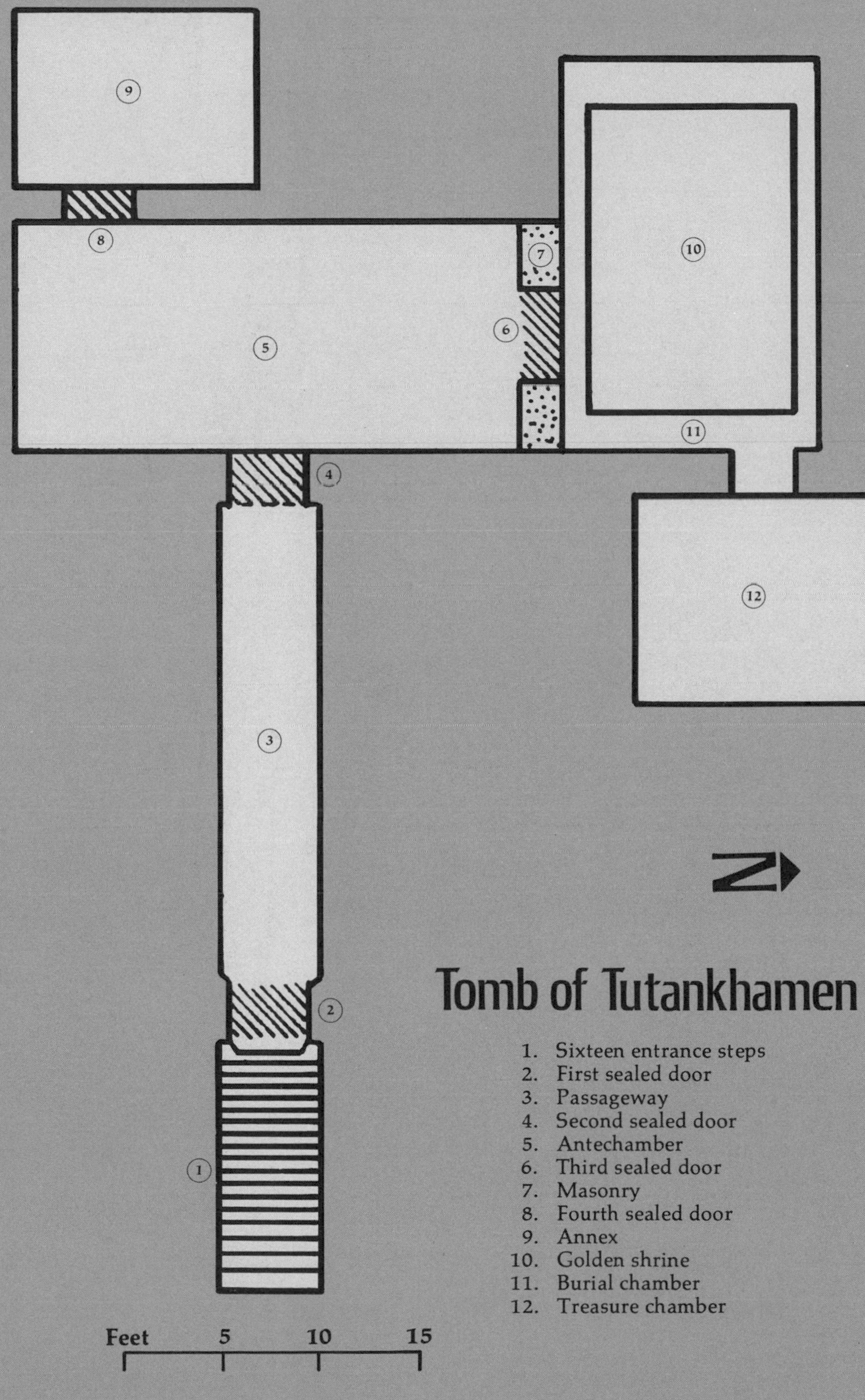

*Adapted from Kurt Schroeder, *Guide to Egypt* (Cairo, 1965), by permission.

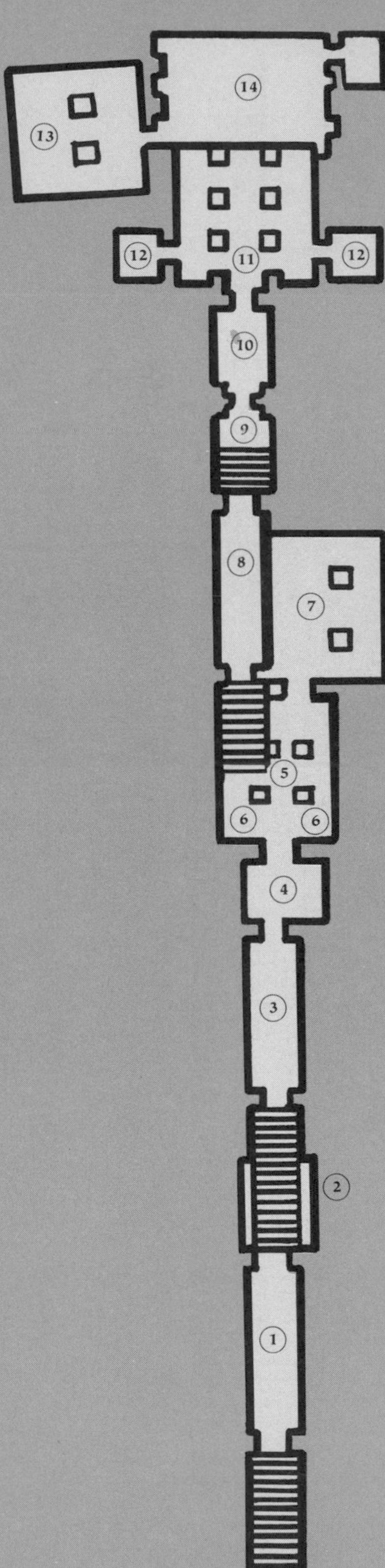

Tomb of Seti I

1. First corridor
2. Second corridor
3. Third corridor
4. Antechamber
5. Chamber
6. Walls portraying the sun's voyage through the underworld
7. Unfinished room, perhaps a decoy to deceive would-be robbers
8. Corridor
9. Corridor
10. Antechamber
11. First section of burial chamber, with 6 pillars
12. Side chambers
13. Sacrificial room
14. Sarcophagus

*Adapted from Kurt Schroeder, *Guide to Egypt* (Cairo, 1965), by permission.

The three coffins, totaling a weight of 3,030 pounds, were placed on a low lion-shaped bed of gold-gilt wood in a quartzite sarcophagus. This was in turn covered with four golden burial shrines – oak wood overlaid with gold, fitted together like Chinese boxes, one into another. The largest shrine – nearly filling the 13-by-21 foot room of the tomb – measured 10 feet 10 inches by 16 feet 5 inches by 9 feet and was made of gilt wood inlaid with blue lapis lazuli and glass paste. The shrines were separated by veils decorated with flowers, and each shrine was decorated with beautiful reliefs of flowers, gods, and hieroglyphic texts. The smallest shrine covered the sarcophagus and was inscribed with the names and titles of the king. Each corner was decorated with a beautiful high relief of a goddess protectively spreading her wings – in similar style to the ark of the covenant carried through the wilderness by the Israelites (Exod. 25:10-22).

In the room called the "treasury" was found a shrine guarded by goddesses about 2½ feet high: Isis, Nephthys, Neith, and Serket. In the shrine was an alabaster chest in which were four canopic urns, each containing a miniature coffin 15 inches long and made in the same shape as the innermost gold coffin. These small coffins contained the mummified viscera of the king: liver, lungs, stomach, and intestines. Only the heart was left in Tutankhamon's body, which was facing the east.

It was a surprise to find two small anthropoid coffins in the treasury room. In them were smaller gold coffins, and in each was the mummy of a fetus preserved like a fully developed infant. One was a six-month and one a seven-month fetus. The smaller had a gold mask.

The paintings on the walls of the burial room are beautiful and well preserved. On a dark ochre background, under a band representing the sky of Egypt, tall human figures painted in bright colors – predominantly yellow, red, white, and black – occupied the full length of three of the walls.

Pharaoh Tutankhamon was not a famous leader in Egypt. He was 9 years old when he came to the throne at the end of the Eighteenth Dynasty. He died in January, 1343 B.C. At the beginning of his reign he was at Tell el Amarna and his name was *Tutankhaton*, but he moved the capital back to Thebes and changed his name to *Tutankhamon*. Nebkheprure was his "first" or "coronation" name. He was married to Princess Ankheshamun, a daughter of Akhenaton. He died when he was 18 years old and was relatively unimportant. He became very important, however, when Howard Carter discovered his tomb, still intact, the first discovery of its kind. Inasmuch as his tomb is the smallest of the kings' tombs in the Valley of the Kings, one can imagine the huge store of treasures that would have been buried in the larger tombs of the more famous pharaohs.

Thus Tutankhamon, son of the god Amon, was prepared with his elaborate burial to rejoin the god who created him. Although not the most famous pharaoh in life, he has become one of the most famous in death.

TOMB OF SETI I (no. 17). This 700-foot-long tomb, with its passageways, halls, and staircases, is the largest and one of the best preserved in the Valley of the Kings. The burial chamber is 150 feet below the entrance to the first staircase. It dates from the Nineteenth Dynasty (1313-1298 B.C.).

The tomb was discovered in 1817 by the Italian Giovanni Battista Belzoni, and in 1881 the mummy of Seti I was found in a "cachette" at Deir el-Bahri. It is now in the Egyptian Museum and is considered to be the most lifelike of all mummies of kings discovered to this date. The alabaster sarcophagus is in the Soane Museum in London. The paintings on the walls are well preserved high reliefs and show the sun-god, Isis, Nephthys, Hathor, Osiris, Egyptians, Asiatics, Libyans, and others. They begin at the entrance and continue throughout the tomb. Some of the paintings are unfinished. Burial chamber walls with text and pictures describe the voyage of the king as he traveled through the underworld, aided along the way by the sun-god. Signs of the zodiac decorate the ceiling of the burial chamber.

The **TOMB OF AMENHOTEP II** (no. 35) is, with little doubt, one of the most impressive and best preserved tombs in the Valley of the Kings. Amenhotep reigned in the Eighteenth Dynasty, about 1447-1420 B.C. Because of its unique construction, which includes a deep shaft in the corridor to mislead robbers, the tomb is sometimes called the "Tomb of Safety." When it was discovered in 1898 by M. Loret, there was still a number of mummies buried here, including the mummies of Amenhotep IV, Thutmose IV, and Seti II.

This is one of the most ancient of the tombs open to the public. The walls are painted with various scenes from the "Book of the Underworld," and the blue painted ceiling is decorated with yellow stars. The papyrus-yellow tint of the walls creates a unique atmosphere. At the lower level the body of Amenhotep II still lies in the sarcophagus, undisturbed for 3,300 years.

Left of the sarcophagus is a small chamber where three mummies can be viewed. The one on the left is an elderly woman, possibly Queen Taa, wife of the pharaoh, but considered by some to be Hatshepsut, moved to his tomb for safety during the time of the great tomb robberies during the reign of Ramses X (1117-1114 B.C.). The second is a youth of about 14 years of age, possibly a son. The second is a girl, either a daughter or wife of the pharaoh.

TOMB OF RAMSES V AND VI (no. 9). This tomb was originally built for Ramses V of the Twentieth Dynasty (1160 B.C.), but when Ramses VI was unable to build a tomb because of his short reign, the priests placed his mummy in one grave with Ramses V. A broken granite sarcophagus may still be seen in the burial

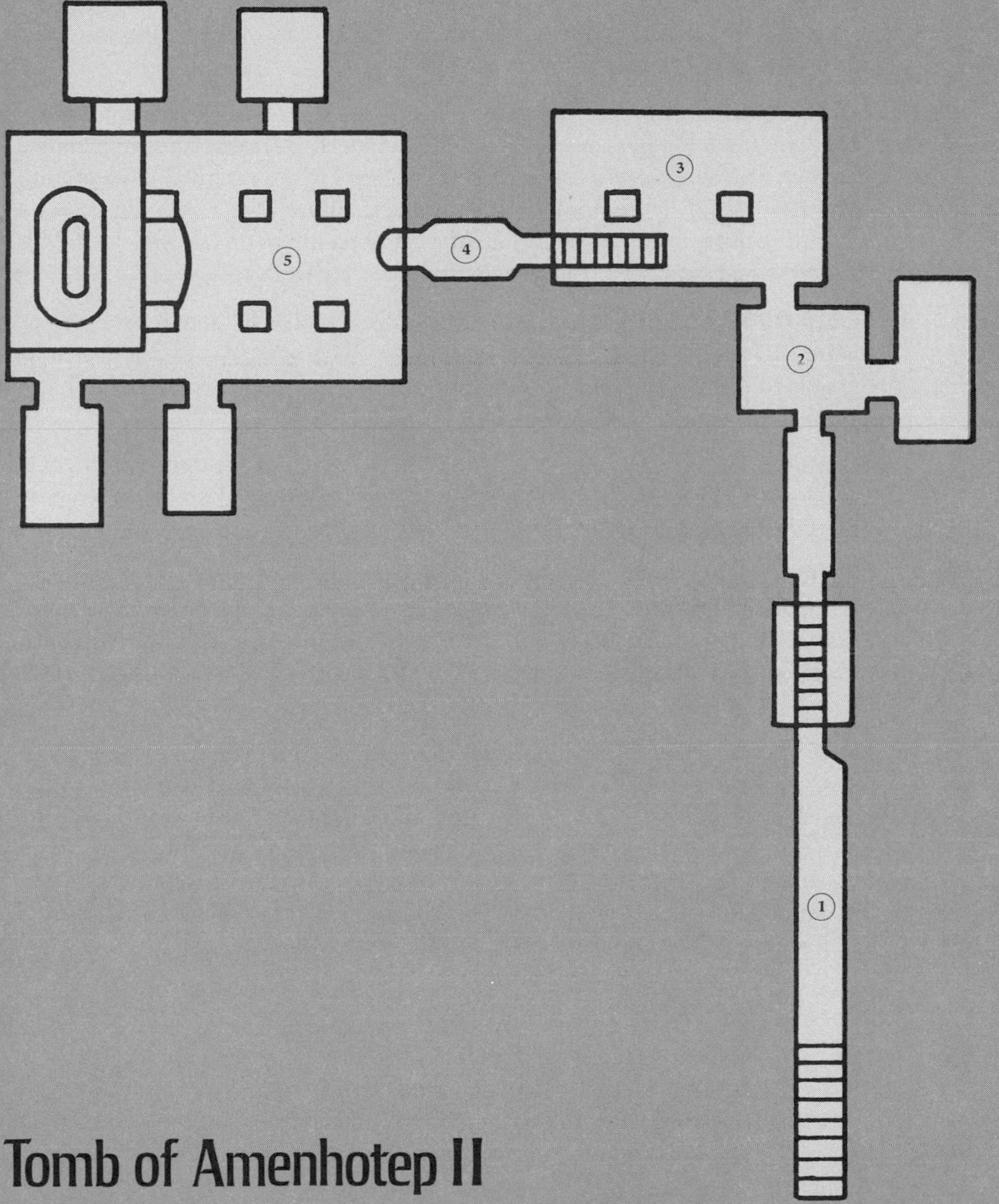

Tomb of Amenhotep II

1. Passageway
2. Bridge over pit
3. Room with 2 pillars
4. Stairs and passageway
5. Burial room

*Adapted from Kurt Schroeder, *Guide to Egypt* (Cairo, 1965), by permission.

chamber. The freshness of the colored reliefs is remarkable. The decoration of the roof with astronomical figures and the huge arched body of the sky goddess Nut giving birth to the sun is also interesting.

TOMB OF RAMSES I (no. 16). Ramses I had a very short term as pharaoh, and as a result his tomb was not completed when he died. He was buried in a small inner chamber, which one reaches after descending two flights of stairs. A pink granite sarcophagus is still in the burial chamber, but the mummy was removed by priests to a hiding place at Deir el-Bahri for safety. The paintings on the wall, including pictures of gods and the journey of the sun-boat, are well preserved.

TOMB OF RAMSES III (no. 11). Originally commenced by Setnakht, father of Ramses III, this tomb is one of the largest in the Valley of the Kings. Ten niches on the sides of the first and second corridors are quite unique. The mummy is in the Egyptian Museum and the sarcophagus is in the Louvre.

TOMB OF HARMHAB (no. 57). Noted for its scenes of the underworld, this tomb is worth a visit. It was cut in the Nineteenth Dynasty, and the sarcophagus is still in the burial chamber.

OTHER TOMBS. Similar to the ones already described but of less importance are the tombs of **RAMSES X** (no. 6), **RAMSES IV** (no. 2), **RAMSES IX** (no. 6), **MERNEPTAH** (no. 8), **SETNAKHT** (no. 14), **SETI II** (no. 15), **HATSHEPSUT** (no. 20), **THUTMOSE III** (no. 34), **THUTMOSE I** (no. 38), and **AMENHOTEP III** (no. 23), in the western valley.

MORTUARY TEMPLE OF SETI I AND RAMSES II. On the northeast corner of the Acropolis is a temple dedicated to the god Amon. Seti I started to build it near the end of his reign (1290 B.C.) for him and his father, but it was finished by Ramses II. Most of the courts and the pylons are in ruins, but the 155-foot-long temple, with its 6 papyrus pillars, inner sanctuary, and miscellaneous chambers, still exists. The temple complex was originally 520 feet long. Reliefs of Ramses II and the three deities Amon-Ra, Mut, and Khons decorate the walls.

LUXOR TO ASWAN

Esna

The city of Esna, 33 miles south of Luxor, may be reached in 1 hour by train from Luxor. It has approximately 40,000 inhabitants and is located on the west bank of the Nile. The town dates back to the Eighteenth Dynasty, or 1580 B.C. At this point in the river there is a 2,870-foot dam that helps to control the Nile waters.

The **TEMPLE OF KHNUM** is the ruin of antiquity that is of interest, but since most of it is buried under the houses of the city the exposed part is small. Khnum, a god of Upper Egypt, usually portrayed with a ram's head, is the god of this Ptolemaic period temple. A temple of Thutmose III was apparently built on the site previously. Khnum's temple has beautiful columns and inscriptions on the walls depicting various Roman emperors, including Decius (A.D. 251), worshiping the god Khnum. The temple seems to have been built between 180 B.C. and A.D. 250. The relief showing Decius is the last representation of a pharaoh found in Egypt.

Edfu

Seventy miles south of Luxor is Edfu. It is approximately halfway between Luxor and Aswan and takes about 2½ hours to reach by train. As the temple is on the west bank, the river must be crossed.

The **TEMPLE OF HORUS** at Edfu is practically intact and is perhaps the best-preserved monument in Egypt. It was built between 237 and 57 B.C., under the direction of Ptolemy III, Euergetes I, Philopator, Philometor, and Euergetes II. The god Horus is shown as a great falcon with a double crown. Beautiful columns, reliefs, inscriptions, and a view from the top of the temple make a visit to Edfu worthwhile.

Kom Ombo

Kom Ombo is 105 miles south of Luxor and 30 miles north of Aswan on the east bank of the Nile. A visit to Kom Ombo is best made by train from Aswan. Cotton and sugarcane are important crops of the community.

The **TEMPLE OF HARUAR AND SEBEK** was dedicated to the worship of the hawk-headed god Haruar and the crocodile god Sebek. To avoid giving offense to either of these two patron gods of the town, a twin temple was constructed. The one on the left was for Haruar and the one on the right for Sebek. They were built during the Ptolemaic period, in the second century B.C. The columns, capitals, and low reliefs are very beautiful. In places there are sketches for reliefs which were never sculptured.

ASWAN AREA

Aswan, *Syene*

Aswan, at the First Cataract, is located 550 miles from Cairo and 136 miles south of Luxor. *Aswan* means "market." It is Egypt's southern-most winter resort and attracts many tourists. According to tradition, the first Egyptian pharaohs came from here, including the builders of the Pyramids of Giza. Because of the new Aswan Dam construction, the population swelled during the 1960s. Present population is over 200,000.

The **ASWAN HIGH DAM**, *Sadd el Aali* was built by 30,000 Egyptian workers, the aid of Russian finances, and 2,000 technicians during the years 1960-71. The total cost was over $1. billion. It was begun January 9, 1960, by President Gamal Abdel Nasser detonating the first dynamite blast and was dedicated by President Anwar Sadat on Nasser's birthday, January 15, 1971 – nearly four months after Nasser's death.

Ranking as one of the largest and highest dams in the world, it is more than 2 miles long (11,811 feet), 364 feet high, and 3,215 feet thick at its base. A highway 131 feet wide crosses over the top. Fifty-five million cubic yards of rock fill were used in the construction – enough to build seventeen Cheops pyramids – making it the world's tenth largest rock-fill dam. It backs up the waters of Lake Nasser, and instead of the 5,400 million tons of water that the old dam held, the new dam holds 165,000 million tons. Lake Nasser is 310 miles long, averages 6 miles in width, and is 500 feet deep in places.

The Nile Delta received its last full-scale flood in the summer of 1964, and with the new dam the annual flood has come to an end. A power station of 12 turbines capable of producing 10,000,000 kilowatt hours of electricity per year is an important part of the project. By 1970, all the electricity consumed in Cairo, 550 miles away, was being produced at the Aswan High Dam. A million new acres of agricultural land has been brought into production because of the new dam. Another million acres will be able to produce three crops instead of one. A whole new complex of industry is expected to locate in Aswan because of the abundance of water and power. A steel plant is projected to use the iron mined in the nearby desert.

Some feel, however, that although the dam brings many benefits it may also be disastrous to the Egyptians, because of the blood fluke disease – *schistosomiasis* – spread by snails that invade the quiet, slow, warm waters now available in secondary and tertiary canals and ditches. Malaria will probably increase, farmers have to use artificial fertilizers, the salt content and temperature of the Eastern Mediterranean may harm the fishing industry, and other negative factors cause some to doubt the value of the Aswan High Dam.

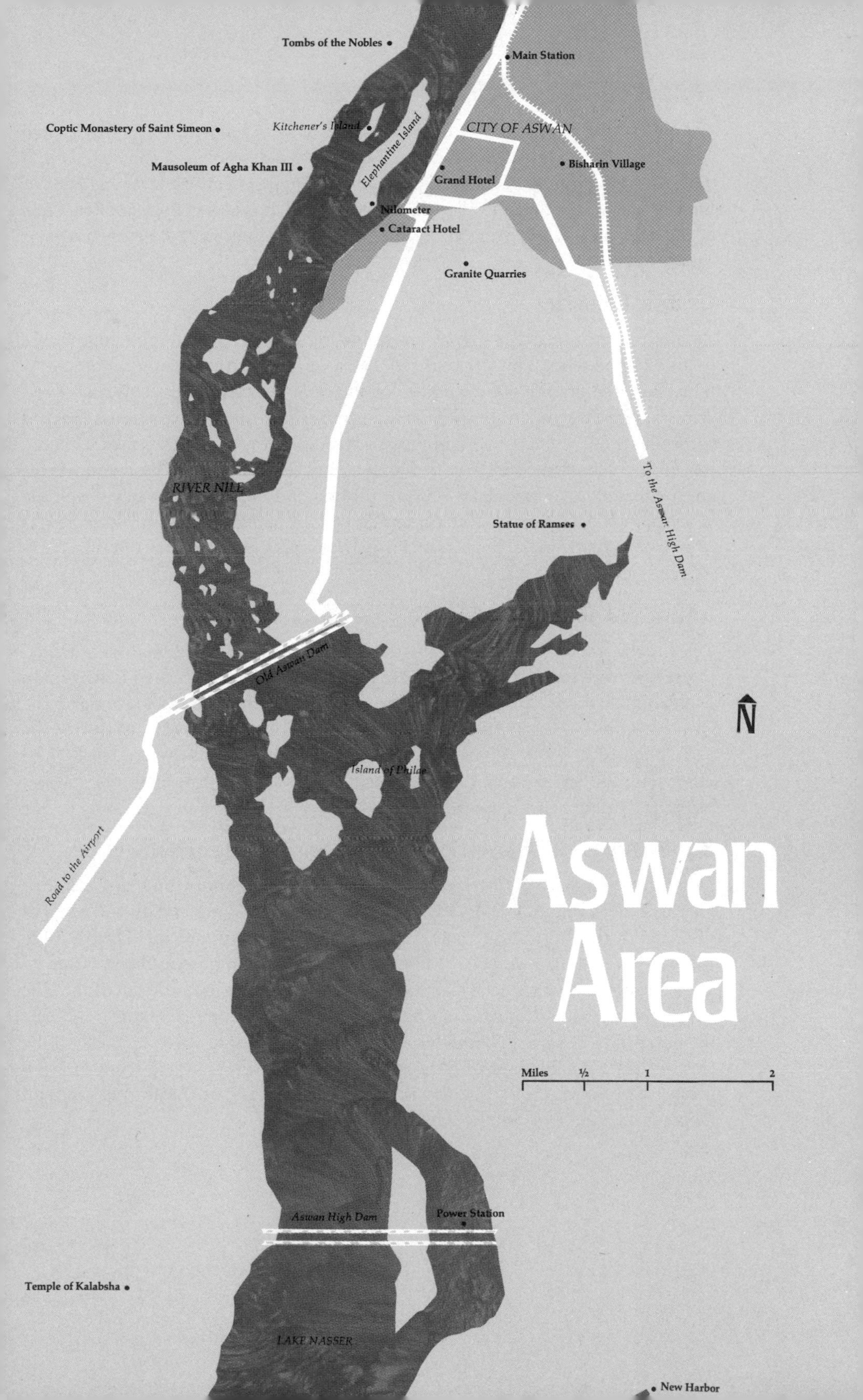

Aswan Area

Tombs of the Nobles
Main Station
Coptic Monastery of Saint Simeon
Kitchener's Island
Elephantine Island
CITY OF ASWAN
Mausoleum of Agha Khan III
Grand Hotel
Bisharin Village
Nilometer
Cataract Hotel
Granite Quarries
RIVER NILE
To the Aswan High Dam
Statue of Ramses
Old Aswan Dam
N
Island of Philae
Road to the Airport
Miles ½ 1 2
Aswan High Dam
Power Station
Temple of Kalabsha
LAKE NASSER
New Harbor

The **OLD ASWAN DAM** was originally completed in 1902 but was heightened twice: once in 1912 and again in 1933. Located 4½ miles north of the new dam, it marked the beginning of modern irrigation in Egypt. It is 7,062 feet long and for many years was the biggest valley dam in the world. It is 68 feet high, 100 feet thick at the base, and 36 feet wide at the top. It made a reservoir that covered over 11 square miles.

Granite Quarries

Twenty minutes south of Aswan are the world-famous granite quarries, whose granite can be seen in far-off Istanbul, Lebanon, Cyprus, Israel, and other countries. Here the granite was quarried for the pyramid passageways, obelisks, and sarcophagi. Still lying in the quarry is an unfinished obelisk, which was cracked before it could be excavated completely. It shows how the obelisks were carved out of the rock. It measures 137 feet long and 14 feet wide at the base and weighs approximately 1,170 tons. Had it been finished and used it would have been the tallest obelisk ever erected. A second quarry to the south has uncompleted blocks of granite that are interesting to see. From the heights here one may obtain a magnificent view.

Island and Temples of Philae

One may be rowed by boat from Shellal to the Island of Philae. Mostly submerged in the reservoir except from July to November, the island is located between the two dams at a point 2 miles south of the old Aswan Dam. The chief temple on the island was built to the goddess Isis, her husband Osiris, and son Horus during the period 600 B.C.-A.D. 138. The large pylons, sanctuaries, relief-covered walls, and other temples, arches, and ruins are very impressive. An international call has been made to save the temples of Philae.

ELEPHANTINE ISLAND, *El Gezira;* the Temple of Yahweh

Opposite the Cataract Hotel is the mile-and-a-half island called *El Gezira*, or Elephantine Island. A **TEMPLE BUILT BY TRAJAN** was erected on the ruins of the temples of Thutmose III and IV and Ramses II. This and the **TEMPLE OF KHNUM** are not in a very good state of preservation. On the south end of the island are ancient and modern **NILOMETERS** to record the rise and fall of the Nile River. The ancient Nilometer has both Greek and demotic markings to indicate the water level. Near the Nilometer is a **MUSEUM**, housing artifacts found in the area. A **MUMMY OF A SACRED RAM**, representing the ram god Khnum, is on display. The southern end of the island also has traces of the former town of Elephantine, the "Door of the South."

A well-preserved papyrus document located in the Turin Museum and written about 1150 B.C. tells of the "Elephantine Scandal," wherein a priest of the Temple of Khnum was charged with thefts, bribery, sacrilege, and adultery. He was also charged with the misappropriation and sale of sacred Mnevis calves.

The famous *Elephantine Papyri* that were found here are partly Aramaic and partly Hebrew documents of the fifth century B.C. (oldest 495 B.C.). They are contemporary with Ezra, Malachi, and Nehemiah. Published by A. H. Sayce and A. E. Cowley between 1906 and 1911, they have become of great importance to the biblical period of Ezra and Nehemiah. From the papyri it was discovered that a Jewish military colony existed at Elephantine as early as 495 B.C.

The Jews built a temple to their god Yahweh (Yahu) on Elephantine Island. That a Jewish temple stood in Elephantine in the fifth century B.C. is surprising. The law of Deuteronomy, which Josiah had put in force in 621 B.C., prohibited any altar save one, which was located at Jerusalem. One of the prize pieces of papyri, however, was a letter from the Jews at Elephantine to Bagoas, governor of Judah, appealing for his aid in obtaining a restoration of the temple of Yahweh, which had been destroyed in 410 B.C. at the instigation of the priests of Khnum, the ram-headed patron divinity at Elephantine. Calling Elephantine a "fortress," the letter describes how the temple was destroyed. It also indicates that "our fathers built this temple in the fortress of Elephantine in the days of the kings of Egypt and when Cambyses entered Egypt [525 B.C.], they found the temple already built."

Another document of importance is the so-called *Passover Papyrus*, a letter dated 419 B.C. ordering the Jews in the name of Darius II to celebrate the feast of "Unleavened Bread." Since the Temple of Khnum was right next to the Jewish temple, it was probably to avoid an offense to the worshipers of Khnum, the ram god, that the Jews had failed to sacrifice the Passover lamb. Papyri found more recently show that the Elephantine temple was probably restored.

The Jews who settled at Elephantine may have come here as a part of the Diaspora, after their captivity in Babylon under Nebuchadnezzar. Many Jews were left in Canaan at that time (2 Kings 25:22), organized under the leadership of Gedaliah; but he was assassinated by Ishmael, who tried to organize a fresh revolt against Babylon (2 Kings 25:23-25). Dreading the almost certain consequences, many fled to Egypt against the wishes of Jeremiah (Jer. 42:14-22) and took the old prophet Jeremiah with them (2 Kings 25:26; Jer. 43:1-7). They settled in the city of Migdol – near the spot where the Israelites had crossed the Red Sea (Exod. 14:2; Num. 33:7) – Pathros (Upper Egypt) (Isa. 11:11; Jer. 44:1, 15; Ezek. 29:14; 30:14), Tahpanhes, Memphis (Noph), and Elephantine. They soon cultivated the vices of the Egyptians, and Jeremiah attacked his fellow Jews in Egypt for their apostasy

(Jer. 42:13-46:28; Lam. 5). According to tradition, Jeremiah was beaten to death for uttering the attacks.

Some feel the Elephantine Jewish colony was established under Pharaoh Amasis between 569 and 526 B.C. and disappeared from view after the Persian control of Egypt came to an end in 404 B.C.

Kitchener's Island, *the Botanical Island*

From Elephantine Island a short boat ride takes one to this beautiful island formerly owned by Lord Kitchener. It has beautiful gardens, with trees from tropical regions, especially India.

Tombs of the Nobles

On the west bank, opposite the north end of Elephantine Island, are tombs cut into the face of the cliffs and dating from the Sixth to the Twelfth dynasties. Some of the reliefs are in bright colors. The most interesting tombs are those of **PRINCE MEKHU** (no. 25, Sixth Dynasty); **PRINCE SERENPITU** (no. 31, Twelfth Dynasty); **PRINCE PEPI NEKHT** (no. 35); **PRINCE SERENPITWA** (no. 36), the Governor of the South in the Twelfth Dynasty; **SABNI** (no. 26), the Ruler of the South; and **HER KHOF**.

Coptic Monastery of Saint Simeon, *Anba Somaan*

This monastery lies in the desert about 2 miles from the Nile River and near the Agha Khan Mausoleum. It was dedicated to Anba Hadra, a local saint of the fifth century. The monastery was built in the sixth century and abandoned in the tenth. The walls still have paintings of Jesus and the saints.

Bisharin Village

Just east of Aswan is this Bedouin village. The Bisharin are a Hamitic race, related to the Ethiopians. They are darkskinned, thin, and rugged, and their language and customs are different from those of other Nile Valley people. Men wear their hair in a thick fuzzy mop, and the women wrap theirs in numerous little oil-soaked plaits.

Mausoleum of Agha Khan III

This large mausoleum dominates a desert height on the Nile River, beyond Elephantine Island, at Aswan. Agha Khan III was the leader of the Ismaili Community, a sect of Islam. He spent two months of every year at Aswan, and when he died in 1959 his body was placed in the white marble tomb. He claimed direct descent from Fatima, daughter of Muhammad. His widow lived in a villa on the bank of the Nile near the tomb. His son, Ali Khan, married the American movie actress Rita Hayworth.

Temples of Lake Nasser

When it was decided to build the Aswan High Dam, the Egyptian government appealed to the United Nations to aid in the preservation of some of the monuments that were threatened with a watery tomb at the bottom of Lake Nasser. Twenty temples were relocated on higher ground, and some of the monuments were dismantled and taken to other nations.

The region around Lake Nasser is called Nubia, and the inhabitants have their own Nubian language. Nubia covers the desert and steppe-land between Aswan and Khartoum, Sudan. During the Twelfth Dynasty Egypt conquered the Nubians and built temples and fortresses along the Nile. But by 1100 B.C. the Egyptian influence declined and the Ethiopians came to power.

The following temples are some of the more important ones that were saved for future generations to view:

The **TEMPLE OF KERTASSI** has been dismantled and rebuilt near the Aswan High Dam by the United Arab Republic.

The **TEMPLE OF BEIT-EL-WALI** has been moved to a site near the Aswan High Dam by the joint efforts of the Oriental Institute of Chicago and the Swiss Institute of Cairo. It was hewn out of solid rock under the direction of Ramses II in the thirteenth century B.C., and many beautiful reliefs adorn the walls.

The **TEMPLE OF KALABSHA** is one of the finest sandstone Nubian temples to be saved. It was 30 miles south of Aswan, but was removed to its present site near the Aswan High Dam in a super-human task. The 13,000 blocks removed by the federal government of West Germany weighed a ton each. Next to the temple of Abu Simbel, this is the largest and finest temple in Nubia. It was erected during the reign of Augustus (27 B.C.-A.D. 14) in honor of the god Mandulis.

The **TEMPLES OF DENDUR, ELLESIYA, DEBRID,** and **TAFA** were given to the United States, Italy, Spain, and Holland respectively for their contribution in the salvage of the Nubian monuments.

The **TEMPLE OF DAKKA** has been removed to a site at Wadi es Sebua by the Academy of Sciences of Leningrad and the United Arab Republic. It was located originally on the west bank, 77 miles from Aswan.

The **TEMPLE OF WADI OF SEBUA** has been removed to higher ground near the site by the efforts of the United States, the United Arab Republic, and the French and Swiss Archaeological Institutes of Cairo. It was built by Ramses II and dedicated to the god Amon and the sun-god Ra-Harakhte. The building has two rows of lion-sphinxes wearing the double crown. Scenes on the walls are similar to those on other temples. Many reliefs were painted over by Christians. Over the central statue of the Egyptian deities the early Christians placed a painting of Saint Peter with the key of heaven.

The **TEMPLE OF EL-DERR**, built by Ramses II, has been removed to a site at Amada.

The **TEMPLE OF EL-AMADA** was erected under the direction of Thutmose III and Amenhotep II (1500 B.C.). King Akhenaton defaced the reliefs, but King Seti restored them in the fourteenth century B.C. Early Christians whitewashed the reliefs, which helped to preserve them. The West German Institute of Cairo was given the responsibility of preserving the temple from the water of Lake Nasser, and it was rebuilt on higher ground near the site.

The **ROCK-TEMPLE OF ABU SIMBEL** is the most famous temple in Nubia and is 180 miles south of Aswan. It is carved out of solid sandstone rock and faces the east to let the light of the rising sun penetrate the innermost sanctuaries, "the heart of the Holiest of Holies." It was built by Ramses II between 1300 and 1233 B.C. and dedicated to the gods Amon-Ra of Thebes and Harakhte of Heliopolis. On each side of the temple entrance are two colossal 66-foot-high statues of Ramses II. To the right and left of each statue are statues of other members of the royal family: Queen Tue, Ramses' mother, on the left of the second colossus; and Nefertari, his wife, on the right. The rock temple is 181 feet in length, and a large hypostyle hall has 8 huge 33-foot-high statues of the god Osiris. Reliefs on the walls show victory scenes.

When it was realized that the waters of Lake Nasser, behind the Aswan High Dam, would completely cover the Temple of Abu Simbel, the problem became an international concern. In 1959 UNESCO answered the United Arab Republic's appeal to save the Nubian monuments. The salvage project began in 1963 and cost $36,000,000. The United States offered to pay one-third of the cost.

In what has been one of the most interesting and expensive projects ever undertaken to preserve the beautiful art work of the Egyptians, Swedish engineers designed a plan to cut the statues and temples in sections and reassemble them in a natural setting on the plateau above. The project was completed in September 1968.

Visitors in Aswan may go to Abu Simbel by a hydrofoil boat in 5 hours and return the 180 miles to Aswan in the same day. Daily air service is also available.

The **ROCK-TEMPLE OF HATHOR**, north of the Great Temple of Abu Simbel, was also built by Ramses II and dedicated to the goddess Hathor and Ramses' wife, Nefertari. The arcade is hewn to imitate a pylon. Two large statues represent the king and queen, with smaller statues of their children beside them. Mural reliefs decorate the walls.

THE RED SEA AREA (WEST SIDE)

The Red Sea is over 1,200 miles in length. It divides Africa and Arabia, and the two northern projections, the Gulf of Suez and the Gulf of Aqaba, embrace the Sinai Peninsula. The mean depth of the sea is 1,600 feet; it is 7,200 feet deep in the main basin.

- *The Red Sea parted to save the Israelites. Baal-zephon is the traditional place, but the site is unknown (Exod. 14:2, 9; Num. 33:7; Neh. 9:9; Ps. 106:7, 9, 22; Acts 7:36; Heb. 11:29).*
- *The same incident is mentioned in the Doctrine and Covenants (8:3).*

Port Said, *Bur Said*

After Alexandria, Port Said is the most important port in Egypt. It is located at the entrance to the Suez Canal from the Mediterranean Sea and was founded in 1860 during the construction of the canal. Since its business is taking care of passing ships, it has been called "the town that never sleeps."

Ismailia, *Ismaileya*

This town is situated on the north shore of Lake Timsah and was the center of operations when the Suez Canal was being constructed.

Suez, *El Suweis*

Suez is a "canal town," 80 miles east of Cairo, at the south end of the Suez Canal and the north end of the Red Sea.

Ein Sukhna

This is the nearest beach to Cairo – 2½ hours by car. It is 35 miles south of Suez. It is one of the most beautiful white sandy beaches on the Red Sea, and all kinds of water sports can be enjoyed here.

Zaafarana

About 80 miles south of Suez, Zaafarana is the starting point to visit **SAINT ANTHONY'S MONASTERY** and **SAINT PAUL'S MONASTERY**. Both monasteries date from the fourth century A.D. and have ancient and rare manuscripts.

SINAI PENINSULA

This triangular tongue of land 175 miles wide and 250 miles long is located between deserts on the north and the two arms of the Red Sea – the Gulf of Aqaba on the east and the Gulf of Suez on the west. It is a rugged, little-watered desert with impressive mountain scenery. It has very little human population.

Sculptured stelae near turquoise mines of the Wadi Magharah date back to the First Dynasty (3100 B.C.). Most of them have been removed to the Cairo Museum. A **TEMPLE OF HATHOR** still exists near the mines at a place named Sarabit el Khadim.

Mount Sinai, in the south end of the peninsula, is composed of red and gray granite and gneiss, and schists of various kinds: horn-blende and talcose, and chloritic overlying them. Later rocks, such as diorite and basalt, penetrate the rocks. Vegetation is confined to the valleys, especially near water springs.

It is difficult to imagine one or two million Israelites spending forty years of their lives in the wilderness of the Sinai Peninsula.

- *Abraham crossed the Sinai Peninsula (Gen. 12:10).*
- *Joseph, Jacob, and Jesus crossed the Sinai Peninsula to get to Egypt (Gen. 37:28; Gen. 46:1-7; Matt. 2:14).*
- *Moses fled to the Sinai Peninsula after killing the Egyptian (Exod. 2:11-15).*
- *The Midianites in Sinai were of the same people that sold Joseph into Egypt (Gen. 37:28, 36).*
- *Midian was a son of Abraham by Keturah (Gen. 25:1-2).*
- *After helping the daughters of Jethro at the well, Moses lived with Jethro (Reuel) in this area for the second forty years of his life (Exod. 2:15-3:1).*
- *Zipporah, daughter of Jethro (Reuel) became Moses' wife (Exod. 2:21; 3:1).*
- *The Israelites crossed the Red Sea (Exod. 14:1-15:21).*
- *The Israelites were fed quail and manna in this area (Exod. 16; Num. 11:1-3, 31-32).*
- *Water came forth from a rock at Horeb (Meribah) (Exod. 17).*
- *Sinai is called the "great and terrible wilderness" (Deut. 8:15).*
- *Abraham crossed the Sinai Peninsula (Abr. 3:15).*
- *Moses received the priesthood under the hand of Jethro (D&C 84:6).*
- *God appeared to Moses on the top of an "exceedingly high mountain." Here Moses was transfigured and saw every particle of the earth. The Lord said his work and glory was to "bring to pass the immortality and eternal life of man" (Moses 1).*

  (For further scripture references on this area, see the section on Mount Sinai, below.)

There are four place names that are used in a general way to mean a large area and sometimes to designate a smaller area: *Shur*, the region between Egypt and

Said
Port Fuad
MEDITERRANEAN SEA
Sabkhat el Bardawil
Khan Yunis
Rafah
Beersheba
El Arish
Nahal Yam
Negev
Bir Hama
El Qusaima
Kadesh-Barnea
Bir Gafgafa
Bir Hasana
Gidi Pass
Ras el Gindi
Mitla Pass
Suez
El Shatt
Aiyun Musa
(Marah)
El Nakhl
Kuntilla
Ras Sudr
El Thamad
Ras Matarma
Ras Abu Darag
Ezion-Geber (Eilat)
Taba
The Fjord
Elim (Wadi Gharandal)
Hammam Faruon
Zaafarana
GULF OF SUEZ
Abu Zeneima
Sarabiel Khadim
Merkhah Port
Nuweiba
Magharah
Abu Rodeis
Wadi Feiran
Neve Feiran
Tomb of Sheikh Nebi Saleh
Jebel Sirbal
Mount Sinai
Saint Catherine's Monastery
Mount Catherina
Dhahab
GULF OF EILAT
N
Tor
Sinai
Peninsula
Oasis of Nabk
Tiran Island
Sharm el Sheikh
10
25

Canaan (Gen. 16:7; 20:1; 25:18; Exod. 15:22; 13:20; Num. 33:8; 1 Sam. 15:7; 27:8); *Paran*, the territory between Kadesh and Sinai (Gen. 21:21; Deut. 33:2; 1 Sam. 25:1; 1 Kings 11:18; Hab. 3:3); *Sin*, a dry strip of white chalky land west of Sinai and reaching to the Gulf of Suez (Exod. 16:1; 17:1; Num. 33:11-12); *Zin*, the territory east of Paran, close to Kadesh-Barnea and west of Mount Seir (Num. 13:21; 20:1; 27:14; 34:3, 4; Deut. 32:51; Josh. 15:1, 3).

The following place names are listed in the order in which a traveler would visit them if he traveled from Cairo to Saint Catherine's Monastery and returned to Gaza via Tor, Sharm el Sheikh, Eilat, El Nakhl, Mitla Pass, Kadesh-Barnea, and El Arish.

EL SHATT

A frontier corps station is located at this point 11 miles from Suez.

- *At some point on the Red Sea, the Israelites crossed when fleeing from the pharaoh of Egypt (Exod. 14:1-15:21).*

AIYUN MUSA ("*Moses' Well*"), Marah

Eleven miles south of El Shatt is this small oasis with palm groves and still pools. A dozen springs supply brackish yet palatable water. Two of them are very bitter. Tradition links this site with the first stop of the Israelites after they fled from the pharaoh in Egypt. The largest and southernmost spring is said to be the spring which Moses sweetened.

- *Moses sweetened the water by casting a limb of a tree into it (Exod. 15:23-25).*
- *Tradition has it that at this location Moses' sister Miriam taught the women of Israel "the song of triumph" (Exod. 15:20-21).*

Ras Sudr, *Sidr*

Sultan Saladin built a fortress here that dominated the neighboring wadis and oases. Very little of the fortress remains today. It is 38 miles from Suez.

Hawara

On the slope of a ridge, a small thicket of stunted palms shading a spring of brackish water marks the site of Hawara.

ELIM, *Wadi Gharandal*

This is the traditional site of Israel's second camp after crossing the Red Sea (Exod. 15:27). It is located 63 miles from Suez. It had several fine springs and many palm trees.

Hammam Faruon

About 74 miles from Suez, at the foot of Jebel Hammam Faruon, there are several hot springs of sulphurous water. The Arabs believe the springs have healing qualities.

Abu Zeneima, *Abu Zenima*

This village is identified by some to be an Israelite encampment on the Red Sea. It is now a mining port and a village of the Sinai Mining Company, which extracts manganese from the neighboring Mount Om Bagma, 2,400 feet high. Ancient Egyptian inscriptions found at el-Maghra, on Gebal Habashi, indicate that the area was occupied as early as the First Dynasty, about 3100 B.C.

Sarabiel Khadim, *Sarabit el Khadim*

This is the site of ancient turquoise mines and inscriptions of crude Canaanite pictures, from which some of our alphabet may have evolved. They date from about 1500 B.C. Also in the area is the Egyptian **TEMPLE OF HATHOR**, dating back to the nineteenth century B.C. Stones with hieroglyphs eulogize the Egyptian kings and the goddess Hathor.

Magharah

Here were the oldest Egyptian copper mines that supplied the pre-dynastic cultures. Here also are **STELAE** commemorating the daring mining enterprises of Egypt and praising her pharaohs. There are also some early **HEBREW CHARACTERS**.

Abu Rodeis *and* Merkhah Port

Abu Rodeis has beautiful palm trees and is a center for Sinai's oil industry. It serves as a rest stop for tours to Mount Sinai.

Wadi el-Maktab (*Valley of Writings*)

The road winds between granite cliffs to the great valley where huge granite blocks are inscribed with Greek and Arabic writings and pictures of gazelles, camels, crosses, boats, stars, and so on. By taking the route via Wadi Feiran, one will bypass Wadi el-Maktab. Visitors may go to Sinai via Wadi Feiran and return via Wadi el-Maktab.

Wadi Feiran, Feiran Oasis (*biblical Paran and Rephidim?*)

The Wadi Feiran (Paran) is 81 miles long and is one of the longest, most beautiful, and most famous wadis in Sinai. It begins in the region of Jebel Musa, where it is called Wadi el Sheikh, and its mouth is located about 18 miles southeast of Abu Rodeis.

Because this wadi is one of the most important routes to Mount Sinai, pilgrims from the third century onwards have traveled this route and left inscriptions on the rocks that line the wadi.

POINTS OF INTEREST

HESSY EL KHATTATIN. One of the first objects of special interest in the wadi is the Hessy el Khattatin – the miracle of water in Rephidim (Exod 17:6). On the right bank, a large block of fallen granite stands at a sharp angle to the valley, surrounded with heaps of pebbles and small stones. Similar heaps are seen on the surrounding rocks, placed here by the Bedouins to remember a tradition concerning the site. According to the tradition, it was from this rock that water was supplied to the Israelites when Moses smote it with the rod. As the Israelites rested at this site they amused themselves by throwing pebbles upon the surrounding piece of rock. Arabs today believe that healing qualities are associated with the rock and the throwing of pebbles.

FEIRAN OASIS. In the wadi, about 28 miles from its mouth, is the 3-mile-long, beautiful, palm-laden Feiran Oasis, about 2,000 feet above sea level. It is the Eden of Sinai. Thousands of date palms have attracted settlers to this site since ancient times. The Gabaly tribe of Bedouins, originally from Romania, inhabit the oasis, and the women wear beautiful, long, golden-colored veils that completely cover the face from the nose down. They are very timid when being photographed. The Sinai bishopric maintains a small farm and church at the oasis, with a monk in charge.

In the second century A.D. Claudius Ptolemaeus spoke of the town of Paran as an episcopal see and the central point of the monastic and anchorite fraternities of the peninsula. There are numerous old monasteries and hermits' cells on the rocky slopes and plateau of the Serbal Mountains surrounding the Feiran Oasis.

JEBEL EL TAHUNA. On the right side of Wadi Feiran is Jebel el Tahuna (mountain of the mill), covered with tombs, monk cells, and chapels. Traditionally this is the mountain from which Moses viewed the battle with the Amalekites (Exod. 17:8-16).

MOUNT SERBAL. To the south of Wadi Feiran is Mount Serbal, which rises 4,000 feet above the valley.

- *Some regard Wadi Feiran as the site of Rephidim of the Bible, where Moses smote the rock and water came forth (Exod. 17:1-7; 19:2; Num. 33:14-15).*

- *Some believe that Wadi Feiran is the biblical Paran, where the Israelites stayed during the Exodus (Num. 10:12; 12:16; 13:3, 26; Deut. 1:1; 33:2; 1 Sam. 25:1; 1 Kings 11:18).*

Wadi el Sheikh

From Feiran Oasis the road goes to the most important valley of the peninsula, Wadi el Sheikh, followed by Saint Catherine's Monastery, 30 miles away.

Tomb of Sheikh Nebi Saleh

This tomb, the Mecca of Sinai, is considered to be the most sacred in Sinai. It is 7 miles from Saint Catherine's Monastery and consists of a small, whitewashed chamber with a domed roof. Nebi Saleh, a companion of Muhammad during the seventh century, is buried in the building. He is extolled in the Qur'an as a venerable patriarch. Every May a great festival takes place at the tomb of Nebi Saleh, and is considered the national event of the year. Bedouins come brightly dressed from all parts of the peninsula. Sheep are sacrificed, camels compete in races, and a lively festival is held.

Saint Catherine's Monastery

In the sixth century A.D. the emperor Justinian built the fortress-monastery of Saint Catherine at the foot of a mountain in Sinai to protect the life and property of the numerous monks living in the region. It is built like a miniature city and is little changed now after 14 centuries. It has a fine Greek Orthodox Church of the Transfiguration, with beautiful sixteenth-century mosaics, a small Muslim mosque (A.D. 1106), living quarters, a library, a bakery, and living quarters for pilgrims. The 33 to 49-foot-high walls are 279 feet by 312 feet in length. The monastery is 5,012 feet above sea level.

Catherine was born Dorothea, in Alexandria, in the 3rd century A.D. She was a beautiful and well-educated daughter of an aristocratic family. Converted to Jesus Christ by a Syrian monk, she was baptized as Catherine. During the persecutions of Christians by Maximinus in the 4th century, she persisted in her faith and was executed. Her body disappeared. Tradition has it that angels transported it to the highest peak in Sinai (just south of Mount Sinai, Mount Catherine towers over 1,000 feet higher). Three centuries later monks from Justinian's monastery found her body and brought it down and placed it in a golden sarcophagus in the church.

In times past the only way to get into the monastery was by the use of a hoist that lifted the visitor 90 feet to an opening in the wall. The hoist is still used for heavy loads and supplies.

Saint Catherine's Monastery, Mount Sinai

The monks in the monastery observe long periods of self-mortification. Prayers, light housekeeping duties, and small tasks make up their daily routine. Usually about a dozen to two dozen monks live in the monastery, but in the past between 100-400 monks have lived here at the same time.

Visitors may climb 3,000 steps, built out of rock by monks as a penance, to the summit of the mountain, where tradition says Moses received the Ten Commandments.

Sinai bedouins of the Jebelia tribe live near Saint Catherine's. They speak Arabic and claim they are descendants of Wallachian and Egyptian slaves who were settled here by Justinian in the sixth century A.D. to guard the monastery and act as servants to the monks.

Muhammad, the Arab caliphs, Turkish sultans, and Napoleon all took the monastery under their protection. It has never in its long history been conquered, destroyed, or even damaged!

POINTS OF INTEREST

The **BYZANTINE CHURCH OF THE TRANSFIGURATION** is richly adorned with icons. Legend says the church was built by Helena, mother of Constantine, in A.D. 342, as the Chapel of the Burning Bush, which burning bush was reputed to have been found here by early Byzantine monks. The traditional original site of the burning bush is found inside the Chapel of the Burning Bush, but the roots of the bush have been replanted outside the chapel and carefully nurtured. Not only do the monks believe they found the burning bush, but according to tradition they also located Mount Sinai, the well where Moses found Jethro's seven daughters (inside the northern part of the monastery), the path of Moses, the spot where Moses broke the tablets of stone, the site where the earth swallowed up Korah, the hill of Aaron, and the burial place of the golden calf.

Near the **CHARNEL HOUSE**, in the garden outside the monastery wall, is a small **BURIAL GROUND**, 15 feet square. After monks have been buried here for about one year, their bones are moved to the charnel house to be added to the heaps of skulls and bones that are already there. Reasons for collecting them in the bone house are (1) the difficulty of digging graves in the stony ground, and (2) constant reminder to monks of their coming death. Remains of archbishops are kept in special niches.

The **SKELETON OF SAINT STEPHANOS**, the monastery sexton who died in A.D. 580, may be observed seated on a chair in the charnel house. Since he spent his life guarding the steps leading to the mountain of Moses, he was rewarded by having his skeleton seated in the charnel house, fully dressed in his habit.

A special treasure of the monastery is a copy of a **SCRIPT SIGNED BY MUHAMMAD**. The story is told that a young camel driver sought refuge one night, and the monks realized that the driver was the prophet Muhammad. In return for their hospitality the prophet signed a scroll ordering his followers never to violate the monastery. This document was signed by the print of the prophet's hand. The original was taken by a Turkish sultan, but a facsimile is shown to visitors.

The monastery **LIBRARY**, one of the oldest and most valuable in the world, contains some 3,000 manuscripts and 5,000 books (two-thirds in Greek, others in Arabic, Syriac, Persian, Slavonic, Georgian, Armenian, Coptic, and Ethiopian). One of them is the *Evangeliarium Theodosianum*, presented to the monastery by the emperor Theodosius III in A.D. 766. The lettering is in gold and it has pictures of seven saints. The famous *Codex Sinaiticus* was found here by Tischendorf in 1844. Parts of the Codex were in a wastebasket and were nearly used to start a fire. They proved to be one of the two oldest vellum manuscripts then known. Dating from about A.D. 340, the Codex contains all of the New Testament, the apocryphal New Testament books of the Shepherd of Hermes and the Epistle of Barnabas, plus parts of the Old Testament. The Codex came into the hands of the Russians, but the British Museum purchased it in 1933 for 100,000 pounds. In 1950 an American expedition microfilmed 2 million pages of documents written in twelve different languages. The expedition was led by Dr. Aziz Atiya, who in 1959 founded the Middle East Center at the University of Utah (which contains over 100,000 volumes – one of the finest Middle East libraries in America).

The library also houses many ancient and valuable icons ("icon" is Greek for "image"); in fact, it is the most important collection of icons extant (over 2,000). In the eighth century, the issue of whether or not the veneration of icons constituted idolatry erupted into a civil war that shook Byzantium. Imperial decrees ordered the smashing of every holy image; hence our word *iconoclast*, "Icon smasher." The rising tide of Islam, however had isolated Saint Catherine's from Constantinople, and the monastery's collection escaped destruction. A seventh-century icon of Peter holding the keys is one of the most beautiful icons in existence. The icon of the baptism of Jesus in the Jordan River shows Jesus immersed in the water.

In 1958 a team of experts under the direction of Dr. Kurt Weitzmann restored the art work at Saint Catherine's.

MOUNT SINAI, *Mount Horeb*

Jews, Christians, and Muslims have sought to identify the Mountain of God, where Moses received the Ten Commandments. And though there are still differences of opinion, research tends to strengthen the case for locating Mount Sinai in the south end of the peninsula.

The other name for Mount Sinai is Horeb. The Hebrew *Khorev* means desolation, wasteland – dry, parched land, desert, depopulated. (The Hebrew translation of *The Book of Mormon* uses the same term in Mormon 4:1; the land of Desolation is *eretz Khorbah.*) Mosiah 13:5 says that great Jehovah revealed himself and his law on "the mount of Sinai."

The Mount Sinai range rises abruptly from the Wadi el-Sheikh and is composed of several high peaks in a mountain mass 2 miles long and 1 mile wide. The range runs from northwest to southeast, and Saint Catherine's Monastery is in the center of the northeast side.

RAS SUFSAFEH, the northernmost peak of the Mount Sinai range, is 6,830 feet high. It "dwells apart" from the mountain mass, and many feel that it was from this peak that Moses gave the law to the Israelites who were camped on the **PLAIN OF RAHAH**, northwest of the peak. This plain is about 2 miles long and ½ mile wide. The mountain peak is about 1,870 feet above the plain of Rahah, and is very difficult to climb.

JEBEL MUSA, Arabic: **MOUNT OF MOSES**, is 7,363 feet above sea level. Since the sixth century A.D., this has been the traditional site where Moses received the Ten Commandments. On top of the peak is a small, Christian church standing next to a mosque. A small grotto alongside the chapel is the traditional site where Moses received shelter while on the mount. Camels are provided for the visitor who desires to go to the top of the mountain. The camels go as far as **ELIJAH'S CHAPEL**, and steps lead from there to the summit. Just below the Chapel of Elijah and the splendid cypress trees, on the route of descent by stairs, is the arched gateway of Saint Stephanos, where he sat in the same attitude in which his skeleton now sits in the charnel house, quizzing the traveler as to his worthiness to ascend the mount. This trip to the top of Jebel Musa and back takes about half a day (5 or 6 hours).

Some have believed that **JEBEL SERBAL** is Mount Sinai. It is located northwest of Jebel Musa and is the most imposing peak in the chain. Although it is lower than the others (6,759 feet), it stands in solitary grandeur, and would seem an appropriate mountain to be identified with Mount Sinai.

In addition to those already named, **JEBEL KATHERINA** is the highest peak in this range – nearly 9,000 feet above sea level. Being the highest, it was identified as Mount Sinai as early as the fourth century B.C.

Those who believe the route of the Israelites was via Migdol and Baalzephon, parallel to "the way of the Philistines," or on the old caravan route not too far from the seacoast, believe Mount Sinai to be Jebel el Halal, 25 miles west of Kadesh-Barnea, or possibly Jebel Libni, Jebel el Maghara, or another one in the area.

- *Mount Sinai was near Mount Seir (Deut. 33:2; Judg. 5:4-5).*
- *Near Mount Sinai Moses watched the flocks of Jethro and saw God in the burning bush (Exod 3:1-4:17).*
- *Moses spent 40 days on Mount Sinai, receiving the Ten Commandments as part of the Law, and then delivered the Law to the Israelites (Exod. 18-40; Leviticus and most of Deuteronomy).*
- *Jethro met Moses at Mount Sinai and suggested that judges be appointed (Exod. 18).*
- *Instructions for a tabernacle were received on the mount (Exod. 25-31).*
- *Here the golden calf was made and worshiped (Exod. 32).*
- *The children of Israel stripped themselves of ornaments, and Moses went outside the camp and interceded for them (Exod. 33:6-23).*
- *Moses went the second time to Mount Sinai to receive again what was written on the first tablets he had broken (Exod. 34; Deut. 10:2).*
- *Elijah was visited by the Lord on Mount Horeb, the mount of God (1 Kings 19:8-18).*
- *The words on the second set of tablets were the same as those on the first set Moses had broken, "save the words of the everlasting covenant of the holy priesthood" (JST Deut. 10:2).*

Tor, *el Tur* (*"mount"*)

This is one of the largest settlements in southern Sinai. The people are mostly Muslim, but some of them are Greeks who own fishing boats. In the town are a hotel, a hospital, stores, and a quarantine station for pilgrims going to Mecca. The monastery and Greek Orthodox church here are attached to Saint Catherine's monastery. Two miles north of the town are hot springs, called in Arabic *Hammam Musa*, or the hot baths of Moses. It is believed the water has healing properties.

Sharm el Sheikh

On the extreme southeast corner of the Sinai Peninsula, where a small tongue of land splits the coast in two, lies Sharm el Sheikh, one of the beauty spots of the Red Sea coast. It was never inhabited until recent times, and in the near past it was used as a small military post for the Egyptians.

Tiran Island

Located 130 miles south of Eilat is an island 9 by 5 miles in size, with mountain ranges up to 1,600 feet high. Reefs between the island and the mainland leave only narrow, deep passages for shipping. It has thus become a very important military station. In the Israeli-Egyptian conflict the Egyptians set up their batteries of guns here to prevent Israeli shipping from passing through the straits. There is no water or vegetation on the island and no evidence that it was ever occupied by man in early times.

Oasis of Nabk, *Nabq*

About 20 miles north of Sharm el Sheikh, this abandoned oasis has small date palms and a well.

Dhahab

About 50 miles north of Sharm el Sheikh is Dhahab, an oasis inhabited by a sparse Bedouin population. There is a concentration of copper slag, indicating that ancient mines were once located in the area.

Nuweiba *and* **Taba**

These are identifiable points along the coast of the gulf of Aqaba. Nuweiba is approximately 45 miles south of Eilat and Taba is 5 miles south. Taba was the scene of an Israeli-Egyptian border dispute in recent years; international arbitrators decided in favor of Egypt.

Coral Island, *Yi Haalmogim, Jezirat Pharaun* (*"Island of Pharaoh"*)

This small island, 9½ miles south of Eilat, may have been an ancient outpost of Ramses II and Ramses III. It has ruins of a Crusader fortress dating from the twelfth century which was lost to Saladin in 1170. Later, Turks and now Egyptians have rebuilt the fortress.

EZION-GEBER, Eilat, *Elath*

Eilat is a port city founded in 1949 and today vies with Tiberias as Israel's leading winter tourist resort.

- *This was King Solomon's port (1 Kings 9:26-28).*
- *The children of Israel, under Moses' leadership, passed this way (Deut. 2:8).*
- *The Queen of Sheba must have landed here (1 Kings 10:1-13).*
- *Lehi and his family are said to have traveled "in the borders near the Red Sea" in 600 B.C. (1 Ne. 2:5; 16:14).*

Valley of Inscriptions

In the hills southwest of Eilat, at Ras el Nagb, near the "Pilgrim's Way" and the Egypt-Israel border, is the Valley of Inscriptions. On the walls of a canyon are inscriptions that include a seven-branched **CANDELABRUM** with an adjacent ram's horn – ancient Jewish emblems. Some Jewish Aramaic inscriptions are in Nabataean characters.

El Thamad

This is a point about 40 miles west of Eilat on the "Pilgrim's Way" (Darb el Haj). The Darb el Haj starts at Suez, goes east through Mitla Pass and the Gulf of Eilat, and to Mecca, in Arabia.

El Nahkl, *Qal'at el Nakhl*

This **FORTRESS** is near the center of the Sinai Peninsula, on the "Pilgrim's Way," where a road comes to this point from the north and El Arish. It is midway between Eilat and Suez and is known as the "Fortress of Date-Palms." The main structure was built by Sultan Selim I in the course of his conquest of Egypt in A.D. 1517. It was used as a hospice for Muslim pilgrims. The mosque of the fortress is in several stages of construction. East of the fortress is a sheikh's tomb, and around it are hundreds of Arab graves. It would seem that this site is not pre-medieval.

Ras el Gindi

Near the junction of three desert routes, about 15 miles north of Mitla Pass, is a **FORTRESS** built by Saladin in the twelfth century A.D. It is built on a summit of a 2,142-foot mountain. In some respects it is similar to Masada, near the shores of the Dead Sea. A 30-minute hike to the northwest corner of the preserved wall will bring the visitor to the main gate, with a Shield of David engraved in the arch over the gateway. A large mosque and a number of large buildings are in the fortress, in addition to an enormous roofed cistern and great underground cisterns.

Mitla Pass

About 25 miles east of Suez is Mitla Pass. Near the pass are the remains of ancient buildings that possibly belonged to an Amorite settlement and date to the Middle Bronze Age (Patriarchal Period). They are north of the road junction of Sudr el Haitan on the slopes of Ruweiset el Akheider, not far from the memorial of the former governor of Sinai, Colonel A. C. Parker.

Bir Hasana

This is a point in the Sinai Peninsula where the road from El Arish to El Nakhl crosses over the road that runs between Mitla Pass and El Qusaima.

KADESH-BARNEA, El Qusaima, *Ain el Qudeirat, near El Muweilah and Ain Qadeis*

Only in the El Qusaima area are there enough greenstuffs and water to sustain a body of people the size of Israel at the time of the Exodus. Here is the largest spring in North Sinai. This must be the wilderness of Zin and Kadesh-Barnea. It is 150 miles from Ramses in Egypt, 140 miles from Mount Sinai, or the "uttermost" border of Edom, on the south border of Canaan, in the wilderness of Zin (Num. 20:1, 16; 33:36-37; Deut. 1:2). Of all the sites visited during the travels of the Israelites in the Sinai Peninsula, this one has the most unanimous agreement among the scholars as to its location. The area is approximately 40 miles south and a little west of Beersheba.

Here the Israelites made their headquarters for 38 years, from the sending of the spies until they entered Canaan. Here was the springboard for the invasion of Canaan. Here Moses wrestled for the destiny of his people, and here his own destiny was decided. This area played a major role in the desert wanderings of the Israelites.

Ain el Qudeirat and Ain Qadeis are separated by 12 miles and seem to be the two main points identifying Kadesh-Barnea. *Kadesh* means "holy," and *Barnea* means "desert of wandering." There is a series of wells in the area. Remains of an ancient fort on a small tell were found in the neck of Wadi el Ain by Woolley and Lawrence and dated by Glueck to the early Hebrew monarchy. The tell is 200 by 120 feet in size. The Egyptians, like the Nabataeans of old, developed a small experimental farm here, and there is a very interesting communal olive press located in a vacant house at El Qusaima. It is very similar to those described in the Mishna, with two heavy stone rollers which move on a solid base about 7 feet in diameter. The rollers were turned by a camel or a pair of donkeys.

Most scholars believe Mount Hor, where Aaron died (Num. 33:38), was near Kadesh-Barnea and not near Petra in Jordan, as the Arab Muslims and Josephus believe. Some feel that the present Jebel el Madra, a limestone peak by Maale-Aqrabim, is the peak Mount Hor. This is in the center of the Nahal Zin (Wadi Fikra). It was in the borders of Edom (Num. 20:23; 33:37) and was the first stopping place of Israel's wanderings after they left Kadesh-Barnea (Num. 20:22; 33:37).

Those who believe the Israelites came directly to the Kadesh-Barnea area via the Mediterranean seacoast believe that Mount Sinai was 25 miles west of Kadesh-Barnea – possibly Jebel el Halal.

- *Chedorlaomer and his confederates smote the Amorites and Amalekites here (Gen. 14:1-7).*
- *When Hagar fled from Sarah's wrath, she stopped at a well and an angel told her she would bear a son, Ishmael. The well was located between Kadesh and Bered (Gen. 16:6-14).*
- *Abraham dwelt between Kadesh and Shur after the destruction of Sodom and Gomorrah (Gen. 20:1).*
- *Here was the center of the wanderings of the tribes of Israel (Num. 20:1; Deut. 1:46).*
- *Spies were sent into the promised land from here, and here Israel sinned (Num. 13-14; 32:8; Deut 9:23).*
- *Here Caleb gave a positive report on the land of Canaan (Num. 13:30; 14:6-9; Josh. 14:6 – 15).*
- *This was the scene of the rebellion of Korah, the murmuring of the people, and the budding of Aaron's rod (Num. 16-17).*
- *Here Miriam died. She had watched Moses in the ark of bulrushes (Exod. 2:4), had led the women in the song of victory at the Red Sea (Exod 15:20), and had been both punished by leprosy and healed of it (Num. 12:1-15; 20:1; Deut. 24:8-9). (Some traditions have Moses buried here also).*
- *Here Moses smote the rock and water came forth (Num. 20:11).*
- *Here Moses was told he could not enter the promised land (Num. 20:12; 27:14; Deut. 32:48-52).*
- *A delegation was sent from here to the king of Edom (Num. 20:14-21; Judg. 11:17).*
- *Here the final journey into the promised land began via Mount Hor (Num. 20:22).*
- *It was on the southern border of Judah (Josh. 15:3; Ezek. 47:19).*
- *Kadesh was mentioned by David (Ps. 29:8).*

EL ARISH (*"the booth"*)

This is a town on the Mediterranean seacoast, 50 miles southwest of Gaza. Here the Wadi el Arish, called the "River of Egypt," flows into the Mediterranean. It is located on "the way of the land of the Philistines," or the "way of the sea." El Arish is known as the capital of Sinai. Its population is mostly Muslim, with a few Coptic Christians.

- *Tradition indicates that when Jacob left Canaan and went to Egypt (Gen. 46:5-6) he built a booth and rested here.*

EGYPT – HELPFUL TERMS TO KNOW

alabaster - a fine, granular, white or translucent gypsum used for ornamentation.

Amon or Amen - chief god of Egyptian pantheon at Thebes; sometimes, Amon-Ra.

ankh - the sign of life, often connoting eternal life.

Apis - sacred name of the ancient bull worshipped at Memphis; identified originally with Ptah, later assimilated with Osiris to form Hellenistic period Serapis (burial place of the embalmed bulls = the Serapeum).

Aton or Aten - the one and only god of Akhenaton at el Amarna; the sun disc.

cartouche - French for "royal ring"; an oval or oblong figure enclosing characters representing the name of a Pharaoh.

cataract - point on the Nile River where cliffs and mountains close in on the river and make it quite narrow causing the water to flow very rapidly.

citadel - (Latin) fortress on commanding height for defense of a city (Gr: acropolis).

colossus (pl. colossi) - Greek, a statue of gigantic size and proportions (e.g., "Colossi of Memnon;" many of Ramses II - as at Memphis, Abu Simbel, Luxor, Tanis, etc.)

Copts - Greek Aigyptios; Coptic Kyptios; native Egyptians, descended from the ancient Egyptians, members of the Coptic (Christian) Church. Coptic is the nearly extinct language of Egypt that developed from ancient Egyptian, still used in liturgy.

demotic - a simplified form of the Egyptian hieratic writing, similar to shorthand.

dynasty - a succession of rulers belonging to one family.

Egypt, Upper and Lower - Upper Egypt (southern Egypt) is the Nile River region from the first cataract to modern Cairo; Lower Egypt is the Delta. "Upper" and "Lower" are used due to the south to north flow of the Nile.

falouka - a Nile sailboat.

fellah (pl. fellahin) - peasant(s); lit. tiller of the soil.

hieratic - cursive form of ancient Egyptian hieroglyphics.

hieroglyphics [Gr. hiero = holy, sacred + glyphein = to carve] - a system of writing using pictorial characters.

Hyksos - nomadic Amorite tribes who invaded Egypt from the north about 1750 B.C. and ruled for a century and a half; Hequ khoswe = rulers of foreign lands.

hypocephalus (pl. hypocephali) [Gr. hypo = under + cephalo = head] - as Facsimile #2, Book of Abraham; often an inscription from the Book of

Breathings, round in shape, placed at burial under the head of an important person.

hypostyle [adj. & noun, Gr. hypo = under, beneath + stylos = pillar] - a roof resting on rows of columns.

mastaba - a later period word [Arabic = stone bench] used to describe an Egyptian tomb from the time of Memphite dynasties.

necropolis - Gr. literally "city of the dead;" a large, elaborate cemetery of an ancient city (usually to the west of the city, where the sun sets.)

obelisk - giant, monolithic [one-stone], four-sided shaft or pillar with a pyramidal apex, said to represent a ray of sun.

Osiris - judge of the dead, god of resurrection.

ossuary - Gr. "bone box"; about a year after interment, with subsequent decomposition, bones were removed from the sarcophagus and placed in an ossuary.

papyrus - a plant of the Nile Valley which was cut into strips and pressed into writing material: ancient paper.

parchment - animal skin prepared for writing on.

pylon [Gr. = gate] - a massive gateway building in a truncated pyramidal shape.

pyramid - a massive structure built of stone, usually with square base and sloping sides meeting at an apex, such as those that ancient Egyptians built as royal tombs.

Ra or Re - the sun god of ancient Egypt.

saqiya - waterwheel, usually powered by an ox.

sarcophagus (pl. sarcophagi) - Gr. lit. "flesh-eating stone" i. e., a stone coffin; so called because in it the flesh gradually decayed, dried, and essentially vanished.

scarab - a beetle held sacred by the ancient Egyptians, an image of which was cut from a stone or gem and worn as a charm or a personal stamp.

shaduf - mechanical device raising water to higher ditches for irrigation; long pole with rope and bucket at one end and counterweight at the other.

sphinx - an Egyptian statue or figure that has a body of an animal and head of a man.

stele or stela (pl. stelae) - an upright stone slab or pillar often with inscription boasting of victory over enemies.

tambour - Archimedes' screw; used to raise Nile water to a higher level.

Notes

1 Mormon travelers will be especially interested in the **Lion Couch**, which resembles the one upon which Abraham is portrayed as lying when he was nearly sacrificed (Facsimile no. 1 of the Book of Abraham; Abr. 1:12-14).

2 Necho also reigned about the same time as the Book of Mormon prophet Lehi is said to have left Jerusalem with his family. Josiah Quincy, mayor of Boston, Massachusetts, reported that in May of 1844 the Mormon prophet Joseph Smith identified one of the four mummies he owned as that of Pharaoh Necho, king of Egypt. Most students give little credence to Quincy's report, however.

Certain scholars of The Church of Jesus Christ of Latter-day Saints (Mormon) have believed that tomb number 33 could well be the tomb from which one of their sacred scriptures, the Book of Abraham, was taken. The French (Piedmontese) Antonio Lebolo procured a license from Mehemet Ali (Muhammad Ali), then viceroy of Egypt, under the direction of Bernardino Drovetti, the French consul, sometime in the period A.D. 1818-23. After employing 433 men for four months and two days, he entered the catacomb. It was approximately 60 feet below the surface and had a large room or "grand cavity." In fact, it was so large that there were said to be several hundred mummies in the catacomb. About 100 of the mummies were embalmed after the "first order" and placed in "niches." Two or three hundred, embalmed after the "second" and "third" orders, were so badly decomposed that they could not be removed. Eleven of the well-preserved mummies, however, were taken from the tomb and eventually came into the hands of Michael Chandler, reported to be a nephew of Lebolo. From Chandler four of the mummies passed into the hands of Joseph Smith, the Mormon leader, at Kirtland, Ohio, in the year 1835. With the mummies were two rolls of papyrus with black and red Egyptian characters written on them. Joseph Smith said the records contained the writings of Abraham and Joseph while they were in Egypt, and that the rolls had been deposited with two of the mummies.

Mormons consider the Book of Abraham, translated by Joseph Smith, as sacred scripture, on par with the Bible. The story of Abraham contained in the Book of Abraham parallels the Bible in many respects, and adds a number of details on the youth of Abraham and his journey into the "promised land" and into Egypt. It also contains an interesting discussion concerning a premortal life of man, comments on man's purposes on the earth, and pointedly affirms the divine mission of Jesus Christ as the Son of God.

In 1967 leading newspapers in the United States and Egypt carried an announcement on the front page that intrigued both Mormons and non-Mormons alike. Long-lost manuscripts of papyrus that are now associated with the Book of Abraham had been discovered in the New York Metropolitan Museum of Art by Dr. Aziz S. Atiya of the University of Utah. The papyri were given to The Church of Jesus Christ of Latter-day Saints, and after 96 years Mormons had tangible evidence of at least a portion of the papyri from which Joseph Smith was said to have translated the Book of Abraham.

Mormons present a number of reasons for associating tomb 33 with the Book of Abraham:

(1) Oliver Cowdery, who helped Joseph Smith translate the Book of Abraham, said the mummies were taken from one of the catacombs of Egypt, near the site of ancient Thebes.

(2) Warren R. Dawson, author of *Who Was Who in Egyptology*, indicated that while in Thebes in 1818 Antonio Lebolo discovered at Gournah a "pit tomb" containing a number of mummies.

(3) The catacomb in question had to be a "grand cavity" and had to hold several hundred mummies. It had to be a large tomb. Tomb 33 is not only the largest in the area, but it appears to be the only tomb of the size described. According to Oliver Cowdery's description, it also had to have "niches," or recesses, large enough to house a hundred mummies of the first order.

(4) Emma Smith's document that accompanied the sale of the papyri in 1856 stated that the mummies were found in catacombs sixty feet below the surface of the earth. Tomb 33 fits that description.

(5) In 1824, Giulio di San Quintino, curator of the Royal Egyptian Museum at Turin, Italy, gave an account of Lebolo's mummy discovery in a 73-page monograph published in *Lezioni Archeologiche.* He said that Lebolo removed 11-12 mummies from a pit tomb near Gournah. He also said that the pit tomb was deep, partially constructed of brick, and internally adorned with various wall paintings. This early report of Lebolo's activities also substantiates the identification of tomb 33.

Dr. Ross T. Christensen, professor of archaeology at Brigham Young University, in Provo, Utah, was the first person to suggest the possibility of identifying pit tomb number 33 with the Book of Abraham. Dr. Lynn Hilton visited the site a few months later in 1961, and finally in January of 1970 he and his friend Don Blackwelder became the first Latter-day Saints to enter the tomb. They apparently visited the first two rooms. Then on April 5, 1970, Dr. LaMar C. Berrett led the first BYU Travel Study group (46 persons) ever to go through the tomb. They visited all the large rooms and took photographs of the inside of the tomb.

Jordan

Jordan is about the size of Ohio, with a population around four million, with 2.5 million living in greater Amman, the nation's capital.

HISTORY

Before the Israelite Conquest

Before the conquest of Canaan by the Israelites, the area on the east side of the Jordan River encompassing the present-day country called Jordan was divided into the following five districts (see map).

BASHAN

Between the Jabbok and the Yarmuk rivers, northern Gilead extends north and south for about 35 miles. The land of Bashan, north of the Yarmuk, reaches to Mount Hermon and eastward to the northern slopes of the Hauran and to the city of Salecah. At the time of the conquest this kingdom was ruled by Og, who was said to have been a giant (Deut. 3:11). Og was defeated by the Israelites at Edrei (in Syria), and his territory of Bashan and North Gilead was assigned to half the tribe of Manasseh (Deut. 1:4; 3:1-14). Og's territory passed from David to Solomon and was lost during the Syrian wars, to be regained by Jeroboam II (2 Kings 14:23, 25). Beginning with the time of Tiglath-pileser III, king of the Assyrians, it passed into foreign control (2 Kings 15:29).

Megalithic graves, or *dolmens*, were once used for burying the dead. These famous great stone graves consisted of tall stones, built in oval formation and every now and then roofed over with a heavy transverse block. They are called locally "giants' beds." In 1918 Gustaf Dalman discovered a dolmen in the neighborhood of Amman, the modern capital of Jordan.

The Bible says about the giant King Og: "Behold, his bedstead was a bedstead of iron; is it not in Rabbath of the children of Ammon [Rabbath-Ammon]? nine cubits was the length thereof, and four cubits the breadth of it, after the cubit of a man" (Deut. 3:11). The size of the dolmen discovered by Dalman corresponded approximately to these measurements. The "bed" consisted of basalt, an extremely hard, gray-black stone. The appearance of such a burying place may have given rise to the biblical description of the giant king's "bedstead of iron."

- *Bashan was ruled by Og the giant (Deut. 3:1, 11).*
- *It was taken by the Israelites and assigned to half the tribe of Manasseh (Deut. 1:4; 3:1-14).*
- *It was lost during the Syrian wars, but regained by Jeroboam II (2 Kings 14:23, 25).*
- *From Bashan came the story of Og's giant bed (Deut. 3:11).*

SYRIA
Sea of Galilee
El-Himmeh
Gadara (Um Qeis)
Irbid
Ramtha
N
Jabesh-Gilead
Ajalon (Ajlun)
Um el Jimal
Mafraq
Wood of Ephraim
Jerash
Nablus
Succoth (Tell Deir'Alla)
Mahanaim
Peniel
Jabbok River (Wadi Zerqa)
Qasr Hammam
OCCUPIED TERRITORY
Adam (Damiya)
Zarqa
Ramoth Gilead (Salt)
River Jordan
Amman
Naur
Al Azraq
Abel-Shittim
Bethabara
Heshbon
Qasr Amra
Mount Nebo
Mashatta
Jerusalem
Mukhaiyat
Jiza
Medeba (Madaba)
Zerka Main
Desert Road
Machaerus
Hebron
DEAD SEA
Dibon
Aroer
River Arnon (Wadi Mojib)
SAUDI ARABIA
Mazra
Qasr
Rabbah
Qatrana
Karak
Mauta
Mazar
Wadi Hasa
Khirbet et Tannur
Labban
Tafila
Desert Road
Bayir
SRAEL
King's Highway
Jurf ed Darawish
Shaubak
Uneiza
Petra
Mount Hor
Ain Musa
El Jafr
Ma'an
Gharandal
Ras en Naqb
Wadi el Arabah
SAUDI ARABIA
at
Wadi Rum
Aqaba
Jordan
Miles 5 25 50

- *It was taken from Israel by the Assyrians, and the inhabitants were carried into captivity (2 Kings 15:29).*
- *The Old Testament has several references to the "oaks of Bashan" (Isa. 2:13; Ezek. 27:6; Zech. 11:2).*
- *The Book of Mormon (Isaiah) also refers to the "oaks of Bashan" (2 Ne. 12:13).*

GILEAD

The term *Gilead* is used loosely in the Old Testament. In Numbers 32:33 the territory assigned to Gad, Reuben, and half the tribe of Manasseh included the kingdoms of Sihon, king of the Amorites, and of Og, king of Bashan, comprising all the territory between the Arnon and the Yarmuk rivers and beyond. The word *Gilead* is employed for the whole of this territory, as well as for part of it (2 Kings 10:33). The Jabbok River divides it in two.

The territory of Sihon, king of the Amorites, extended from the Arnon north to the Jabbok. The Israelites, having been refused permission to pass through Edom and Moab along the King's Highway went around these two kingdoms as they headed north. When they reached the river Arnon, which was the south border of the Amorites, they again asked permission to use the King's Highway. Sihon refused permission, and the Israelites attacked his kingdom. This marked the beginning of the conquest of Canaan by force of arms.

The original Ammonite kingdom consisted of a small, strongly fortified, fairly fertile strip south of the Nahal Jabbok (Wadi Zerqa) and reaching eastward to the desert. Among the most striking of Ammonite fortifications were strongly-built circular towers of megalithic construction, which – sometimes alone, but usually in conjunction with rectangular or square fortifications, also built of large blocks of stone – provided the defenses of the Ammonite kingdom and particularly of the approaches to the capital city of Rabbath-Ammon. Usually the large, rectangular flint (or limestone) blocks were not dressed or smoothed beyond the roughly hewn state. A puzzling question is how the Ammonite builders moved these large, heavy stones into position after the stones had been prepared for use. If earthen ramps were used, no traces of such have ever been reported.

Typical wall construction technique consisted of laying blocks at the corners in headers and stretchers, while between the corners, stones were placed in rude courses, with smaller stones interspersed to make the rows fairly even.

- *Ahab, king of Israel, was mortally wounded at Ramoth Gilead. (1 Kings 22:29-40).*
- *The conquest of Canaan began when Sihon, king of the Amorites, refused Israel permission to cross his territory (Num. 21:21-24).*

MOAB

Moab was a district east of the Dead Sea with its boundaries north and south about even with the ends of the Dead Sea from Wadi Hasa to Wadi Mojib (Arnon River). It was about 35 miles long and 25 miles wide. The area lies 3,000 feet above sea level and 4,300 feet above the Dead Sea. Deep gorges were formed by rivers draining into the Dead Sea. Here are mounts Nebo and Pisgah (Deut. 34:1; Num. 21:20).

The Moabites, like the Ammonites, descended from Lot, the nephew of Abraham. The Amorites and later the Arabs took over this area, causing the Moabites to lose their identity. The chief god of the Moabites was Chemosh, who was worshiped by human sacrifice (2 Kings 3:26-27).

- *Genesis speaks of the Moabites' origin (Gen. 19:30-38).*
- *Israel avoided them as they approached Canaan (Deut. 2:9; 2 Chron. 20:10).*
- *Moses saw the promised land from Mount Nebo, where, it is said, he died (Deut. 32:48-52; 34:1-8).*
- *Saul smote Moab (1 Sam. 14:47).*
- *David's parents were protected there while Saul persecuted David (1 Sam. 22:3-4).*
- *Moab was defeated by Jehoshaphat (2 Kings 3).*
- *Ruth came from Moab (Ruth 1:4).*
- *Amos reproved Moab (Amos 2:1-3).*

EDOM

The area which was once the territory of Edom (also known as Seir) is located east of the Rift Valley and extends from the Dead Sea to the Gulf of Aqaba. Its mountains rise to 5,900 feet. The ancient inhabitants were descendants of Esau (Gen. 14:6; Deut. 2:22). In the Iron Age, Edom was a prosperous, civilized kingdom. It was an enemy to Israel (Num. 20:14-21; 21:4; Deut. 23:7-8).

- *Edom was located near and around Seir (Gen. 32:3).*
- *Edom would not let Moses and the Israelites pass through (Num. 20:14-21).*
- *Saul, David, and Amaziah each defeated Edom in war and David garrisoned the country (1 Sam. 14:47; 2 Sam. 8:13-14; 2 Kings 14:7-10).*
- *Edom acknowledged the supremacy of Judah (1 Kings 11:14-25; 2 Kings 3:6-26; 2 Kings 14:7).*
- *Edom was severely criticized by the prophets (Lam. 4:21; Ezek. 25:12-14; 35; Obadiah).*

MIDIAN

It appears that this land area, which extends both east and west of the eastern arm of the Red Sea, was inhabited by the Midianites. These people took their name from Midian, one of the sons of Abraham and his wife Keturah (Gen. 25:1-2), who, with his brothers and their families, had gone away from Isaac into the "east country" (Gen. 25:6; 1 Kings 11:18; Judg. 8:11; Num. 32:42; Ex. 3:1). There is a very close relationship between the Midianites and Ishmaelites (descendants of Hagar), to the point that these two names are sometimes used interchangeably (Gen. 37:25, 28, 36; Judg. 8:22, 24).

- *Moses fled to Midian, where he met Jethro and received a wife from him. From here he was sent to deliver Israel (Exod. 2:15-21; 3:1-10; 4:19).*
- *Israel wandered in the area (Num. 10:29-36).*
- *The Midianites joined Balak in seeking a curse on Israel (Num. 22-24).*
- *Israel sinned by intermarriage with the Midianites (Num. 25; 31:2-18).*
- *Gideon overthrew them and saved Israel after seven years' oppression (Judg. 6-8; 9:17; Ps. 83:9; Isa. 9:4; 10:26; Hab. 3:7).*
- *Hadad and many of Israel dwelt in Midian (1 Kings 11:14-22).*
- *Moses received the priesthood from his father-in-law, Jethro (D&C 84:6).*

Ancient Times

Until modern times, Jordan was always an appendage to more powerful kingdoms and empires. After Israel conquered Canaan, the northern districts east of the Jordan River became Israelite territory, occupied by the tribes of Manasseh, Gad, and Reuben. These Israelite lands went as far south as the middle of the Dead Sea. South of that point, the Moabites and Edomites possessed the land. During the 6th century B.C. Nabataeans established Petra and preserved independence while the north became Greek (Seleucid). In the 4th and 3rd centuries B.C. hellenistic centers like Philadelphia and Gerasa flourished. In the first century A.D. all Transjordan became part of the Roman Empire.

Modern Times

The Hashemite Kingdom of Jordan became independent as Transjordan in 1946, then as the independent Hashemite Kingdom of Jordan in 1949. King Amir Abdullah reigned over Jordan from 1946 until 1951, when he was assassinated. His son King Talal then ruled, but was not competent. King Hussein, grandson of Abdullah, has ruled since 1953. Young Hussein received his education in Egypt and England. Since ascending the throne in 1953, he has survived several attempts on his life. In 1993 the country celebrated the 40th year of his reign (then the longest-ruling monarch in the world).

Religion

The country is predominantly Muslim, but Arab and non-Arab Christians comprise a small percentage of the population and represent a number of Catholic and Protestant denominations, the largest group being Greek Orthodox.

JORDAN TODAY

Jordan is largely an agricultural country, and many of its people are engaged in raising grain and livestock. The country on the whole is fairly dry, with most of its precipitation occurring in the winter season; the highest concentration of rainfall is in the northwest. Eighty-eight percent of the land is desert or wasteland, 11% is agricultural and 1% is forested. Although the Jordan Valley comprises only .6% of the country's agricultural land, it produces 50% of the fruits and vegetables needed in Jordan and 90% of its export crops. Use of plastic greenhouses further increases crop yield.

The government of Jordan is considered a constitutional monarchy, and Jordan's Independence Day is May 25.

The Jordanian unit of currency is the *dinar*, divided into 1,000 *fils*.

Water resources

1.The East Ghor Canal is the major irrigation project in Jordan (and the first hydraulic project in this land since the days of the Roman Empire). Waters of the Yarmuk River are channelled south in open, concrete-lined canals for over 70 miles, watering Jordan Valley agricultural land.

2.In the Rift Valley Basin the Jordan River has a large catchment area, with several tributaries feeding it. The Yarmuk River at Jordan's northern border is the main tributary; the second major tributary is the River Zerqa (the Jabbok of the Bible).

3.In the Dead Sea Basin there are four major wadis: Zerqa Ma'in is fed by a series of mineral springs (called Callirhoe anciently, and made famous by Herod the Great's use); Wadi Wala; Wadi Mujib (Biblical Arnon); and Wadi Hasa (Biblical Zered).

Dams in Jordan

The biggest thus far is the King Talal Dam on the Jabbok, with a total storage capacity of 56 million cubic meters (used for irrigation and drinking). The biggest proposed dam (Al-Wahda) is on the Yarmuk with a capacity of 200 million cubic meters. Additional water is needed for irrigation, but also to be pumped up to the capital, which is suffering severe problems in water quality and quantity.

Industry

Jordan's single most expensive industrial enterprise is the Dead Sea Potash Scheme, which reached in the mid-1980s its full productive capacity of over a million tons of potash per year. Other economically viable mining operations include phosphates, iron, copper (east side of the Arabah), and manganese.

Tourism

Tourism brings hundreds of millions of dollars annually; export income is even more.

Before the Gulf War of 1991, Jordan's largest source of income for many years was money sent home by over 400,000 skilled Jordanians employed in other countries, mainly Saudi Arabia and Persian Gulf countries. Following the war those workers were repatriated and that source of income dried up.

Gross national product in the early 1990s was around $5. billion, and per capita income was $1400.

Population

By 1993 there were an estimated four million people in Jordan, with 2.5 million living in greater Amman. Ninety percent of the people live on ten percent of the land, with the greatest concentration in the north-west. Urban population is over 60%. In the past thirty years Jordan has experienced a population increase of over 650%, on a very limited resource base. Ninety-two percent is Sunni Muslim and eight percent Christian. Over half of the population are Palestinians, and the greatest social distinction in the country is Palestinian/native Jordanian. Before 1900, bedouin constituted the majority of the population of Transjordan, but now they are rapidly diminishing (though they still comprise the core of the Jordanian army).

Half of the population is under fifteen years of age. Ninety-five percent of school-age children attend school, and many continue until age twenty. Jordan has four universities and nearly 40 community colleges. Literacy rate is 80%.

The dependency ratio in Jordan is 1:5 (one of the world's highest), meaning that a working person must support himself and four others.

Natural increase is 3.7%, one of the highest in the world.

Average number of children per mother: 7.1.

Life expectancy for males is 70 years; females 73 years.

Infant mortality is about 38 per 1,000 births.

CITIES AND SITES

AMMON, RABBAH, RABBATH (*"great"*), *Philadelphia*, Amman

Amman, the capital city of Jordan, is 25 miles east of the Jordan River and 45 miles northeast of Jerusalem, at an altitude of 3,000 feet (500 feet higher than Jerusalem). About 1200 B.C. it was the capital of the Ammonites. The Israelites did not occupy Rabbath (the city's biblical name) after David took the city, but left it in the possession of the Ammonite king, who became David's vassal.

The first dramatic change to affect Amman came with the victorious arrival, in the third century B.C., of Ptolemy II (Philadelphus) of Egypt (265-263 B.C.), who rebuilt Amman and named it Philadelphia. The Seleucids conquered Amman in 218 B.C., and in 30 B.C. Herod the Great took the city for Rome. Herod embarked on an extensive building program, leveling off the Citadel, surrounding it with a wall, and building a massive temple to Hercules.

During the Roman period Amman was a member of the Decapolis. Centuries later, during the Byzantine period, it became the seat of a Christian Bishopric of Petra and Philadelphia. After the Arab conquest of the seventeenth century the city flourished, but gradually it declined in importance until, when Abdullah moved the seat of his newly formed government there in the 1920s, it was only a village.

It is now the seat of the government, however, and the hub of commercial activity. The population of the city is nearing three million, including thousands of Palestinian refugees who flocked into the city after 1948.

POINTS OF INTEREST

1. A **ROMAN THEATER**, with a seating capacity of 6,000, dates from the second or third century A.D. It is located right behind the Philadelphia Hotel. Outdoor festivals are held in the theater during the summer. Only a few columns remain of the **ROMAN FORUM**, and east of the hotel there is a small theater called the **ODEUM**. On the west was the **NYMPHAEUM**.

2. The **CITADEL** is the site of ancient Rabbah or Rabbath-Ammon. While Israelite armies were storming its walls, David had one of his officers named Uriah intentionally left in a vulnerable position so he would be killed (2 Sam. 11:1, 14-17). The citadel was built on a plateau (Jebel Hussein) where once stood a temple to Hercules (second century A.D.). **A BYZANTINE GATE** stills stands, and on the outside of the **ROMAN WALLS** is a rock-carved cistern that supplied the fortress with water when the fortress was under attack. North of the Citadel is **EL-QASR** (the Castle), dating back to the Umayyad period (sixth and seventh centuries).

3. The **AMMAN ARCHAEOLOGICAL MUSEUM** is located on Citadel Hill. Archaeological artifacts include Nabataean pottery and Dead Sea Scrolls, especially the original Copper Scroll from the Qumran community.

4. The **BASMAN PALACE** is the "working" palace of King Hussein. It stands on a hilltop facing the Citadel, and Circassian soldiers wearing red and black uniforms guard the king.

Roman Theatre, Amman

5. **REFUGEE CAMPS** near the city are the pathetic results of war. Thousands of Palestinian refugees have lived in these camps for nearly fifty years and raised their families in very humble circumstances. The United Nations has been the agent of mercy to these poor Arabs.

The **SHOPPING CENTER**, **KING HUSSEIN SPORTS CITY**, and **QUEEN MOTHER PALACE** are also of interest.

- *The ancient nation of the Ammonites, with their capital at Amman, were descendants of Lot. They lived on the east of the Jordan and the Dead Sea, between the rivers Arnon and Jabbok. Their chief god was Molech, to whom they offered human sacrifices (2 Kings 3:26-27; Lev. 20:2-5; Deut. 2:19).*
- *Og's bedstead might still be seen here (Deut. 3:11). Some believe this refers to a large dolmen still visible not far from Amman.*
- *The city was mentioned in defining the boundaries of Gad (Josh. 13:24-25).*
- *Amman oppressed Israel and was overthrown by Jephthah (Judg. 11:4-33).*
- *The city was taken by David. In one of the battles Uriah, the husband of Bathsheba, was killed (2 Sam. 11; 12:26-29; 1 Chron. 20:1).*

- *Amman showed mercy to David, a fugitive (2 Sam. 17:27-29).*
- *It was hostile to Israel (2 Chron. 20:1-25; 27:5; 2 Kings 24:2; Neh. 4:1-12; 2 Kings 25:22-26; Jer. 40:13-41:4).*
- *Solomon married an Ammonite woman, whose son, Rehoboam, succeeded him (1 Kings 14:21, 31; 2 Chron. 12:13).*
- *The cruelty of the Ammonites was denounced by the prophets (Jer. 49:1-6; Ezek. 21:28-32; Amos 1:13-15; Zeph. 2:8-11).*
- *Amman was one of the cities of the Decapolis (Mark 7:31).*

NORTH FROM AMMAN

RAMOTH GILEAD (*"heights of Gilead"*)

Under Solomon, Ramoth Gilead was the seat of the governor of the province north of the Yarmuk River and may have been the most important Israelite city east of the Jordan. The location is uncertain.

- *Here Ahab was wounded and died (1 Kings 22:1-35; 2 Chron. 18).*
- *Elisha sent a young prophet here to anoint Jehu king of Israel (2 Kings 9:1-10; 2 Chron. 22:7).*

ADAM (*"of the ground"*), **Damiya**, *Kiriathaim, Tell ed-Damiyeh*

This is a natural fording-place near Zaretan, 25 miles northwest of Amman, beside the Jordan River upstream from where the Israelites crossed.

- *The waters were "cut off" so the Israelites could cross the Jordan River (Josh. 3:14-17).*

JABBOK (*"flowing"*), **Wadi Zerqa** (*"the blue river"*)

This is a clear river that crosses the territory of Gilead. It flows at the bottom of a great cleft, cutting the land of Gilead in two.

- *Here Jacob wrestled and was given the name Israel, as he returned from Padan-aram (Gen. 32:22-32).*
- *Sihon ruled to the Jabbok (Josh. 12:2).*
- *The place is mentioned elsewhere in the Old Testament (Num. 21:24; Deut. 2:37; 3:16; Judg. 11:13; 11:22).*

SUCCOTH (*"booths"*), **Tell Deir 'Alla**

Succoth was a town of Gad, 4 miles east of the Jordan and somewhat over 1 mile north of the brook Jabbok.

- *Jacob built a house for his family and booths for his cattle after separating from Esau (Gen. 33:17; Josh. 13:27).*
- *Gideon and his army punished the people of Succoth after the people refused to give bread to the army (Judg. 8:4-7, 15-17).*

Amman
N
To Jerash and Damascus
To Airport
AL RAZI STREET
SUKEINA STREET
KING HUSEIN STREET
ASMA STREET
KHALID BEN AL WALID STREET
QASSAM STREET
AL RAZI STREET
ABU OBEIDAH STREET
MAAMOUN STREET
AL HUSEIN BEN ALI STREET
KING HUSEIN STREET
IBRAHIM TOUKAN STREET
AIESHEH EL BAOUNIEH STREET
SHAREA COLLEGE STREET
MOHAMMAD ABDO
JAREER STREET
SALT STREET
SALAH EDDIGE STREET
WADI AL HADADEH STREET
MUSEUM STREET
KING ABDULLAH STREET
PRINCE MOHAMMAD STREET
MUTANABI STREET
ABU TAMMAM STREET
ABU FERAS STREET
QUEEN ZEIN STREET
SHABAN STREET
JORDAN STREET
OTHMAN STREET
KING FEISAL STREET
SHABSOUGH STREET
MUNICIPALITY STREET
ABU BAKER AL SADEEA STREET
BUHTORY STREET
OMAR BEN KHATTAB STREET
IMMAM ALI STREET
MUHAJEREEN STREET
RAS EL AIN STREET
KING TALLAL STREET
1
2
3
4
6
7
8

1. Roman theatre
2. Citadel
3. Amman Archeological Museum
4. Basman Palace
5. Refugee camps
6. Shopping center
7. King Hussein Sports City
8. Queen Mother Palace

- *Solomon cast bronze vessels for worship in the Temple in this area because the rich deposits of clay on the plain of the Jordan River were suitable for casting bronze (1 Kings 7:45-46; 2 Chron. 4:16-17).*
- *Succoth is referred to in the Psalms (Ps. 60:6; 108:7).*

PENIEL (*"face of God"*), **PENUEL**, *Tubeleth Drahab*

Peniel is a place on the east side of the Jordan near the brook Jabbok (Gen. 32:22, 30), possibly near Succoth.

- *Here Jacob wrestled all night with the angel (Gen. 32:22-32).*
- *Peniel was beaten down by Gideon (Judg. 8:4-17).*
- *It was fortified by Jeroboam (1 Kings 12:25).*

MAHANAIM (*"two camps"*)

This was a town east of the Jordan River and south of the Jabbok River. It was a Levitical city of Gad.

- *It was located on the east of the Jordan and on the border between Gad and Manasseh (Josh. 13:24, 26, 29-30).*
- *Jacob came to this place before crossing the Jabbok (Gen. 32:2, 22).*
- *It was the capital of Ish-bosheth (2 Sam. 2:8, 12, 29).*
- *Here Abner made Ish-bosheth, son of Saul, the king (2 Sam. 2:8-9).*
- *Here David took refuge from his rebel son Absalom (2 Sam. 17:24, 27; 19:32).*
- *Solomon placed Ahinadab in authority over this city (1 Kings 4:7, 14).*

Jerash, *Gerasa, Jarash*

Of the cities east of the Jordan River that were a part of the Decapolis, Damascus was the largest and Jerash was second in size. The Decapolis was an association of ten Greek cities (deca = ten, and polis = city) to the east and south of Galilee. The cities were Greek in the sense of having a predominantly Greek or hellenized culture. In the New Testament, the Decapolis is mentioned two additional times (Mark 5:20 and 7:31). Jesus travelled and performed miracles among the Greeks, some of whom became disciples. The ten cities included Damascus, Raphana, Dion, Hippos (Heb. Susita), Gadara, Scythopolis (former Beth-shean), Pella, Gerasa (today's Jerash), Philadelphia (today's Amman), and Abila or Canatha.

Jerash is 30 miles north of Amman, and lies 2500 feet above sea level. It has two-and-a-half miles of walls, with towers at each turn, and eight gates – just as the old city of Jerusalem.

Here is one of the most complete ruins of any Greek-Roman city in the world. It was founded by Alexander the Great about 332 B.C. and continued as an important city until about A.D. 300, when a shift in trade routes helped to cause its decline.

The city as it now stands was chiefly the product of the first and second centuries A.D., but many conquerors had a hand in its making. The city thrived as an important trade route city and had abundant water, with springs running all year round and a river whose banks were green.

But when Rome declined, so did Jerash. It had a Byzantine Christian recovery, but late in the eighth century earthquakes destroyed much of the city and hastened its decline. The Crusaders used the city as a fort, and when they left, the city became deserted. In 1878 some Turks – Circassians from the Caucasus – settled the east side of the site.

Jerash has been called the "Pompeii of the East" or "City of a Thousand Pillars." In the 1920s the site was excavated by Lankaster Harding (who worked 12 years here); only 15% of the total site is now excavated. Jordanian archaeologists and teams from eight other countries have excavated and restored various quarters of the ancient city since 1982.

POINTS OF INTEREST

The ruins include the following:

TRIUMPHAL ARCH. This was built in A.D. 129 to celebrate Hadrian's visit. It is 39 feet high.

HIPPODROME. Largest structure at Jerash; could hold nearly 15,000 spectators.

TEMPLE OF ZEUS. This temple was built in the second century A.D.

The **SOUTH THEATER** held over 4,000 people (first century A.D.).

The **FORUM**, with its 56 columns, is the only Roman forum ever discovered that is oval-shaped. It is beautifully reconstructed and very photogenic (first century A.D.).

STREET OF COLUMNS. This is the *Cardo* or main street of Jerash, lined with 75 beautiful columns (second century A.D.). It starts at the Forum and runs the en-

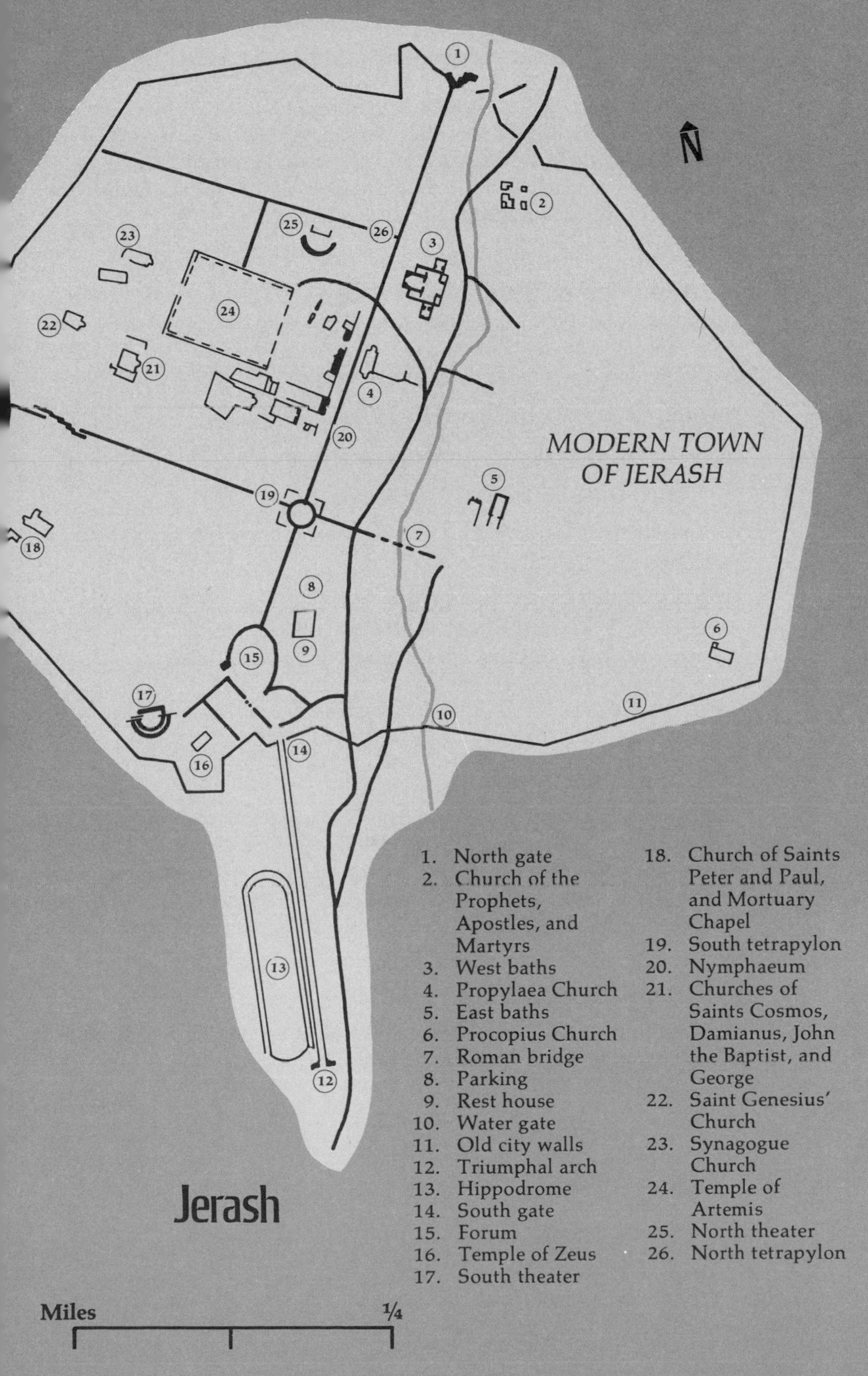

N
MODERN TOWN OF JERASH
1
2
3
4
5
6
7
8
9
10
11
12
13
14
15
16
17
18
19
20
21
22
23
24
25
26
1. North gate
2. Church of the Prophets, Apostles, and Martyrs
3. West baths
4. Propylaea Church
5. East baths
6. Procopius Church
7. Roman bridge
8. Parking
9. Rest house
10. Water gate
11. Old city walls
12. Triumphal arch
13. Hippodrome
14. South gate
15. Forum
16. Temple of Zeus
17. South theater
18. Church of Saints Peter and Paul, and Mortuary Chapel
19. South tetrapylon
20. Nymphaeum
21. Churches of Saints Cosmos, Damianus, John the Baptist, and George
22. Saint Genesius' Church
23. Synagogue Church
24. Temple of Artemis
25. North theater
26. North tetrapylon
Jerash
Miles
¼

tire length of Jerash to the North Gate, nearly 2400 feet. Notice broad sidewalks and shops along the sides of the Cardo, the deep grooves rutted by Roman chariot and wagon wheels in the street, and the sewerage system running the full length with stone manhole covers. In the heart of the city the Cardo intersected with a colonnaded side street, the Decumanus.

NYMPHAEUM. This is the fountain and temple of the nymphs.

The **TEMPLE OF ARTEMIS** was built in the second century A.D. for the god Artemis, the local god of Jerash. This is the most impressive ruin of the site, with its 45-foot-tall columns and beautiful Corinthian capitals. The **VIADUCT CHURCH** is built over the forecourt of the temple.

The **ROMAN BATHS** were built in the second century A.D.

The **NORTH THEATER** is a small theater that seats 1,200.

The **NORTH GATE** marks the north end of the city.

The **CEMETERY** is north of the city walls. A small **THEATER** and **SPRING** are located there.

THIRTEEN BYZANTINE CHURCHES have been excavated at Jerash. The fourth-century **CATHEDRAL CHURCH** is probably the oldest.

- *People from Decapolis followed Jesus during his travels in Galilee. He must have been well known in Jerash (Matt. 4:23-25).*
- *Jesus traveled through the midst of the coasts of Decapolis and could have visited Jerash (Mark 7:31).*

AJALON, AIJALON, Ajlun

Located 46 miles north of Amman, and northwest of Jerash about 10 miles, is the town of Aijalon. Today a **BAPTIST HOSPITAL** is there. A **MOSQUE** has been built on the site of a church, and a **FORTRESS** built by one of Saladin's emirs may be visited. The castle stands on top of a 4,068-foot mountain, the highest in northern Jordan, and is one of the few Arab castles remaining from Crusader days.

WOOD OF EPHRAIM (*"to be fruitful"*)

Northwest from Jerash is a locality called "Wood of Ephraim," where Absalom in revolt against King David, his father, was killed by Joab (2 Sam. 18).

JABESH-GILEAD

The approximate site of this chief city of Gilead is about 5 miles northwest of Aijalon, on Wadi Yabis, which preserves the name (*Yabesh* means "dry"). Several important events of Israelitish history took place there.

- *Israel had vowed at an assembly that they would not give any of their women to the Benjaminites. The men of Jabesh-gilead did not come to the meeting, however, whereupon Israel sent an army to Jabesh-gilead, which slew every living thing in the city except four hundred virgins, whom they brought back as wives for Benjamin (Judg. 21:8-14).*
- *The men of Jabesh-gilead removed the bodies of Saul and his sons from the wall of Beth-shan and burned and buried them in Jabesh. The men were blessed by David (1 Sam. 31:11-13; 2 Sam. 2:4-7; 1 Chron. 10:11-12).*
- *When Saul was king, Israel failed to support him. When the men of Jabesh-gilead asked Saul for aid against the king of Syria, however, Israel rallied behind Saul and he was recognized as king (1 Sam. 11).*
- *David took the bones of Saul and Jonathan, Saul's son, from the men of Jabesh-gilead (2 Sam. 21:12).*

Pella, *Pehal, Tabaqat Fahl*

Directly across the Jordan Valley to the east of Scythopolis (Beth-shan) is Pella, today's *Tabaqat Fahl*, meaning literally "terraces of Pella," because it is situated on a terra rosa plateau or terrace overlooking the valley. Pella was one of the cities of Decapolis. It is the place, according to Eusebius' *Ecclesiastical History* (III 5, 3), to which Christians fled the imminent onslaught at Jerusalem in AD 70.

Irbid (*Arbila*)

Refugees from Palestine swelled the population of Irbid. It is located 45 miles north of Amman. The city of **BARHA**, to the west, is a part of greater Irbid. There are no important archaeological ruins in Irbid.

GADARA, Hammath Gader, El Hamma, El Himmeh, *Gader, Muqes*, Umm Qeis

Approximately 5-6 miles southeast of the south end of the Sea of Galilee is Gadara, the area of the Gadarenes. Its territory probably extended to the Sea of Galilee. It has not been excavated to any extent. Its capture by Antiochus III (218 B.C.) is the first mention of it in history. It was taken by the Jews under Alexander Jannaeus (103-76 B.C.) but was liberated by Pompey in 63 B.C. It joined the federation of Greek cities called the Decapolis. It was famous for its hot springs at nearby Hammath Gader (El Hammeth).

- *Here Jesus cast the evil spirits out of the man (Matt. 8:28-34; Mark 5:1-20; Luke 8:26-39).*

Um el Jimal, *Al Jamal*

Approximately 10 miles east of Al Mafraq are the ruins of this ancient Nabataean city, dating from the first century B.C. It is now a mass of black basalt, but there are towers and houses from a later period that are still in a good state of preservation.

SOUTH FROM AMMAN

Important geographical note: inhabited Transjordanian highlands extend eastward from the Jordan Valley for about 25-30 miles before entering the great Syrian desert. There are two major highways that traverse this territory north-south: the **King's Highway**, which runs through the farmlands of Gilead, Ammon, Moab, and Edom, and the **Desert Road**, which circumnavigates four big, deep wadis, by running north-south about twenty miles further out in the desert. The two highways intersect at one point: Rabbath-Ammon (modern Amman), which has been, therefore, of critical strategic importance throughout history.

Beyond Jordan

"And he arose from thence, and cometh into the coasts of Judaea by the farther side of Jordan" (Mark 10:1).

The "farther side of Jordan" is the same phrase rendered seven other times as "beyond Jordan," meaning "across the Jordan" (Greek: *peran tou Jordanou*). The word *peran* is an adverb of place, and its cognate noun *Peraea* is known to stand by itself as a regional name, especially in the writings of Josephus. Directions are given by Bible writers as if standing looking east. Beyond Jordan, then, would be on the east side of the river.

"And there followed him great multitudes of people from Galilee, and from Decapolis, and from Jerusalem, and from Judaea, and from beyond Jordan [that is, from Peraea]" (Matthew 4:25).

Since all toponyms in the above passage are regional names (besides Jerusalem), it follows that "beyond Jordan" is also a regional name.

Both Galilee and Peraea were provinces ruled by Herod Antipas. Later Antipas would have John the Baptist incarcerated and put to death in the prison-fortress of Machaerus in southern Peraea.

Al Azraq

Sixty-eight miles east of Amman is this desert oasis, with an eighth-century Arab castle, whose walls are covered with frescoes of people, birds, animals, and flowers.

Mashatta, *Qasr el Mushatta*

Eighteen miles southeast of Amman is an eighth-century Arab castle in the desert, probably used as a hunting lodge.

BETHABARA (*"place of passage"*), *Bethabara,* **Bet ha Arava**

This location, 7 miles southeast of Jericho, is the possible crossing point of Israelites entering Canaan (Josh. 3:14-17), and where Elijah and Elisha crossed over the Jordan (2 Kings 2:4-15), and it is the traditional site of Jesus' baptism.

Bethabara appears on the Medeba Map at the natural fording place east of Jericho entering Peraea. In Hebrew Beth-abara or Beth-avara means place of crossing or fording. At such an important juncture along a major east-west travel route John could have taught all the souls coming from the regions of Judaea, Peraea, Galilee, Decapolis, and Phoenicia.

- *This place is perhaps connected with the Beth-barah of Judges (Judg. 7:24).*
- *Here John baptized Jesus (John 1:28-34).*
- *It was accessible to Jerusalem and all Judaea (Mark 1:5).*
- *Lehi said that John baptized Jesus in Bethabara (1 Ne. 10:9.)*

HESHBON (*"stronghold"*), **Hisban**, *Hesban*

Approximately 14 miles southwest of Amman, on the Eastern Plateau, are these extensive Roman ruins. This was the capital of Sihon and the Levitical city of Reuben and Gad. It belonged to Moab and then to Ammon.

- *Heshbon was the former capital of the Amorite king Sihon (Num. 21:21-30).*
- *It was taken by the Israelites and assigned to Reuben (Deut. 2:30; Num. 32:27-37; Josh. 13:15-17).*
- *It was supposedly in the hands of Israel for over 300 years (Judg. 11:26; Neh. 9:22).*
- *This is the location of the famous pools described in the Song of Solomon: "...thine eyes like the fishpools in Heshbon..." (Song of Sol. 7:4).*

MOUNT NEBO (*"height"*), **Syagha**

Directly east of the north end of the Dead Sea, on the edge of the Eastern Plateau, is Mount Nebo. It is the highest point of a ridge called *Pisgah* ("overlook point") in the Abarim range of mountains. It is 27 miles southwest of Amman, 6 miles southwest of Heshbon, and 6 miles northwest of Madeba. Byzantine ruins on Mount Nebo include a sixth-century church and a monastery. The local name *Siyagha* means "monastery" in Aramaic.

- *The children of Israel pitched their tents before Nebo (Num. 33:47).*
- *It was in this area that the incident involving Balaam and the "talking ass" took place (Num. 22:21-31).*
- *Here Moses first viewed the "Promised Land" (Num. 27:12-14; Deut. 32:49).*

- *Here Moses is said to have died (Deut. 34:5-6).*
- *Moses is thought by some to have been translated (Al. 45:18-19; see also Matt. 17:3).*

Zerka Main, *Callirhoe, Zarka Ma'in, Zarqa Main*

From Madeba and Mount Nebo a road runs southwest to the hot mineral springs of Zerka Main, about 14 miles from Madeba and 2½ miles from the Dead Sea. The springs consist of a series of large and small pools that were made famous when used by Herod the Great. In classical times the springs had the name Callirhoe.

Mukhaiyat

About 2 miles southeast of Mount Nebo is the site of the largest mosaic floor ever found in Jordan. It dates back to the sixth century. It portrays twisting grapevines and men gathering and treading the grapes. It also has scenes from the sea, mythology, music, bulbs, trees, animals, and a fire altar. A long inscription gives the names of founders and contributors.

ABEL-SHITTIM, SHITTIM (*"meadow of acacias"*), **Tell el-Hamman** (*Hamma*), *Abila*

Eighteen miles southwest of Ammon and 4 miles northwest of Mount Nebo is Abel-shittim, a site where Israel camped before crossing the Jordan River.

- *Abel-shittim was the last camping site of the Israelites on their journey from Egypt to Canaan (Num. 33:49).*
- *From here Joshua sent spies to Jericho (Josh. 2:1).*
- *Here the Israelites sinned with Moabite women (Num. 25:1).*
- *Here the Lord told Moses that Phinehas, son of Eleazar, was given "the covenant of an everlasting priesthood" (Num. 25:10-13).*
- *The Israelites were numbered here (Num. 26:3-4).*
- *Joshua was set apart to take Moses' place as the prophet. Moses "set him before...all the congregation" and "laid his hands upon him, and gave him a charge" (Num. 27:18-23).*
- *Prophets spoke of Shittim (Joel 3:18; Mic. 6:5).*

MEDEBA, Madaba, Madeba

Twenty miles south of Amman, on the King's Highway, is the Ammonite, Moabite, Nabataean, Greek, Roman, and Byzantine city of Madeba. The town stands on rising ground in the middle of a plain, which has been the scene of many battles. Its slight eminence is due to its being on a vast mound made up of all the earlier Madebas since the Middle Bronze Age (1580-200 B.C.)

Madeba reached the height of its glory during the Byzantine era (fifth and sixth centuries A.D.), and most of its famous mosaics date from this period. It was destroyed by Persians in 614, then occupied by Arabs. An earthquake in A.D. 747 caused the town to be abandoned until the early nineteenth century, when 2,000 Christians from Kerak settled there. In rebuilding the city the settlers uncovered priceless mosaics that have made Madeba famous. There are houses and churches built over many of the Byzantine church mosaic floors. One floor has a picture of a modern Greek church.

Perhaps the most important and famous mosaic is a map of Egypt and Palestine, with a detailed map of Jerusalem that dates back to the sixth century A.D. It is located in Saint George's Greek Orthodox church. The beautiful map is the only one in the world that shows that area during the early sixth century. The inscriptions are all meant to be read by a person facing east. Its coloring is very vivid: a row of white cubes on black lines depicts a road; roofs are indicated with pink, striped in carmine; church facades are lemon yellow; doors and windows are black outlined with white. Of the principal buildings depicted in this map of Jerusalem, the most interesting is the Church of the Holy Sepulcher. The walls and gates of the city are very clear. Fish in the Nile and Jordan rivers are portrayed like those on Egyptian temple walls.

Saint Catherine's Monastery at Mount Sinai and other monasteries are shown on the map. The church was built over the map in 1896, on the site of another basilica. The floor is estimated to include approx. 2,300,000 cubes of colored stone, and probably took over 11,000 hours to lay.

See on Mosaic Map:

1. HAGIA POLIS IEROYCA(LEM) = Holy City of Jerusalem (oval shape in middle with colonnaded cardo and single column at today's Damascus Gate).

2. Identify (with a little help from someone who knows Greek): Bethabara, Jericho, Efrata, Bethlehem, Gehenna, Aceldama, Benjamin, Beth-horon, Shechem (CY XEM)

Also: note the bridge crossing the Jordan, the fording place, the Byzantine Church visible at Nebo, and the Arnon and Zered Rivers.

Opposite the police station is a small **MUSEUM.** Among other items of interest, it contains a large mosaic showing Achilles, Pan, and Bacchus, of Greek mythology.

Some houses with mosaics are open to the public for a small fee.

There is a rest house in Madeba, where refreshments can be purchased.

- *Medeba was a Moabite city captured by King Sihon and then by Israel (Num. 21:24-30).*
- *It was assigned to Reuben (Josh. 13:7-9, 15-16).*

- *It fell into Ammonite hands during David's time (1 Chron. 19:7).*
- *The Moabite Stone (see section on Dhiban, below) says Medeba was held by Omri and Ahab for 40 years.*

MACHAERUS, Mukawir, *Mekawer, Makhwar*

Eight miles south of Madeba, on the west side of the road, is a high, isolated hill called Libb. At this point, a road goes west 9 miles to Machaerus (Mukawir), a site on the east side of the Dead Sea, on a height about halfway between Wadi Zarka Main and Wadi el Mojib (Arnon River).

This was a fortress built by Alexander Jannaeus and enlarged and strengthened by Herod the Great. According to Josephus, when the wife of Herod Antipas heard of her husband's intention to get rid of her and wed Herodias, she retired to this place and from here escaped to her father, Aretas, king of the Nabataeans. Josephus also reported that it was here that John the Baptist was imprisoned, Salome danced, and John was beheaded.

The fort was one of the last to be taken by the Romans. The site has not been thoroughly excavated. Machaerus offers a magnificent view of the Dead Sea area and even of the city of Jerusalem on a clear day.

- *This is a traditional site of the imprisonment and beheading of John the Baptist (Matt. 14:3-11; Mark 6:17-28); see Josephus, Antiquities of the Jews, XVIII 5:2.*

DIBON ("*river course*"), Dhiban, *Dibon-gad*

This Moabite city was located about 2 miles north of Arair, on the edge of the Arnon valley (Wadi el Mojib), 15 miles south of Madeba and 13 miles east of the Dead Sea. It was apparently the home of King Mesha of Moab, and it also achieved importance in Roman times.

The large mound of Dhiban, north of the modern village, was excavated by Nelson Glueck, and it was found that the site dates back to 3000 B.C., and that the Early Iron Age site was northeast of the main area of excavation. The whole surface of the mound is covered with early Byzantine and Arab ruins, immediately below which are remains of the Romans and Nabataeans.

In 1868 a missionary, F. A. Klein, found the *Moabite Stone* (Mesha Stone) at Dhiban. It is now in the Louvre. The stone is dated at approximately 830 B.C., and its great importance lies in its close correspondence with the Old Testament narrative. The inscription on the stone commemorates victories of Mesha, king of Moab, over Israel (2 Kings 3:4-5). The revolt took place in the later years of Ahab's reign.

The stone refers to the present-day city of Madeba and to Chemosh, the national god of Moab. Mesha tells of the Israelite prisoners and the ditches they dug for him. He fought against Israel to take Nebo and slew 7,000 men, boys, and girls. The inscription reads like a chapter of the Old Testament, and as an external evidence of the Old Testament scriptures the stone is significant.

- *Sihon, king of the Amorites, took Dibon from the Moabites (Num. 21:26, 30).*
- *It was assigned to Reuben and built by Gad (Josh. 13:7-9, 15, 17; Num. 32:1-7, 34).*
- *It was a Moabite town (Isa. 15:1-2; Jer. 48:18, 20-22).*
- *It was taken by Moab under King Mesha, as mentioned in his stela, the Moabite Stone.*

AROER (*"juniper"*), Arair

This is a town high above the northern bank of the Arnon River, 3½ miles southeast of Dhiban. It belonged to Reuben's tribe.

- *It was a town on the Arnon River (Josh. 12:2; 13:9, 16; Judg. 11:26).*
- *It was taken by the Israelites from King Sihon (Deut. 2:32-34, 36; 4:46-48).*
- *The census of David began here (2 Sam. 24:1, 5).*
- *Hazael occupied Aroer when he overran Transjordan (2 Kings 10: 32-33).*
- *On the Moabite Stone, Mesha records that he fortified Aroer and built a road through the Arnon.*

RIVER ARNON, Wadi el Mujib, *Wadi Mojib, Wadi el Mojib*

This is a valley 2 miles wide and 1700 feet deep. The stream gathers water from many tributaries as it flows to the Dead Sea. It was the border between Moab and the land of the Amorites on the north. On the way to Wadi Mojib the traveler will notice two **ROMAN MILESTONES**.

- *It was mentioned as the north border of Moab and the south border of the Amorites (Num. 21:13).*
- *Isaiah referred to it as it flowed between high perpendicular rocks near the Dead Sea. He called it the "fords of Arnon" (Isa. 16:2).*

Qasr, *El Qasr* (*"the castle"*)

Ten miles south of Wadi Mojib are ruins of a small Nabataean temple, on a plateau near the road. Some pieces of sculpture from the temple have been incorporated into houses in the village.

Rabbah, *Rabba*

Three miles south of Qasr is the site of this ancient Moabite city. In biblical times, *Rabbah* was the name of the present capital city of Amman. Some believe this was also the site of the Roman acropolis. Fine columns and a temple facade are the chief remains. There are also remains of Byzantine houses.

KIR-HARESETH, *Crac de Montreal,* **Karak**, *Al Karak, Kerak*

Forty miles south of Madeba, 10 miles east of the Dead Sea, on the Wadi Karak, is the city of Karak. It is situated on a plateau 3,400 feet above sea level, and the "Mountain Road" to Karak follows the crest of the Moabite range. This was a chief city of Moab, dominating the main caravan route linking Syria to Egypt and Arabia.

An ancient citadel, Le Crac de Montreal, dates back to the Crusader period and offers an excellent reconstruction of the life of the Frankish knights, who held it from A.D. 1142 to 1187. This was a part of the Crusader system of fortification by which they dominated the area until Saladin conquered the Citadel in A.D. 1187.

The site is also known as Kir of Moab or Kir-Heres.

- *It was a strong, important place in Moab (2 Kings 3:24-25).*
- *Israel mourned for Kir-hareseth (Isa. 15:1; 16:7-11; Jer. 48:31, 36).*

Mauta *and* **Mazar**

Six miles south of Karak is Mauta, where the first clash between the Islamic and Byzantine forces occurred in A.D. 632. The Arab leaders killed in the battles were buried in the village of Mazar, 2 miles south of Mauta, where a very large mosque has been built over the tomb of Jaafar ibn Abi Taleb.

WADI HASA

Wadi Hasa was the northern limit of Edom (*Seir*), where Esau wandered after losing his birthright (Gen. 36:6-8).

Khirbet et Tannur

About 15 miles directly south of Karak is Jebel Tannur (mountains of Tannur), on the peak of which there is a temple accessible only on the southeast side by a single steep path. The temple dates from the first century B.C. and is one of the very few Nabataean temples ever to have been excavated. The temple was richly decorated with carving and sculpture, most of which is now housed in the museum at Amman.

KING'S HIGHWAY, Mountain Road

The King's Highway was an old trade route which extended from Syria on the north to Elath on the Gulf of Aqaba. The route traversed Edom, Moab, Ammon, and Gilead, and was used through the entire Old Testament period. The modern name of the King's Highway is the *Mountain Road.* It runs parallel to and west of the *Desert Road,* with a strip of land about 20 miles wide between them.

- *The Edomites refused Moses and Israel permission to cross Edom via the King's Highway (Num. 20:14-21).*

- *When permission to use the King's Highway to cross Amorite territory was refused, this led to the first battle of the conquest (Num. 21:21-24).*

Shaubak, *Montreal*

Sixteen miles northeast of Petra and 46 miles south of Karak is Shaubak, a fortress built by Baldwin I in A.D. 1115 to control the road from Damascus to Egypt. It was called Montreal (*Monte Reale* = "Royal Mountain") because a king founded it. Saladin captured it in 1189, and it was restored by the Mamelukes in the fourteenth century. The circle of walls and the gateway of the castle are complete, but within is only the modern village.

MA'AN

It is believed by some that Ma'an, 20 miles southeast of Petra, was the scene of the healing of the children of Israel by the miracle of the brazen serpent.

- *Moses set a serpent of brass upon a pole (Num. 21:4-9; John 3:14).*
- *This incident is also mentioned in the Book of Mormon (Al. 33:19; Hel. 8:14-15).*

MERIBAH, Ain Musa

A crystal clear cool spring of water gushes forth from the grounds in Wadi Musa, about 3 miles east of Petra. Muslims believe this is where Moses struck the rock and water came forth (Num. 20:7-13).

Sela (*"rock"*), SELAH, Petra (*"rock"*), *Joktheel*

The rose-red Nabataean city of Petra is located 169 miles south-southwest of Amman and 50 miles south of the Dead Sea. It is in the canyon of Wadi Musa, surrounded by the rugged mountains of Edom, and was once the capital of Edom. Petra was probably the land of the biblical Horites around 2000 B.C. (Gen. 14:6; 36:20-21, 29-30). Esau, Jacob's brother, migrated to this region and was the ancestor of the Edomites.

The valley is entered by the Siq, a narrow defile in the red sandstone cliffs that rise 200-300 feet. This narrow entrance is only 8 feet wide at some places, and is something less than 2 miles long. Visitors usually ride into Petra on horseback.

About 300 B.C. the Nabataeans from North Africa settled in Petra and carved their homes in the red sandstone. They plundered caravans going between Arabia, Syria, and Egypt, and hid the stolen goods in the caves of Petra. Later they stopped plundering but exacted a high toll for safe passage of the caravans. The Nabataeans prospered and extended their kingdom as far north as Damascus. A Nabataean governor ruled Damascus when Paul was converted. From 63 BC to AD 106 the Nabataeans were a client kingdom of the Roman Empire. (During this period, the land was divided roughly into two regions: the Decapolis in the north and the Nabataean Kingdom in the south.) Nabataean culture was a strange amalgamation of Arabic speech, Aramaic writing, Semitic (and apostate) religion, and Graeco-Roman art and architecture.

The Romans under Trajan conquered Petra in A.D. 106 and carved homes, baths, palaces, shops, and an amphitheater that seats 3,000-5,000 persons in the living rose-colored sandstone. During the Roman period there were as many as 7,000 people living in Petra.

The Byzantines lived here in the fourth century, then later the Crusaders, followed by the Muslims. When Petra flourished, there were as many as 6,000 to 7,000 people dwelling in the rock-hewn houses of Petra. It was a wealthy Nabataean city in the days of Jesus. Not only was it the Nabataean capital but it was the center of the caravan trade during the Christian era.

Petra was lost to the world for hundreds of years until 1812, when Johann Burckhardt, posing as a Muslim who had vowed to sacrifice a goat at the altar of Aaron, looked with wonder into the valley. The huge temples and buildings are an artistic and engineering marvel. The city remains a provocative mystery to every visitor. All monuments now visible date from the Nabataean and Roman periods, and all the structures except one (the so-called "Qasr el Bint," a Roman temple which was constructed) were carved from the native stone.

The University of Utah (under the direction of Professor Philip C. Hammond) has been excavating Petra for years; Brigham Young University has also been involved.

POINTS OF INTEREST

The **SIQ** is the narrow winding defile that leads from the east into the area of Petra. It is in Wadi Musa, on the dry riverbed. The Queen of Sheba and Cleopatra both rode through the narrow Siq.

The **TREASURY** (Al Khazneh) is Petra's most exquisite building, ornamented with rock-carved 50-foot Corinthian columns, goddesses in niches, floral pediments, and topped by a rock urn. It is the first large building the visitor sees as he progresses through the Siq.

The **ROMAN THEATER** was carved into a 300-foot stone, and the facades of ancient tombs were cut away to provide seats high in the cliffs. It seats 3000 people and dates from the second or third century.

The **PALACE TOMB** is one of Petra's largest buildings. It is on the right as you near the **PROCESSION STREET** and **TRIUMPHAL ARCH**. Three stories high, it is believed to be a copy of a Roman palace. Four doors lead into small rooms.

The Treasury, Petra

The **URN TOMB** is to the right of the Palace tomb. It opens onto a paved courtyard with a rock-cut colonnade. A unique feature of this tomb is the extension of the courtyard outward on vaults two stories high. A Greek inscription painted on the walls says that this building was used as a Christian church in A.D. 447.

The **CORINTHIAN TOMB** is between the Palace Tomb and Urn Tomb.

The **TEMPLE**, near the rest house, is the only free-standing building that remains in Petra.

UM EL BIYARA, the Edomite acropolis, is a huge, flat-topped rock rising a thousand feet above the Petra basin. Similar to Masada in Israel, it dominates Petra as it dominated the ancient caravan routes. Biblical scholars believe this was the Selah from which King Amaziah cast down 10,000 Edomites. When Obadiah refers to the Edomites living "in the clefts of the rock" (Obad. 1-4), it is very possible that the "rock" has reference to the **EDOMITE FORTRESS** on top of Um el Biyara, around which the Nabataeans later built their capital city.

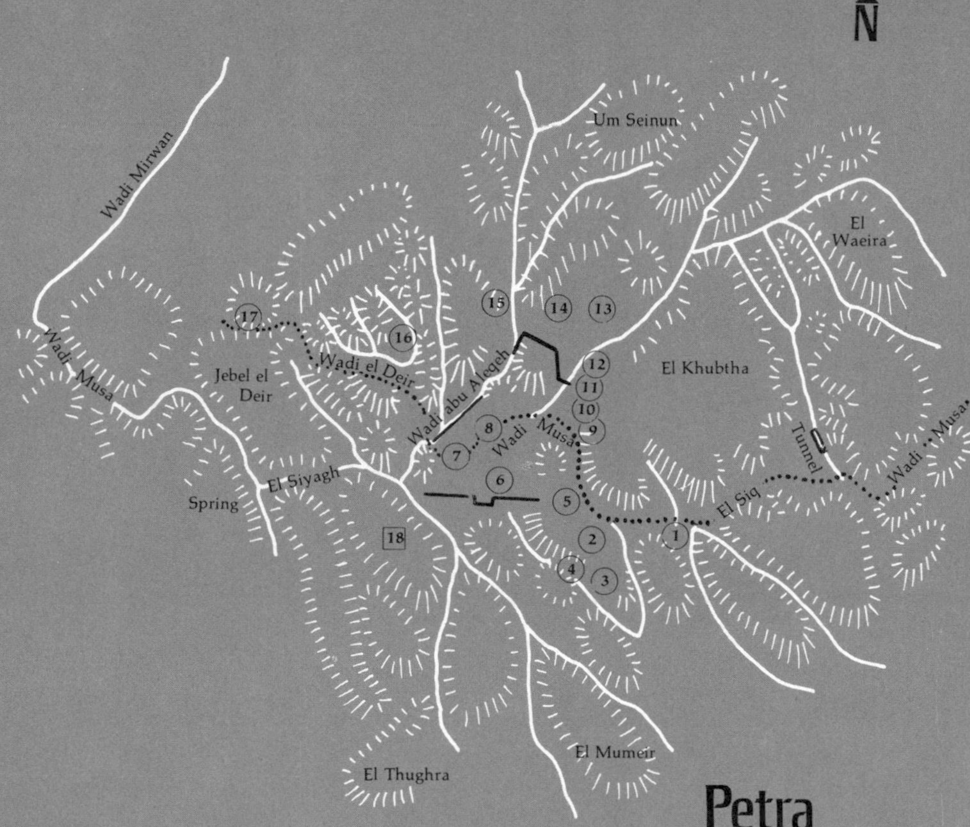

Miles ½ 1

Enclosing hills or plateaus

1. Treasury
2. High place
3. Garden tomb
4. Statue tomb
5. Roman theater
6. City wall
7. Temple
8. Triumphal arch
9. Urn tomb
10. Corinthian tomb
11. Palace tomb
12. Florentine tomb
13. Places of the Christians
14. Circular high place
15. Tomb with Nabataean inscription
16. Lion tomb
17. El Deir Monastery
18. Um el Biyara

The **MONASTERY** (El-Deir) is located northwest of the rest house, at the head of Wadi el Deir. This is Petra's most gigantic building, carved 165 feet wide and 148 feet high into a mountaintop cliff. It is believed to have been a temple, but at one time was used as a Christian church, as indicated by crosses carved into its walls. It probably dates from the second or third century A.D. The **LION TOMB** may be seen on the way to the monastery. From the top of the wadi above the monastery, the Mountain of Aaron, **MOUNT HOR**, can be seen in the west. A small mosque marks the traditional site of the tomb of Aaron.

EL BARID, the "little Petra," has rock-cut halls and elaborate facades. It also has huge subterranean cisterns for water storage. El Barid is accessible only by two passages so narrow that only one person can pass at a time.

REST HOUSES. At the new rest houses just outside the Siq, visitors can be accommodated with meals and beds.

- *The Edomites incurred the displeasure of God for refusing passage of the children of Israel through their land (Num. 20:14-21; Obad. 10; Amos 1:11; Ezek. 25:12-14).*
- *Amaziah of Jerusalem took Selah by war (2 Kings 14:1, 7).*
- *It is very probable that the expression "thou that dwellest in the clefts of the rock" refers to the Edomites who dwelt in ancient Petra (Isa. 42:11; Jer. 49:16-17; Obad. 3).*
- *Isaiah mentioned Sela (Isa. 16:1).*

MOUNT HOR, Jebel Harun

From the peaks of Petra, Mount Hor can be seen 2 miles to the west at an altitude of 4,780 feet. It is ascended from Petra.

Tradition since the days of Josephus says that Mount Hor in Jebel Harun is the "Mountain of Aaron" above Petra. Arabs regard this as the mountain where Aaron, the brother of Moses, died and was buried, and they have erected a tomb under a small dome on the top of the peak. Modern scholars doubt the tradition and fix other sites, such as Jebel Madra, northwest of Ain Qadeis (Kadesh-Barnea), as the place where Aaron died.

- *Aaron died at Mount Hor (Num. 33:37-39).*

RAS EN NAQB, *Ras el Negeb*

This was the site of an Edomite fortress that forced the Israelites to go through the wilderness on their journey to Canaan. It is 20 miles southwest of Ma'an.

- *The Israelites had to go around Edom (Num. 21:4).*
- *The road north from Ras en Naqb follows the ancient Roman road built over the King's Highway of the time of Moses (Num. 20:17).*

WADI EL ARABAH

The huge depression, a rift zone, extends from the Dead Sea to the Gulf of Aqaba. In ancient times the wadi was rich in copper and other minerals. The copper mines there were one of the sources of Solomon's wealth. Copper was exported and used within Israel for such things as the construction of Solomon's Temple and palace in Jerusalem.

- *The promised land contained an area full of iron and copper (translated as "brass") (Deut. 8:9).*
- *The harbor at Ezion-geber was a base for Solomon's trading fleet (1 Kings 9:26; 1 Kings 10:11, 22).*
- *Work in the copper mines began after David captured Edom (2 Sam. 8:13).*

AQABA

Located 210 miles south of Amman, at the southern end of the Arabah and at the northeast corner of the Gulf of Aqaba, is Aqaba, Jordan's only seaport. Aqaba seems to have been founded in the thirteenth century B.C., as the southernmost city in the kingdom of Edom. The Phoenicians converted it into an important seaport under King Hiram of Tyre. During the Roman period (first to fourth century A.D.) Aqaba was an important stop on the great Roman road which ran from Damascus to Egypt. In A.D. 639 the great Arab caliph Omar visited Aqaba on one of his tours and stayed with its bishop. About A.D. 1116, the Crusaders occupied Aqaba under Baldwin I and built a small fortress, whose remains still stand on an island off the coast. Saladin and the Arabs came next, followed by the Mamelukes, who are credited with having built a fort in the fifteenth or sixteenth century A.D. During the First World War, King Faisal made Aqaba his headquarters after the Arabs captured the base from the Turks.

Like its closest neighbor to the west, Eilat, Aqaba is also a resort city. Fishing, swimming, water-skiing, skin diving, and boating in glass-bottom boats are pastimes in Aqaba. The temperature in winter rarely falls below 68 degrees Fahrenheit; in summer the temperature averages about 95 degrees Fahrenheit and sometimes in late July and August may rise as high as 120.

- *The Queen of Sheba undoubtedly disembarked in the general area (1 Kings 10:1-13).*

Wadi Rum

Thirty miles east-northeast of Aqaba and 190 miles south of Amman is the spectacular "valley of the moon." This was the desert setting for the film "Lawrence of Arabia." Travelers usually visit this site in jeeps or on camels.

Sheikh tent, Wadi Rum

JORDAN - HELPFUL TERMS TO KNOW

Useful vocabulary to know at four cities of the Decapolis:
Philadelphia (Amman), Pella (Fahl), Gadara (Umm Qeis), and Gerasa (Jerash)

acropolis (cf. Latin: citadel) - usually a high, fortified hill of a city.

amphora (pl. amphorae) - ceramic jar or vase with large oval body, narrow neck, two handles; if flat-bottomed, usually for grains; if pointed, for liquids (oil or wine).

apse - half-domed recess in the front of a basilica.

Artemis - Greek goddess (Roman Diana) of hunting and archery, and (paradoxically) protectress of wild animals, children, weak things; provider of fertility.

basilica (Latin from Greek "basilikos" = royal) - a rectangular Roman building with a broad nave and colonnaded aisles used for court or public assembly; later adopted as the shape of early Christian church buildings.

cardo maximus (lit. the "heart") - the main street of a Roman city.

Decapolis - a loose federation of ten Greek cities granted independence by Pompey in 63 BC.

decumanus maximus - a paved and colonnaded street which intersects at right angles with the major street (the cardo).

exedra - open recess in the wall of a basilica or other public building.

forum (Gr. agora) - the main marketplace or square/plaza.

loculus (pl. loculi) - long burial recess or niche cut into interior wall of a tomb.

mausoleum - a large, often ornate burial house (named after Mausolus of Caria, whose magnificent tomb at Halicarnassus was one of the seven wonders of the ancient world).

nymphaeum - sacred water fountain or pool dedicated to the nymphs (mythological Greco-Roman water maidens or goddesses).

odeon (from Gr. song, ode) - a small, usually circular and covered theater.

Pax Romana - period of relative peace in the Roman era.

prophylaeum - a street-front, stately gate or entrance.

temenos - a sacred precinct.

tetrapylon - four-arched, monumental gateway at intersection of streets.

thermae - baths, including:

- apodyterium - disrobing or changing room.
- frigidarium - cold pool.
- tepidarium - tepid (luke-warm) pool.
- caldarium - hot bath.
- hypocaust system - heat from fire blown by bellows under tile floor supported by stone pillars (hypocaustae) producing a sauna effect.

triclinium - couch around a three-sided, U-shaped table (or a dining room furnished with a triclinium).

Tyche - Greco-Roman city goddess and goddess of fortune.

vomitorium (pl. vomitoria) - concentric, barrel-vaulted internal passageway of a theater; a portal.

Appendix

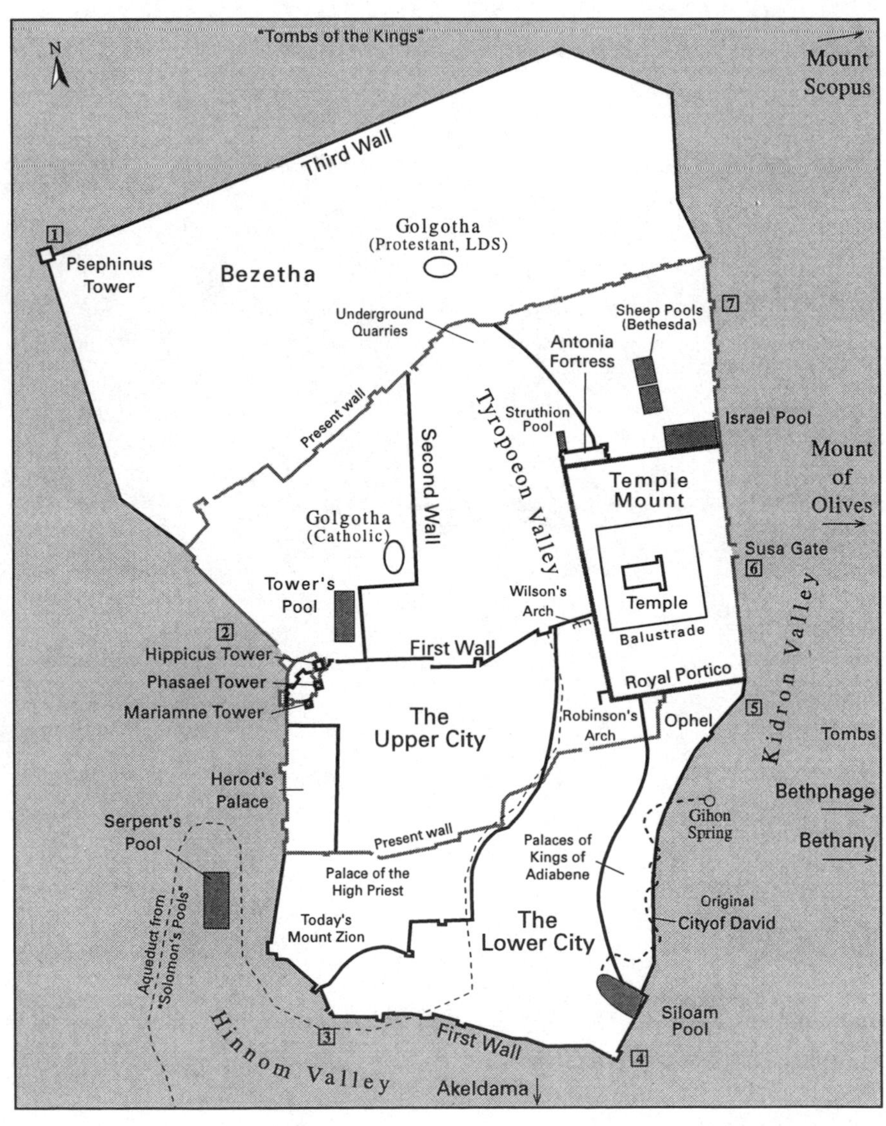
"Tombs of the Kings"
N
Mount Scopus
Third Wall
Golgotha (Protestant, LDS)
1
Psephinus Tower
Bezetha
7
Sheep Pools (Bethesda)
Underground Quarries
Antonia Fortress
Present wall
Second Wall
Tyropoeon Valley
Struthion Pool
Israel Pool
Mount of Olives
Temple Mount
Golgotha (Catholic)
Susa Gate
6
Tower's Pool
Wilson's Arch
Temple
Balustrade
2
Hippicus Tower
First Wall
Phasael Tower
Royal Portico
Mariamne Tower
The Upper City
Robinson's Arch
Ophel
5
Kidron Valley
Tombs
Herod's Palace
Bethphage
Gihon Spring
Serpent's Pool
Present wall
Bethany
Palaces of Kings of Adiabene
Palace of the High Priest
Original City of David
Today's Mount Zion
The Lower City
Aqueduct from "Solomon's Pools"
Siloam Pool
3
First Wall
4
Hinnom Valley
Akeldama

GUIDE TO THE MODEL CITY AND TO NEW TESTAMENT JERUSALEM

The Model City was conceived and executed in the 1960s with the encouragement of the late Mr. Hans Kroch, owner of the Holyland Hotel. The mastermind behind its construction was Professor Michael Avi-Yonah of the Hebrew University, prolific scholar and writer of Second Temple period art, architecture, and archaeology. The work is continued by Hebrew University professors (especially Yoram Tsafrir).

Materials used are true to ancient originals: the local limestone, some marble, wood, copper, and iron.

Jerusalem is a complex archaeological site, perhaps the most investigated and excavated site in the world (having seen fifty to sixty expeditions in the past century and a half). The Model remains up-to-date through reconstruction whenever necessary to comply with the latest archaeological discoveries.

Time Period

The model represents the City of Jerusalem a little more than three decades after the death of Jesus – about A. D. 66, just before the Jewish Revolt and the destruction of the Temple and city by the Roman legions. The Temple referred to is often called the "Second Temple." The First Temple (Solomon's) was destroyed by the Babylonians in 586 B. C. Upon the Jews' return from exile they built a second Temple under the direction of Zerubbabel, Haggai, and Zechariah. This same Temple, though in considerable disrepair, was still standing when Herod announced his intention to reconstruct it. The "Second Temple Period," then, includes the Early Roman Period.

Sources for the Model

Josephus' *Antiquities of the Jews* (Book 15, Chapter 11 "Description of the Temple Mount") and *Wars of the Jews* (Book 5, Chapter 4 "Description of Jerusalem" and Chapter 5 "Description of the Temple"); the *Mishnah* and other volumes of the *Talmud; The New Testament*; and recent archaeological discoveries.

Scale

One-fourth inch equals one foot (two centimeters = one meter). At that scale an average man would be nearly one and a half inches (three and a half centimeters) tall. The Model is also properly oriented to the four points of the compass and is topographically accurate.

Size and Population

At that time period Jerusalem covered approximately 300 acres and contained between 100,000 and 200,000 residents. It was the biggest walled city in the Holy Land and one of the biggest in the entire Near East.

Growth of the City

The original Old Testament period Jerusalem (Zion, the City of David) was located on a spur of land south of the Temple Mount and consisted of no more than 15 acres. With the construction of the First Temple in the mid-10th century B. C., the city began to expand northward, and during the following two centuries residential districts were established to the west and northwest – all within what Josephus called the "First Wall." (See City Plan.) By the Roman period and Jesus' day the city had extended even farther northward to the point of today's Old City walls (at Damascus Gate – the beginning of the Tyropoeon Valley) – an area encompassed by what Josephus called the "Second Wall." The construction of a "Third Wall" was begun as a defensive measure by King Agrippa (A. D. 41-44). It was not completed until A. D. 66, the year the Great Revolt broke out, and during the Romans' initial advances on the city this wall was destroyed. Sections of the wall have been uncovered in front of and immediately east and west of the American Consulate in East Jerusalem (just north of the Garden Tomb).

TOUR

[1] **PSEPHINUS TOWER** – an octagonal tower located at the northwest corner of the Third Wall. This wall and the tower protected residents of the New Quarter or Bezetha. The houses and buildings between the Third and Second Walls are not substantiated archaeologically; they merely represent the fact that this New Quarter was somewhat populated during these few decades.

According to Josephus one could stand on the Tower (115 feet high – 35 meters) and, if the atmosphere was clear, see both sides of the country, from the Mediterranean to the hills of Transjordan.

In this area Titus pitched his own tent during the siege of Jerusalem, A. D. 66-70.

[2] **HEROD'S TOWERS** – Today's Jaffa Gate – this is the junction of the three walls. Just ahead, a little to the left, and outside the Second Wall (see City Plan) is a quarrying area believed by many to be the place of Jesus' crucifixion (the view of Catholics and others). In the 4th century A. D. Constantine's mother Helena indicated that this was the location of the Lord's death and subsequent burial and resurrection, so the Church of the Holy Sepulchre was constructed over the physically altered site. (See LDS view under "Moriah – The Mount of Sacrifice.")

Herod the Great (the great builder and great murderer who reigned from 37 to 4 B. C.) erected fortresses and royal cities and impressive structures all over the Holy Land and in many parts of the Roman Empire. He was the grandest builder the City of Jerusalem ever knew in ancient times. He constructed in Jerusalem all that other great cities of the Hellenistic-Roman period had.

THE TOWERS – The largest of Herod's towers at the north end of his palace was named after his brother Phasael (148 feet – 45 meters). Some of this tower remains today in the Citadel at Jaffa Gate; the one in back of it, to the east (132 feet – 40 meters), was named in honor of a friend, Hippicus; and the feminine-looking tower (90 feet – 27 meters) was named after his beloved wife Mariamne whom he had executed (because of suspicion of her involvement in some treachery). The towers had luxurious residential quarters in the upper sections, and the Hippicus tower even held a deep water reservoir above its base.

HEROD'S PALACE – The king's royal palace was built in 23 B. C. at the highest spot in the city. The three towers were erected to secure his palace, which also had a protective wall on all sides (to provide protection not only for the city in general on the west, but also protection from his own subjects on the east). On the north end of the palace complex were military barracks, a camp for his guards. The rest of the palace consisted of banquet halls, guest apartments, baths, etc. – some of which sported lovely mosaics and frescoes. Landscaping included groves of trees, aqueducts, pools, water-spouting statues, and fountains.

Some believe that Jesus' trial before Pontius Pilate occurred here. It is likely, however, that Herod Antipas (visiting from Galilee) would have stayed at the *Herodian* palace, whereas Pilate (up from the Roman seat of government, Caesarea) would be housed in the *Roman* Fortress of Antonia.

Outside the palace to the east was the *Agora* (Greek: marketplace; Latin for the same: *Forum*), a colonnaded shopping mall with open plaza in the middle.

The area east and south of Herod's palace was known as the *Upper City*, in contrast to the lower city: the eastern hill, the ancient Zion or City of David.

The Upper city boasted a wealthier Jewish housing district with Hellenistic town-planning: well laid-out streets and houses built around courtyards with gardens and cisterns.

3 "MT. ZION," AND VIEW TO THE WESTERN WALL – The term Zion originally referred to the eastern hill of ancient Jerusalem, the City of David. The name then shifted to the Temple Mount. Now, ever since the Second Temple/Roman period, people have been calling this western hill "Mt. Zion" because they supposed that this hill was the original City of David. Thus we have "David's Tower" at Jaffa Gate and "David's Tomb" on this hill (the actual site of Old Testament Jerusalem, the lower eastern ridge, had apparently been forgotten). The traditional Tomb of

David is represented in the Model as a monumental structure with a pyramidal top.

Today, Mt. Zion is *outside* the Old City wall, but in the Roman period the hill was included inside the city's wall.

Though not depicted in the Model City, the longest and strongest traditions indicate that this hill is the location of the *Upper Room*, where Jesus instituted the Sacrament (Matt. 26:26-29; Luke 22:15-20), where he gave special meaning to the washing of feet (John 13:2-17), and where he revealed who would betray him (Matt. 26:20-25; John 13:18-30).

In finding the guestchamber, a furnished upper room (Luke 22:11-12 [located in the Model about where David's Tomb is positioned]), Jesus instructed Peter and John to follow a *man* bearing a pitcher of water (from the Gihon Spring or the Pool of Siloam). Though women usually did the water-carrying, this man may have been part of the semi-monastic Essene community that resided in that part of the Upper City. The apostles proceeded as Jesus had directed them and prepared the room for celebrating the Passover – the last legitimate Passover celebration in history. West of David's Tomb is a low-lying palace complex identified with the High Priest Caiaphas, where some members of the Sanhedrin convened illegally at night before the high holy day for the trial of Jesus. Inside the outer walls of this palace is where Peter would have denied knowing Jesus as he warmed himself at a fire during the cool early morning hours (Luke 22:55-62; John 18:15-18). Archaeologists label this site as *Caiaphas' Palace.* It is on the grounds of the Armenian cemetery just outside – south – of today's Old City wall, though the traditional site visited is eastward, down the slope at "St. Peter in Gallicantu" (Latin: cock-crowing).

Looking up toward the Temple Mount, the Western (or "Wailing") Wall is visible. It is important to remember that the *Western Wall* is a *retaining wall* around the hill of the Temple, not part of the Temple proper. Jesus' prophecy that not one stone would be left standing on another (Matt. 24:2) was literally fulfilled: the Temple itself was completely leveled. Several sections of the retaining walls remain to this day.

Running between the Temple Mount and the Upper City was a deep valley; the only name which has survived is the one Josephus used: the "Tyropoeon" (Cheesemakers).

The bridge built by the Hasmoneans which connected the Temple Mount with the Upper City (over the Tyropoeon Valley) is now named after its last-century British discoverer Charles Wilson: thus *Wilson's Arch.* Compare the height of the arches in the Model with the very little upper portion now visible at the Western Wall plaza!

The bridge projecting out from the southwest corner of the Temple Mount is named *"Robinson's Arch,"* after the 19th century American scholar and explorer Edward Robinson, who stood at ground level (then!) and examined, measured, and postulated over the purpose of the arched bridge. Though once it was considered another bridge spanning the valley over to the Upper City, it is now known through archaeological excavation that the bridge was in fact an arched stairway leading down into the Tyropoeon Valley.

Note the *red arrow* on the Western Wall. Only a portion of the wall seen in the Model is visible to the visitor today. Nineteen courses of beautifully carved stones with Herod's characteristic marginal dressing are now underground (it is possible to look down to the foundations inside Wilson's Arch). The top portion of Herod's Wall is also not to be seen today, having been destroyed by the Romans, though the Ottoman Turkish ruler Suleiman in the early 1500's restored the upper courses of stone along with the ramparts. His work is quite inferior to the work of Herod's engineers over 1500 years earlier. The original retaining walls were 30 meters above the paved roads (as high as a modern 10-story building) and the towers were 35 meters high. The prodigious undertaking of bringing into position all of Herod's massive pre-cut building stones is evidenced by the finding of one stone which measure 12 meters long, 3 meters high, 4 meters thick, and weighs over 500 tons!

4 **THE CITY OF DAVID** – Proceeding from Point **3** to Point **4** the topography of ancient Jerusalem is clear: one must descend from the Upper City. One particular stairway leading up to St. Peter in Gallicantu which dates to the Hasmonean period (167-63 B.C.) has been uncovered. It may have been that very stairway up which Jesus was taken when led to Caiaphas' Palace after his arrest in Gethsemane.

Point **4** is the confluence of three valleys (wadis) of ancient Jerusalem. The Model ends at the walls, so it is important to keep in mind that while we walk on the sidewalks we would actually be *below* the level of those walls (and not able to view the model). While walking on the west and south we are hundreds of feet below Mt. Zion in the Hinnom Valley. While walking the sidewalk to the east of the Model we are far below the City of David and Temple Mount in the Kidron Valley.

Again, Point **4** is the confluence where the Hinnom, Tyropoeon, and Kidron come together. From there the wadi is called the Kidron for another twenty miles through the Judean Desert, eventually emptying into the Dead Sea.

Looking north the *Tyropoeon Valley* is visible, and at its southern end is the colonnaded *Pool of Siloam*, where Jesus one day sent a man blind from birth (John 9). He answered the man's plea for sight by making a mud paste, putting it on his eyes, and instructing him to go to the pool and wash it off. The blind man obeyed and was healed. The Pool of Siloam stands at the end of the ancient city's most unique hydro-technical project, *Hezekiah's Tunnel* (see City Plan). In the year 701 B. C. King Hezekiah, encouraged by the lone voice of the Prophet Isaiah, prepared for the attack of the Assyrian King Sennacherib's forces by repairing the city walls and carving out of solid limestone an underground water channel nearly 1800 feet long (one-third mile), in order to camouflage the Gihon Spring, the city's water source, and bring its waters inside the city for safe access.

The ridge of the hill east of the Tyropoeon and south of the Temple Mount was the original Old Testament Jerusalem [though the Luke 2/Nativity account calls Bethlehem the "City of David" (as it was David's hometown), yet "City of David" refers almost exclusively to Jerusalem]. No more than 15 acres in area, it served as King David's administrative capital for an empire extending from the River of Egypt to the Euphrates in Mesopotamia. Somewhere on this hill, likely nearer the north end adjacent to the hill top of Moriah where the great Temple would stand was David's Royal Palace (not represented in the Model). One warm evening he was walking on a roof or balcony looking out over his city. His eyes fell on a woman bathing herself within the enclosed courtyard of her home in the city below. Her husband, Uriah, was a Hittite man and warrior in David's army – then fighting a strategic battle at Rabbath-Ammon (today's Amman, capital of Jordan). David sent for her and the tragedy ensued (2 Samuel 11).

Another person with whom we're acquainted who lived on this hill some four centuries later was an important official and record-keeper named Laban (1 Nephi 3-4). It was in this city that Nephi and brothers planned their approach for securing the scriptural and genealogical records on the plates of brass. An angel appeared outside these walls and chastised the unbelieving and complaining brothers. One of the tactics tried by Lehi's sons was to go down to the land of their inheritance, gather what things of value they could, and return again into the city to Laban's house. Some Israelite houses from this very time period (600 B.C . – just before the Babylonian siege and destruction) have been recently uncovered on the eastern slope as part of the City of David archaeological excavations.

The buildings seen in the middle of this same hill in the Model are palaces of a Mesopotamian royal family (of Adiabene) who converted to Judaism in the first century B. C. (Their tombs are also in Jerusalem, north of the Garden Tomb, at the intersection of Saladin and Nablus Roads; they are called the "Tombs of the Kings.") South of their palaces was the "Synagogue of the Freedmen [KJV: Libertines]," or Alexandrians, possibly mentioned in Acts 6:9.

5 **SOUTHERN WALL OF THE TEMPLE MOUNT** – The main entrance and exit to the Temple Mount were the two sets of gates (called the "Huldah Gates") leading in and out of the Temple Mount from the south. Through the one on the

right a person would enter to perform the holy work in the Temple, after having gone through some ritual washings or cleansings accomplished in small pools or fonts just outside the retaining walls of the sacred enclosure. And through the one on the left a person would exit following the conclusion of the Temple work or service.

Now partly visible after the archaeological restoration done in recent years is a beautiful stone staircase leading up to the wall. Here it was where rabbis sometimes taught the people. Jesus could have taught from this stairway also, at one point in his scathing condemnation of hypocrites (Matt. 23) even gesturing eastward over the Kidron toward the city's necropolis [burial place] and comparing those hypocrites to whited sepulchres, radiant and impressive on the outside but on the inside full of dead men's bones and corruption.

The southeast corner is the highest point along the whole length of the Temple Mount retaining walls (211 feet – 64 meters; measuring from the top of Herod's portico to the bottom of the Kidron was over 400 feet!). It is the traditional "*Pinnacle of the Temple*" to which Jesus was brought while in the Spirit (JST Matt. 4:5-6, 8). Satan then came along and tempted him to misuse his divine power by throwing himself off the dizzying height and counting on angels to rescue him from the fall.

Some researchers consider the south*western* corner of the Mount to be a more logical location for the temptation of Jesus since that corner has a much better angle for looking out over the city, and a specially-carved platform stone was discovered in the toppled ruins indicating by a Hebrew inscription where a herald would blow the shofar to signal holy days.

6 **THE TEMPLE MOUNT** – The Temple of Herod was constructed with the help of 10,000 workmen, including 1000 priests, and 1000 wagons for transporting materials. The courtyards and porticoes were eight years under construction and the Temple proper a year and a half. It was said that whoever had not seen the Temple of Herod had never seen a beautiful building. No other temple complex in the Greco-Roman world compared with it in expansiveness and magnificence.

Herod had nearly doubled the size of the Temple Mount from what it was during the period of the First Temple (Solomon's), making it in Jesus' day approximately 40 acres in area (compare Salt Lake Temple Square's *10* acres). To expand so much he had to extend the platform of the mount, particularly to the north, to the west, and to the south. Below floor level to the north and west was earth-fill, but to the south he supported the floor with vaults, rows of arched colonnades. Under the floor of the southeast portion of the Temple courtyard, then, it is hollow. There is a large, columned chamber erroneously called "*Solomon's Stables*" (since it was constructed by Herod, the place didn't exist in Solomon's day, though it was later used by the Crusaders for stabling horses).

The Temple Mount was a very large space measuring more than 144,000 square meters. Above ground on all sides were extraordinary colonnaded *porticoes* or *porches* (also called *cloisters*; i.e., covered walkways with colonnades opening to the inside). Each portico hosted a double row of Corinthian columns, each column a monolith; i. e., cut from one block of stone, and rising to over 37 feet high. According to Josephus, Herod was responsible for extending the mount northward, westward, and southward and erecting porticoes inside his newly positioned walls, but the eastern portico (not visible to those standing on the sidewalk looking west) was built up by Herod in the same position as the previous Temple Mount. It is this eastern portico which is called "*Solomon's Porch*" (1 Kings 6:3) where Jesus, having come to the Passover at age 12 to become a "son of the law," taught the learned rabbis (JST Luke 2:46), and where he later walked and taught at the Feast of Dedication (Hanukkah) and testified that he was God's Son and the Jews tried to stone him (John 10:22-39). Also Peter and John, after performing a miracle at the gate of the Temple, drew a large crowd in Solomon's Porch and preached and called for repentance following the denying and killing of the Holy One and were arrested by temple police and Sanhedrin officials (Acts 3:1-4:2).

The southern portico – grander than the others – is often called Herod's *Basilica*. The word "basilica" (from the Greek *basileus*, "king," therefore a royal portico) meant a public hall which was rectangular in shape and had colonnaded aisles (a similar ground plan was adopted for early Christian churches). The Royal Basilica or Portico contained a total of 162 Corinthian columns. At its foot were the ramps leading onto the Temple courtyard from the south.

The eastern gate of the Temple Mount was called the *Susa Gate*. It faces eastward toward Susa, which was the Persian capital where the Biblical stories of Daniel, Esther, Nehemiah, and others in part unfolded (called Shushan in the Bible – Dan. 8:2; Esth. 1:2; Neh. 1:1). This gate was said to have been lower than the other gates so that the priests across the bridge on the Mount of Olives for the sacrifice of the Red Heifer might still look directly into the Temple.

COURTS OF THE TEMPLE – The outer court was called the *Court of the Gentiles*, where Jesus cast out the money-changers. As Judea was a cross-roads country the money-changers were legitimate characters involved in changing foreign and local coins with pagan symbols and effigies of political rulers into Temple coinage. Non-Jews were allowed to enter thus far onto the Temple Mount (similarly, non-"Mormons" are allowed onto Temple Square in Salt Lake City to within a certain proximity of the Temple). Surrounding the Temple proper was a balustrade (Heb. "soreg"), an elevated stone railing about 4.5 feet (1.5 meters) high with posted inscriptions in Greek and Latin warning Gentiles not to pass beyond.

Roman authorities conceded to the Jewish authorities control of the sacred inner area to the point of capital punishment for non-Jews who passed beyond the stone railing. A fortified inner wall with towers and gates surrounded the *Court of the Women*, Israelite women being permitted to enter into this area and not further, except for sacrificial purposes. The main gate into the Court of the Women was called the *Beautiful Gate* because of its rich decoration. It was at this gate that Peter and John, on their way to do some Temple work or worship, stopped to hear the petition of a lame man. Peter dramatically healed the man, who joined them into the Temple – "walking, and leaping, and praising God" (Acts 3:1-11). The Women's Court was a large space, nearly 200 feet square. In the four corners were chambers which served various functions. The eastern chambers served the Nazarites, where those who had made special vows could prepare their sacrifices, and another for storing wood. The western chambers were used for store of olive oil and for purification of lepers, with their own private ritual bath.

In was perhaps to this Court of the Women that Joseph and Mary brought the infant Jesus five to six weeks (40 days) after birth in order for him as a first-born to be redeemed and for Mary to be ceremonially cleansed.

This whole court was surrounded by porticoes. Against the walls inside the porticoes were chests for charitable contributions, likely the place called "the Treasury," where the widow cast in her mites (Mark 12:41-44), and where Jesus taught during the Feast of the Tabernacles (John 8:20). Here Jesus bore witness of his own Divinity; dealt mercifully with the woman taken in adultery; proclaimed himself the Light of the World, the Messiah; and bore testimony that he was the God of Abraham. Jews tried to stone him again (John 7-8).

Fifteen curved steps and then the *Gate of Nicanor* (green) led into the innermost court. Nicanor was a wealthy Jew from Alexandria in Egypt who donated the ornate doors of the gate. Only priests and other authorized Temple officiators would enter this court. To the sides of its porticoes were the Chamber of Hewn Stone where the Sanhedrin met (where Stephen was transfigured before them - Acts 6:12-15; and where Paul testified before them – Acts 22:30 - 23:10), and the Chamber of the Hearth, where priests on duty could spend their nights.

On the north side of this court, which is actually a double court (first the Court of the Men of Israel, then the Priests' Court) was the Place of the Slaughtering. On the south side was the giant brass wash basin (the *Laver*) supported on the backs of twelve lions. For all the water needs of the Temple Mount millions of gallons of water were brought in from "Solomon's Pools," south of Bethlehem, and stored in a connected series of rock-cut reservoirs (cisterns). Near the Laver the great horned *Altar of Sacrifice* or Burnt Offering stood, measuring 48 feet square and 15 feet high! (Some think that the huge rock-mass inside the Dome of the Rock – which now measures approximately 40 x 50 feet x 7 feet high – once formed the base of the Altar of Sacrifice. At least it is clear from scripture [2 Samuel 24:18-25] that King David purchased the Rock in order to build an altar to the Lord.) The Altar stood off center in the court so that the priest sacrificing the Red Heifer on the Mount of Olives could see straight into the giant entry-way of the Holy Sanctuary, which stood 66 feet high and 33 feet wide (20 x 10 meters). The Sanctuary or Holy Place was made of marble. Two columns in front were named Jachin and Boaz (meaning "He will establish" and "In him is strength") after those of Solomon's Temple. The Temple proper was over 150 feet high (the Dome of the Rock reaches a height of just over 100 feet), and it was surmounted by golden spikes to discourage birds from landing there and tarnishing the stone.

Inside the Holy Place was the veil leading to the most sacred chamber, the Holy of Holies. That same Temple veil was torn from top to bottom at the death of Jesus (Matt. 27:51).

Thus the Temple area consisted of a series of rising platforms: from the Court of the Gentiles one ascended stairs to the Court of the Women; from there one ascended the fifteen curved stairs to the Court of the Men of Israel and of the Priests; and finally an ascent was requisite to enter the Holy Place itself. The three courtyards surrounding the holiest place where the Divine Presence could be manifest may appropriately be compared to three degrees of glory and three settings for instruction in modern Temples: Telestial, Terrestrial, and Celestial. It is not enough to progress into the third courtyard or heaven, but to actually enter into the highest degree of that realm: to symbolically enter into the Presence and be exalted.

Remember that immediately east of Point **6**, across the Kidron, is the slope of the Mount of Olives where the Garden of Gethsemane was located (see City Plan). The Garden was appropriately named *Gat Shemen*, which in Hebrew means oil press. For just as the blood [juice] of the grape or olive is pressed and crushed by the heavy stone in the oil press, so the heavy burden of the sins of the world pressed the blood of the Anointed One from his body.

In Gethsemane, among the olive trees which were themselves symbolic of the people of Israel, was accomplished the most important and most selfless suffering in the history of mankind.

There, in the darkness of that agonizing night, Jesus was arrested by a party of temple police and Sanhedrin officials led by the betrayer, Judas Iscariot.

At the northwestern corner of the Temple Mount stood the massive governmental and military headquarters called the *Antonia Fortress*, previously constructed by the Hasmoneans but now reconstructed and fortified by Herod and named after Mark Antony. The Fortress was also called in the New Testament the

"Praetorium" (Mark 15:16 – Latin: governor's courtroom or Hall of Judgment, as translated in John 18:28, 33). Another name was the "Castle." Jesus' trial before the Roman governor took place in the Antonia Fortress, in Pilate's hall of judgment (John 18:28 - 19:16), on what John called the Pavement (John 19:14; Hebrew-Aramaic: *Gabbatha*; Greek: *Lithostrotos*). Though some have proposed that the Roman military presence would have been housed in barracks at Herod's Palace on the west side of the city, it is more likely that soldiers were stationed at the Antonia, the biggest fortress in Roman Jerusalem, so they could keep watch over the Temple Mount, which was their main reason for coming to Jerusalem. Roman soldiers, then Temple guards took Paul down to the Sanhedrin at their meeting hall in the Temple and returned with him back up into the Fortress, "the castle." Two stairways are visible in the Model at the northwest corner of the Temple Mount. (Note interesting details of movement back and forth between the Temple and the Roman Fortress in Acts, chapters 21-23.)

[7] **POOL OF BETHESDA** – The Third Wall, running north from the Temple Mount and then west, was begun by Herod Agrippa (A. D. 41-44) and finished by the Jewish Zealots during the First Revolt, just before the Romans destroyed it. The gate in the wall at Point **7**, then, is the work of Herod Agrippa about a decade after the Crucifixion – at least the gate was not there yet when Stephen, a short time after Jesus, was stoned to death for defending his testimony that Jesus was the Messiah. Though some traditions identify this as "St. Stephen's Gate" (now also called the "Lions Gate"), outside of which he was stoned, yet older tradition suggests his martyrdom outside the *northern* gate of the city (what today is called "Damascus Gate"), where there was an execution place – where Jesus had also been martyred (see below, "Moriah - The Mount of Sacrifice").

Inside the city wall at this point is a double pool called the Sheep Pool or *Pool of Bethesda*. Some think that the reference in John 5:2 to the sheep market or the sheep *gate* (today, either the Lions Gate or the gate leading directly onto the Temple Mount) relates to sheep brought in and washed in the pool before being taken onto the Temple Mount for sacrifice. There were five porticoes or porches surrounding the twin pools, four around the sides and one dividing them. Here Jesus met an invalid man, lame or paralyzed for thirty-eight years. On the Sabbath Day he raised him up, completely healed (John 5:1-16).

MORIAH – THE MOUNT OF SACRIFICE – Also at Point **7** a couple of the most poignant, awe-inspiring, and eternally important events in the history of humankind can be brought together visually – the two sacrifices on Moriah and Golgotha.

Abraham had made the long, strenuous trek (53 miles, uphill, for a man of over 100 years of age) from Beersheba to the top of Moriah, later to be known as the Temple Mount (2 Chron. 3:1). Although he himself had nearly been sacrificed earlier in his life to the idolatrous gods in his old Chaldean homeland, and he knew how repulsive human sacrifice was and how foreign such a practice is to the true worship of our heavenly Father, yet the command was given to sacrifice his son; the test was perfectly designed for Abraham. He had waited so many years for his and Sarah's most precious possession, that covenant son whom he loved. Now the Lord called on him to sacrifice, to give up, that beloved son. Paul wrote that "by faith, Abraham, when he was tried, offered up Isaac: and he that had received the promises offered up his only begotten son" (Heb. 11:17).

Abraham was going to learn to a degree the magnitude of the Sacrifice that God our Father made in giving up His Beloved Son. Abraham's offering of his son Isaac was a "similitude of God and His only Begotten Son" (Jacob 4:5). And they were both accomplished at the same location. By following the Mount of Moriah northward to just outside the Second Wall a prominence is visible whereat the Son of God was executed by crucifixion. The place was called *Golgotha*, from the Hebrew "gulgoleth," meaning skull. Another name-title is *Calvary* (Luke 23:33), from Latin "calva," also meaning skull. The site may have had the physical appearance of a skull (though a *hill* is not mentioned in the New Testament), or else there were skulls lying around from those previously killed. It should be noted, however, that JST Matt. 27:35 indicates that Jesus was taken to "a place called Golgotha, that is to say, a place of *burial*."

When Abraham and Isaac approached Moriah, Isaac reminded his father that they had the wood for the sacrifice, but where was the sacrifice? Abraham prophetically responded, "My son, God [*Elohim* in the Hebrew text] will provide himself a lamb . . ." (Gen. 22:7-8). When Abraham's test was passed, and the angel of the Lord sent to stop the sacrifice of the son, a ram (not a *lamb*) was substituted. But 2000 years later, on the northern extension of the same mountain, God did provide a lamb - the Lamb of God was sacrificed. (It is interesting to note that when a lamb was slain on the great altar of the Temple, it was slain on the *north* side of the altar – Lev. 1:11.)

Abraham knew something of the meaning of his similitude-sacrifice. He had uttered prophetically – not unintentionally or accidentally – that our heavenly Father would provide a lamb as a sacrifice for sin, and he knew that the Son would be that sacrifice, to be made at that very place. Said Jesus in the Temple courtyard, "Your father Abraham rejoiced to see my day: and he saw it, and was glad" (John 8:56).

Thus *the* Passover Lamb was slain at Passover time on the north of the Altar of Moriah as an Atonement for sin, which was the symbolic and typical purpose of all the lambs slain on the Temple altar over the centuries; they all prefigured that greatest Sacrifice.

Additional Points of Interest

1. Near the foot of the western entrance to the Antonia Fortress are two octagonal *market pavilions*, designed after similar structures found in Roman Africa.

2. Just north of Herod's Towers (today's Jaffa Gate) is a monumental *Tomb of the Hasmonean King John Hyrcanus* who ruled the Holy Land from 135 to 104 B. C. The Hasmoneans (or the "Maccabees" as they are popularly called) were a priestly family who initiated a revolt against Seleucid (Syrian) forces then dominating the land. Mattathias and his five sons carried out a series of guerrilla raids which eventually culminated in the better part of a century of independence for the Jews. Simon, the last of the original family, was the father of John Hyrcanus.

3. Immediately north of Hippicus Tower is the *Tower's Pool*, an open reservoir sometimes called "Hezekiah's Pool." The nearby gate was appropriately called the "Water Gate."

4. East of Mariamne Tower was the *Palace of the High Priest Annas*, father-in-law of Caiaphas, who was involved in the trial of Jesus and of the apostles later (Luke 3:2; John 18:13; Acts 4:6). Farther east, nearer the Temple Mount (just west of the Tyropoeon Valley), was the Royal *Palace of the Hasmoneans*. South of the Hasmonean Palace is a possible location of *Herod's Theater* (note: an *amphitheater* is circular in shape; a theater is semi-circular).

5. At the southwest corner of the Temple Mount is a *hippodrome* (the Greek word used for a horse and chariot-racing track). It was also built by Herod's construction workers. Its position in the Model City is speculative; there is no evidence for its exact location in the ancient city.

6. Just south of the southern wall of the Temple Mount is a monumental tomb with pyramidal top identified as the *Tomb of the Prophetess Huldah*. It was to Huldah, a prophetess living in this quarter of Jerusalem and contemporary of Jeremiah and Lehi, that Josiah sent to inquire of the Lord whether or not He would carry out the predicted judgments recorded in the Scriptures they had just found in the Temple. The Lord's word was forthright: "I will bring evil upon this place, and upon the inhabitants thereof . . . Because they have forsaken me, and have burned incense unto other gods . . . therefore my wrath shall be kindled against this place, and shall not be quenched" (see 2 Kings 22:3-20). The hundreds of cultic objects involved in pagan idol worship found in archaeological excavations right near the Temple Mount attest to the corruption of Judah's religious practices and the validity of Huldah's pronouncement.

7. North of the Pool of Bethesda stands a *Monument to the Hasmonean King Alexander Jannaeus* (103-76 B. C.) It was during his reign that the kingdom expanded to the size of the former Solomonic kingdom.

Index

EGYPT

ISRAEL

JORDAN